LIKE ANDY WARHOL

LIKE ANDY WARHOL
LIKE ANDY WARHOL
LIKE ANDY WARHOL

JONATHAN FLATLEY

The University of Chicago Press
Chicago and London

The University of Chicago Press, Chicago 60637
The University of Chicago Press, Ltd., London

Published 2017
Paperback edition 2022
Printed in the United States of America

31 30 29 28 27 26 25 24 23 22   1 2 3 4 5

ISBN-13: 978-0-226-50557-2 (cloth)
ISBN-13: 978-0-226-82394-2 (paper)
ISBN-13: 978-0-226-50560-2 (e-book)
DOI: https://doi.org/10.7208/chicago/9780226505602.001.0001

Library of Congress Cataloging-in-Publication Data

Names: Flatley, Jonathan, author.
Title: Like Andy Warhol / Jonathan Flatley.
Description: Chicago ; London : The University of Chicago Press, 2018. | Includes index.
Identifiers: LCCN 2017033940 | ISBN 9780226505572 (cloth : alk. paper) | ISBN 9780226505602 (e-book)
Subjects: LCSH: Warhol, Andy, 1928–1987.
Classification: LCC N6537.W28 F58 2018 | DDC 700.92—dc23
LC record available at https://lccn.loc.gov/2017033940

♾ This paper meets the requirements of ANSI/NISO Z39.48-1992 (Permanence of Paper).

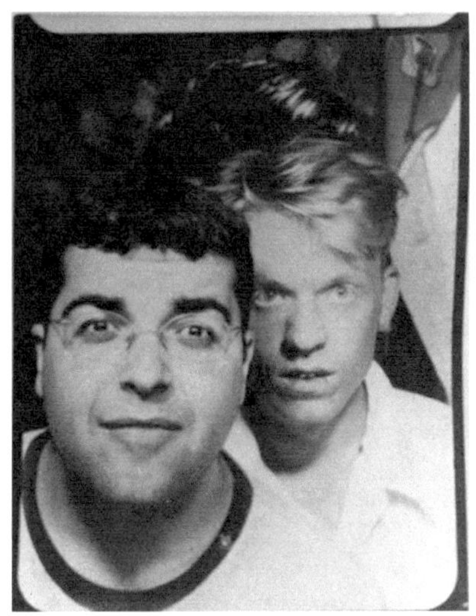

For José Esteban Muñoz

Contents

Introduction: Like

WARHOL: Someone said that Brecht wanted everybody to think alike. I want everybody to think alike. But Brecht wanted to do it through Communism, in a way. Russia is doing it under government. It's happening here all by itself without being under a strict government; so if it's working without trying, why can't it work without being Communist? Everybody looks alike and acts alike, and we're getting more and more that way.

I think everybody should be a machine.

I think everybody should like everybody.

Is that what Pop Art is all about?

WARHOL: Yes. It's liking things.

And liking things is like being a machine?

WARHOL: Yes, because you do the same thing every time. You do it over and over again.

Andy Warhol, "What Is Pop Art?"[1]

The like is not the same.

Jean-Luc Nancy[2]

It was no secret that Andy Warhol liked liking things. He liked to say things like "I like everything" and "I like everybody."[3] In response to questions about his favorite artist, movie star, movie, or TV show, he would generally

1 "What Is Pop Art?," interview by G. R. Swenson, *Art News* 62, no. 7 (November 1963); reprinted in *IBYM*, 16–20, 16. Gerard Malanga reported that Warhol was more open and expansive in this interview because Gene Swenson (an art critic and Warhol's friend) hid the tape recorder under the table and Warhol did not know he was being recorded. Patrick S. Smith, *Warhol: Conversations about the Artist* (Ann Arbor: UMI Research Press, 1988), 165.

2 *The Inoperative Community*, ed. Peter Connor, trans. Peter Connor, Lisa Garbus, Michael Holland, and Simona Sawhey (Minneapolis: University of Minnesota Press, 1991), 33.

3 See, among many examples, *A: A Novel* (New York: Grove Press, 1968), 324.

refuse to state a preference, instead insisting, "I like them all."[4] When a photo of Warhol eating from an open can of Campbell's soup next to one of his Campbell's Soup Can paintings appeared in a 1962 *Time* magazine story on Pop Art, the caption read: "WARHOL: 'JUST BECAUSE I LIKE IT.'"[5] His friends and associates noticed that Warhol not only liked liking but had a positive talent for it. Recalling his collaborations with Warhol in the 1960s, Ronald Tavel (who wrote the scenarios for several Warhol films) remembered that he frequently disagreed with Warhol about whether the films had to be boring. The problem, Tavel suggested, was that Warhol did not get bored like everyone else; he always found something to like.[6] In *Andy Warhol's Exposures*, his 1979 book of "photographs and profiles" of friends, Warhol writes that the publicist Susan Blond "told me the reason she takes me out so much is because I'm easy to please. She said, 'No matter what kind of music I take you to see, it's your favorite kind of music. You like everything,

4 For instance, on films, in 1965: "Oh, I like them all" (*IBYM*, 65). And see Glenn O'Brien, "Interview: Andy Warhol," *High Times*, August 24, 1977; reprinted in *IBYM*, 233–64 (on painters, 238; on movie stars, 254: "I like them all—I mean anyone who's in a movie"). Asked in 1986 if he collected art, his response was "I like everybody's art" (*IBYM*, 358). In a 1977 interview: "I like everybody" (*IBYM*, 272). At the end of a longer exchange in 1981, Edward Lucie-Smith asked Warhol, "Do you ever allow yourself to dislike people then?" Warhol responded, "No . . . I try . . . I really try not to" ("Conversations with Artists: Andy Warhol Talks with Edward Lucie-Smith," January 27, 1981, BBC Script, 17).

5 "The Slice of Cake School," *Time*, May 11, 1962, 52. The story also featured short reports on Wayne Thiebaud, Roy Lichtenstein, and James Rosenquist. Warhol, the only artist pictured, is quoted as saying, "I just paint things I always thought were beautiful, things you use every day and never think about. I'm working on soups, and I've been doing some paintings of money. I just do it because I like it."

6 Personal communication during "Warhol Week in Moscow" conference and film festival, Moscow, 2001. Tavel told David James that Warhol "would sit and watch [his own films] for endless hours with one leg crossed over the other and his face in his hands and his elbows on his knees, with absolute fascination and he was puzzled why the public wasn't equally fascinated. When we stopped off at a screening of *Empire* to see how it was doing, and there were six people in the theater, he said, 'Well, look at that. They'll just pile in to see'—and he referred to some Hollywood blockbuster, you know—'and nobody comes to see *Empire*.' It was a genuine remark, he was not dissembling. He said to me, 'Why don't they come in droves to see *Empire*?' So we should not think that these films were not interesting to him or that he didn't want them to be interesting." James, "The Warhol Screenplays: An Interview with Ronald Tavel," *Persistence of Vision* 11 (1995): 51; quoted by Douglas Crimp, *"Our Kind of Movie": The Films of Andy Warhol* (Cambridge, MA: MIT Press, 2012), 140. Also see Tavel's remarks in "Banana Diary," in *Andy Warhol Film Factory*, ed. Michael O'Pray (London: BFI, 1989).

Tavel was a novelist, playwright, screenwriter, poet, and essayist who wrote the scenarios for several films directed by Warhol, including *Vinyl* (1965), *Horse* (1965), *Kitchen* (1965), and *The Life of Juanita Castro* (1965). On Tavel, see Matthias Haase and Marc Siegel, "Do It Again! Do It Again! An Interview with Ronald Tavel," in "Jack Smith: Beyond the Rented World" (special issue, ed. Marc Siegel), *Criticism* 56, no. 2 (Spring 2014), and Douglas Crimp, "Coming Together to Stay Apart," in *Our Kind of Movie*.

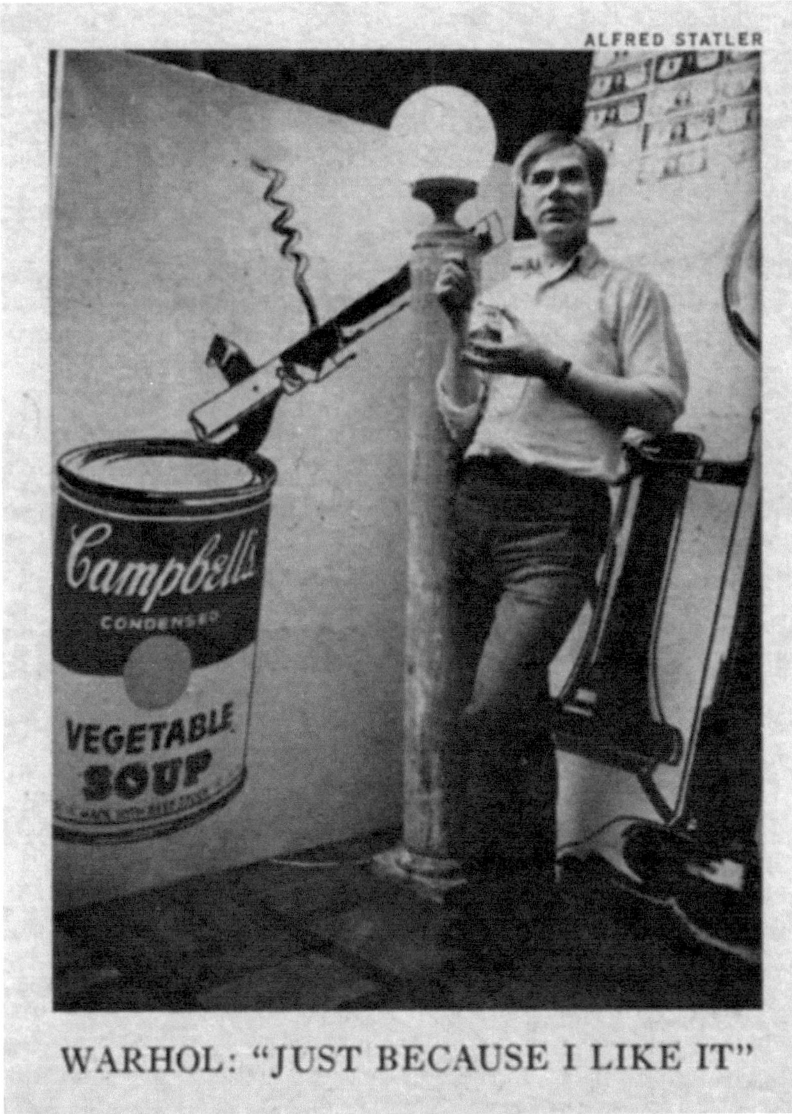

0.1 "Just Because I Like It," *Time*, May 11, 1962, 52. Photograph: Alfred Statler, *Andy Warhol in his studio at 1342 Lexington Avenue, New York City*, April 1962. Collection of the Andy Warhol Museum, Pittsburgh. © The Andy Warhol Museum, a museum of Carnegie Institute.

Andy.'"[7] Vito Giallo, a onetime Warhol studio assistant who later became an antiques dealer, had a similar take on Warhol's passionate collecting: he

7 She then adds, "You would make a *great* publicist." *Andy Warhol's Exposures: Photographs by Andy Warhol*, text by Warhol with Bob Colacello (New York: Andy Warhol Books/Grosset and Dunlap, 1979), 201. Another friend, Tony Berlant, recalls walking with Warhol in New York on West Broadway: "He looked up at the stoplight and said,

"was interested in everything and I was just floored by the amount of things that he bought and the diversity of his interests."[8]

Like Andy Warhol examines Warhol's liking. It contends that for Warhol, "liking things" was a project to be pursued, involving abilities that could be nurtured and educated. Liking constitutes a fundamental value judgment, one that people make continually and often automatically: Will I eat the banana or the apple? Which of my fellow subway riders draws my eye? Should I keep reading this book? Will I nod my head and sway my hips to the rhythm of this music? Liking is less a discrete emotion than an elemental attraction, the most basic positive feeling one can have, a readiness to pay attention to something and be affected by it. As such, it is also an implicit affirmation of something's existence. A chief claim of this book is that Warhol's impressive commitment to liking constitutes a coherent organizing principle running through his enormous and diverse body of work in many media, including drawing, painting, film, video, photography, writing, graphic design, tape-recording, performance, and collecting.

In analyzing Warhol's work as an archive of his liking, I suggest an alternative to a certain commonsense view that understands his art (and its machine-like use of repetition, for instance) as a defense *against* being affected. *Like Andy Warhol* presents Warhol's liking as a praxis, a de-instrumentalized affective labor, which aimed to engage and transform the world in a context where (as Warhol put it) "it would be so much easier not to care."[9] It discerns a pedagogical effort in Warhol's promiscuous liking as well, an ambitious attempt to initiate others into its pleasures: "I think everybody should like everybody" (*IBYM*, 16).

Warhol's primary method for pursuing liking as a project was an inventive and varied production of and attention to ways of being, acting, and looking *alike*. He expanded the force and reach of his liking through an array of aesthetic practices aimed at revitalizing what Walter Benjamin called the mimetic faculty, our "gift for seeing similarity," which has its origins in a "once powerful compulsion to become similar and to behave mimetically."[10] Miriam Hansen emphasizes that for Benjamin, "the mimetic is not a category of representation, pertaining to a particular relationship with a refer-

---

'Streetlights, they're just so great.' You know, he could use that particular Warhol take on anything." In *Possession Obsession: Andy Warhol and Collecting*, ed. John Smith (Pittsburgh: Andy Warhol Museum, 2002), 120.

8 In Victor Bockris, *The Life and Death of Andy Warhol* (London: Fourth Estate, 1989), 415.

9 Lane Slate, "USA Artists: Andy Warhol and Roy Lichtenstein" (1966), in *IBYM*, 81; he repeats the line in Gretchen Berg, "Andy Warhol: My True Story" (1966) in *IBYM*, 96.

10 "On the Mimetic Faculty," *SW2*, 720–22, 720. Although a preoccupation with the mimetic faculty runs through his work (from "One Way Street" and "Berlin Childhood" to "The Image of Proust" and "The Work of Art in the Age of Its Technological Reproducibility"), Benjamin's most focused account occurs in a series of related and overlapping short pieces written in 1933, including also "On Astrology" (*SW2*, 684–85) and "Doctrine of the Similar" (*SW2*, 694–98).

ent, but a *relational* practice—a process, comportment, or activity of 'producing similarities' (such as astrology, dance, and play)."[11] For Benjamin, it is by way of the mimetic faculty that we relate and connect to the world; affinity and affiliation, correspondence and conviviality, are made possible by its operations. "Experiences," he wrote, "are lived similarities."[12] As for Benjamin, for Warhol too, there can be no liking without the capacity to perceive likenesses and to be alike.

It is important to emphasize that this being *alike*, this "lived similarity," is both experientially and conceptually distinct from being equal or identical. As Jean-Luc Nancy concisely observes, "The like is not the same [le semblable n'est pas le pareil]."[13] Indeed, when something is *like* something else, it means precisely that it is *not the same* as it. Things that are alike or similar are neither incommensurate nor identical; they are related and resembling, yet distinct. Similarity is thus a discrete concept aside from the same-different opposition, and insofar as it lies at the core of Warhol's liking, it is a concept we need for understanding his practice.

If, as Eve Sedgwick remarks, "nothing, in Western thought, isn't categorizable and deconstructible under 'same' and 'different,'" then Warhol's replacement of this opposition with a roomier orientation toward likeness should have powerful effects on our apprehension of a whole range of problems (as Benjamin, Nancy, and Kaja Silverman have proposed), including the concept of "identity," the constitution of collectivities, and our sense of what art is and what it does.[14] Perhaps most significantly, it made space for Warhol to conceive of attraction, affection, and attachment without relying on the homo/hetero opposition so central to modern ideas of sexual identity and desire.

Like Andy Warhol investigates Warhol's efforts to produce similarities and draw our attention to them in his famous serial paintings of celebrities (Marilyn, Elvis, Liz, Jackie, Mao), commodities (Campbell's soup, Coke, shoes), and "deaths and disasters" (suicides, electric chairs, car crashes, "race riots"), but also across the wide range of his aesthetic commitments, including his affection for bad acting, his imitation of the machine, his fascination

11 Hansen, *Cinema and Experience: Siegfried Kracauer, Walter Benjamin, and Theodor W. Adorno* (Berkeley: University of California Press, 2012), 147.

12 Benjamin, "Experience," *SW2*, 553. The concept of the mimetic faculty was central to Benjamin's attempt to theorize the conditions of possibility for what he called experience "in the strict sense of the term" (*Erfahrung*), which he discusses in the opening sections of "On Some Motifs in Baudelaire." On *Erfahrung*, see Hansen, *Cinema and Experience*, xiv, 81–82, 171–73, and Flatley, *Affective Mapping: Melancholia and the Politics of Modernism* (Cambridge, MA: Harvard University Press, 2008), 67–70.

13 Nancy, *Inoperative Community*, 33. Similarly, Hansen writes, "Benjamin's similitude works on the order of affinity (*Verwandschaft*), rather than sameness, identity, copy, or reproduction" (*Cinema and Experience*, 147–48).

14 Sedgwick, *Epistemology of the Closet* (Berkeley: University of California Press, 1990), 157. See Silverman, *Flesh of My Flesh* (Stanford, CA: Stanford University Press, 2009).

with drag queens, his promotion of boredom, and his energetic collecting, which encompassed not only "collectible" things like cookie jars, jewelry, cutlery, art, furniture, and Native American rugs, but also vast numbers of photographs (his own and others), perfumes, his own drawings of feet and cocks, his Polaroids of genitalia, thousands of hours of tape recordings made with his Norelco tape recorder (which he called his "wife"), the 472 Screen Tests he filmed between 1964 and 1966, his thousands of commissioned portraits, and his 612 Time Capsules, cardboard boxes filled with printed matter that passed through Warhol's hands—mail, photographs, newspaper clippings, poems, invitations, magazines—along with drawings, clothes, toys, the occasional food item, and just about anything else he did not want to throw out (or that had no other collection to welcome it).[15] Inasmuch as it assembles groups of like-beings (or *semblables*) through a practice of everyday liking, Warhol's collecting vividly dramatizes a mode of attraction based not on lack but on accumulation and plenitude.

To be sure, liking things, never mind liking *everything* and *everybody*, is an unexpected, almost scandalous, project to set for oneself. It certainly represents a departure from scholarly skepticism, and it is directly opposed to what we usually think of as the exercise of aesthetic taste or political judgment (both of which involve liking some things and not liking others). Yet, I think Warhol's energetic commitment to liking and likeness makes most sense if we understand it not only as a provocation. Instead, I see a utopian impulse animating Warhol's liking. It offers what José Muñoz (borrowing from Ernst Bloch) called an "anticipatory illumination" of a world that did not (and does not) yet exist, a world that was appealing to the extent that it promised to repair the inadequacies, injuries, and losses that mar this one.[16]

Perhaps Warhol could only imagine himself being liked in a world where everything and everybody is likable, where nobody is not, at least in some way, alike, and where therefore everybody can enter into relations of imitation and resemblance with everybody else. Embedded in Warhol's "I like everybody" may be the wish "Everybody likes me."[17] Like Walt Whitman, whose affirmative impulse was also inextricable from his capacity for imaginative imitation, Andy Warhol's tendency toward liking and promotion of likenesses may have been a response to "hours of torment" when he won-

15 On the Time Capsules, see *Andy Warhol's Time Capsule 21*, ed. John W. Smith and Matthew Wrbican (Pittsburgh: Andy Warhol Museum, 2003); Matt Wrbican, "Warhol's 'Time Capsule 51,'" in "Andy Warhol" (special issue, ed. Jonathan Flatley and Anthony Grudin), *Criticism* 56, no. 3 (Summer 2014); and Scott Herring, *The Hoarders: Material Deviance in Modern American Culture* (Chicago: University of Chicago, 2014), chap. 2, "Pathological Collectibles." I discuss Warhol's collecting in chapter 1.

16 Muñoz, *Cruising Utopia: The Then and There of Queer Futurity* (New York: NYU Press, 2009), 3.

17 Such a wish is embedded in the history of the word itself: the current usage ("I like it") only gradually replaced an older, now obsolete sense: "to please" or "to be pleasing" (in effect, "it likes me").

dered (as Whitman put it) if "other men ever have the like / out of the like feelings," if indeed "there is even one other like me."[18]

Instead of seeing a world of normal and stigmatized persons, of identities improper either to be or to desire, Warhol seems to have done his best to see and create collections of similars who do have "the like feelings." In this sense, Warhol's liking is an attempt to imagine new, queer forms of affection and relationality and to transform the world into a place where those forms could find a home. It seems probable that this was one of Warhol's ways of managing or repairing his sense of his own stigmatizing weirdness, of being unable to fit into what he called "stock roles." The embarrassing "problems" that he felt needed managing were multiple: his sexual attraction to men and his identification with femininity, but also his baldness, his immigrant, working-class background, and his odd and unusually white skin. Instead of seeking a way to "fit in," Warhol sought to see and make a world in which nobody fit properly, where everybody was "somehow misfitting together."[19] In such a world, Warhol's sometimes flamboyant queerness would lose its stigmatizing effect to the extent that he became one misfit among many.

Both antiassimilationist and antiseparatist, refusing to affirm an identity while also stubbornly avowing his attraction to the male body and more generally making room for nonnormative feelings, attractions, and ways of life, Warhol's liking is queer, and queer as distinct from gay.[20] Or, as Eve

18 "Live Oak with Moss" (1860), in *The Portable Walt Whitman*, ed. Michael Warner (New York: Penguin, 2004), 208. On the utopian and compensatory quality of Whitman's affirmative impulse, see Warner's introduction to the volume, and Peter Coviello, "Intimate Nationality: Anonymity and Attachment in Whitman," *American Literature* 73, no. 1 (March 2001): 85–119.

19 "I was reflecting that most people thought the Factory was a place where everybody had the same attitudes about everything; the truth was, we were all odds-and-ends misfits, somehow misfitting together" (*POP*, 219). See Douglas Crimp's brilliant reading of the double screen *Chelsea Girls* as an allegory and instantiation of what this might mean: "Misfitting Together," in *Our Kind of Movie*, 97–109.

20 I am borrowing here from Eve Kosofsky Sedgwick, "Foreword: T Times" and "Queer and Now," both in *Tendencies* (Durham, NC: Duke University Press, 1993). Among the writings in the large queer studies archive that have most influenced my usage of "queer" here and throughout the book are, in addition to Sedgwick's essays in *Tendencies*, her "Shame, Theatricality and Queer Performativity: Henry James's *Art of the Novel*" and "Paranoid Reading and Reparative Reading, or, You're So Paranoid You Probably Think This Essay Is about You," in *Touching Feeling: Affect, Pedagogy, Performativity* (Durham, NC: Duke University Press, 2003); the writings of Judith Butler, especially "Imitation and Gender Insubordination," in *Inside/Out: Lesbian Theories Gay Theories*, ed. Diana Fuss (New York Routledge, 1991) (reprinted in *Lesbian and Gay Studies Reader*, ed. Henry Abelove, Michèle Aina Barale, and David M. Halperin [New York: Routledge, 1993]), and "Critically Queer," in *Bodies That Matter* (New York: Routledge, 1993); Douglas Crimp, "Right On Girlfriend!" *Social Text*, no. 33 (1992), 2–18; Michael Warner, "Introduction," in *Fear of a Queer Planet: Queer Politics and Social Theory* (Minneapolis: University of Minnesota Press, 1993); Lauren Berlant and Warner, "Sex in Public," in *Intimacy*, ed. Berlant (Chicago: University of Chicago Press, 2000); Cathy Cohen, "Punks, Bulldaggers and

Sedgwick said of the "immemorial current that queer represents," of which Warhol's liking would appear to be a paradigmatic instance: "Keenly, it is relational, and strange."[21]

Liking Being Alike

Just think about all the James Deans and what it means.

The Philosophy of Andy Warhol

The indispensable starting point for thinking about Warhol's liking is his well-known 1963 interview with Gene Swenson, "What Is Pop Art?" (cited in the epigraph at the beginning of this introduction). There, Warhol and Swenson connect being alike to liking by playing with different meanings and forms of "like." In asserting that he wants "everybody to think alike" and that "everybody looks alike and acts alike," Warhol begins with the adjectival or adverbial "alike" that indicates similarity, resemblance, or analogy. He then moves to the transitive verb ("liking things," "liking everybody"), which can refer to a range of positive feelings, including attraction, finding something pleasing, and taking pleasure. The narrative sequence implies that the abundance of likenesses, and our related capacity to think, act, and look alike sets the stage for liking.

The connection between the different senses of "like" resonates through the word's history, as if there were a moment in the past when it was obvious that liking and being-like were immanent to each other, when feelings of attraction toward an object that promised pleasure or enjoyment were understood to be essentially related to the imitation of or assimilation into that object.[22] By bringing the different meanings together, the word "like"

Welfare Queens: The Radical Potential of Queer Politics?" *GLQ* 3 (1997): 437–65; José Esteban Muñoz, *Disidentifications: Queers of Color and the Performance of Critique* (Minneapolis: University of Minnesota Press, 1999) and *Cruising Utopia*; Roderick Ferguson, *Aberrations in Black: A Queer of Color Critique* (Minneapolis: University of Minnesota, Press, 2003); Heather Love, *Feeling Backward: Loss and the Politics of Queer History* (Cambridge, MA: Harvard University Press, 2007) and "Queers ___ This," in *After Sex? On Writing since Queer Theory*, ed. Janet Halley and Andrew Parker (Durham, NC: Duke University Press, 2010); Michael Snediker, *Queer Optimism* (Minneapolis: University of Minnesota Press, 2008); Mel Chen, *Animacies: Biopolitics, Racial Mattering and Queer Affect* (Durham, NC: Duke University Press, 2012); and Ann Cvetkovich, *Depression* (Durham, NC: Duke University Press, 2012).

21 "T Times," viii.

22 Like a homograph, "like" is a word of the same written form as another but of different meaning; we discern which "like" is meant by its place in a grammatical structure and by its semantic context. But unlike a homograph, the different meanings seem to share an origin and may be confused with each other. On the homograph in relation to the reading of "homosexuality," see Lee Edelman, *Homographesis* (New York: Routledge, 1994).

itself makes the chiastic double assertion that to be pleased by something is to feel like it, and that feeling similar to something is itself pleasing. Literary critics Bruce Smith and Stephen Burt both call attention to the origins of "like" in the Old and Middle English *lich*, meaning "body" or "form."[23] "Beneath all the modern uses of 'like,'" Smith writes, "is the fundamental idea of con-formity, of fitting something with the body or fitting the body with that something" (10). On some basic level, in its various meanings, "like" means to correspond, to fit together, to be-with.

It is fitting, then, that Warhol begins the interview sequence mimetically by asserting that, like Brecht, he "want[s] everybody to think alike." In so doing, Warhol appears to dramatize the imitative substitution that brings his desiring "I" into being.[24] This is what Rene Girard called "mimetic" or "triangular" desire, where a subject desires an object only through the imitation of another subject's desire for that object.[25] Desire thus triangulated or mediated (which for Girard is all desire) tends to produce a mimetic rivalry over the object (as, for example, in the son's Oedipal desire for the mother), a wanting to "be" or "replace" that other person, since only one person can "have" the object of desire. For Warhol too there is no genuine self-generated desire because no desire comes into being except by way of imitation. Yet, Warhol here neatly sidesteps the central drama of Girard's model, avoiding rivalry in his imitation of Brecht because what Warhol "likes" (like Brecht) is not an object over which they might compete, but "thinking alike" itself. In thereby wrapping liking and being-like together Warhol fulfills Brecht's want by imitating it. Instead of producing mimetic rivalries over objects that

23 The body indicated could be dead or alive; thus, for instance, the Lichyard is the grave yard. See Smith, *Phenomenal Shakespeare* (Chichester: Wiley-Blackwell, 2010); Burt, "'LIKE': A Speculative Essay about Poetry, Simile, Artificial Intelligence, Mourning, Sex, Rock and Roll, Grammar, Romantic Love," *American Poetry Review* 43, no. 1, https://www.aprweb.org/article/quotlikequot-speculative-essay-about-poetry-simile-artificial-intelligence-mourning-sex-rock.

24 On Warhol's "I" as an imitative effect, see his 1966 interview with Lane Slate, where he says, "It's so exciting not to think anything. I mean, you should just tell me the words and I can just repeat them because I can't . . . uh . . . I can't . . . I'm so empty today. I can't think of anything. Why don't you just tell me the words and they'll just come out of my mouth" (*IBYM*,80). He makes a similar comment to Gretchen Berg the same year: "The interviewer should just tell me the words he wants me to say and I'll repeat them after him" (*IBYM*, 61). The matter of Warhol's mode of self-presentation in his interviews, as well as the poetics of his interview performances, is a fascinating topic in its own right, smartly treated by Wayne Koestenbaum in his short afterword to *IBYM*, and Nicholas de Villiers, in his insightful *Opacity and the Closet: Queer Tactics in Foucault, Barthes and Warhol* (Minneapolis: University of Minnesota Press, 2012).

25 See Girard, *Deceit, Desire and the Novel* (Baltimore: Johns Hopkins University Press, 1965). Rosalind Krauss reads Warhol in terms of mimetic desire in "Carnal Knowledge (1996)," in *Andy Warhol*, ed. Annette Michelson (Cambridge, MA: MIT Press, 2001), 111–18, and in chap. 6 of Krauss, *The Optical Unconscious* (Cambridge, MA: MIT Press, 1993).

one either has or lacks, Warhol's liking combines attraction and imitation: "When you want to be like something, it means you really love it."[26]

Warhol is explicit about one way that being-like replaces the being-versus-having model in a passage from the "Love" section of his *Philosophy*:

> If you see a person who looks like your teenage fantasy walking down the street, it's probably not your fantasy, but someone who had the same fantasy as you and decided instead of getting it or being it, to *look like it*, and so he went to the store and bought the look that you both like. So forget it. Just think about all the James Deans and what it means. (53)

That is, the person you like is *already* like you—in fact, that is *why* you like him or her, even if you do not know it. She or he had the same fantasy you had, and failed (like you) to get it or be it. Each of you has internalized the old fantasy object, although through different strategies: you have the image nostalgically tucked away as an imaginative and affective aid as you look at people on the street; the person who looks like your fantasy has kept an attachment to the fantasy alive by modeling her- or himself after it. Both processes (distinct from "desire," but akin to Freud's descriptions of melancholic identification) involve a mimetic copying in response to an experience of loss.[27] We are all miming what we miss. As Lacan put it, "What one cannot keep outside, one always keeps an image of inside."[28]

Perhaps the first objects we keep inside in this way—because they are the first objects we lose—are our first caretakers, typically our parents. Melancholic incorporation is what enables us to keep an emotional tie alive in the absence of this caretaker, on whom our very survival, after all, depends. This is one way to understand Freud's observation that identification is the first emotional tie.[29] This imitative incorporation allows us to tolerate our caretaker's absence and to recognize her or him when s/he returns. The "self" is at once the instrument and creation of this imitative incorporation: we only need a "self" in order to deal with the rupture of the originary form

26 *Phil*, 53.
27 On melancholia and identification, see "Mourning and Melancholia," in *The Standard Edition of the Complete Psychological Works of Sigmund Freud*, vol. 14, trans. and ed. James Strachey (London: Hogarth Press, 1957), 243–58. Freud revised his understanding of melancholic identification in *The Ego and the Id* (1923; *Standard Edition*, 19:29). See also *Group Psychology and the Analysis of the Ego*, trans. and ed. James Strachey (New York: Norton, 1959). I discuss this in *Affective Mapping*, esp. 41–50.
28 *The Four Fundamental Concepts of Psychoanalysis* (New York: Norton, 1978), 243.
29 "Identification is known to psychoanalysis as the earliest expression of an emotional tie with another person" (*Group Psychology*, 46). See also Diana Fuss, *Identification Papers* (New York: Routledge, 1995), and Mikkel Borch-Jacobsen, *The Emotional Tie: Psychoanalysis, Mimesis and Affect* (Stanford, CA: Stanford University Press, 1992). For another take on the relation between identification and desire, see Leo Bersani, "Sociability and Cruising," in *Is the Rectum a Grave?* (Chicago: University of Chicago Press, 2009).

of relationality at the basis of our being. The self, as Jacques Derrida puts it, "appears to itself only in this bereaved allegory, in this hallucinatory prosopopoeia."[30] Out of this moment, where I have created inside me (*as* "me") a likeness of the person to whom I am affectively attached, springs a psychic formation in which "liking" someone else is dependent on my ability to "be like" her or him. That is, in order to like someone, I need to perceive a resemblance in them such that they can seem imitable to me as the condition of possibility for recognizing them and surviving their absences.[31] Emotional attachment requires a capacity for noticing and prioritizing resemblances. "Love is the power to see similarity in the dissimilar," Adorno remarked (echoing Aristotle's famous observation that the creation of a metaphor requires "an intuitive perception of the similarity in dissimilars").[32] This is a power we are all evidently born with but that is increasingly policed and even damaged as we "grow up" (on which, more below).

So when Warhol says "so forget it" about the person you find attractive on the street whom you think might be your fantasy, he is not advising you to forget your attractions or to refrain from picking up the person who looks like your fantasy. Rather, what you need to forget is the idea that you can ever have or be your fantasy object, because you never *are* a subject without some internalized object you are imitating, and we only like those objects that look like ones about which we have already fantasized. ("People's fantasies are what give them problems"; *Phil*, 55.) Warhol is encouraging us to forget the sense that we must relate to others by way of *either* identification ("being") or desire ("having"), which itself relies on the opposition between same and different. Instead, he seems to be reminding us, since our selves

30 "The specular reflection never closes on itself; it does not appear *before* this *possibility* of mourning, before and outside this structure of allegory and prosopopoeia which constitutes in advance all 'being-in-us,' 'in-me,' between us, or between ourselves. The *selbst*, the *soi-meme*, the self appears to itself only in this bereaved allegory, in this hallucinatory prosopopoeia—and even before the death of the other *actually* happens, as we say, in 'reality.' The strange situation I am describing here, for example that of my friendship with Paul de Man, would have allowed me to say all of this *before* his death. It suffices that I know him to be mortal, that he knows me to be mortal—there is no friendship without this knowledge of finitude." Derrida, *Memoires for Paul de Man* (New York: Columbia University Press, 1988), 28–29.

31 Borch-Jacobsen makes a similar point in *The Emotional Tie*: "To affirm that 'the earliest emotional tie with another person' is identification is, in effect, to assert that affect as such is identificatory, mimetic, and that there is no 'proper' affect except on the condition of a prior 'affection' of the ego by another. Another does not affect me because I feel such and such an affect in regard to him, nor even because he succeeds in communicating an affect to me by way of words. He affects me because 'I' *am* that 'other,' following an identification that is my affection, the strangest alteration of my proper autoaffection. My identity is a passion. And reciprocally, my passions are always identificatory" (73).

32 Adorno, *Minima Moralia: Reflections on a Damaged Life*, trans. E. F. N. Jephcott (1974; London: Verso, 2005), 191; Aristotle, *Poetics*, sect. 22, in *The Basic Works of Aristotle*, ed. Richard McKeon (New York: Random House, 1947), 1479.

are formed from a process of imitation, so too our likes are always repetitions of past likes, "transferences," as Freud called them, of earlier attractions or past emotional ties onto an object in the present.[33] The new object need only be perceived as similar to the old one, and the similarity can be slight (more important is that our capacity for perceiving that similarity remain active and robust). In this sense affects and attractions never occur for the first time. They always appear as (what Freud called) "facsimiles or new editions" of old emotional ties.[34] We are, each of us, going back to the Marilyn or Elvis or James Dean model (which we may see as themselves repetitions of earlier "imagos" of our parents) and reprinting it on new material. The fact that in our mass-mediated society plenty of other people will be repeating the same models means that there are going to be people out there who look like your fantasy, and that there is a good chance someone will like the look that you bought too. (One can imagine how, for Warhol, who did not see himself as attractive, this may have been a comforting insight.[35])

What makes us all "look and act alike," then, is a shared relation to and reliance on consumption (going to "the store and [buying] the look that you both like"), which banks on and repeats the basic (melancholic) structure of human relationality, ever and again offering the promise of being like the object you did not get and could not be. But, whereas for Girard the fact that we all want the same objects only ratchets up the competitive nature of mimetic desire (we are all trying to keep up with the Joneses),[36] for Warhol,

33 See also Sandor Ferenczi's writings on introjection, especially "Introjection and Transference (1909)," in *Sex in Psycho-Analysis* (New York: Dover, 1956). Ferenczi coined the term "introjection" to designate the opposite of projection; in this mode of transference, external objects are brought "inside," inasmuch as they substitute for their (internalized) models. He argues that introjection is a strategy for "mollifying free floating affects by extension of the circle of interest."

34 "What are transferences? They are new editions or facsimiles of the tendencies and fantasies which are aroused and made conscious of the progress of the analysis; but they have this peculiarity, which is characteristic for their species, that they replace some earlier person by the person of the physician." Freud also refers to the transferences as "new impressions or reprints," noting that in some cases there are "revised editions." *Dora: An Analysis of a Case of Hysteria* (New York: Collier Books, 1963), 138.

35 From the *Diaries*: "When I saw myself in those home movies we took on the Cape last weekend I hated myself so much. Every simple thing I do looks strange. I have such a strange walk and a strange look. If I could only have been a peculiar comic in the movies, I would have looked like a puppet. But it's too late. What's wrong with me?" (Saturday, May 30, 1981, 385). Or later, on seeing a tape he did for a TV show: "I was terrible. Reeeallly reeeallly peculiar. I'm just a freak. I can't change it. I'm too unusual" (January 25, 1983, 481). See also Tony Scherman and David Dalton, *Pop: The Genius of Andy Warhol* (New York: HarperCollins, 2010), 8.

36 *Deceit, Desire and the Novel*, esp. 223, where Girard asserts that in consumer society, "the value of the article consumed is based solely on how it is regarded by the Other. . . . More recently, David Riesman and Vance Packard have shown that even the vast American middle class, which is as free from want and even more uniform than the circles described by Proust, is also divided into abstract compartments. It produces more and

if we are able to follow his advice to "forget" the being-having fantasies (a not inconsiderable "if," to be sure), our mass culture–produced similarity makes it easier for us to imagine imitating and also liking each other.

Happily, Warhol is a gifted forgetter. (Indeed, he bragged, "my mind is like a tape recorder with one button—Erase."[37]) He is especially good at forgetting reified or ideologically freighted oppositions and instead noticing or creating resemblances across them. Such resemblances then make a hospitable site for nonhierarchical analogies. As Kaja Silverman reminds us (in her reading of Gerhard Richter's work), "An analogy brings two or more things together on the basis of their lesser or greater resemblance," a relation that neutralizes our habitual "identity-antithesis" mode of thinking.[38] So, for instance, in the Swenson interview, where Brecht wanted to pursue thinking alike "under Communism," Warhol notes that it is "happening here all by itself," since "everybody looks alike and acts alike, and we're getting more and more that way." Casually puncturing the celebratory rhetoric of American "individuality" and subverting the Cold War logic that opposed it to Soviet homogeneity, Warhol reminds us that industrial modernity in both places involves the proliferation of similarities, at the level of work (in the Fordist factory) and of consumption.[39] Even if cars and soups and celebrities mostly differed across the Cold War divide, people were shaped in both places by the experience of sharing with millions of others common objects of emotional attachment in their everyday lives.[40] People in the

more taboos and excommunications among absolutely similar but opposed units. Insignificant distinctions appear immense and produce incalculable effects."

37 *Phil*, 199.

38 Analogy, Silverman writes, is Richter's "name for a special kind of relationship, one that has become more capacious with each new development in his art making. An analogy brings two or more things together on the basis of their lesser or greater resemblance. I say 'lesser or greater' because although in some of Richter's analogies similarity and difference are evenly balanced, in others similarity outweighs difference, or difference, similarity. But regardless of the form they take, these couplings neutralize the two principles by means of which we are accustomed to think: identity and antithesis" (*Flesh of My Flesh*, 173).

39 See Susan Buck-Morss on shared practices and fantasies of modernity in the United States and the Soviet Union in *Dreamworld and Catastrophe: The Passing of Mass Utopia in the East and West* (Cambridge, MA: MIT Press, 2000). On the basic logic and origins of mass culture, see Richard Ohmann's indispensable *Selling Culture: Magazines, Markets and Class at the Turn of the Century* (New York: Verso, 1998), where he demonstrates that beginning around the turn of the twentieth century in the United States, modern mass culture, in the form of magazines (and later radio, film, and television), had created a situation in which, for the first time, thousands, even hundreds of thousands or millions, of people, could and did experience the same cultural objects simultaneously or nearly so.

40 For an interesting reading of Warhol's "commonism" in relation to the visual modes of the Cold War, see John J. Curley, *A Conspiracy of Images: Andy Warhol, Gerhard Richter and the Art of the Cold War* (New Haven, CT: Yale University Press, 2013), esp. chap. 2, "The Development of Andy Warhol's Pop Eye."

United States and Soviet Union were alike precisely in their experience of likenesses.

Warhol replaces the opposition between capitalism and communism with a commitment to "commonism," an early neologism (reportedly favored by Warhol) for what would become known as Pop Art.[41] At the time, it referred to artists' representation of common things, the "comics, picnic tables, men's trousers, celebrities, shower curtains, refrigerators, Coke bottles—all the great modern things that the abstract expressionists tried so hard not to notice at all" (*POP*, 3). But it also aptly names Warhol's focus on the being-in-common enabled by the compellingly mutual relations of resemblance. The "like-being" (*semblable*), Nancy writes, "resembles me in that I myself 'resemble' him: we resemble together, if you will."[42]

Warhol's commonism also has a certain leveling effect, which is described in an oft-cited passage from his *Philosophy*:

> What's great about this country is that America started the tradition where the richest consumers buy essentially the same things as the poorest. You can be watching TV and see Coca-Cola, and you can know that the President drinks Coke, Liz Taylor drinks Coke, and just think, you can drink Coke, too. A Coke is a Coke and no amount of money can get you a better Coke than the one the bum on the corner is drinking. All the Cokes are the same and all the Cokes are good. Liz Taylor knows it, the President knows it, the bum knows it, and you know it. (100–101)

Overlooking the differences in lived experiences between the "richest" and the "poorest" (of which he was keenly aware), Warhol asserts a commonality achieved through a shared consumption of Coke. Indeed, Warhol points out that this Coke-commonism's negation of difference in particular experience is the source of its charm; in fact, it is the appeal of consumption (and spectatorship) more generally.[43] This attraction, as Lauren Berlant and Michael Warner have argued, mimics the way citizenship also offers one access to a

41 See Nathan Gluck in Smith, *Conversations*: "You know, at one time, when the movement first got started, he wanted to call his stuff 'Commonist Painting.' Meaning, it was common. . . . I know there was this plug about 'Commonist Art' because they were going to paint common things, but 'Pop' stuck and it never got off the ground, and of course it sounded like 'Communist'" (67). Brief discussions of the term can also be found in Wayne Koestenbaum, *Andy Warhol* (New York: Viking, 2001), 63; Blake Stimson, "Andy Warhol's Red Beard," *Art Bulletin* 83, no. 3 (September 2001): 527–47; Caroline Jones, *The Machine in the Studio: Constructing the Postwar American Artist* (Chicago: University of Chicago Press, 1996), esp. 204–5; and Scherman and Dalton, *Pop*, 100–101.

42 *Inoperative Community*, 33.

43 He extends his point about Coke to include hot dogs, and then TV and film, noting that "rich people can't see a sillier version of *Truth or Consequences* or a scarier version of the *Exorcist*. You can get just as revolted as they can—you can have the same nightmares" (*Phil*, 101).

self-abstracted space of the "person in general," where bodily particularity can be left behind (and seen as if from a distance) and matters of common concern can be deliberated. (As such, it is especially appealing to minoritized subjects who have been denied access to the abstracted personhood promised by citizenship.)[44] And even as (or to the precise extent that) Warhol knew and resented the fact that certain bodies—such as female ones, or queer ones, or nonwhite ones—had a difficult time accessing that sphere of abstracted "personhood" (the "stock role" par excellence), and even though he knew that the promise of transcendence into a realm where everything is good serves to cover over the inequalities of access to that goodness, Warhol all the more avowed and directed our attention to those sites of commonality that did exist. For it was precisely here, as Muñoz powerfully suggests in *Cruising Utopia*, that Warhol sought to illuminate the potential of a different life-world, a "restructured sociality."[45] Thus, Warhol approved when college student Suzy Stanton described what he was "saying" in his Campbell Soup paintings in this way: "I love soup, and I love it when other people love soup too, because then we can all love it together and love each other at the same time."[46] Stanton's reading of Warhol may sound naïve, but it is worth remembering that it accurately, if optimistically, describes one of the structures of feeling supporting the social movements of the 1960s. Many of the struggles of the civil rights movement—for example, at lunch counters—were about asserting similarity in the face of its denial at sites of consumption.[47]

In fact, despite the language of universality Warhol sometimes invokes, his commonism is organized, on the level of content, precisely around the experiences of marginalized or devalued subjectivities. For instance, not only does Warhol depict celebrities well known for their queer fans (James

44 See Berlant, "National Brands/National Bodies: Imitation of Life," and Warner, "The Mass Public and the Mass Subject," both in *The Phantom Public Sphere*, ed. Bruce Robbins (Minneapolis: University of Minnesota Press, 1993). I write about the appeal of publicity and consumption in "Warhol Gives Good Face: Publicity and the Politics of Prosopopoeia," in *Pop Out: Queer Warhol*, ed. Jennifer Doyle, Jonathan Flatley, and José Esteban Muñoz (Durham, NC: Duke University Press, 1996).

45 *Cruising Utopia*, 7.

46 Stanton wrote the essay for a college art class and sent it to Warhol, who liked it so much that he reprinted it in its entirety as an invitation to his first New York exhibition at the Stable Gallery. The archives at the Warhol Museum in Pittsburgh have an original copy of the essay/invitation. Cited in *CR1*, 70. Stephen Burt's observation echoes Stanton's: "The more often I like what you like, the more likely it becomes that you are like, and that you will like, me" ("LIKE," n.p.).

47 One might also consider that the antiwar movement and the countercultures that surrounded it were in part formed through shared incorporation of and attunement to "a market mediated form of popular expression (rock music) inflected with the rebellious sentiments of the working class and oppressed peoples, particularly African Americans." Howard Brick, *Age of Contradiction: American Thought and Culture in the 1960s* (Ithaca, NY: Cornell University Press 2000), 114.

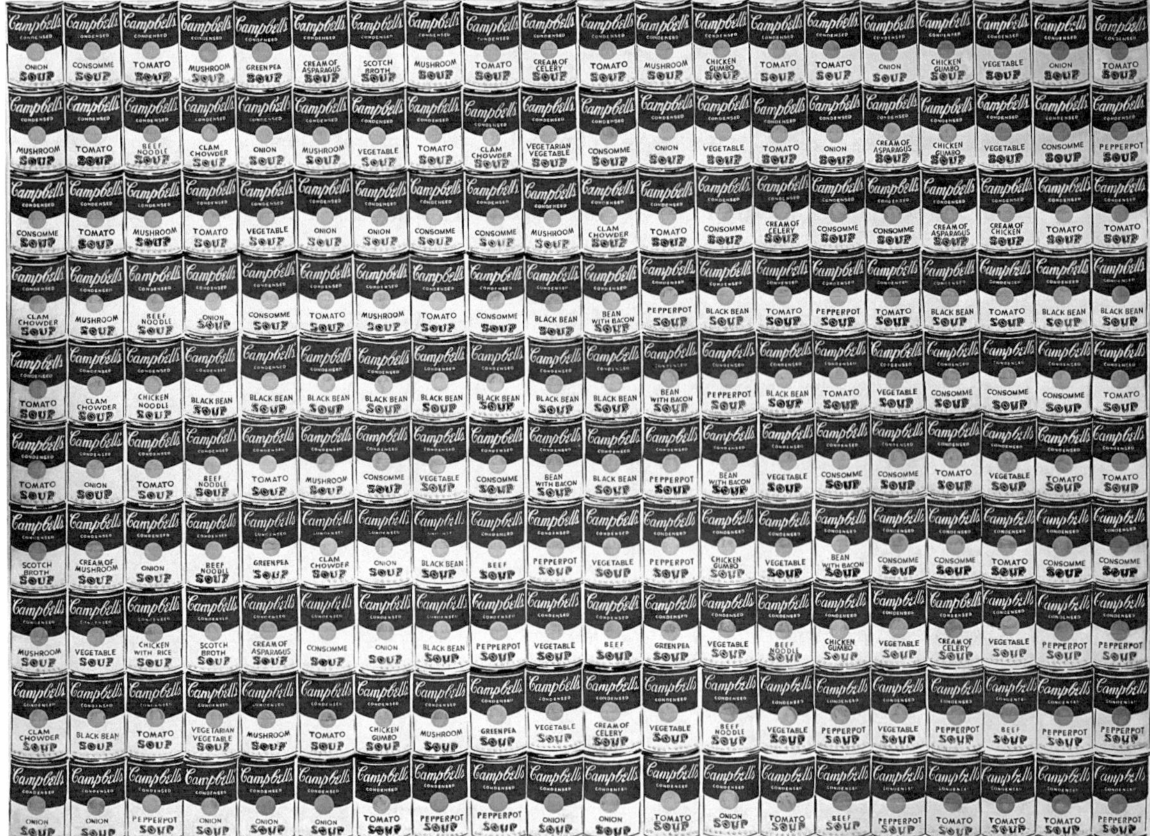

0.2 Andy Warhol, *200 Campbell's Soup Cans*, 1962. Synthetic polymer paint and silkscreen ink on canvas, 72 × 100 inches. © 2016 Andy Warhol Foundation for the Visual Arts/Artists Rights Society (ARS), New York.

Dean, Troy Donahue, Marilyn Monroe, Liz Taylor, Jackie Kennedy).[48] But, as Anthony Grudin has shown, his interest in all the "great modern things" is also an interest in objects—from comics to Coke, Brillo Pads to Campbell's soup—that "were deployed and widely understood as class-specific images, explicitly targeted at a working-class audience."[49]

The persistent focus of Warhol's work was the world of common objects as a world of common feeling, one that contributed to the sixties mood in

48 On James Dean (of whom Warhol made at least two drawings in the 1950s) in particular, see Roy Grundmann's excellent "Andy Warhol, James Dean, and White Gay Men," in *Andy Warhol's Blow Job* (Philadelphia: Temple University Press, 2003), 132–63.
49 "'Except Like a Tracing': Defectiveness, Accuracy, and Class in Early Warhol," *October*, no. 140 (Spring 2012), 139–64, 141. Grudin demonstrates how this is evident in Warhol's source images, especially for his earliest Pop works, which were usually "the cheapest and most accessible images available—images marketed to and associated with a working-class demographic."

which, as Warhol said, "everybody got interested in everybody else" (*Phil*, 26). But then, he added, "drugs helped a little there." They helped first of all because amphetamines, marijuana, and LSD were themselves common objects sought out because they increased one's ability to "get interested" in other people. For instance, Warhol describes kids on acid staring at each other for hours at the Central Park Be-In.[50] But also, since each drug changes perception, sensation, affect, and experience in specific ways, using a given drug is a quick way to become like other people whose perception and experience have also been altered by it.[51] Taking amphetamines (as Warhol and many of his friends did in the 1960s) was a technique Warhol valued because the drugs created magic circles of "lived similarity." In Warhol's Factory, this magic circle formed a particular collectivity of "A-men" or "Mole People" with its own protocols and tendencies. Although "the Factory A-men were mostly fags," along with a "notorious dyke" (Warhol's longtime friend Brigid Berlin) (*POP*, 62), membership in this collectivity was not defined by pregiven or stable identities so much as it was created by a shared decision to take amphetamines and in so doing become like the others.[52] In this, the A-men constitute a kind of paradigm for Warhol: voluntary practices of becoming-alike that create a way to belong and be with others without depending on existing norms or on one's capacity to *be* an identity.

Anti-Likeness

As we know, there was also a world outside these magic circles where liking and likeness were not valued, which is precisely what made Warhol's techniques for noticing and producing resemblances attractive. What he posits in his interview with Swenson as a self-evident or given historical fact—that we are all *already* thinking and acting alike, that imitation and likeness *already* abound—was, at best, underappreciated at the moment Warhol was speaking (in the context of the Cold War and the civil rights movement) and, at worst, actively discouraged or ignored. If the imitation of others and the experience of a mimetic "we-centric" space that allows for affective attunement and relationality is in some sense basic, even automatic, it is nonetheless the case that this shared space can be negated.[53]

50 Discussed in chapter 3.

51 See Juan A. Suárez, "Warhol's 1960s Films, Amphetamine, and Queer Materiality," and Chelsea Weathers, "Drugtime," both in *Criticism* 56, no. 3 (Summer 2014; Warhol special issue).

52 See Mary Woronov's compelling memoir, *Swimming Underground: My Years in the Warhol Factory* (Boston: Journey Editions, 1995). On the A-men, see Scherman and Dalton, *Pop*, 203–7. For a related discussion of queer imitation and initiation, see Michael Moon's brilliant *A Small Boy and Others: Imitation and Initiation in American Culture from Henry James to Andy Warhol* (Durham, NC: Duke University Press, 1998).

53 Paolo Virno makes an argument along these lines in "Mirror Neurons, Linguistic Negation, Reciprocal Recognition," in *Multitude: Between Innovation and Negation* (New

Indeed, as Walter Benjamin argued, we need not look far to see ways in which modernity has suppressed the mimetic faculty, and how this suppression can have negative implications for the possibilities of emotional attachment and engagement. As Susan Buck-Morss emphasizes in her important essay "Aesthetics and Anaesthetics: The Artwork Essay Reconsidered," Benjamin's analysis of modernization's impact on the mimetic faculty centers on the experience of shock. Benjamin generalized Freud's analysis of traumatic "shell shock," arguing that "in industrial production no less than modern warfare, in street crowds and erotic encounters, in amusement parks and gambling casinos, shock is the very essence of modern experience."[54] In the factory, workers must adapt their movements to a dangerous, automated process indifferent to the particularities of distinct bodies, sensations, and feelings; to be affectively open to this compulsory mimesis would be nearly suicidal. To survive the factory setting, the mimetic response becomes a defensive reflex: imagination is paralyzed, memory replaced by conditioned response, learning by "drill," skill by repetition—"practice counts for nothing."[55] Outside the factory, the mimetic faculty is challenged even by the simple experience of riding on a bus or train, which puts people "in a position of having to stare at one another for minutes or even hours on end without exchanging a word."[56] We would be emotionally drained, to the point of collapse, if we were affectively open to all the people we encounter on city streets or public transportation, never mind the wars, murders, floods, earthquakes, terror alerts, and bombings we see on the news. In response to this affectively demanding sensory assault, the primary function of consciousness, Benjamin argues, is to insulate us from disruptive emotional experiences. Thus, "rather than incorporating the outside world," mimetic capacities "are used as a deflection against it. The smile that appears automatically on passersby wards off contact, a reflex that functions as a mimetic shock absorber." Instead of affective attunement or mimetic correspondence, our faculties are increasingly oriented toward anaesthetization.[57] The drug trade

York: Semiotext(e), 2008), 175–90. This is also a persistent focus of Jean-Luc Nancy's writing, in *Inoperative Community, Being Singular Plural*, trans. Robert D. Richardson and Anne E. O'Byrne (Stanford, CA: Stanford University Press, 2000), and elsewhere.

54 Buck-Morss, "Aesthetics and Anaesthetics: Walter Benjamin's Artwork Essay Reconsidered" *October*, no. 62 (Fall 1992), 3–41, 17.

55 Benjamin, "On Some Motifs in Baudelaire," *SW4*, 329.

56 Georg Simmel, "Excursus on the Sociology of Sense Perception" (1911), in *Sociology, Inquiry into the Construction of Social Forms*, vol. 1, trans. and ed. Anthony J. Blasi, Anton K. Jacobs, and Mathew Kanjiranthinkal (Leiden/Boston: Brill, 2009), 573; cited in Benjamin, "On Some Motifs in Baudelaire," 341. See also Simmel, "The Metropolis and Mental Life"(1903), in *Georg Simmel on Individuality and Social Form*, 324–39 (Chicago: University of Chicago Press, 1971).

57 Buck-Morss, "Aesthetics and Anaesthetics," 17. In such a situation, Buck-Morss argues, our assemblage of cognitive, affective, and perceptual systems for interacting with and processing the world reverses its role. Instead of mimetic openness, "its goal is to

correspondingly expands. Everybody can relate to Joey Ramone's plea: "I wanna be sedated."

Yet the dulling of the mimetic faculty, the distance from the world that an etherized life entails, gives rise to a newfound pleasure in the experiences that manage to break on through to the other side, which the modern subject finds on offer in the *phantasmagoria*, the total spectacle designed to overwhelm the senses. Borrowing from Buck-Morss, Miriam Hansen observes that the hyperstimulation offered by Wagner's total work of art and the Luna Parks' rollercoasters, as well as the blockbuster Hollywood action film, was "designed to pierce the defensive shield of consciousness in the momentary experience of shock, awe, or vertigo," but this piercing instead "further contributed to the thickening of the protective shield and thus effectively exacerbated sensory alienation." In a negative feedback loop, the pleasurable piercing of the defensive mimetic shield only amplifies the need to fortify the shield, which requires that the stimulus become yet stronger, which ratchets up the defenses again. "By the 1930s," Hansen writes, "this dialectics of anaesthetics and aestheticization had impaired human faculties of experience, affect, and cognition on a mass scale, thereby paralyzing political agency and the collective ability to prevent the deployment of technology toward self-destructive ends."[58]

It was toward overcoming this paralysis and figuring out how to stimulate collective affective involvement in a shared world that much of Benjamin's thought is directed.[59] That is, Benjamin's aim is not to lament the mimetic faculty's "dying out" so much as to try to figure out how "the gift for producing similarities . . . and therefore also the gift of recognizing them, have changed in the course of history."[60] How might we discern "a transformation that has taken place" in our ability to see and produce similarities? "In the course of the centuries both the mimetic force and the mimetic mode of vision may have vanished from certain spheres, perhaps only to surface in others," Benjamin suggests.[61] The task, shared by Benjamin and Warhol, is

---

numb the organism, to deaden the senses, to repress memory: the cognitive system of synaesthetics has become, rather, one of anaesthetics" (18).

58 Hansen, *Cinema and Experience*, 79–80.

59 Hansen helpfully summaries Benjamin's position: "The alienation of the senses that abets the deadly violence of imperialist warfare and fascism can be undone only on the terrain of technology itself, by means of new media of reproduction that allow for a collective and playful (that is, nonfatal) innervation of the technologically transformed physis" (ibid., 80). At the same time, Benjamin was interested in how Baudelaire responded to this situation by becoming a traumatophile, actively seeking to break through the anaesthetic defense, dramatizing for his readers the lengths to which one had to go to have an experience, and showing us why we usually do not. In this way, Benjamin suggests in "On Some Motifs in Baudelaire," we could at least experience the loss of our ability to have an experience.

60 *SW2*, 720.

61 *SW2*, 684.

to find where the mimetic force has surfaced and help it to flourish. Benjamin well describes the world Warhol also saw—one where, in general, one feels that "it would be so much easier not to care"—and sought to change through a pointed and constant attempt to stimulate and awaken a slumbering mimetic faculty. In so doing, Warhol is also showing us how we might disrupt, short-circuit, or otherwise circumvent the discourses, institutions, and practices that discourage or inhibit our mimetic faculties and our imitative behaviors.

For it is not only this anaesthetizing dynamic that has made the mimetic faculty "increasingly fragile," so that the similarities we are now capable of perceiving "in buildings and plant forms, in certain cloud formations and skin diseases, are nothing more than tiny prospects from a cosmos of similarity" (*SW2*, 684). The promulgation of any number of equivalences and incommensurabilities tends also to distract us. For starters, "identity," the idea that some things are "equal," lies at the basis of logic itself but, as Nietzsche wrote, suppresses similarity because it requires that we "treat as equal what is merely similar" ("an illogical tendency, for nothing is really equal").[62] The universal standard of equivalence established by money is then only "logical," as is the compensatory valorization of the "genuine" and "authentic. The related ideology that holds that we should be independent, self-owned individuals (a version of which is found in the art world premium on originality) disparages imitation as a sign of weakness and dependence. Only "logical," too, is our personal "identity," which we must guard against theft and stand ready to "prove"—to the state, to the police, to our employer. In many everyday contexts, a fixed and verifiable personal identity is compulsory: whether signing and cashing checks, crossing the border, driving a car, signing a lease, filing taxes, reporting to work, signing a work of art, or authoring a text, there must be no confusing you and your likeness; playing someone you are not invites all kinds of trouble (trouble Warhol actively courted). The discourses, institutions, and norms regarding gender, sexual, and racial identity are also crucial sites where, as we grow up, we are schooled quite carefully and deliberately concerning the proper objects of imitation and correct modes of mimetic comportment.

In response to these anti-likeness, anti-liking forces, Warhol (like Benjamin) "envisions a regeneration of affect by means of mechanically produced images, that is, the possibility of countering the alienation of the human sensorium with the same means and media that are part of the technological proliferation of shock anaesthetics-aestheticization."[63] As Warhol told an interviewer in the mid-1960s: "Mechanical means are *today*, and using

62 Friedrich Nietzsche, *The Gay Science*, trans. Walter Kaufmann (New York: Vintage, 1974), 171. On the suppression of similarity in logic, and on identity and nonidentity, also see sections 510–12 and 515–17 of *The Will to Power*, trans. Walter Kaufmann and R. J. Hollingdale (New York: Vintage, 1967), 276–80.

63 Hansen, *Cinema and Experience*, 153.

them I can get more art to more people. Art should be for everyone."[64] *Like Andy Warhol* is an examination of Warhol's various strategies for combating this alienation of the human sensorium and nourishing and stimulating the mimetic faculty. For the most part, Warhol engaged in this project "less by demonstrating found similarities than by replicating the processes which generate such similarities" (*SW2*, 694).

We can see Warhol exploring the artistic resources for visually representing relations of resemblance in his practical, formal decisions about how to make paintings, as Georg Frei and Neil Printz document in volume 1 of *The Andy Warhol Catalogue Raisonné*. Thus, as he sought to find ways around painting or drawing with his hands, in an early Pop work such as *200 Campbell's Soup Cans* (1962), Warhol used stamps and stencils to produce a series of images of cans that appear to be nearly identical, but for the fact that they are different kinds of soup. The serial repetition itself makes it clear that it is not "representation" in the usual sense at work here: this is not a painting *of* 200 Campbell's soup cans. The painting's frame is not a window. Instead, Warhol is "doing a reproduction of the thing," mechanically simulating the image of the can, based on a model.[65] Whereas re-presentation involves a substitution for (and accompanying negation of) the thing represented, which is *not* here, simulation involves a repeated effort to be like the model. What we see in Warhol's painting are a collection of similars; these soup can images are all imitating a model, which makes them all like each other as well. As Foucault (optimistically) wrote in the final lines of his short book on Magritte, "A day will come when, by means of similitude relayed indefinitely along the length of a series, the image itself, along with the name it bears, will lose its identity. Campbell, Campbell, Campbell, Campbell."[66]

Although the insistence on similarity and nonidentity is apparent in these earliest serial paintings, the silkscreen technique Warhol adopted in 1962 with his Dollar Bill paintings much more vividly foregrounds the similarity of the images.[67] Warhol liked the technology (which he appears to

64 Andy Warhol, "Underground Films: Art or Naughty Movies," interview by Douglas Arango, *Movie TV Secrets* (June 1966); cited by Benjamin Buchloh in "Andy Warhol's One-Dimensional Art: 1956–1966," in Michelson, *Andy Warhol*, 1–46, 5.

65 Warhol made the reproduction remark in his 1985 interview with Benjamin Buchloh (*IBYM*, 323). Apropos simulation, Jean Baudrillard writes, "Here it is a question of a reversal of origin and finality, for all the forms change once they are not so much mechanically reproduced but *conceived from the point-of-view of the their very reproducibility*, diffracted from a generating nucleus we call the model." Baudrillard, *Simulations* (New York: Semiotext(e), 1983), 100 (also, for comments on Warhol specifically, 136, 144, 158–59).

66 Michel Foucault, *This Is Not a Pipe* (Berkeley: University of California Press, 1981), 54.

67 Somewhat ironically, because photographs of money cannot legally be reproduced, these first silkscreens were based on Warhol's drawings of money. Shortly thereafter, Warhol began to work mainly with photo-based silkscreens. On the twists and turns in production methods during this period, see the fascinating discussion in *CR1*, esp.

have used in this way before other painters, and would use for the rest of his career) precisely because, in contrast to the stamp or stencil, similarity-producing mistakes and irregularities were overtly built into the process. "With silkscreening," he wrote, "you pick a photograph, blow it up, transfer it in glue onto silk, and then roll ink across it so the ink goes through the silk but not through the glue. That way you get the same image, slightly different, each time" (*POP*, 22). Thus, while Warhol understood that repetition itself degrades or undoes identity—remarking, for example, that he "liked the way the repetition changed the same image" (*IBYM*, 193)—his choice of the silkscreen process clearly indicates that he wished to draw attention to a mechanically produced "slightly different" similar.[68] This effect is especially evident in his late 1962 silkscreens of celebrities such as Troy Donahue, Warren Beatty, Natalie Wood (figure 2.1), Marilyn Monroe, and Elvis Presley.

Of course, Warhol was not the only artist working with seriality or repetition during this period. As Benjamin Buchloh noted in a 1985 interview with Warhol, "serial form had become increasingly important in the early 1960s" (*IBYM*, 324), and it had precedents in the abstract art of the 1950s as well. In the interview, Warhol expresses his admiration for Josef Albers ("like, you know, the guy who just does the squares . . . I like his work a lot") and the black-on-black paintings of Ad Reinhardt ("the person I really like"). Buchloh mentions Yves Klein's exhibition of identically sized but differently priced blue paintings in 1957, Arman's accumulations, and John Cage "and the concept of musical seriality" as other possible precedents.[69] Warhol says, however, that he was not thinking about any of these examples when he adopted the serial forms that came to characterize his work. Instead, ironically enough, his embrace of a technique that performed and thematized imitation and similarity was motivated by the need to *distinguish* his work in the competitive New York art market. Like Roy Lichtenstein, Warhol had been painting comics (such as *Nancy*, *Popeye*, *Superman*, and *Dick*

131–50 (on the Dollar Bills) and 205–6 (on the first photo-silkscreened paintings). For an extended reading of these paintings and drawings, see Printz, "Making Money/Printing Painting: Warhol's Dollar Bill Paintings," in *Criticism* 56, no. 3 (Summer 2014; Warhol special issue).

68 Gerard Malanga observes, "When you're working with a silk screen, you don't get everything worked out *totally* in advance in what you're going to do, in terms of what you want the *effect* to be. So, everything is going to come out chancy. I mean, sometimes we'd make a mistake, and there'd be a slight space between the image here, let's say. It wouldn't be a seamless thing. And that was an accident! We missed it. Andy took all of those accidents into account, as being part of the art." In Smith, *Conversations*, 170. See also Malanga's description of the process in Scherman and Dalton, *Pop*, 127.

69 I think Buchloh here is probably referring to seriality as a repetitive structuring principle in the most general sense, not to serialism (as developd by Arnold Schoenberg) in the sense of twelve-tone music, which orders the twelve notes of the chromatic scale, which is then used as the basis for composition. Thanks to Charles Kronengold for pointing this out.

Tracy), but without knowing that Lichtenstein was doing it too.[70] As soon as he saw Lichtenstein's paintings, and their reproduction of the Ben Day dots, Warhol decided "that since Roy was doing comics so well, that I would just stop comics altogether and go in other directions where I could come out first—like quantity and repetition" (*POP*, 18). Indeed, this proved to be a canny assessment of the market, as Warhol would later be taken on by the prestigious Leo Castelli gallery, which had initially refused him precisely because his work was too similar to Lichtenstein's.

While Warhol's use of "quantity and repetition" did distinguish him from other pop artists (like Jim Dine, Claes Oldenburg, and James Rosenquist) and the already famous proto-Pop artists Robert Rauschenberg and Jasper Johns, to whom he was in other respects (such as the appropriation of recognizable everyday images and representation of common objects) very similar, his use of serial forms also made him like artists who might initially seem quite different, such as Albers and Reinhardt. With the emergence of minimalist and conceptual art practices in the 1960s, where serial forms and procedures were also common, Warhol's proliferation of similarities itself became a point of similarity and analogy, as I examine in chapters 2 (on Warhol and Sol LeWitt) and 3 (on Warhol and Donald Judd). Thus, even his effort to distinguish himself (by going in the direction of quantity and repetition) is one that sought to do away with the need to distinguish oneself (by creating a world in which everybody is similar).[71] Still, Warhol's use of repetition remains particular because of its place in his overall effort to maximize liking. It is one of his several strategies for emphasizing and producing likenesses as distinct from samenesses (rather than an organizing principle as such), the project (I have been arguing) that organizes his work (as in his promotion of bad acting or his collecting) throughout his career.

To return to Warhol's silkscreens, we can see that on a formal level, the serial images in paintings such as *Marilyn Diptych* or *Red Elvis* are perfor-

70 For a brilliant reading of these fantastic early Pop paintings, see Michael Moon, "Screen Memories, or, Pop Comes from the Outside: Warhol and Queer Childhood," in Doyle, Flatley, and Muñoz, *Pop Out*, 78–100, reprinted in Moon, *A Small Boy and Others*, 95–116.

71 For the emphasis on liking and likeness as itself a point of similarity, also see Dan Graham's 1969 *Likes: A Computer Astrological Dating-Placement Service*, an advertisement placed in a local newspaper that used a set of "like relations," based partly on astrological categories, to "define what you are like" and "what you would like your date to be like." Also see his *Like* (1971), a performance in which "Two performers have been instructed to convince the other (the ways in which) he is like him (and him is like the first performer)." It is designed to "communicate parts of likenesses: gesture, verbal dialogue, hand or skin manipulation," ideally producing a "continuous, gradual coming together until a point where this development is arrested and reverses is reached (perhaps at boundaries of self)." Both works are documented in Garry Neill Kennedy, *The Last Art College: Nova Scotia College of Art and Design, 1968–1978* (Cambridge, MA: MIT Press, 2012), 20, 94–95.

mances of multiple attempts to *be like* a model Marilyn or model Elvis. As such, they are allegories of our melancholic incorporation through consumption of their looks: like Warhol's smudged and blotted silkscreened images of Marilyn, Elvis, Natalie Wood, Troy Donahue, Warren Beatty, Elizabeth Taylor, Robert Rauschenberg, and Jackie Kennedy, our own subjectivities are produced from repeated, imperfect simulations. Like the screened images we see, so too our singularity derives, not from some internal essence, but from the quality of our flaws and mistakes and their accumulation and juxtaposition, the places we fail to match up to our models, when too much ink was squeezed through or caked on, or when the pressure was a little uneven. Each of us has internalized a slightly different Marilyn, one that produces more imperfections and interstices each time we imitate it, destabilizing identity anew. In their emphasis on the productivity of imitation, their suggestion that celebrity is itself constituted by the multiple imitations it inspires, these paintings invert the meaning of "original" and "copy."[72]

"Stars of the Out-take"

As Warhol suggests in his remark about "all the James Deans," orienting oneself toward resemblance and the plural singularities it makes apparent may be especially rewarding in the sphere of sexual attraction. It is appealing to the precise extent that it also requires forgetting the oppositions between the same and the different, desire and identification, being and having, that are so central to the dominant discourses of sexuality, which have reinscribed these oppositions with regularly damaging effects.

Consider, for instance, the influential idea of the "invert," the person with the soul of the "opposite" sex trapped in her or his body. A dominant discourse for describing women sexually attracted to women and men sexually attracted to men in the first half of the twentieth century, this model of gender-liminality persists in the figures of the sissy, the fairy, and the butch, among others. Within the discourse of the invert, writes Eve Sedgwick, desire "by definition subsists in the current that runs between one male self and one female self, in whatever sex of bodies these selves may be manifested."[73] That is, even as it describes attractions between persons of the

72 As Judith Butler put it, borrowing from Derrida (but referring to the imitation of sexual identities), such an "imitation does not copy that which is prior, but produces and inverts the very terms of priority and derivativeness" ("Imitation," 313).

73 *Epistemology*, 87. Sedgwick is here borrowing from Christopher Craft, "'Kiss Me with Those Red Lips': Gender and Inversion in Bram Stoker's *Dracula*," *Representations*, no. 8 (Fall 1984), 107–34, esp. 114. Foucault influentially placed this psychological/medical model of "contrary sexual sensations" at the origin of the idea of sexual *identity* as such (a placement that Sedgwick complicates in *Epistemology*). The new homosexual identity is characterized, Foucault wrote, "less by a type of sexual relations than by a certain quality of sexual sensibility, a certain way of inverting the masculine and the feminine in oneself" (*History of Sexuality*, vol. 1, *An Introduction* [New York: Random House, 1978], 43). This

"same" sex, the model of the invert maintains the heterosexuality of desire. A similar binary logic underwrites Freudian thought about sexuality and desire, especially when Freud is writing about the Oedipal drama of (nuclear) family life and its formative effects (even though he is also attentive to the imitative and melancholic quality of identification, a point emphasized by Judith Butler, Mikkel Borch-Jacobsen, and Adam Phillips[74]). For Freud, Diana Fuss argues, "desire for one sex is always secured through identification with the other sex; to desire and identify with the same person at the same time is, in this model, a theoretical impossibility." In such a theory, "homosexual desire [is] inherently contradictory, since desire can only be for the other and never for the same."[75]

As Chris Nealon and Heather Love have demonstrated, modern gay and lesbian literature is filled with examples of how the inversion model only partially, and often damagingly, pictured queer lives and feelings. At issue is not only the sense of stigma or pathology attached to the figure of the invert, but also the incoherence generated by the discourse's reinscription of the opposition between the same and the different along the lines of identification and desire. If desire as such is understood to be fundamentally for the "opposite" sex, then desire *for* the invert appears as an incomplete or misdirected desire for an "actual" or "natural" man or woman. The invert appears as a copy that cannot as such *be* an object of desire.[76] The damaging effects of this disqualification from desirability are famously dramatized in

---

discourse of inversion, central to any account of modern sexuality, finds early, influential articulations in the works of Karl Ulrichs, Richard von Krafft-Ebing, and Havelock Ellis. For one historical account of this discourse, see George Chauncey, "From Sexual Inversion to Homosexuality: Medicine and the Changing Conceptualization of Female Deviance," *Salamagundi*, nos. 58–59 (Fall 1982/Winter 1983), 114–45. On the centrality of the idea of inversion, and the related concept of the "intermediate sex" to the "fairy," a relevant identity formation for Warhol, see Chauncey, *Gay New York: Gender, Urban Culture and the Making of the Gay Male World 1890–1940* (New York: Basic Books, 1994), esp. 47–63.

74 See Butler, *Gender Trouble* (New York: Routledge, 1990) and *The Psychic Life of Power* (Stanford, CA: Stanford University Press, 1997), including Adam Phillips's response to Butler within that book; Borch-Jacobsen, *Emotional Tie*.

75 Fuss, *Identification Papers*, 11, 12. This is not to say that the distinction is maintained even in Freud. The effort to reconceptualize gender and sexuality within queer theory (especially in the work of Judith Butler) has refocused attention on the precariousness of the opposition between desire and identification within psychoanalysis, especially around Freud's attempts to understand affect and the "emotional tie." While Freud himself would complicate the tension between identification and desire in various ways (as he complicates so many of his theories and concepts), especially when he turns his attention to the emotional tie (of which identification is seen as the earliest instance) instead of "desire," the opposition between desire and identification, especially concerning "same sex" object choice, persists.

76 Jason Edwards lucidly describes the incoherent logic of the inversion model in his excellent *Eve Kosofsky Sedgwick*, Routledge Critical Thinkers (London: Routledge, 2009), 26–28.

Radclyffe Hall's *The Well of Loneliness*, in which we see the mannish female heroine Stephen loved and then left by a series of women (who leave her for "actual" or "natural" men). On the one hand, the novel embraces the discourse of the invert (which Stephen finds in the writings of Kraft-Ebbing), in a paradigmatic instance of what Foucault calls a "'reverse' discourse."[77] The discourse gives Stephen a way to understand her desire and her gender dysphoria, as well as a language with which to conceive (with some difficulty) of social and political alliance with other similarly stigmatized inverts (including male ones). At the same time, the novel dramatizes how the discourse of inversion blocks her from imagining her body, indeed her being, as wantable. In a famous scene, Stephen looks at herself in the mirror and grieves for her "body that must worship yet never be worshipped in return by the creature of its adoration."[78] She is left with the "riddle of her unwanted being."[79] The model of the invert renders her failed imitation of masculinity ontologically unintelligible; she is an "unviable (un)subject," as Judith Butler puts it.[80]

Like most men attracted to other men who grew up in the first half of the twentieth century in the United States, Warhol (who was born in 1928) would have had to reckon with the discourse of inversion (or of the "fairy") in coming to an understanding of his sexual attractions and pleasures.[81] This would have especially been so given Warhol's apparently fairly consistent identification with femininity, which he sometimes publicly affirmed, as when he remarked that he copied Edie Sedgwick's silver hair ("I wanted to look like Edie because I always wanted to look like a girl"; *IBYM*, 113), referred to himself as "Miss Warhol" in a radio interview, or pretended to be Mrs. Geldzahler welcoming guests on the steps of the Metropolitan Museum at the opening of Henry Geldzahler's famous exhibition *New York Painting and Sculpture: 1940–1970*.[82] But Warhol does not embrace the discourse of inver-

77 Foucault, *History of Sexuality*, vol. 1, 101.

78 Radclyffe Hall, *The Well of Loneliness* (1928; New York: Doubleday, 1990), 187. See Heather Love's brilliant reading of this scene and its critical reception in *Feeling Backward*, 114–24. On Stephen's masculinity, see also Esther Newton's groundbreaking "The Mythic Mannish Lesbian: Radclyffe Hall and the New Woman," *Signs* 9 (1984): 557–75. For an important reading of Stephen as transsexual, see Jay Prosser, *Second Skins: The Body Narratives of Transsexuality* (New York: Columbia University Press, 1998).

79 Hall, *Well of Loneliness*, 203.

80 "Imitation," 312.

81 See Chauncey, *Gay New York*, chap. 2, "The Fairy as Intermediate Sex."

82 For the radio appearance, see Jean Stein, *Edie: American Girl* (edited with George Plimpton) (New York: Grove Press, 1982), 203–4; for the "Mrs. Geldzahler" story, Emile de Antonio and Mitch Tuchman, *Painters Painting* (New York: Abbeville Press, 1984), 129–30. See also the powerful photographs by Christopher Makos of Warhol in drag, and Warhol's assertion that as a little boy he wanted to be a tap dancer like Shirley Temple: "I never wanted to be a painter; I wanted to be a tap dancer" (*IBYM*, 89). On Warhol and Temple, see Blake Stimson, *Citizen Warhol* (London: Reaktion, 2014), 88–100. For critical commentary on Warhol's identification with women, including his mother,

sion nor the logic underlying it. He thereby offers an interesting alternative to the phenomenon persuasively described by Chris Nealon in *Foundlings*. Nealon examines how many lesbian and gay persons who felt "exiled from sanctioned experience" sought to work around the pathologizing discourses to which they were subject by seeking "a reunion with some 'people' or sodality who redeem this exile and surpass the painful limitations of the original 'home.'"[83] Though Warhol certainly took pleasure in the existence of a gay and lesbian lifeworld in New York City, both before and after Stonewall, he resisted the turn to the minoritizing model of a gay and lesbian "people."

Instead, as Douglas Crimp argues, Warhol "disdains and defies the coherence and stability of all sexual identity."[84] And he does this inasmuch as he imagines a world where, as Leo Bersani writes, the "very opposition between sameness and difference becomes irrelevant as a structuring category of being."[85] Thus, rather than a "people" brought together by a shared (minority) identity, Warhol sees like-beings brought together by a shared *failure* to "be" an identity in a world constituted by what Bersani calls "networks of inaccurate replication."[86] Thus, for Warhol, the (inverted) feminine male or mannish woman is not a failed unsubject but a successful imitator, indeed a beacon of mimetic talents. In this way, Warhol anticipates Butler's well-known argument for the disruption of the regulative, policing "matrix of intelligibility" constituted by identity categories.[87] If, as Butler points

---

see Koestenbaum, *Andy Warhol*, esp. chap. 2, "Pussy Heaven"; Neil Printz's dissertation "Other Voices, Other Rooms: Between Andy Warhol and Truman Capote, 1948–1961" (CUNY, 2000); and Lucy Mulroney, "One Blue Pussy," *Criticism* 56, no. 3 (Summer 2014; Warhol special issue). On his identification with his mother and on "Warhol-as-she" and "Warhol-as Mom," see Hilton Als, "Basquiat and I," in *Andy Warhol Jean-Michel Basquiat Collaboration Paintings* (New York: Gagosian Gallery, 2002).

83 *Foundlings* (Durham, NC: Duke University Press, 2001), 1.

84 Crimp, "Getting the Warhol We Deserve," *Social Text*, no. 59 (Summer 1999), 49–66, 64.

85 Bersani and Adam Phillips, *Intimacies* (Chicago: University of Chicago Press, 2010), 86. For Bersani, it is by way of the homoness of homosexuality, the love of "the same" (which inevitably fails to be or stay the same), that we might be "free us from an oppressive psychology of desire as lack" and move to a place where "the antagonisms between the different and the same no longer exist" (*Homos* [Cambridge, MA: Harvard University Press, 1995], 59). In contrast, Warhol's promotion of similarity, precisely as distinct from sameness, more directly proposes an alternative to the discourses and institutions supporting the same-different binary and the logic of identity.

86 *Homos*, 146.

87 Such identity categories, Butler argues, "tend to be instruments of regulatory regimes, whether as the normalizing categories of oppressive structures or as the rallying points for a liberatory contestation of that very oppression" ("Imitation," 308). But, she argues, while such identities may be dominant and compulsory, they are not in any sense natural; in fact their ontological status is precarious because they come into being as an effect of the repeated performances of them: "How and where I 'play' at being [a lesbian] is the way in which that 'being' gets established instituted, circulated and confirmed" (311). Nevertheless, such categories exert a regulative function on these performances,

out, "it is already true that 'lesbians' and 'gay men' have been traditionally designated as impossible identities, errors of classification, unnatural disasters within juridico-medical discourses," then perhaps "these sites of disruption, error, confusion, and trouble can be the very rallying points for a certain resistance to classification and to identity as such." For Warhol, such a resistance took form in a revaluation of disqualification and error.[88]

Warhol's practice is oriented, as Joseph Litvak put it, toward "taking the terror out of error, at making the making of mistakes sexy, creative, even cognitively powerful."[89] As I mentioned, he valued the "mistakes" of messy printing in the silkscreened simulations of Liz or Elvis or Jackie, which powerfully represented attempts to be like these stars, emphasizing how both similarity and singularity emerge precisely from the inaccuracy of the imitations, an inevitable failure to match up to the model experienced in common by all the images arranged in series across the canvas. Similarly, Warhol enthusiastically embraced performances that highlighted their own inauthenticity, that staged the failure to "be" an identity in a kind of demonstration of sympathy for the unviable (un)subjects who cannot or do not want to fit into available identity models. Thus, Warhol could "only understand really amateur performers or really bad performers," preferring "the wrong person for the part" since "no person is ever completely right for any part, because a part is a role is never real" (*Phil*, 82, 83). Instead of feeling bad for our failures to fit our roles, bad performers allow us to feel like them by failing (to be right for the part) with them.

Warhol was committed to a practice in which "mistakes can be good rather than bad surprises."[90] And where he sees no mistakes, he imagines them: "When I see an old Esther Williams movie and a hundred girls are jumping off their swings, I think of what the auditions must have been like and about all the takes where maybe one girl didn't have the nerve to jump when she was supposed to, and I think about her left over on the swing. So that take of the scene was a leftover on the editing room floor—an out-take—and the girl was probably a leftover at that point—she was probably fired—so the whole scene is much funnier than the real scene where everything went right, and the girl who didn't jump is the star of the out-take" (*Phil*, 93). In Warhol's imagination, even scenes of aesthetic conformity become occasions to conjure up failures of nerve and action, which he sees as "much funnier" than

---

which are, as Butler emphasizes, more or less compulsory, the entry ticket for being a subject at all.

88 "Imitation," 309–10. Like Warhol, Butler makes the case for "de-instituting" (315) re-performances of those identities, performances that avowedly fail to achieve a proper identity. For a related examination of the suggestion in popular representations of gay men that "there is something hypermimetic about our behavior," see Moon, *A Small Boy and Others*, 9–14.

89 Litvak, personal communication, cited by Sedgwick, "Paranoid Reading," 147

90 Ibid.

"the real scene where everything went right." In fact, Warhol's films could be seen as a series of attempts to produce scenes in which we can appreciate the "stars of the out-take."

It is not hard to see in Warhol's practices an attempt at "loosening the traumatic, inevitable-seeming connection between mistakes and humiliation."[91] That effect may be best achieved in settings where mistakes and failures bring one together with others. In the 1960s (as I discuss in chapter 1), Warhol seemed to relate to the Factory as a place where "stars of the out-take" could come together and, in so doing, find their best audience. Around Warhol and his friends, the failure to fit in, usually an isolating and alienating condition (the girl who didn't jump "was probably fired"), could instead be the basis of shared experience. Giving us a sense of his affective attachment to the Factory as a space and a situation, Warhol reflects in *POPism* (which he wrote with Pat Hackett in the late 1970s) on a moment in 1967 when the Factory became "the target for some very aggressive attacks on drugs and homosexuality" in the press. "Naturally, the Factory had fags; we were in the entertainment business and—That's Entertainment!" While "the Factory had more gays than, say, Congress," he notes, "it probably wasn't even as gay as your favorite TV police show." The Factory was a place "where you could let your 'problems' show and nobody would hate you for it. And if you worked up your problems into entertaining routines, people would like you even more for being strong enough to say you were different and actually have fun with it" (222). Warhol speculated that the attacks were directed precisely at these reparative deflections of identification: the way "gays in the Factory" refused to "play along and be hypocritical and covert," but instead found ways "have fun with" their problems. The Factory was filled with what Valerie Solanas called "faggots who, by their shimmering, flaming example, encourage other men to de-man themselves."[92] Unsurprisingly, this "incensed a lot of people who wanted the old stereotypes to stay around." But why, Warhol wondered, don't these people "care about all the miserable people in the world who just can't fit into stock roles?" (*POP*, 222–23).

Warhol knew how it felt to be one of those miserable people. The attacks on the Factory recalled his earlier experience of not fitting the role of "major painter," also recounted in *POPism*. Just before the beginning of his Pop

91 Ibid.

92 *SCUM Manifesto* (San Francisco: AK Press, 1996), 41–42. Because it encouraged identity failures, the Factory was a place where a misfit like Solanas, who refused to play the "Daddy's girl" role she vehemently critiqued in *SCUM Manifesto*, could imagine finding room to pursue the "absorbing, emotionally satisfying, meaningful activity" she saw as the "actual female function": "to relate, groove, love, and be herself, irreplaceable by anyone else . . . to explore, discover, invent, solve problems, crack jokes, make music—all with love. In other words, create a magic world" (6, 14). Inasmuch as it suggests a capacity for correspondence and connection, Solanas's emphasis on the female ability to "groove" and female "grooviness" forms an interesting point of analogy with Warhol's liking.

career, Warhol had asked Emile de Antonio why Jasper Johns and Robert Rauschenberg "cut [him] dead" whenever he saw them. "De" told Warhol that he was "too swish, and that upsets them" (11). "The *major painters*," De observed, "try to look straight; you play up the swish—its like an armor with you" (12).[93] This rejection by Johns and Rauschenberg had a particular sting because, as de Antonio noted, Warhol *wanted* to "be like them": he saw in them examples of a role he might actually fit into. Here, after all, were two apparently gay men, in a couple, who (like Warhol) made money as window dressers, but who had also developed careers as "major painters," while rejecting abstract expressionism and its macho ethos.[94]

The Johns-Rauschenberg rejection seems an instance of what Erving Goffman called "identity ambivalence," a concept Heather Love puts to illuminating use in *Feeling Backward*. "The stigmatized individual," Goffman writes, "may exhibit identity ambivalence when he obtains a close sight of his own kind behaving in a stereotypical way, flamboyantly or pitifully acting out the negative attributes imputed to them."[95] Precisely because they are (or may be seen to be) like the "fruity" and "effeminate" Warhol, Johns and Rauschenberg are repelled and embarrassed by him.[96] Even as Warhol sometimes responded to such rejections with paranoia of the why-don't-they-like-me sort, he refused to give in to the double-consciousness-like identification with dominant norms that animates identity ambivalence. Here, Warhol's efforts to like and be alike did not lead to an attempt to "blend in" or fade into the background, as in Roger Caillois's famous analysis of mim-

93 This rejection echoed his earlier rejection by the Tanager Gallery, which refused to show his homoerotic drawings in 1956, underscoring the point that Warhol's fey self-presentation and depictions of male-male eroticism were persistent obstacles to his ascent to the role of "artist." In *You Got to Burn to Shine* (New York: High Risk Books, 1994), John Giorno writes, "The art world was homophobic, and an ever-present threat. Anyone who was gay was at a disadvantage. An artist overtly with a boyfriend was at a complete disadvantage, and could ruin his career. De Kooning, Pollock, Motherwell, and the male power structure were mean straight pricks. No matter their liberal views, they deep down hated fags. Their disdain dismissed a gay person's art. On top of it, those guys really hated Pop Art" (132–33). See Trevor Fairbrother's groundbreaking "Tomorrow's Man," in *"Success Is a Job in New York": The Early Art and Business of Andy Warhol*, exh. cat., ed. Donna de Salvo (New York: Grey Gallery, 1989), on the Tanager Gallery episode and on his homoerotic drawings from that period, which were exhibited in the (less prestigious) Bodley Gallery. Gavin Butt considers the centrality of gossip (between de Antonio and Warhol) to the episode in *Between You and Me: Queer Disclosures in the New York Art World, 1948–1963* (Durham, NC: Duke University Press, 2005), 112–15.

94 De Antonio noted that Rauschenberg and Johns "opened up another world and different sensibility which Warhol thought he could latch on to or identify with. And this is why he not only wanted to meet then, but be like them" (Smith, *Conversations*, 192).

95 Goffman, *Stigma: Notes on the Management of Spoiled Identity* (New York; Touchstone, 1986), 107–8, cited in Love, *Feeling Backward*, 102.

96 These are de Antonio's words, from Smith, *Conversations*: "Andy was too effeminate for Bob and Jap" (189), "he was just too fruity for them" (192).

icry.[97] Instead, like his brightly colored camouflage paintings, which invoke the workings of mimicry while dynamically (even expressively) standing out from the white gallery walls, Warhol insisted on being the "right thing in the wrong space and the wrong thing in the right space" (*Phil*, 158).[98] "I certainly wasn't a butch guy by nature, but I must admit, I went out of my way to play up the other extreme" (*POP*, 13). Where Johns and Rauschenberg sought to disavow their similarity to Warhol so they could feel better about "looking straight" and fitting into the role of "the major painter," Warhol wanted to make such disavowals less necessary (and less possible) by seeing everybody as similar to everybody else, precisely inasmuch as they *cannot* fit in. If Warhol held that "no person is ever completely right for any part, because a part is a role is never real," then he directed his swishy aggression at those who pretended to be real "viable" subjects, the people who made it seem like we *should* all be able to fit the stock roles. It was fun just to "watch the expressions on people's faces," he wrote, as they reacted to his fey self-presentation (*POP*, 12). Warhol *wanted* to embarrass Johns and Rauschenberg for refusing to recognize their similarity to him, for pretending to be above such abjection. In this, we might see an effort at what Sara Ahmed calls "queer pride," a "refusal to be shamed by witnessing the other as being ashamed by you."[99] This refusal, however, does not necessarily abolish

97 See Caillois, "Mimicry and Legendary Psychasthenia," *October*, no. 31 (Winter 1984), 16–32. For a fascinating analysis of seriality and mimicry that draws on Caillois—and does *not* lead to liking everybody—see Mark Seltzer, *Serial Killers: Death And Life in America's Wound Culture* (New York: Routledge, 1998), esp. 48–52 on the "mimetic compulsion."

98 For a different view of these works, see Brenda Richardson's very helpful "Hiding in Plain Sight: Warhol's Camouflage," which argues for seeing these paintings, and his camouflage self-portraits in particular, as documents of Warhol's desire to blend in. In *Andy Warhol, Camouflage* (New York: Gagosian Gallery, 1998). For a queer reading of Warhol's camouflage self-portrait, see Muñoz, *Cruising Utopia*, 138–40. And see Magda Szcześniak's smart reading of camouflage in Jack Smith, Warhol, and elsewhere in "Blending In and Standing Out: Camouflage and Masking as Queer Tactics of Negotiating Visibility," *View: Theories and Practices of Visual Culture* 5 (2014).

99 Ahmed, *The Promise of Happiness* (Durham, NC: Duke University Press, 2010), 116. This passage is quoted to powerful effect in Maggie Nelson's *The Argonauts* (Minneapolis: Graywolf Press, 2015), 18. See also Michael Warner's proposition in *The Trouble with Normal* (Cambridge, MA: Harvard University Press, 1999) that queer scenes are the true "*salons des refuses*": "A relation to others, in these contexts, begins in an acknowledgment of all that is most abject and least reputable in oneself. Shame is bedrock. Queers can be abusive, insulting, and vile toward one another, but because abjection is understood to be the shared condition, they also know how to communicate through such camaraderie a moving and unexpected form of generosity. No one is beneath its reach, not because it prides itself on generosity, but because it prides itself on nothing. The rule is: Get over yourself. Put a wig on before you judge" (35).

Along such lines, one of the things Warhol allowed himself to *not* like were assertions of normative individuality that pretend to be above any similarity with everybody else, and artists who seem *not* to like what they paint. See, for instance, his remarks about

shame so much as signal a desire to pluralize it, and thereby mitigate its isolating effects. One might also see Warhol's flamboyant swishiness as an invitation to be embarrassed (and stigmatized) together.[100]

Warhol's flamboyant performance of the "wrong" identity with Johns and Rauschenberg, his embrace of leftovers and fags and amphetamine users, his celebration of the "stars of the out-take," were all efforts to "care about all the miserable people who just can't fit into stock roles"—not least himself. His was an attempt to create not only a "federation of the shamed, the alienated, the destitute, the illegitimate, and the hated" (as Love compellingly describes the dream of queer studies at its most expansive[101]), but a commonist space where shamed, alienated, and illegitimate ways of being and feeling could be repaired, rewarded, and valued. To the precise extent that some found this exciting or restorative, others found it disturbing and threatening, all the more so because Warhol was not at all "covert" in his efforts, instead determinedly promoting himself and his friends in the public eye.

As a reparative response to his avowed failure to fit into stock roles, Warhol not only valued misfitting as such but actively mocked and subverted "fitting in." If he could not play the role of major painter, why not get one of his friends to perform it in his place? In 1967 Warhol found himself having committed to speak at a number of colleges and universities. Since he was "too shy and scared" himself, as he explained in *POPism*, he would bring along a group of friends, including Viva, Ultra Violet, Brigid Berlin, Paul Morrissey, and Allen Midgette, and they would answer questions while he sat quietly on stage. Warhol was not exactly playing the role he was supposed to play—"it was more like a talk show with a dummied-up host"—but at least he was present at the events. This was not the case later in the year when Warhol decided it would be better just to send Midgette to lecture *as* Warhol. "Allen was so good-looking," not to mention younger, "they might even enjoy him more." Moreover, Warhol reasoned, "we'd been playing switch-the-superstar at parties and openings around New York for years, telling people that Viva was Ultra and Edie was me and I was Gerard—sometimes people would get mixed up all by themselves . . . and we just wouldn't bother to correct them, it

Edward Kienholz: "I don't think I really like him . . . he seems kind of moral to me. . . . I don't think he really likes the things he does like he doesn't really like—greasy hamburgers" (*IBYM*, 138).

100 On the vital topic of queer shame and queer embarrassment see, among many others, Eve Kosofsky Sedgwick, "Queer Performativity: Henry James's *Art of the Novel*," *GLQ* 1, no. 1 (1993); Warner, *Trouble with Normal*; Crimp's discussion of queer shame in *Screen Test No. 2* (starring Mario Montez), in *Our Kind of Movie*, esp. 35; and Heather Love (on both) in *Feeling Backward*, esp. 13–14.

101 Love, "Queers ___ This," 183. See also Cohen, "Punks, Bulldaggers and Welfare Queens," for a related vision of queer politics.

was too much fun to let them go on getting it all wrong—it seemed like a joke to us. So these antistar identity games were something we were doing anyway, as a matter of course." Unfortunately, when "somebody at one of the colleges happened to see a picture of [Warhol] in the *Voice* and compared it to the one he'd taken of Allen on the podium," Warhol got caught, and soon realized that what for him had been a classic Pop "put-on" was "what some people would call 'fraud.'" Warhol was surprised at how upset people got at the identity games he had the habit of playing, but recognized their powerfully unraveling effect when he was on "the phone with an official from one of the other colleges on that tour, telling him how really sorry I was when suddenly he turned paranoid and said: 'How can I even be sure this is really you on the phone right *now*?' After a pause while I gave that some thought, I had to admit, 'I don't know.'"[102] Warhol had to refund the lecture fees; a verifiable identity is required where money and contractual obligations are involved. He realized that it might be a good idea to stop playing his identity games and "start acting more grown-up," at least in some contexts, even if he tried to treat "grown-up" as just another not-real role.

Warhol's identity games are an apt example of the mimetic and reparative practices "that emerge from queer experience but become invisible or illegible under a paranoid optic," as Sedgwick puts it.[103] If your concern is finding a way to be sure about who Warhol "really" is, his mimetic confusions and identity deflections become interference, noise to cut through. Sometimes, in their attempt to figure out the real Warhol, his critics seem to echo the paranoid college official, who, after all, models the critical and suspicious mode of attunement to which we are most accustomed in the academic profession. What was Warhol's "real" sexual identity? Are his paintings a critique of consumer capitalism or a cynical affirmation of it? Was he as naïve as he appeared to be in interviews or was he "actually" smart?[104] During his life, in interviews, Warhol regularly and brilliantly deflected such questions and the modes of knowing they presume, as Wayne Koestenbaum and Nicholas de Villiers have each shown, often turning attention back to the interviewer's line of inquiry itself or producing what Koestenbaum calls an "ambient destabilization."[105] For the most part, the attempts to find stable ground from which to determine the real Warhol obscure his actual

102 *POP*, 247–48. For Midgette's later recollections of these events, see Scherman and Dalton, *Pop*, 394–96

103 "Paranoid Reading," 147.

104 See Kelly Cresap's smart *Pop Trickster Fool: Warhol Performs Naiveté* (Urbana: University of Illinois Press, 2004) on Warhol's performance and the critical preoccupation with his apparent stupidity.

105 Koestenbaum, "Afterword: Warhol's Interviews," in *IBYM*, 395–97; De Villiers, *Opacity and the Closet*, esp. chap. 3, "'What Do You Have to Say for Yourself?' Warhol's Opacity."

practices, whose queer appeal and queer effects vanish under this identificatory gaze.[106]

Warhol's Affect Theory: How to Like More

I think we could like a lot more people than we do.

Adam Phillips, "The Value of Frustration"[107]

When Warhol talks about "liking things" or "liking everybody," what understanding of liking, and of affect and feeling more generally, is he working with? What kind of a feeling is liking? While we have an abundance of theories of love at our disposal, like the "minor feelings" Sianne Ngai examines in *Ugly Feelings*, liking has tended to fly below the theoretical radar. This is not to say that one does not find it in some key locations. For instance, in his translation of Kant's *Critique of Judgment*, Werner Pluhar uses "liking" for *Wohlgefallen*, Kant's "most generic term for positive rather than negative feeling."[108] Kant's frequent reference to "the liking that determines a judgment of taste," which may or may not be devoid of interest, which may or may not be universal, makes it hard to ignore the need for a term to refer to this most basic level of feeling, although his primary interest is in distinguishing between different kinds of liking rather than considering the

106 In a way, the most reparative and nonparanoid Warhol criticism has been accomplished by the two major recent catalogue raisonné projects: Callie Angell's work on Warhol's films, which showed how careful and considered his choices were, how he was constantly trying out new techniques and exploring the possibilities of the medium, and Neil Printz's careful scholarship on the paintings and sculpture, which demonstrates Warhol's assiduous move toward the silkscreen method and the explosion of activity that resulted from its discovery. In their precise descriptions of Warhol's practices, Warhol's weird and surprising specificity can be apprehended. Although quite distinct from these publications, Douglas Crimp's *"Our Kind of Movie"* engages in a reparative description of Warhol's specific filmic practices that allows their queer aims and effects to be apprehended as such; the chapter titled "Spacious" is especially ambitious and effective in this regard.

107 "The Value of Frustration," an interview with Adam Phillips, Jane Elliot, and John David Rhodes, *World Picture* 3, 2009; http://www.worldpicturejournal.com/WP_3/Phillips.html (accessed October 2, 2015).

108 Robert Hullot-Kentor, translator of Adorno's *Aesthetic Theory* (Minneapolis: University of Minnesota Press, 1997), also uses "liking" for *Wohlgefallen*. Paul Guyer and Allen W. Wood, translators of Kant's *Critique of the Power of Judgment* (New York: Cambridge University Press, 2000), explain their different choice thus: "Kant's many terms connected with pleasure and pain also presented problems. Meredith's 'delight' for Wohlgefallen, which Kant uses as his most generic term for positive rather than negative feeling, seemed dated and too specific, and Pluhar's use of 'liking' as a noun seemed unnatural. We have chosen to translate the nouns Wohlgefallen and Mißfallen as 'satisfaction' and 'dissatisfaction' respectively, using 'pleasure' and 'displeasure' for Lust and Unlust, 'enjoyment' for Genießen, and 'gratification' for Vergnügen" (xlviii).

nature of the feeling in itself.[109] In American psychology, "liking" has often similarly referred to a basic, mostly automatic reaction that guides humans (and other animals) to either approach or avoid a given stimulus. Robert Zajonc and Jonathan Haidt, for instance, have made efforts to understand how liking might be manipulated and how it appears to function independently from the processes that guide knowledge and recognition.[110]

But on the whole, even where liking is presumed to be basic and fundamental, it rarely receives critical attention as such, as if it were *so* basic as to be beneath analysis. And where liking is not taken for granted, it is regularly treated as unimportant, weak, or even degraded, often in contrast to other, more serious feelings. For instance, in describing the way most photographs either "please or displease" him in *Camera Lucida*, Roland Barthes writes that the "*studium* is that very wide field of unconcerned desire, of various interest, of inconsequential taste: *I like/I don't like*." Setting up the more complex and affecting *punctum*, which ruptures the *studium* by "pricking" or "piercing" the viewer, Barthes writes that "the *studium* is of the order of *liking*, not of *loving*; it mobilizes a half desire, a demi-volition; it is the same sort of vague, slippery, irresponsible interest one takes in the people, the entertainments, the books, the clothes one finds 'all right.'"[111] Even though (or precisely because) it describes the general or "*average* affect" that he feels most often, the vague, ambient, passive liking remains for Barthes not only uninteresting as a feeling (either to have or to think about), but an "irresponsible" path of least resistance, complicit with the manipulations of consumer culture, indeed with "culture" itself as a means of social control.[112]

109 Thus, for instance, chapters 2–5 of Pluhar's *Critique of Judgment* (Indianapolis: Hackett Publishing, 1987) are "The Liking That Determines a Judgment of Taste Is Devoid of All Interest," "A Liking for the Agreeable Is Connected with Interest," "A Liking for the Good Is Connected with Interest," "Comparison of the Three Sorts of Liking, Which Differ in Kind."

110 Zajonc, "Feeling and Thinking: Preferences Need No Inferences," *American Psychologist* 35, no. 2 (February 1980): 151–75; Haidt, *The Happiness Hypothesis: Finding Modern Truth in Ancient Wisdom* (New York: basic Books, 2006). Zajonc describes a set of experiments that show that "mere exposure" to a stimulus increases the chances we will like it, even if the exposure was so brief that it did not produce recognition; liking is thus autonomous from knowledge and recognition.

111 *Camera Lucida: Reflections on Photography*, trans. Richard Howard (New York: Farrar, Strauss, Giroux, 1981), 27. Barthes uses the English "like" in the French as well, as if the very concept and feeling is named best by the English and is even, perhaps, somehow fundamentally American. "Le studium, c'est le champ très vaste du désir nonchalant, de l'intérêt divers, du goût inconséquent : j'aime/je n'aime pas, I like/I don't. Le studium est de l'ordre du to like, et non du to love; il mobilise un demi—désir, un demi—vouloir; c'est la même sorte d'intérêt vague, lisse, irresponsable, qu'on a pour des gens, des spectacles, des vêtements, des livres, qu'on trouve « bien»."

112 For another interesting critical comment on liking, see Adorno: "If one seeks to find out who 'likes' a commercial piece, one cannot avoid the suspicion that liking and dislik-

Where Barthes seems mainly uninterested in liking, the writer Jonathan Franzen is firmly opposed to it. In his 2011 commencement speech (which became an opinion column), "Liking Is for Cowards, Go for What Hurts," Franzen makes an *ethical* case against liking, which he sees as "commercial culture's substitute for loving."[113] It names the feeling we have about new purchases, especially technological devices which seek to compensate for an indifferent world of "hurricanes and hardships and breakable hearts" by offering in its place "a world so responsive to our wishes as to be, effectively, a mere extension of the self." Unlike his Blackberry, "serious art and literature" (like "jet engines [and] laboratory equipment") is "simply itself," since its makers "aren't fixated on your liking it." The dominance of liking and likability in the world of consumer goods, Franzen suggests, may also tempt one into seeking to *be* likable, an undertaking that leads down a slippery slope to a life "without integrity, without a center," indeed to "pathological narcissism," a danger typified by Facebook and its "Like" button.[114]

In opposition to this culture of liking, Franzen makes a case for "actual love," which involves feeling "bottomless empathy" for another person, an identification with "his or her struggles and joys as if they were your own." Loving a specific person requires that you "surrender some of your self," risking rejection, disappointment, or loss. "To expose your whole self, not just the likable surface, and to have it rejected, can be catastrophically painful. The prospect of pain generally, the pain of loss, of breakup, of death, is what makes it so tempting to avoid love and stay safely in the world of liking." Liking is superficial and safe. It is lazily complicit with the worst consumerist and narcissistic aspects of our culture. So, Franzen advises, don't be a coward; be tough and have integrity and don't care so much about what

ing are inappropriate to the situation, even if the person questioned clothes his reactions in those words. The familiarity of the piece is a surrogate for the quality ascribed to it. To like it is almost the same thing as to recognize it. An approach in terms of value judgments has become a fiction for the person who finds himself hemmed in by standardized music goods." Adorno, "On the Fetish-Character in Music and the Regressions of Listening," in *Essays on Music* (Berkeley: University of California Press, 2002): 288–317, 288.

113 *New York Times*, May 28, 2011, http://www.nytimes.com/2011/05/29/opinion/29franzen.html?_r=0 (accessed May 31, 2015).

114 Franzen describes Facebook's Like button as "the transformation [of] a feeling to an assertion of consumer choice." Of course, Facebook (like all forms of mass culture) sells its users' attention to advertisers: when one "likes" something on Facebook, one is generating income for Facebook by producing data that helps advertisers learn about its users' tastes, turn-ons, anxieties, and emotional ties and how these may be directed, indeed manipulated, as in Facebook's notorious mood experiment. "For one week in January 2012, data scientists skewed what almost 700,000 Facebook users saw when they logged into its service. Some people were shown content with a preponderance of happy and positive words; some were shown content analyzed as sadder than average. And when the week was over, these manipulated users were more likely to post either especially positive or negative words themselves." Robinson Meyer, "Everything We Know about Facebook's Secret Mood Manipulation Experiment," *Atlantic*, June 28, 2014.

other people think and give yourself over to loving that one special person, even though that risks the pain of rejection or loss.

Franzen's familiar romance of serious and authentic individual feeling, opposed to the debased, narcissistic world of commercialization, but deeply committed to the virtues of love as it is experienced in the couple form, was already well-worn if hegemonic in the early 1960s. Warhol's enthusiastic embrace of what Franzen calls "the world of liking," his liking all "the great modern things" that the abstract expressionists "tried so hard not to notice at all" (*POP*, 3), presents a forceful rejoinder to Franzen-style moralizing.

Where Franzen presents liking as a weak and debased feeling that could and should be avoided, and Barthes sees liking as "inconsequential," I think Warhol used the word to refer to the simplest judgment—"I like this"—essential to *any* engagement with the world. As I suggested above, for Warhol (as in some psychological uses of the word), liking is not so much an emotion as a force propelling us toward something instead of away. As such, it is the condition of possibility for being affected by something. Like interest, it prepares us to pay attention. And it is a basic affirmation: *like* me, this is here, and it is here *with* me. As a form of attraction, it is also anticipates pleasure. Warhol suggests that, for him, liking is an open-ended way of being "affectionate."[115] As Stephen Burt points out, it is a transitional feeling. In discussing the way children and teenagers say, "X likes Y," Burt suggest that this "'like' is more than, or other than, friendship, but it is not exactly love." Instead, it is "something liminal, undefined, 'transitional' in Winnicott's sense: the word 'like' can do so much work . . . only if, and only because, nobody insists on knowing everything that it can mean."[116] Like Winnicott's transitional object, liking is an opening into the world more generally: it indicates potentiality. In this sense, liking is not a debasement of love (as Franzen would have it); it is its precondition. Yet Warhol does not promote liking as a preliminary step toward love ("first comes like," as the online dating site Zoosk has it), but as a feeling that is valuable in itself. "I don't really believe in love; I sort of believe in liking" (*IBYM*, 226).

Where the (so-called) social media instrumentalize and financialize liking, Warhol's project aimed to deinstrumentalize, proliferate, and maximize it to a well-nigh universal scale: like everything, like everybody. (Perhaps, as I mentioned, this allowed him to imagine a world in which it is possible to like Andy Warhol, too.) He sought to do this by directing us right to the apparently debased places—the commodity, celebrity, mass entertainment,

115 See Lucie-Smith, "Conversations with Artists":

ELS: Do you ever feel affectionate about people, or is that against feeling too?
AW: Well, no, I like everybody, so that's affectionate.
ELS: What . . . that the great thing is to feel affectionate toward everybody in the world.
AW: Yes.

116 Burt, "LIKE," n.p.

pornography—where our liking is already stimulated and instrumentalized, in order to reclaim, pervert, and expand this liking. This approach to liking is more disruptive and less passive than it may at first appear. Think, for instance, of the function of the Like button on Facebook, which has based its algorithms on the (correct) presumption that most people (unlike Warhol) are not trying to like everything. Liking is selective. The person who likes *everything* on Facebook no longer provides information that is useful to advertisers.[117] Liking everybody and everything—especially if everybody did it—would not only disrupt Facebook's financial model, it would challenge the basic model for mass culture more generally, where the audience attention that is sold to advertisers is valuable *only* to the extent that it is selectively exercised, indicating preferences that could be directed toward a purchase.

Or consider the way that, as Pierre Bourdieu has famously argued, "taste classifies, and it classifies the classifier."[118] If, like Warhol, we all tried to like as much as we could, taste could no longer serve this invidiously classificatory function. Of course, Warhol's departure from "good taste" was read by many as an embrace of "bad taste," if a disorienting one. But Warhol's efforts to like everything and encourage others to like like him actively imagines a world where taste ceases to function as a means of marking and making class positions.

Even if we are unable to achieve Warholian levels of liking (and not even Warhol managed to like everything and everybody), and see that in our everyday lives liking is manipulated and financialized, it does not logically follow that we should somehow try to like *less*, or give up on liking as a feeling *tout court*. That could only lead to an increasing reification of the private world of authentic emotion and a further withdrawal from the world. Disdain for liking is itself an expression of alienation from those *other*—weaker, stupider, duped or deluded—people who cannot resist giving in to (what Franzen terms) the debased "world of liking." If liking things is the basic affective openness necessary for any kind of engagement with the world, and if the Benjaminian analysis of the dulling and withdrawal of the mimetic faculty is correct and we therefore need more ways to experience and

117 The connection between Facebook liking and advertising was dramatized by Mat Honan, who wrote that when he indiscriminately "liked" everything on his Facebook "newsfeed," the feed was transformed from updates about friends and colleagues into nothing but advertisements. "I Liked Everything I Saw on Facebook and Here's What It Did to Me," *Wired*, August 11, 2014, http://www.wired.com/2014/08/i-liked-everything-i-saw-on-facebook-for-two-days-heres-what-it-did-to-me/?mbid=social_fb (accessed May 13, 2015).

118 Bourdieu, *Distinction: A Social Critique of the Judgment of Taste*, trans. Richard Nice (Cambridge, MA: Harvard University Press, 1984), 6. In paintings of Campbell's soup cans or Coke bottles, Warhol also reconnects the apparently or ideally disinterested character of sophisticated artistic taste with what Bourdieu calls "the elementary taste for the flavours of food" (1).

care about the world and other people rather than fewer, then the question of liking and its vicissitudes should be at the center of our critical concerns.

Warhol's promotion of liking is an effort to increase our capacity for affecting and being affected in general. In principle, this risks a range of feelings, not only "positive" ones (on which more in a moment). And while I think Warhol's liking welcomes this risk, I think it also aims, on the whole, toward what Spinoza (and Gilles Deleuze following him) call the joyous affects, the ones that increase what Spinoza calls the "power of acting or force of existing."[119]

For Spinoza, when one body encounters another, its capacities are altered; this is the moment of being affected. This process is continuous and ongoing (sometimes dramatically, other times subtly) in what Deleuze calls "a melodic line of continuous variation," a line that constitutes "what it means to exist."[120] Of this melodic line constituted by affect, Deleuze explains, "Spinoza will assign two poles: joy-sadness, which for him will be the fundamental passions. Sadness will be any passion whatsoever which involves a diminution of my power of acting, and joy will be any passion involving an increase in my power of acting."[121] Affect is thus not a "psychological" category (something that happens "inside" a "me") nor is it reducible to the subject, or ego (both preceding and exceeding it, which is also what makes it different from an "emotion").[122] Instead, affect is a "passage," less

119 Spinoza, *Ethics*, ed. and trans. Edwin Curley (New York: Penguin, 1996), 113 (II, 204). See Deleuze, "L'affect et l'idée," course lecture at the Université de Paris VIII, Vincennes, January 24, 1978; available at www.deleuzeweb.com in the original French and in English translation. See also *Expressionism in Philosophy: Spinoza*, trans. M. Joughin (New York: Zone Books, 1992), esp. chap. 14, "What Can the Body Do?"

120 The subject, then, is something like the set of relations among the parts of a body, which affect each other according to their own melodies, even as they encounter and are affected by objects in the world. Deleuze elaborates on Spinoza's understanding of the body as constituted by the relation among its parts: "A body must be defined by the ensemble of relations which compose it, or, what amounts to exactly the same thing, by its power to be affected [pouvoir d'être affecté]" ("L'affect et l'idée"). Michael Hardt expands on this: "We need to shift perspective so as no longer to consider a body as an entity (or even a cluster of entities) but instead as a relation. When a new relation is added, a larger body is composed, and when a relation is broken, the body diminishes or decomposes. All this simply means that the border between the inside and outside of bodies, and hence between internal and external causes, is fluid and subject to our efforts." Hardt, "The Power to Be Affected," *International Journal of Politics, Culture, and Society* 28, no. 3 (September 2015): 215–22. See Mary Zournazi, "Navigating Movements: An Interview with Brian Massumi," for a lucid gloss on Deleuze's concept of affect, http://www.international-festival.org/node/111 (accessed May 31, 2015); also in Zournazi, *Hope: New Philosophies for Change* (New York: Routledge, 2003).

121 Deleuze, "L'affect et l'idée."

122 The distinction between affect and emotion has been much discussed, with Silvan Tomkins and Brian Massumi offering two influential accounts. For both, affect is irreducible, the more basic kind of feeling, operating according to an "autonomous" logic, not reducible to the logics of cognition, memory, will, or perception, though constantly

a feeling that one *has* than an event that happens. Warhol's "liking" is an affect in this sense. Like Spinoza's joy, it is one way of encountering things in the world.[123] One can prepare for liking and try to maximize it. But one does not "choose" to like something at the moment of encounter.

The trick to living a life in which one maximizes liking, suggests Deleuze, is not just to avoid things that do not "agree" with one (while nonetheless trying to occupy the limit or edge of one's capacity for being affected), but also to actively seek for points of correspondence and commonality, "to form the idea of what is common to the affecting body and the affected body."[124] This itself requires attunement to what Benjamin called the "active mimetic force acting expressly inside things," the "mimetic centers . . . numerous within every being" (*SW2*, 684). Warhol's liking is an attempt to "form the idea of what is common" in what he encounters, and so to compose a melody that brings him into maximal correspondence with the things

interacting with those other logics. Tomkins sees a distinct number of basic affects (shame, interest, surprise, joy, fear, disgust, anger, distress, dissmell), each with its own internal, systemic logic and its own experiential quality (including distinct facial and bodily responses). An emotion, as Tomkins defines it, involves the combination of affects with ideas, with memories, with other affects, to create a kind of composite. Where emotions are widely variable across cultures and historical periods for Tomkins, affects tend to be more or less consistent. Borrowing from Deleuze (and his work on Spinoza), Massumi argues for affect as an unqualified intensity, a kind of presubjective nonconscious energy that the body experiences in relation to stimuli. Emotion is what happens to the affect once it has been "owned" or captured and named in language by the subject as "mine." An emotion is a personal feeling. Until it has been owned in this way, it remains a potentiality. Massumi: "Emotion is the way the depth of that ongoing experience (described by Spinoza) registers personally at a given moment" (Zournazi, "Navigating Movements"). Where does Warhol's liking fit in here? As should be clear, I do not think that liking maps onto Tomkins's affects, although it bears some similarities to his understanding of the affect interest in the way that it prepares us to pay attention and become engaged with something, and with the surprise (or startle) affect in the way that it can mark a transition from one feeling or orientation to another. Liking seems to be more basic and less specific than any of Tomkins's affects. As an opening and a transition, it seems closer to the understanding of affect that Massumi borrows from Deleuze. Yet, even if Warhol's liking may be mostly precognitive and unconscious, it is not an unqualified pure potentiality. There is a subject—Warhol's "I"—doing the liking, even if that "I" is more of a *semblable* than a liberal individual. On the affect-emotion distinction, see also Sianne Ngai, *Ugly Feelings* (Cambridge, MA: Harvard University Press, 2007), esp. 22–30, and Flatley, *Affective Mapping*, 11–19.

123 In this it bears some similarity to Deleuze's efforts to redefine desire (away from a psychoanalytic focus on lack): "For me, desire includes no such lack; it is also not a natural given. Desire is wholly a part of the functioning heterogeneous assemblage. It is a process, as opposed to a structure or a genesis. It is an affect, as opposed to a feeling. It is a haecceity—the individual singularity of a day, a season, a life. As opposed to a subjectivity, it is an event, not a thing or a person." Deleuze, "Desire and Pleasure," *Two Regimes of Madness: Texts and Interviews 1975–1995*, trans. David Lapoujade, (London: Semiotext(e), 2006), 122–34, 130.

124 Deleuze, "L'affect et l'idée."

he finds in the world. In such a world, "you can imitate everyone you know," as John Lennon put it. Warhol's project of liking things is thus an instance of taking what Brian Massumi describes as "practical, experimental, strategic measures to expand our emotional register" so that we might "access more of our potential at each step, have more of it actually available."[125]

However, as I mentioned, liking things is not done consciously at every encounter; it is not a simple question of volition or decision. Agency regarding one's liking is exerted in a mediated, tactical fashion. In his book on happiness, Jonathan Haidt offers us one metaphor for understanding this mediation, something he calls the "like-o-meter," a kind of automatic internal machine that constantly directs our attention one way or another. In relation to any stimulus, the like-o-meter offers a quick response: approach or avoid.[126] ("Liking is like being a machine, " Warhol says, because "you do the same thing every time. You do it over and over again.") I understand Warhol's range of aesthetic practices as (not always successful) attempts to manipulate this like-o-meter machine in order to make it like more things than it otherwise would, to allow it to overcome barriers put up, say, by racism or misogyny or homophobia that might discourage us from liking and feeling alike. We can understand this shift, setting the like-o-meter at the highest level possible, to operate at the level of *mood*. One exercises agency in relation to one's liking by developing practices for getting in the mood for liking.

By mood I am thinking of Heidegger's *Stimmung*, which has a musical connotation and may also be translated as "attunement." For Heidegger, *Stimmung* is the overall atmosphere or medium in or through which our thinking, doing, willing, feeling, and acting occurs. It establishes the conditions for our encounter with the world *before* cognition and volition.[127] Although our moods often escape notice, it is only through mood and by way of mood that we encounter the world: "*the mood has already disclosed, in every case, Being-in-the-world as a whole, and makes it possible first of all to direct one-self toward something.*"[128] Mood discloses the world in the sense that

125 Zournazi, "Navigating Movements."

126 Haidt, *Happiness Hypothesis*, 12, 17, 26–27.

127 "Ontologically mood (*Stimmung*) is a primordial kind of Being for Dasein, in which Dasein is disclosed to itself *prior* to all cognition and volition and *beyond* their range of disclosure" (*Being and Time*, trans. John Macquarrie and Edward Robinson [San Francisco: Harper and Row, 1962], 175). I rely on both this translation and the newer Stambaugh translation (Albany: SUNY Press, 1996), but unless otherwise noted, references are to the Macquarrie and Robinson text. In the German edition (Tubingen: Niemeyer, 1979), pages of which are referenced in both English translations, the primary discussion of *Stimmung* is on pages 134–40.

128 *Being and Time*, 176; italics Heidegger's. The best overall account of *Stimmung* in Heidegger can be found in Charles Guignon, "Moods in Heidegger's Being and Time," in *What Is an Emotion? Classic Readings in Philosophical Psychology*, ed. Robert C. Solomon and Cheshire Calhoun (New York: Oxford University Press, 1984), 230–43. But see also

mood constitutes our openness to the world; it is the situated directionality of that openness and as such shapes the totality of things that we see and that can "matter" to us. As Charles Guignon puts it, "Moods enable us to focus our attention and orient ourselves," and as such they themselves exert a broad but foundational form of judgment.[129] One's mood, moreover, sets the situation in which our particular affects come into being, allowing certain affects, which are more punctual and object-oriented than moods, to attach to certain objects, while foreclosing other affective attachments and relations.[130] If "affect" refers to the transformation or "passage" that occurs in a particular encounter, moods are the force shaping the melodic line of that shifting affect. Where affects tend to be about something in particular, moods are usually about everything in general. Indeed, using the same metaphor as Deleuze (if rather loosely), Heidegger writes that *Stimmung* is the "melody" that "does not merely hover over" our being, but that "sets the tone for such being, attunes and determines the manner and way [*Art und Wie*]" of that being.[131] It attunes us to some things and not others; it is by way of mood that we come to value something, to "care" (*sorgen*), an important word for Heidegger and Warhol alike.[132]

Warhol sought to exert agency first of all over his own mood in order to attune it to likenesses and correspondences, the better to maximize his capacity for having "liking" encounters. But he also sought to arouse liking in his audiences. He put on display the various mechanisms one might use to get in the mood for liking, teaching us how to recognize what is common. Engaging these mechanisms—imagining oneself as a machine, or a celebrity, allowing oneself to relax into boredom, relating to the world as a collector—is itself a kind of affective labor. In this, it is related to the various tactics employed by the flight attendants and other affective laborers

---

Hans Ulrich Gumbrecht, *Atmosphere, Mood Stimmung: On a Hidden Potential of Literature* (Stanford, CA: Stanford University Press, 2012); and Flatley, *Affective Mapping*, esp. 19–24, 109–13, and "How a Revolutionary Counter-Mood Is Made," *New Literary History* 43 (2012): 503–25.

129 Guignon, "Moods," 237.

130 Heidegger writes, "Under the strongest pressure and resistance, nothing like an affect would come about, and the resistance itself would remain essentially undiscovered, if Being-in-the-world, with its state-of-mind [*Befindlichkeit*], had not already submitted itself [*sich schon angewiesen*] to having entities within-the-world 'matter' to it in a way which its moods have outlined in advance" (*Being and Time*, 177).

131 *The Fundamental Concepts of Metaphysics: World, Finitude, Solitude*, trans. William McNeill and Nicholas Walker (Bloomington: Indiana University Press, 1995), 67. As Tavia Nyong'o emphasized (in a private conversation), perhaps melody is the wrong musical metaphor here, since melody stands out from the background; *Stimmung* may be more like the key, major or minor, that is more or less invisible but establishes what sounds good or right.

132 Warhol: "Well, I care . . . I still care, but it would be so much easier not to care" (*IBYM*, 81). Also: "I still think its nice to care about people. And Hollywood movies are uncaring" (*IBYM*, 188).

examined by Arlene Hochschild in her landmark 1983 study *The Managed Heart*.[133] But instead of being directed toward dealing with disgruntled fliers or sustaining a smile so as to keep the clients happy, Warhol is interested in an expanded liking, in which as many things as possible might be encountered as "great" or "exciting." Of course, this project is a compelling one precisely to the extent that one's everyday life is *not* characterized by liking, where one feels the need (like Hochschild's flight attendants) to alter an existing affective atmosphere.

The direction of one's mood toward liking and likeness is not only a kind of work; it also entails its own theory. In attuning himself toward likeness in order to maximize his openness to liking, Warhol creates what Silvan Tomkins calls an "affect theory." Summarizing Tomkins, Sedgwick notes that "all people's cognitive/affective lives are organized according to alternative, changing, strategic and hypothetical affect theories." This "largely tacit theorizing all people do in experiencing and trying to deal with their own and others affects" is a mode of "selective scanning and amplification," where certain affects and relevant information are prioritized.[134] Based on accumulated experience, such affect theories are, among other things, "highly organized way[s] of interpreting information so that what is possibly relevant can be quickly abstracted and magnified, and the rest discarded."[135] In Warhol's affect theory, prioritizing the information that is relevant for liking means first of all setting aside the opposition between the same and the different, scanning instead for similarities, which are then "abstracted and magnified." Instead of asking, Is this person the same as me, or different? Warhol's is an affect theory that wonders, How am I like this? How is this like other things? How can I relate to this thing as somehow imitable? In what way are we alike? How do we (mis)fit together?

For instance, as another way to increase one's powers of acting and feelings of correspondence, Warhol's affect theory looked for, amplified, and promoted experiences that produced sexual arousal or excitement, and not only for that "special person" for whom one has (*par* Franzen) "bottomless empathy." In response to the characterization of his *Blue Movie* (a three-

133 *The Managed Heart: Commercialization of Human Feeling* (1983; Berkeley: University of California Press, 2003). For the best reading of affective labor in relation to aesthetic practices, see the chapter titled "Zany" in Sianne Ngai, *Our Aesthetic Categories* (Cambridge, MA: Harvard University Press, 2012).

134 Sedgwick, "Paranoid Reading," 134, 135

135 Tomkins, *Affect, Imagery, Consciousness*, vol. 2 (1962; New York: Springer, 1992), 433; cited in Sedgwick, "Paranoid Reading," 135. Sedgwick emphasizes the continuity between what we all do in our everyday lives and what academic or philosophical theorists of affect do. We should probably read any given "theory of affect" as, at the same time, an effort to create a workable everyday affect theory. In fact, we might understand the remarkable range of efforts in "academic" affect theory over the last twenty years or so as a response to the felt difficulty of developing workable affect theories in everyday life.

hour depiction of a sexual encounter between Louis Waldron and Viva, who do not appear to be in love but who do seem to like each other) as "hard-core pornography," Warhol (who in *POPism* remarked that "personally, I loved porno") offers a offers a defense of arousal as an aesthetic value and prurience as an aesthetic mode:[136]

> I think movies should appeal to prurient interests. I mean, the way things are going now—people are alienated from one another. Movies should—uh—arouse you. Hollywood films are just planned-out commercials. *Blue Movie* was real. But it wasn't done as pornography—it was an exercise, an experiment. But I really do think movies should arouse you, should get you excited about people, should be prurient. (*IBYM*, 189)

Instead of Hollywood's "planned out commercials," which elsewhere in the interview he calls "uncaring" (perhaps to the degree that they presume normative identities and affects and instrumentalize our affects toward a narrative goal within the film that reinforces its commercial function), Warhol understands himself as experimenting in an effort to find an alternative to "the way things are going now." The arousal that a prurient movie might produce is another way to counter alienation, to "get you excited about people." Warhol's openness to this kind of arousal is also evident in his depictions of sexual encounters and naked bodies in his Sex Parts and Torsos series from the mid-1970s, which registered the ways such an excitement flourished in the expanded, experimental sex scenes of post-Stonewall New York.[137]

Insofar as Warhol's liking is an affective openness that seeks to create correspondences without instrumentalizing them toward a predetermined goal, inasmuch as it is based not on lack but on plenitude (from Campbell's soup, which we can all love together, to the collections of cock drawings and Polaroids I discuss in the next chapter), and insofar as his liking is a promiscuous mode of affection based on acting and looking alike (and, as such, *not* fitting a stock role), rather than being an identity, it is guided by an affect

136 Thanks to Jennifer Doyle for the observation about Waldron and Viva liking but not loving each other. See her "Between Friends," in *A Companion to Lesbian, Gay, Bisexual, Transgender, and Queer Studies*, ed. George Haggerty and Molly McGarry (New York: Blackwell, 2007). On Warhol's love for pornography, see Tom Waugh, "Cockteaser," in Doyle, Flatley, and Muñoz, *Pop Out*, 51–77. In *POPism*, Warhol (and Hackett) write, "Personally, I loved porno and I bought lots of it all the time—the really dirty, exciting stuff. All you had to do was figure out what turned you on, and then just buy the dirty magazines and movie prints that are right for you, the way you'd go for the right pills or the right cans of food. (I was so avid for porno that on my first time out of the house after the shooting I went straight to 42nd Street and checked out the peep shows with Vera Cruise and restocked on dirty magazines.)" (*POP*, 294).

137 On Warhol's Sex Parts and Torso paintings and drawings, and the photo sessions from which they were derived, see Bob Colacello, *Holy Terror: Andy Warhol Close Up* (New York: HarperCollins, 1990), 337–44.

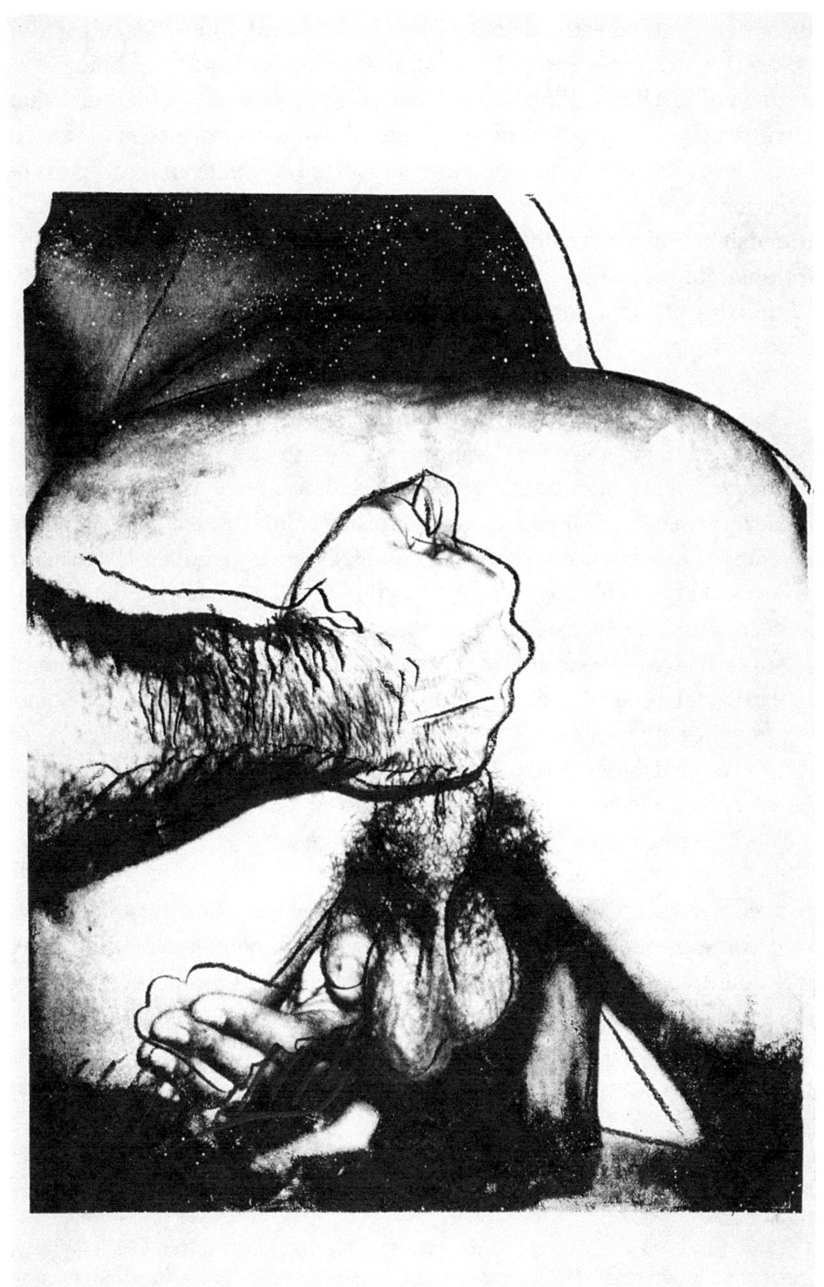

0.3 Andy Warhol, *Sex Parts*, 1978. Screenprint on Ragston S-N paper, 40 × 26 inches. © 2016 Andy Warhol Foundation for the Visual Arts/Artists Rights Society (ARS), New York

theory compatible with what Douglas Crimp called "the ethos of gay liberation regarding the expansion of affectional possibility."[138] Echoing Foucault's enthusiasm for the "new affective and relational virtualities" that might emerge along the "slantwise" lines that queers traverse in the social fabric,[139] Crimp writes that this ethos supported "a great variety of forms of affectional and sexual relationships, a proliferation of variously organized friendships and community relations, which made for a great many options for obtaining pleasure and forming human connection and intimacy."[140] Within this affective world, which Crimp sees at work in the new disco scene of the 1970s,

> coupling was newly seen not as a "happily ever after" compact, but as an in-the-moment union for sharing pleasure. Such pleasure sharing could, of course, lead to all kinds of longer-term relationships: now-and-again casual sex partners, regular fuck buddies, cruising comrades, bar and bathhouse companions, just plain friends, and combinations of any of these and many more. But it didn't have to lead to anything at all. Pleasure was its own reward; it didn't require redemption through "love" or "commitment" or even an exchange of phone numbers. Moreover, two stopped being a magic number: coupling could easily be multiplied to become a three-way, a foursome, group sex. Bathhouses had "orgy rooms," steam rooms, and saunas for those who wanted more than one partner at a time and who might also want a little voyeurism and/or exhibitionism in the mix or the total anonymity of sex in the dark with bodies detached from personhood.[141]

In such a world, "the normative couple was only one of many possibilities, so if you weren't inclined toward that form of connection, you didn't feel weird, left out, and miserable."[142] In composing and promoting an affect theory that does not privilege the normative, monogamous couple as the organizing hub for sociality or the primary site of affective affiliation, comfort, or pleasure—unless that is, you count Warhol's "marriage" to his Norelco

138 Crimp, "Disss-co (A Fragment), from *Before Pictures, a Memoir of 1970s New York*," in "Disco" (special issue, ed. Jonathan Flatley and Charles Kronengold), *Criticism* 50, no. 1 (Winter 2008): 1–18, 15.

139 In "Friendship as a Way of Life" (in *Ethics: Subjectivity and Truth*, ed. Paul Rabinow [New York: New Press, 1997]), Foucault says, "Homosexuality is a historic occasion to reopen affective and relational virtualities, not so much through the intrinsic qualities of the homosexual, but because the 'slantwise' position of the latter, as it were, the diagonal lines he can lay out in the social fabric allow these virtualities to come to light" (138).

140 Tina Takemoto, "The Melancholia of AIDS: Interview with Douglas Crimp," *Art Journal* 62, no. 4 (Winter 2003): 80–90, 86.

141 "Disss-co," 15. See also Samuel Delany, *Times Square Red, Times Square Blue* (New York: NYU Press, 1999), on the modes of conviviality that flourished in the porn theaters of Time Square.

142 Takemoto, "Melancholia," 86.

tape recorder—Warhol's is an effort to create an opening where nonmiserable, even joyous, plural queer singularity could come into being.[143]

Even as he deprivileges the romantic couple and love in aiming to maximize liking, so too Warhol (like Spinoza) "denounces a plot in the universe of those who are interested in affecting us with sad passions."[144] In *POPism*, recalling the moment after President Kennedy's assassination, Warhol said, "I'd been thrilled having Kennedy as a president; he was handsome, young, smart—but it didn't bother me that much that he was dead. What bothered me was the way the television and radio were programming everyone to feel so sad." Warhol recounts trying to rally his friends by taking them out to dinner, but "you couldn't get away" from the programming and so "it didn't work, everyone was acting too depressed." Henry Geldzahler wondered why Warhol was not more upset, and Warhol "told him about the time I was walking in India and saw a bunch of people in a clearing having a ball because someone they really liked had just died and how I realized then that everything was just how you decided to think about it" (*POP*, 60). On the one hand, Warhol here seems to be wishfully overstating the volitional quality of his affective life (which may have been especially attractive as he struggled to come to terms with his failed romance with Charles Lisanby, with whom he had been traveling at the time). But at the same time, he indicates the degree to which he is engaged in self-conscious affect theorizing and affective labor aimed at reducing the effects of mass-media-programmed sadness. This theory and labor involves an attempt to shift the mood by creating a way of being with others—"having a ball," going out to dinner—in which a different set of things matter. Because, as Spinoza (and Deleuze and Massumi following him) emphasized, the sad are more docile, Warhol's mood-shifting opposition to the given programming has clear political consequences.

We might see Warhol's paintings of Jackie Kennedy (1964) and his film *Since* (1966) (in which actors reenact parts of Abraham Zapruder's famous film of the assassination) as illustrations of how the depression-inducing media reactions to Kennedy's death could be altered by finding points of correspondence within the experience of mass grief.[145] The two paintings titled *The Week That Was* and several of the twenty-four works titled *Multiplied Jackies* present a chronologically misarranged montage of mass-mediated images of Jackie before and after her husband's death on variously colored blue, gold, and white canvases: Jackie, in her pillbox hat, smiles broadly during her arrival in Dallas; her downcast face witnesses the swearing in of

143 See Benjamin Kahan's reading of Warhol's marriage to his tape recorder as an instance of his eroticization of objects, and as one of the effects of his "alloerotic celibacy" or "sexualized celibacy," in *Celibacies: American Modernism and Sexual Life* (Durham, NC: Duke University Press, 2013), 129.

144 This is Deleuze describing Spinoza in "L'affect et l'idée."

145 On the Jackie paintings, see *CR2A*, 103–5.

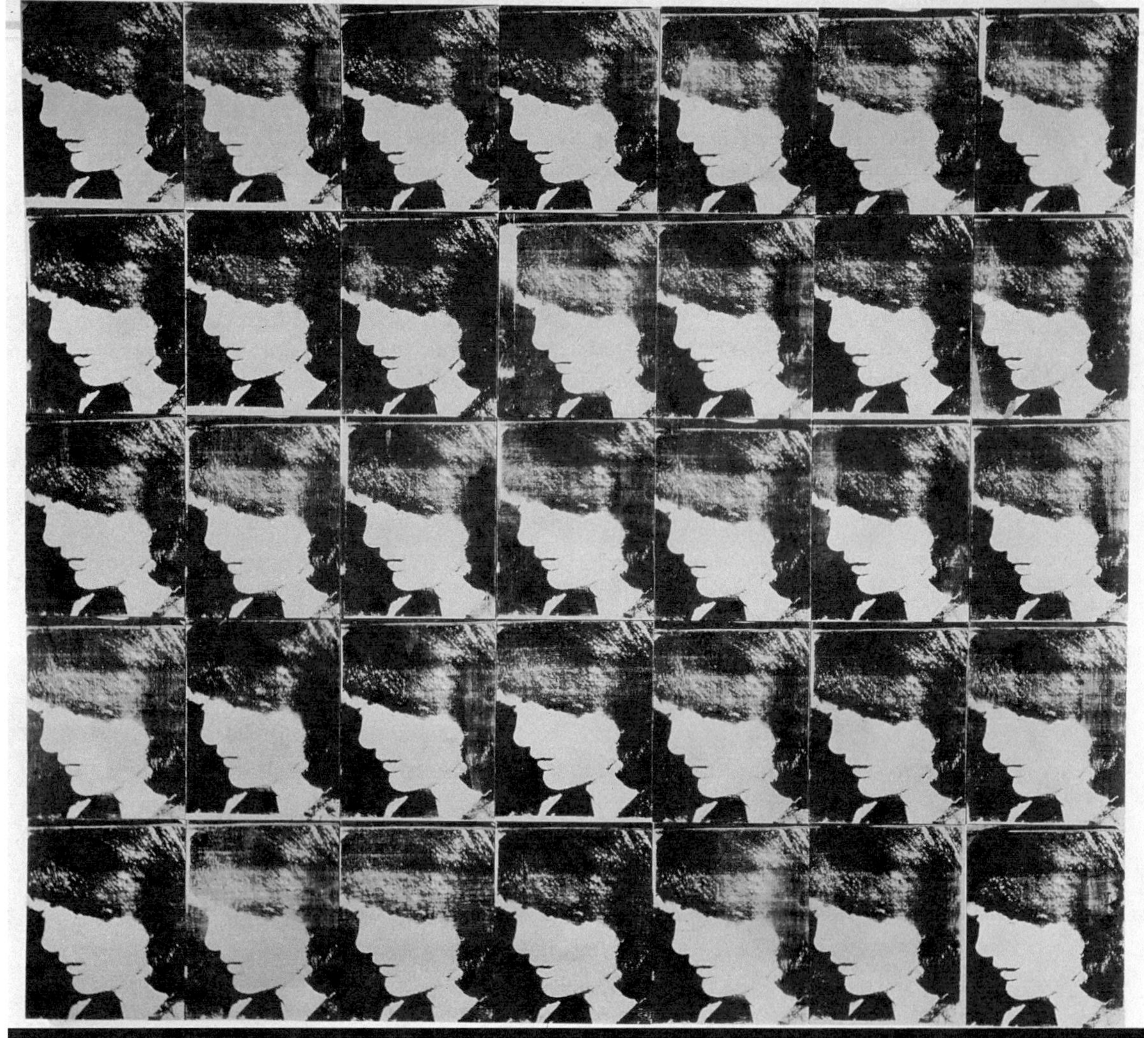

0.4 Andy Warhol, *Thirty-Five Jackies (Multiplied Jackies)*, 1964. Acrylic and silkscreen ink on linen, 100⅜ × 113 inches. © 2016 Andy Warhol Foundation for the Visual Arts/Artists Rights Society (ARS), New York.

Lyndon Johnson; and at the funeral, with and without a veil, she stares ahead with martial grace. The temporal disorder relayed by the stutter from smile to sorrow and back offers a nonteleological series of affective images, one that orients the viewer's apprehension of Kennedy's death squarely toward Jackie's visage and her powerful star persona. What had been an occasion for docile sadness thus becomes an opportunity for a collective mimesis of glamorous mournfulness. This changes the nature of the feeling not only because it allows the public to share a moment of affective intensity with "the most glamorous woman in the world."[146] In allowing one to feel like this powerful, famous, and beautiful woman, Jackie's public displays of grief also provide one with a way to feel like all the others also feeling like her. In this sense, Warhol's paintings of Jackie Kennedy are about the moment when *everybody's* affect was keyed to Jackie's face, which had made itself available as a site of mass-affective imitation and attachment. Inasmuch as she was, at this moment, the object of a nearly universal liking, Warhol could say that her performance of grief was "the best thing she's ever done!"[147]

As Karen Beckman suggests in her brilliant reading of *Since*, the film also presents an actively mimetic nonprogrammed relation to the mass-mediated event of the assassination. Warhol's characters, she writes, respond to the media spectacle "by mimicking the actions they see" through a kind of "watching and rewatching" that turns the Zapruder film strip into "a metaphorical social space of film spectatorship that encourages viewers to mimic and improvise on the content of the strip."[148] Such a spectatorship is a "a kind of doing," one that itself allows for the imagining and enacting of "alternative forms, power relationships and subjectivities." Most significantly for my argument here, the film puts on display (for viewers to study, imitate, or recognize) the process of a media event producing "queer media communities that are forged by idiosyncratic 'inhabitations' of and variations on media experiences." For Beckman (making compelling use of Elizabeth Freeman's concept of temporal drag), what is most important is the way this queer spectatorial community recasts our temporal apprehension of the mass-mediated historical event, but she also points out how this group of mimicking "rewatchers" sexualizes the scene of politics, fosters cross-gender performances (like Mary Woronov as Jack Kennedy), and opens up space for excessive and unanticipated affective investments. Most dramatically, we see Susan Bottomly mimic Jackie Kennedy's crawl across the back of the presidential limousine as she falls "in and out of her different roles, experiencing herself in close corporeal proximity to Jackie Kennedy, 'crawling nearby,' without either becoming her or disavowing her presence."[149] Here, being like Jackie Kennedy allows for a collective queer repossession of an event that had, several years earlier, programmed everyone to feel so sad.

If Warhol's affect theory, centered on liking and likeness, is also a way to be less depressed by the daily news, and by all the ways rulers seek to make the ruled sorrowful and incapable of action, that does not mean it is

146 Gerard Malanga observed that Warhol was attracted to Jackie as "the most glamorous woman in the world, or something like that" (Smith, *Conversations*, 166).

147 "She's so fabulous!" John Giorno reports Warhol saying about Jackie's "electrifying" walk with the black veil (*You Got to Burn to Shine*, 126).

148 *Crash: Cinema and the Politics of Speed and Stasis* (Durham, NC: Duke University Press, 2010), 137–60, 142.

149 Ibid., 159–60.

an attempt to block out an affective experience of the mediated events in question. In the Death and Disaster series from the early 1960s, Warhol depicts grisly car crashes, suicides, electric chairs, white supremacist police violence, and mushroom clouds.[150] On the level of aesthetic experience, we are to "like" these images as well, in the sense that we are to be open to them, to allow ourselves to be affected by them, and to seek ways to correspond with them and with others in relation to them.[151] By reproducing these images and printing them over decorative colors, Warhol removes them from the anaesthetizing negative feedback loop that Benjamin described. As Gerard Malanga remarked, "If you see a UPI photo, you're going to grimace; but if you see it on a canvas with color, you might accept it."[152] One can like the image before the "shock value" of the image has consciously registered; because viewers "don't have to think," Warhol explained, they can "just sort of see the things and they like them and they understand them easier" (*IBYM*, 32). With these images, in some ways "the meaning going away" is a precondition for being affected by them.[153]

The silkscreened similitudes of car crashes, suicides, and police attacks on an unarmed black man also remind us of the plural reception of these disaster images and of their repetitive occurrence in the everyday space of the mass public sphere.[154] In so doing, they deindividualize the consump-

150 Even though (or in part because) they did not sell at first, these are probably Warhol's most critically praised works (as he predicted they would be), in part because it is easier to discern a critique of mass culture and the commodity in his focus on the negative. For two influential readings of these works, see Thomas Crow, "Saturday Disasters: Trace and Reference in Early Warhol," and Hal Foster, "Death in America," both in Michelson, *Andy Warhol*.

151 In suggesting that Warhol's reproductions of these images do not primarily distance us from them, I am proposing an alternative to Foster's strong reading of the paintings as traumatic repetitions of the real. Foster argues that Warhol's repetitions "not only reproduce traumatic effects; they produce them as well (at least they do in me). Somehow in these repetitions, then, several contradictory things occur at the same time: a warding away of traumatic significance and an opening out to it, a defending against traumatic affect and a producing of it" ("Death In America," 72). I think Foster is right to point out that the images produce effects; they are not just shields against affect. But I propose that we see this effect not as "traumatic," at least not in the sense Foster is using the term. See chapter 4 for my discussion of the Race Riots and the "compassion" they solicit as a form of what Jean-Luc Nancy calls "the disturbance of violent relatedness" (*Being Singular Plural*, xiii).

152 Smith, *Conversations*, 163.

153 "The more you look at the exact same thing, the more the meaning goes away" (*POP*, 50). "I just feel the shapes with my eyes and if you look at something long enough, I've discovered, the meaning goes away" (*IBYM*, 95).

154 See Gene Swenson: "Warhol's repetitions of car crashes, suicides and electric chairs are not like the repetition of similar and yet terribly different scenes day in and day out in the tabloids. These paintings mute what is present in the single front page each day, and emphasize what is present persistently day after day in slightly different variations. Looking at the papers, we do not consciously make the connection between today's,

tion of the images, pointing to the way that the anaesthetizing experience of shocking images is itself a point of commonality and correspondence, while reminding us that occasionally, as in the civil rights movement, this collective viewing of violence and suffering can spur political action. Warhol's gambit is that, on the whole, affirming "negative" representations or images, rather than blocking them out, will ultimately be more "joyful" than "sad" (in Spinoza's sense) because we are more capable of acting—and acting with others—if we are open to experiencing these events in the world, affirming them as being in the world with us, instead of either shielding ourselves from them or being traumatized by them.

In other words, even in these representations of violence and death, we can discern a theory of positive affects that tends toward reparation and correspondence. In this sense, Warhol's liking is also hopeful: it anticipates finding or creating the "lived similarities" that constitute experience as such and that allow us to imagine relations of liking and likeness with others. For Warhol, liking and the resembling it entails are themselves active, creative forces that change the being of the liker and the liked. Liking does not only take advantage of already existing similarities. Itself imitative, it also brings them into being. In a world such as ours, where fear, disillusionment, anxiety, and alienation are as present as ever, where caring presents itself as an ongoing challenge, we should not ignore the slantwise potentialities and anticipatory hope opened up by Warhol's deinstrumentalized liking.

* * *

The four chapters of *Like Andy Warhol* examine various of Warhol's tactics for attuning to likeness to get into the mood to like. Chapter 1 considers his energetic collecting practices as one of his chief, everyday methods for liking. In arguing that Warhol tried to relate to as many objects of perception as possible as parts of one collection or another, I examine the range of Warhol's collections, including the many objects auctioned at his death, but also his collections of perfumes, photographs, and tape recordings, as well as his own drawings and photographs of male genitalia. I argue that Warhol's Screen Tests, the short portrait films he made between 1964 and 1966, themselves constitute a collection, one that represents a particular and in some ways ideal version of the collectivity that took shape in Warhol's Factory in the 1960s.

The next two chapters examine two artists who are in some way "like Andy Warhol," Sol LeWitt and Donald Judd, both of whom, as avatars of conceptual art and minimalism respectively, are usually thought of as aestheti-

---

yesterday's, and tomorrow's 'repetitions' which are not repetitions." Swenson, "The Other Tradition," 1966, 36; quoted by Neil Printz in *Andy Warhol Death and Disasters* (Houston: Menil Foundation, 1988), 17.

cally opposed to Pop. Chapter 2, "Art Machine," compares Warhol—who declared that "the reason I'm painting this way is that I want to be a machine, and I feel whatever I do and do machine-like is what I want to do"—with LeWitt, who influentially described conceptual art as a process where "the idea becomes a machine that makes the art." In readings centering on his Dance Diagram paintings, I examine Warhol's dramatization of moments of interface between different systemic logics, especially ones that require translating information from the logics, standards, and materials of one system into another. I argue that these forms of creative mistranslation were one of his key aesthetic tactics for stimulating our perception of similarity. Chapter 3, "Allegories of Boredom," looks at the relation between interest and boredom in the work of Warhol and Judd. Each artist sought to elicit from his audience and produce for himself an apparently mundane form of emotional attachment, which Judd called "interest" and Warhol "liking," with an art that was maximally emptied of subjective or expressive intent. In readings of Judd's metal and Plexiglas "specific objects" and Warhol's film *Sleep*, I argue that, for both Judd and Warhol, it was an affectless art that was most likely to allow for the appearance of affects in their audiences. The absence of affect in the art objects allowed for a relaxation of the mimetic shock-defense dynamic, enabling transferences of affect from everyday life into the space of the art work.

The final chapter takes up Warhol's recurring preoccupation with the color line, focusing on the Race Riot paintings, his early celebrity silkscreens, his 1975 portraits of African American and Latina drag queens (the *Ladies and Gentlemen* series), and his collaborations with Jean-Michel Basquiat in 1984–1985. I argue that Warhol's response to the multifarious and aggressive ideological foregrounding of incommensurable difference sought to recall to us our capacity for perceiving and producing similarities, including and especially across the color line. I make this case by way of an examination of the racial significance of Warhol's use of color and his mediations of skin and skin color.

In focusing on moments of similarity between Warhol and these other artists (LeWitt, Judd, Basquiat) to trace out the historical situations shared by them, these chapters aim to disclose the "there" in which these artists found themselves. By way of these comparisons, I also hope to suggest that Warhol's attention to likenesses might inform a critical practice itself based on liking and analogical thinking, one that would allow the singularity of each artist to come clearly into view precisely to the extent that the artist is seen to be like other artists.

1: Collecting and Collectivity

At bottom, we may say, the collector lives a piece of dream life. For in the dream, too, the rhythm of perception and experience is altered in such a way that everything—even the seemingly most neutral—comes to strike us; everything concerns us.

Walter Benjamin, "The Collector"[1]

There may be no more vivid illustration of Warhol's talent for "liking things" than his energetic and far-ranging collecting practices.[2] An examination of the six-volume catalog of possessions sold at auction after his death reveals an astounding array of collections.[3] One finds Art Deco furniture and silver; Native American blankets, rugs, and baskets; nineteenth-century Americana and folk art (some of which had been exhibited in the 1977 *Folk and Funk* exhibition); jewels, jewelry, and watches; and an art collection that included works by European modernists such as Duchamp, Klee, and Man Ray, as well as Warhol's contemporaries Arman, Johns, Lichtenstein, Twombly, and Rauschenberg. As one looks through the 3,436 lots and sees the hundreds of watches and hundreds of chairs, the cookie jars, the busts of Benjamin Franklin and Napoleon, the ray-gun toys, the Josef Hoffman furniture and Puiforcat tea sets, the Russel Wright dishes and Navajo bracelets, it is not hard to believe that, as several accounts attest, Warhol went shopping for items to add to his collections every day.[4]

Fred Hughes, Warhol's friend and business manager, notes that he had

1 "The Collector," in *The Arcades Project*, trans. Howard Eiland and Kevin McLaughlin (Cambridge, MA: Harvard University Press, 1999), 203–11, 205–6.

2 "Swenson: Is that what Pop Art is all about? / Warhol: Yes. It's liking things" (*IBYM*, 16).

3 *The Andy Warhol Collection* (New York: Sotheby's, 1988): vol. 1, *Art Nouveau and Art Deco*; vol. 2, *Collectibles, Jewelry, Furniture, Decoration, and Paintings*; vol. 3, *Jewelry and Watches*; vol. 4, *American Indian Art*; vol. 5, *Americana and European and American Drawings and Prints*; vol. 6, *Contemporary Art*.

4 Warhol's longtime live-in boyfriend, Jed Johnson, recounts, in "Inconspicuous Consumption" (*Andy Warhol Collection*, vol. 5): "He shopped for two or three hours a day for as many years as I can remember." Also see Bockris *Life and Death*, 415.

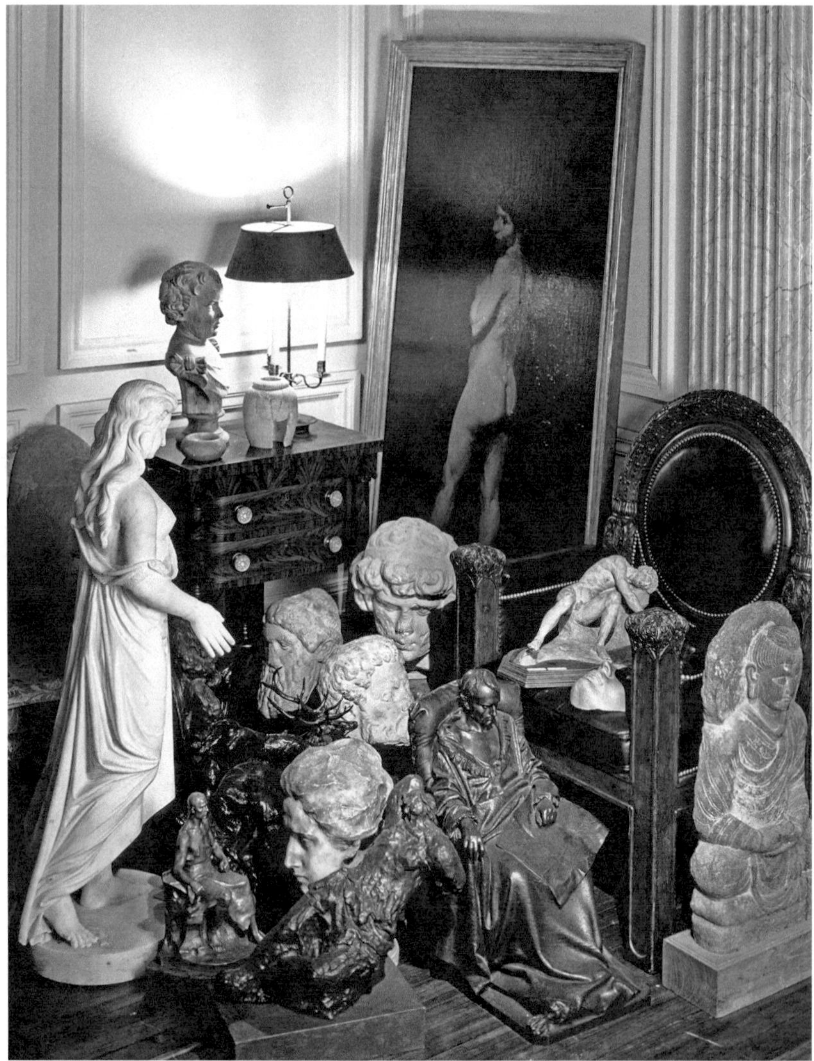

1.1 Norman McGrath, interior of Andy Warhol's house during preparations for the Sotheby's auction of his collections, 1988. Courtesy of Norman McGrath Photos.

been spending more than a million dollars a year just at auctions.[5] He was not only an "indefatigable accumulator,"[6] but an indiscriminate one (as press coverage of the auction sometimes disapprovingly opined): he was "interested in everything," as Vito Giallo noted.[7] While his dedication

5 This figure is cited by Bockris, *Life and Death*, 416. Also see Hughes's comments in his preface to *The Andy Warhol Collection*, where he describes Warhol as "extremely eager and covetous" in his collecting, often displaying a "frenzy" or "childlike" excitement.
6 Henry Geldzahler, "Andy Warhol: Artist and Collector," in *The Andy Warhol Collection*, vol. 6.
7 Giallo, quoted in Bockris, *Life and Death*, 415. As Scott Herring details, the cookie jars and other "kitsch" items, as well as the generally messy and disorganized quality of

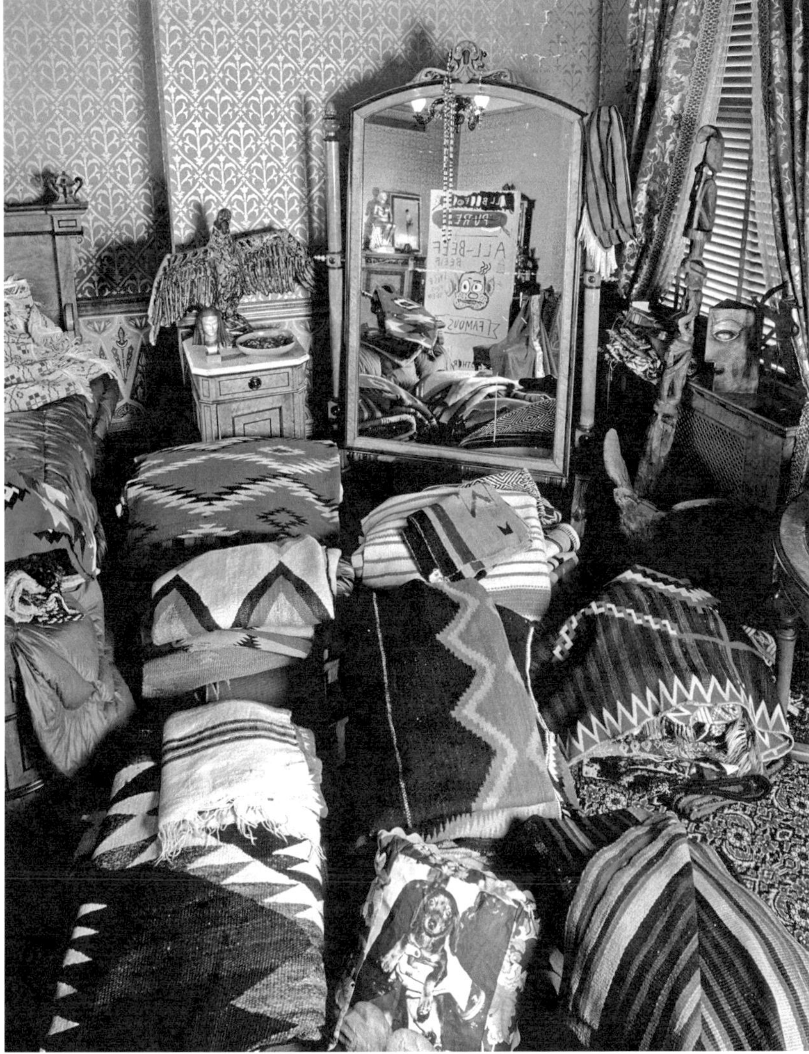

1.2 Norman McGrath, interior of Andy Warhol's house during preparations for the Sotheby's auction of his collections, 1988. Courtesy of Normal McGrath Photos.

to collecting may have increased as he got older (and had more money to spend), it appears that collecting was a lifelong passion, a habit that Warhol developed in childhood, starting probably with film magazines and celebrity memorabilia.[8]

---

his interior received especially negative, indeed pathologizing, attention (*Hoarders*, esp. 68–84).

8 Hughes mentions that "film magazines—he was mesmerized by Hollywood—were an early enthusiasm" (*Andy Warhol Collection*, preface). As a child, Warhol kept a photo album with celebrity photos, including a signed photo of Shirley Temple he had written away for and received when he was eleven, alongside a photo of Mae West. See John Smith, "Hollywood Stars and Noble Savages: Andy Warhol's Photography Collection,"

Warhol's collecting practices were by no means limited to "collectible" items—things that other people collect, creating a market—or even to the realm of purchases. His interest extended to encompass vast collections of photographs (his own and others'), thousands of hours of tape recordings he made with his Norelco tape recorder (which he called his "wife"), an array of perfumes, and his 612 Time Capsules, the boxes he filled with printed matter and whatever else he wanted to save that had no other collection to welcome it.[9] It appears Warhol strove to have a collector's relationship with as many objects of perception, across the senses, as he possibly could, as a matter of general principle and daily habit.

Warhol's artwork is a record and a map of this habit. For instance, his practice of tape recording all of his social interactions gave him the idea for *A: A Novel*, which was to be a transcript of twenty-four hours of taped conversations with his friend Ondine. And when one looks through Warhol's photo collections, one sees the images that formed the basis of his best-known paintings: press photos of car crashes and suicides, the New York City Police Department's *Thirteen Most Wanted Men* pamphlet, and endless celebrity photos, including scores of Marilyn Monroe publicity shots.[10] Collecting was the condition of possibility for Warhol's appropriative painting practice. But Warhol's collections are not only the "source material" for his paintings (and other works); they are also their model. After a photo has been selected from the array of Marilyn photos, for example, the image of her face rejoins a group of others, similar yet distinctly imperfect, within the space of the canvas itself, creating a new collection there. Indeed, the logic of the collection seems to permeate Warhol's aesthetic practices. But what, precisely, is that logic, and what is its appeal?

Walter Benjamin suggests that the collector is motivated by a desire to establish an intimate relationship to the material world, one that could find a home within an economy oriented around consumption but that nonetheless sidesteps capitalist relations to private property. Where (*par* Marx) "private property has made us so stupid and one-sided that an object is only *ours* when we have it—when it exists for us as capital, or when it is directly possessed, eaten, drunk, worn, inhabited, etc.,—in short, when it is used by

in *Andy Warhol Photography*, exh. cat. (Zurich: Edition Stemmle, 1999), 27–30. Bockris reports that, after Warhol was shot, John and Marge Warhola brought him a blue Shirley Temple glass he had owned since he was eight (*Life and Death*, 338). In *The Philosophy*, "B" (Brigid Berlin) remembers how his family and the nuns got Warhol interested in collecting again when he was in the hospital: "The nuns got you interested in collecting stamps, like you did when you were a kid or something. They got you interested in coins again too" (*Phil*, 11).

9 Smith and Wrbican, *Andy Warhol's Time Capsule 21*; Wrbican, "Warhol's 'Time Capsule 51'"; Herring, *Hoarders*, 77–82.

10 Samples of Warhol's photography collection—his own photos and the photos of others—appeared in *Andy Warhol Photography*, and some are reproduced in the exhibition catalog.

us," the collector relates to objects neither as capital nor in terms of use.[11] Indeed, the collector's first move is to "[detach] the object from its original functional relations."[12] Collecting "entails [not only] the liberation of things from the drudgery of being useful" but their transference into a "magic circle" where they can associate with other things that are like them.[13] The collector "brings together what belongs together," creating collectivities of objects based on relations of resemblance.[14]

Being a collector allowed Warhol to ask of each object of perception, What collection does this belong to? This had the salutary function of reorienting perception toward the "active mimetic force acting expressly inside things" (*SW2*, 684). On a daily basis, relating to the world as a collector amplified the similarities and commonalities in any thing he encountered. This may have permitted Warhol's liking to "transfer" from old objects onto new ones along the paths established by likeness.[15] To the extent that each like is a "new edition or facsimile," as Freud puts it, of earlier likes, such that we never like anything for the first time, the very act of liking assembles, as it moves through the world, a collection. Relating to the world as a "collector," then, is a way to amplify this aspect of everyday activity and be certain that liking always has multiple itineraries along which to travel.[16] For the collector, Benjamin notes, "the rhythm of perception and experience is altered in such a way that everything—even the seemingly most neutral—comes to strike us; everything concerns us."[17] In short, collecting was one of Warhol's chief strategies for attuning to similarities and thereby maximizing his capacity for being affected.

If being a collector alters the rhythm of perception and experience so that the patterns of similarity are amplified as one moves through the world, that rhythm is punctuated by the moments when one adds a new object to a collection. The "pleasure of collecting was the act of acquisition," Warhol's

11 Karl Marx, *Economic and Philosophic Manuscripts of 1844* (Moscow: Progress, 1974), 94. Benjamin refers several times to this passage in "The Collector," esp. 209.

12 Benjamin, "Collector," 207.

13 Ibid., 209, 205. Also: "Among children, collecting is only one process of renewal; other processes are the painting of objects, the cutting out of figures, the application of stickers—the whole range of childlike modes of acquisition, from touching things to giving them names" (Benjamin, "Unpacking My Library: A Talk about Collecting," *SW2*, 486–93, 487).

14 Benjamin, "Collector," 211.

15 See also "The Dynamics of the Transference" (1912) and "Further Recommendations in the Technique of Psychoanalysis: Recollection, Repetition and Working-Through" (1914), both in *Therapy and Technique*, ed. Philip Rieff (New York: Collier Books, 1963). Also see Flatley, *Affective Mapping*, 50–64, on transference and affect.

16 Freud writes, as I noted in the introduction, that transferences "are new editions or facsimiles of the tendencies and fantasies which are aroused and made conscious during the progress of the analysis," "new impressions or reprints," or "revised editions." *Dora*, 138.

17 Benjamin, "Collector," 205–6.

friend and colleague Rupert Smith observed, because that is the moment when the collector initiates something or someone into a new existence as a like-being among other like-beings, in a collective space defined by the mutual, nonhierarchical relations of resemblance.[18] There, it experiences a "rebirth," leaving behind its former identity from the everyday world of means-ends rationality and commodity fetishism, entering a territory where it is possible for other "likenesses [to befriend] one another."[19]

Within the collection, the object is involved in a process of varied and variable belonging and becoming. Not only is each new acquisition transformed as it achieves its significance in relation to the collection; it also slightly reorders the collection as a whole, transforming every other item by changing the composition of the group. Because the totality defined by the collection changes with each item added to it (like T. S. Eliot's "tradition," modified by the addition of each new work of literature), there is no Platonic type, no ideal chair or ideal teapot, hovering over Warhol's various collections and bringing them to coherence.[20] Instead, we might say that collecting is a practice for creating a space of commonality shared by all the objects in the collection, constantly changed by the relations of resemblance they participate in.

The collection is "used" in the sense that it is a device that allows one to relate to the everyday world of objects in terms of their similarities and correspondences. Without the collection, there would be no place for collected objects to be initiated into a group existence. It may have been partly for this reason that Warhol had no intention of ever "cashing in" on his purchases, even though he excelled at finding bargains or "sleepers" and took pleasure in speculating about the future value of his acquisitions. Suzie Frankfurt, a friend of Warhol's since the 1950s, remarked that, "as for trading or selling—never, never, never. He believed in holding onto everything, squirreling it all away."[21]

Unlike many collectors, Warhol was not interested in the display of his collections.[22] He kept his collecting private; it was, as his boyfriend Jed

18 Smith, "Acquisition and Accumulation," in *Andy Warhol Collection*, vol. 3.

19 I borrow this evocative phrase from Wayne Koestenbaum's description of Warhol's stitched photographs (*Andy Warhol*, 195).

20 Eliot writes that when a new work enters into the tradition, "the *whole* existing order must be, if ever so slightly, altered; and so the relations, proportions, values of each work of art toward the whole are readjusted." "Tradition and the Individual Talent," in *Selected Prose of T. S. Eliot*, ed. Frank Kermode (New York: Harcourt, Brace and Company, 1975), 37–44, 38–39. This also means that the items in a collection are not "examples" (as Susan Stewart has suggested) of the collected object. Stewart, *On Longing* (Durham, NC: Duke University Press, 1993), 151–54. Koestenbaum makes the case that Warhol "pursued Platonic forms" (*Andy Warhol*, 160). On the collector working with Platonic forms, also see Benjamin, "Collector," 205.

21 Frankfurt, "A Friendship," in *Andy Warhol Collection*, vol. 3.

22 See, as a counterexample, Stewart's discussion of Samuel Pepys, in *On Longing*, 155.

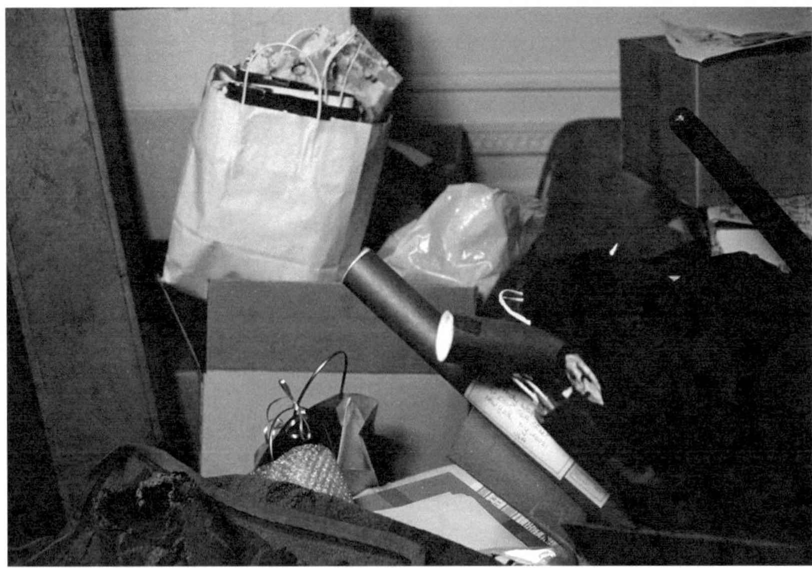

1.3 Steven Bluttal, interior of Andy Warhol's house, 1987. Collection of the Andy Warhol Museum, Pittsburgh.

Johnson described it, "inconspicuous consumption."[23] (Warhol reportedly regretted displaying his collection of folk art in *Folk and Funk*, and seemed to stop collecting in this area after the exhibition.[24]) His purchases eventually transformed his townhouse, which had been carefully and beautifully designed by Johnson, into storage space for unopened boxes, stacks, and assemblages of objects alongside and underneath unemptied shopping bags. Although objects did not have to be physically organized into their collections in order to belong to them, Warhol liked to remind himself of their existence. "He kept most of the rooms locked," Johnson observes. "He had a routine. He'd walk through the house every morning before he left, open the door of each room with a key, peer in, and then relock it. Then at night when he came home he would unlock each door, turn the light on, peer in, lock up, and go to bed."[25] The purpose of the ritual tour was not to pore over the collections, or organize or sort them; nor, I think, was it to luxuriate in the pleasure of possession or ownership as such. Rather, I think this routine reassured Warhol of the presence of this vital and renewable resource, which gave him access to the tremors of becoming and belonging that accompanied each new acquisition.

23 See Johnson, "Inconspicuous Consumption." After Johnson (in 1980) moved out of the townhouse he shared with Warhol, which he had carefully designed, the filling up of rooms with purchases seems to have increased.
24 See John Smith, "Andy Warhol's Art of Collecting," in *Possession Obsession*, 14–21. Also see *Andy Warhol's Folk and Funk* (New York: Museum of American Folk Art, 1977).
25 Quoted in Bockris, *Life and Death*, 395.

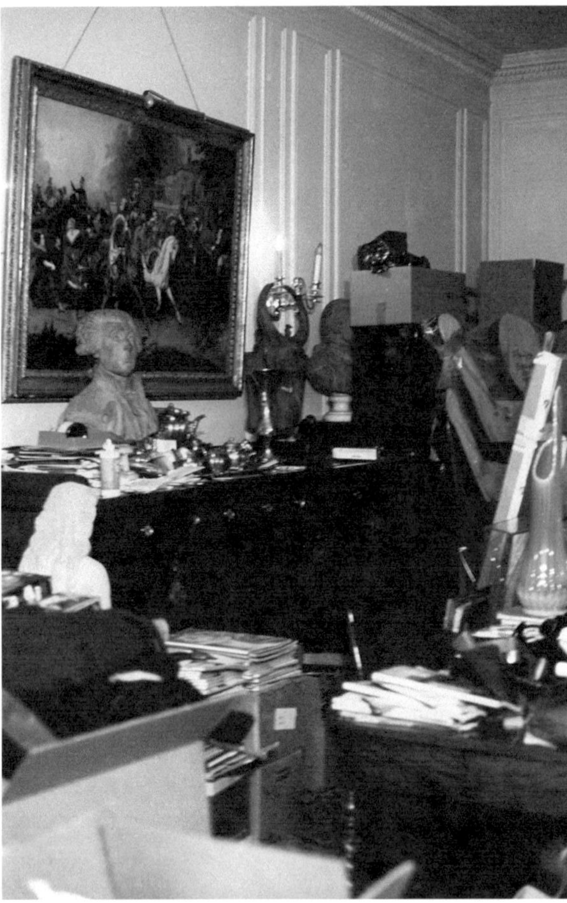

1.4 Steven Bluttal, interior of Andy Warhol's house, 1987. Collection of the Andy Warhol Museum, Pittsburgh.

This belonging and becoming was all the more attractive to the extent that Warhol could imagine his own participation in it. In stimulating his "gift for seeing similarity," his visits with his collections may have also reminded him of the mimetic centers dwelling in everything and everybody, including himself. The sociality and conviviality Warhol felt in the collection was a resource and a model. Its powers radiated outward, inviting others into its orbit. Fred Hughes, for instance, writes that their shared enthusiasm for collecting formed "one of the chief sources of our friendship and collaboration."[26] Warhol liked to like together.

In Warhol's imaginative identification with his like-beings, focusing on the flawed or broken object, the one with signs of wear and use, may have been an aid. Such a preference, not typical among collectors, could be seen clearly in *Folk and Funk*, whose curators noted Warhol's "taste for defects,"

26 Hughes, *Andy Warhol Collection*, preface. Earlier, Warhol had collected "Americana" with Ted Carey; Stuart Pivar appears regularly in his *Diaries* as a flea market and auction companion.

his attraction to "objects which are cracked, broken or somehow marred."[27] In *Raid the Icebox*, the 1970 exhibition Warhol curated from the storage areas of the Rhode Island School of Design Museum of Art, he chose damaged or overlooked items such as a warped table, Windsor chairs that had been kept for spare parts, and storage cabinets filled with old shoes.[28] Traces of use are one of the aspects of the object that draw what Benjamin calls the collector's "physiognomic" interest.[29] Such an interest, an attempt to "read into" the object, to tell its "biography" and predict its fate, stimulates a mimetic attempt to relate to the world from the point of view of the object. Moreover, these signs of wear or flaws, like the mistakes that were part of the silkscreen process (a similarity noted also by the curators of *Folk and Funk*), indicate a way in which these objects fail to match up to their type or model. Like Warhol and his friends, the worn, imperfect, and marred objects in Warhol's collections misfit together.

As I have suggested, Warhol's paintings are themselves often organized as collections, and in several ways. At the beginning of his pop career he often repeated images on a single canvas, in compositions like *Marilyn × 100*, *25 Colored Marilyns*, *Thirty Are Better Than One* (images of Mona Lisa), *210 Coca-Cola Bottles*, or *Black and White Disaster #4*. These paintings, which the *Catalogue Raisonné* calls "serial compositions," contained a fixed number of images on a single canvas. Beginning with his first commissioned portrait, *Ethel Scull 36 Times* (1963), Warhol subtly but significantly changed his approach to seriality. He started to produce "smaller works that could be produced as individual units in a series or assembled as multipanel compositions" (*CR1*, 410). This was a "more flexible and open-ended system" (*CR1*, 437) that allowed him to make more paintings with the same screen and to add to (or subtract from) a given work after the initial printing. Significantly, the single composition had been replaced by a collection of canvases. Warhol made especially effective use of this system in his paintings of Jackie Kennedy; *The Week That Was*, *Jackie Frieze*, and *Sixteen Jackies* are all multicanvas compositions. At least one of the paintings, the surprisingly moving *Thirty-Five Jackies* (which multiplies Jackie's downcast, grieving face), changed form over time, having begun its existence as a set of forty-nine canvases (see figure 0.4). Although Warhol assembled many "multiplied" *Jackies*, he also produced a collection of more than 250 single-image *Jackie* paintings. In its open-endedness, this painting system (of one image

27 *Folk and Funk*, 12. They also note, for instance, that "when Andy shops for American quilts, he chooses strongly stylistic examples, but always ones that show wear. 'I actually like them the best,' he declares" (12).

28 See *Raid the Icebox 1, with Andy Warhol* (Providence: Museum of Art, Rhode Island School of Design, 1969), esp. Daniel Robbins, "Confessions of Museum Director," 8–15, and David Bourdon, "Andy's Dish," 17–24.

29 Benjamin calls collectors the "physiognomists in the world of things" in "Unpacking My Library," *SW2*, 487.

per canvas) functions like a collection that can add or subtract members. Because the work can grow new parts or shrink over time, this mode of composition also slyly, but surely, disrupts the boundedness of the autonomous "work." For instance, Warhol's portrait of Ethel Scull, which had for several years hung in the Scull's library as *Ethel Scull 35 Times* (in five rows of seven canvases), became *Ethel Scull 36 Times* when it was reassembled into four rows of nine in the Metropolitan Museum of Art.[30]

Whether printed multiply on a single canvas or one to a canvas, grouped together into larger compositions or left single, images painted only once are uncommon in Warhol's oeuvre. Often, there are between two and twenty of a given image, but larger collections are also common. For instance, there are 38 Marilyn paintings from 1962 (and more later), 17 paintings of Ethel Scull in addition to *Ethel Scull 36 Times*, 303 canvases of Jackie Kennedy, over 400 *Flowers* (in several series), and over 200 *Ladies and Gentlemen* paintings. This can produce problems for the critic seeking to generalize about Warhol's presentation of any given image, given the multiplicity of such presentations. Often, Warhol put extra paintings, beyond what were exhibited or sold, into storage; with commissioned portraits where the sitter purchased only one or two paintings, there are almost always at least a few more canvases that turned up in storage after Warhol died. To be sure, keeping extra paintings made good business sense: he would be ready when someone decided later that they wanted another portrait or when his paintings (like the disasters or the early celebrity silkscreens) increased in value on the auction market. But it is also hard to miss Warhol's persistent and thoroughgoing commitment to plurality in his painting practice, as if he could not bear to have a painting exist alone.

Reprinting a given image within and across canvases was one of the ways Warhol created groups and represented collectivities. Early works such as the mid-1950s books of drawings *25 Cats Named Sam and One Blue Pussy*, *The Bottom of My Garden*, and *A la Recherche du Shoe Perdu* (themselves composed by groups of friends) depict groups of cats, fairies, and shoes, respectively.[31] Then, one might consider the outlaws, drag queens, Jews, and disciples pictured in *Thirteen Most Wanted Men* (1964), *Ladies and Gentlemen* (1974), *Ten Portraits of Jews of the Twentieth Century* (1980), and the late large series of *Last Supper* paintings, including the serial composition *Detail of the Last Supper (Christ 112 Times)* (1986).[32] Warhol was also interested in what

30 *CR1*, 411. Neil Printz reports that Holly Solomon first purchased eight commissioned portraits, then added a ninth when she and her husband (unhappily) realized that Warhol had screened another canvas. Perhaps wishing her portrait to be a singular, bounded work, she asked Warhol not to produce any more canvases.

31 For a brilliant and carefully researched consideration of the groups represented in his early books, as well as their group composition, see Mulroney, "One Blue Pussy."

32 On *Thirteen Most Wanted Men*, see Richard Meyer, *Outlaw Representation: Censorship and Homosexuality in Twentieth-Century American Art* (New York: Oxford University Press, 2002). On *Ten Portraits of Jews*, see Meyer's exhibition catalog, *Warhol's Jews: Ten*

Koestenbaum calls the "group behavior" of objects, from the famous early paintings of soup cans and sculptures of Brillo boxes through to paintings from the 1980s of eggs, crosses, diamond dust shoes, and strands of yarn.[33]

One large group is constituted by Warhol's hundreds of commissioned portraits. Warhol related to these identically sized portraits not just as paintings of individual persons but as members in an ambitious "Portrait of Society."[34] When some of these paintings were exhibited at the Whitney Museum of American Art in 1979 (with two portraits of each sitter hanging together as a pair), they were roundly criticized for their openly commercial character.[35] They were seen as examples of Warhol's crass indiscriminacy; so long as they were willing to pay (generally $25,000 per canvas), Warhol would "paint anybody. Anybody that asks me," he told Edward Lucie-Smith. "I like everybody. So I don't really . . . decide, you know, whether I like them or not. I really like everybody."[36] This frank willingness to like for hire (just as he offered to "endorse anything" in a *Village Voice* ad in 1966), itself acts as a principle for a self-selecting group—a collection of people who wanted to become "a Warhol" and were willing to pay for it. As Benjamin Buchloh suggests, Warhol thereby manages to provide a picture of "the ruling class" ("industrialists," celebrities, old-world aristocrats, politicians, art dealers, and artists), or at least of the persons capital moved through in animating the art market of the 1970s and 1980s.[37]

But even as these portraits constitute a significant representation of a particular class formation, they also indicate the commonality of the desire to be a star. Just as the richest and the poorest consumers all drink the same

Portraits Reconsidered (New York: Jewish Museum, 2008), which includes his excellent essay "Warhol's Jews."

33 Koestenbaum, *Andy Warhol*, 193. On late Warhol, and the yarn paintings in particular, also see Benjamin Buchloh, "Drawing Blanks: Notes on Andy Warhol's Late Works," *October*, no. 127 (Winter 2009), 3–24.

34 Bob Colacello recalls asking Warhol "why he never would change the size of the portraits to accommodate clients' requests, when he was willing to listen to their suggestions regarding poses and colors." Warhol's response: "They all have to be the same size . . . so they'll all fit together and make one big painting called 'Portrait of Society.'" *Andy Warhol Headshots Drawings and Paintings* (Koln: Jablonka Gallery, 2000), n.p.

35 See my discussion of the portraits in "Warhol Gives Good Face." On the rhetoric of prostitution in the critical discourse on Warhol, see Jennifer Doyle, "Tricks of the Trade: Pop Art/Pop Sex," in Doyle, Flatley, and Muñoz, *Pop Out*, 191–209.

36 Lucie-Smith, "Conversations with Artists."

37 "It is hard to imagine a more accurate collection and depiction of the unique fusion of *arriviste* vulgarity and old-money decadence, the seamless transition from the powers that produce and control corporate culture to those that govern American high cultural institutions than the endless number of commissioned portraits of the American ruling class of the last decade." Buchloh argues that these "corrupted and debased" moments are parodic anticipations of art world trends that enable Warhol to have a distance from and provide a commentary on changes to "which most other artists were still blindly subjected." Buchloh, "The Andy Warhol Line," in *The Work of Andy Warhol*, ed. Gary Garrels (Seattle: Bay Press, 1989), 63.

Coke (as Warhol noted),[38] so too do the wealthy, along with drag queens, future stars, queer working-class kids, industrialists, art dealers, and art critics, draw from the same pantheon of idols for their imitative aspirations. That was the lure offered to potential sitters, of course: by becoming the subject of a Warhol portrait, one would participate in the fame of Warhol's other sitters and of Warhol himself. (John Giorno spoke for them all when he proclaimed, "I want to be like Marilyn Monroe," in response to Warhol's offer to make him the star of his first film.[39]) In paying to be like Marilyn, like Elvis, like Jackie, like Liz, the wealthy sitter "admitted an identity as stand-in, non star, aura seeker."[40] Even if this does not "eviscerate" them, as Koestenbaum suggests, the sitters do thereby succeed in failing, since they do not even manage to match up to their own identities, never mind become stars. For the most part, sitters did not become famous by way of Warhol's commissioned portraits, with the possible exception of Ethel Scull, whose grid of canvases is recognized as an important work in the history of portraiture. (Warhol's movies were more successful in producing celebrity, at least in the short term.) But, then, as David Bourdon noted, perhaps it was in any case a *posthumous* fame they were seeking; all his sitters *have* entered into the particular pantheon defined by this massive Warhol collection, and students of art history and museumgoers will be looking at them looking their best for years to come.[41]

In their display of the *desire* to be a star, all Warhol's sitters also succeed in becoming like Warhol, just as they are like the drag queens Warhol liked so much (as I will suggest in chapter 4) and, for that matter, like everyone else who wants to be a little more glamorous, a little more bedazzled, a little more liked. "Just think about all the James Deans and what it means" (*Phil*, 53).

"I have no memory"

By way of his collecting, Warhol sought not only to alter the rhythm of his perception and experience so that everything would strike and concern him but also to change the state of his memory, indeed to *replace* it with his collections. This impulse is perhaps most apparent in Warhol's passion for perfumes:

> I switch perfumes all the time. If I've been wearing one perfume for three months, I force myself to give it up, even if I still feel like wearing it, so whenever I smell it again it will always remind me of those three months. I never

38 *Phil*, 100–101, discussed in the introduction.

39 Giorno, *You Got to Burn to Shine*, 131.

40 Koestenbaum, *Andy Warhol*, 168.

41 "The commissioning of a Warhol portrait was a sure sign that the sitter intended to achieve posthumous fame." Bourdon, *Warhol* (New York: Abrams, 1989), 324.

> go back to wearing it again; it becomes part of my permanent smell collection. . . . Of the five senses, smell has the closest thing to the full power of the past. Smell really is transporting. Seeing, hearing, touching, tasting are just not as powerful as smelling if you want your whole being to go back for a second to something. Usually I don't want to, but by having smells stopped up in bottles, I can be in control and can only smell the smells I want to, when I want to, to get the memories I'm in the mood to have. Just for a second. (*Phil*, 150–51)

Recalling Marcel Proust's insights about memory and the materiality of sense perception, Warhol suggests that his "permanent smell collection" could be a superior, material, nonsubjective replacement for his memory, one that would give him the ability to transport his "whole being" to a moment in the past, and to thereby "get the memories [he's] in the mood to have." By way of his perfumes, he is able to collect three-month periods of his life.

In Proust's famous example, the taste of the *madeleine* evokes a "*memoire involontaire*" that returns him to a past experience that had been lost, beyond the reach of "voluntary memory," which is under one's control but lacks the power of affective and experiential transport. This involuntary, contingent intrusion of a moment from the past disrupts the progress of clock time and engages one with the materiality of the world. Indeed, one might say that Proust's memory-experience does not really happen *in* the subject, but outside of us in the madeleine itself. This may be because, as Benjamin and Silvan Tomkins (among others) have observed, affecting encounters distribute our being into the materiality of the world.[42] Such a desubjectivizing, mimetic connectedness is an essential component of what Benjamin called "experience in the strict sense," or *Erfahrung*. And it is only these experiences, Benjamin stresses—the ones that connect us by way of affective engagement to the material world in the first place—that are stored in objects as involuntary memory.[43]

The materiality of *mémoire involontaire* and the fact that it lies "beyond the reach of the intellect" leads Proust to be pessimistic about the possibilities of such memory experiences in general, because it is a matter of luck or chance whether one comes across the crucial object that will unlock the past.

42 Between an affect and its object there is what Silvan Tomkins calls a "somewhat fluid relationship": "If an imputed characteristic of an object is capable of evoking a particular affect, the evocation of that affect is also capable of producing a subjective restructuring of the object so that it possesses the imputed characteristic which is capable of evoking that effect. . . . The object may evoke the affect, or the affect find the object." *Shame and Its Sisters: A Silvan Tomkins Reader*, ed. Eve Kosofsky Sedgwick and Adam Frank (Durham, NC: Duke University Press, 1995), 54–55. Also see Benjamin, on the "faults of the beloved"—wrinkles, a lopsided walk—as the material hiding place of love as such. "One Way Street," in *Walter Benjamin Selected Works*, vol. 1 (Cambridge, MA: Harvard University Press, 1996), 449.

43 See Benjamin, "On Some Motifs in Baudelaire," *SW4*, 315.

However, Benjamin suggests that we are reliant on chance in this way only because our capacity for experience as "lived similarity" has been so diminished.[44] In defending ourselves against potentially traumatic or affectively disruptive affecting stimuli, we are overly reliant on a consciousness that does its shielding work by placing experience into a "rosary bead," sequentially ordered memory, which distances us from the world and therefore "retains no trace of that past" (*SW4*, 315). In contrast, Benjamin asserts, rituals, traditions, and festivals once worked like collective, planned tastes of the madeleine: "They triggered recollection at certain times and remained available to memory throughout people's lives. In this way, voluntary and involuntary recollection cease to be mutually exclusive" (*SW4*, 316). With his perfumes, Warhol created a ritual that allowed him reliable (if still private) "voluntary" access to involuntary memory. Even though it allowed Warhol to "get the memories" he was "in the mood to have," it was, in several senses, still only a partial response to the crisis of experience Benjamin identified.

For Warhol, a more satisfactory alteration of the conditions of memory and experience would involve recording *all* of his sensory experiences. He saw his perfume collection as a compensation for his inability to engage in a more complete transfer of his olfactory sensations into a collection. That is, Warhol started collecting perfumes precisely because smells (unlike sounds and images) could not be recorded. "I had to have a kind of smell museum so certain smells wouldn't get lost forever. I loved the way the lobby of the Paramount Theater on Broadway used to smell. I would close my eyes and breathe deep whenever I was in it. Then they tore it down. I can look all I want at a picture of that lobby, but so what? I can't ever smell it again" (*Phil*, 151). As if to underscore the number and range of smell experiences that one cannot record and thus loses, and the degree to which smells are central to our experience of the world, Warhol then offers a page-long list of some of the smells he is aware of as he walks around New York, including things like the "rubber mats in office buildings," the "wood chairs and tables in the N.Y. Public Library," "the donuts, pretzels, gum, and grape soda in the subways," grease-batter, architects' blueprints, souvlaki, pizza, back-issue magazines, and the "good cheap candy smell in the front of Woolworth's" (*Phil*, 151–52).

To the extent that Warhol's perfume collection was an effort to compensate, however incompletely, for his inability to record the smells he loved, ensuring that at least "certain smells wouldn't get lost forever," it points toward a powerful wish motivating his collecting more generally: Warhol sought a nonsubjective, material memory, ordered as a collection, to replace his conscious memory. Where smells resisted this desire, other sensations, such as sound, could be more adequately recorded.

44 Benjamin, "Experience," *SW2*, 553. See my discussion of Benjamin on similarity in the introduction.

At some point in 1964, Warhol acquired a Norelco Carry-Corder, which became so intimately involved in his daily life that he described their relationship as a marriage.[45] ("When I say 'we,' I mean my tape recorder and me. A lot of people don't understand that"; *Phil*, 26.) Warhol explicitly presents his tape recorder as an substitute memory:

> I have no memory. Every day is a new day because I don't remember the day before. Every minute is like the first minute of my life. I try to remember but I can't. That's why I got married—to my tape recorder. That's why I seek out people with minds like tape recorders to be with. My mind is like a tape recorder with one button—Erase. (*Phil*, 199)

Warhol seeks a tape recorder as wife and friends with minds like tape recorders because of a deficit in his own memory—he can't remember anything. But then, noting that he "kill[s] time by watching TV and washing my underwear," he reverses the cause and effect, admitting that "maybe the reason my memory is so bad is that I always do at least two things at once. It's easier to forget something you only half-did or quarter-did" (199). In other words, Warhol's practice is closer to what Nietzsche called "active forgetfulness": having a "bad memory" is for Warhol itself a task and a practice. His tape recording is not an attempt just to compensate for a bad memory, but to make one.

By replacing his memory with his "wife's" recording, Warhol need not try to remember things in the sense of making them available for future recall as voluntary memory. Eliminating this function of consciousness then changes the conditions of his experience. It is as if the emptying or erasure of memory that his tape recorder permits puts him in a maximally receptive state; "every day is a new day," every minute the "first minute of [his] life," like an infant in fullest possession of the gift for affective, mimetic openness. This "wife" is not just a substitute for his own memory, storing his experiences for him; she is also a model for his listening. As Gustavus Stadler observes in his brilliant consideration of Warhol's "strong presence as a listener," Warhol imitates the tape recorder's nonselective relation to sound. Like a tape recorder, which (as Stadler writes) "doesn't get overly focused... doesn't make many choices about what is more and less important as it lis-

45 "I did my first tape recording in 1964" (*Phil*, 94). See Gustavus Stadler, "'My Wife': The Tape Recorder and Warhol's Queer Ways of Listening," *Criticism* 56, no. 3 (Summer 2014; Warhol special issue): 425–56, for the best reading of Warhol's use of "wife" to refer to the tape recorder. Especially interesting is the way the discourse of fidelity brings together companionate marriage and audio recording. See chapter 2 for more on Warhol's use of the tape recorder. See also Melissa Ragona, "Impulse, Type and Index: Warhol's Audio Archive," in *Warhol Live: Music and Dance in Andy Warhol's Work*, ed. Stéphane Aquin (Montreal: Montreal Museum of Fine Arts/Prestel, 2008), 130–35.

tens," which "can't very effectively separate sounds," which is "drenched in the sound of the atmosphere in which the recording is taking place,"[46] Warhol tries to "[let] everything in all at once."[47] Like his tape recorder, Warhol is good at nonselectively "liking" every sound. In the early pages of *POPism*, Warhol recalls playing multiple pieces of music while he was painting, with "rock and roll blasting the same song, a 45 rpm, over and over all day long," along with the "radio blasting opera, and the TV picture on (but not the sound)—and if all that didn't clear enough out of my mind, I'd open a magazine, put it beside me, and half read an article while I painted" (*POP*, 7). Listening to all these different sounds does not confuse him, nor does it fill him up. Instead, it "clears his mind."

This thoroughgoing distractedness was a way to "undermine the presence of the thinking self," as Stadler puts it,[48] one of Warhol's constant projects and the subject of frequent comment. "It's so exciting not to think anything," Warhol told Lane Slate (*IBYM*, 80). We might understand "thinking" here as something like what Benjamin describes as consciousness, which mediates and orders our affective and perceptual interaction with the world. "Not thinking anything" is thus exciting in a specific and literal sense: it excites the senses, activates them, makes them more receptive. At the moment of (non)composition (as I discuss in the next chapter), this not thinking allows the image Warhol is painting to be just another thing he likes; it helps him avoid gesturely, personal comment (as he notes in *POPism*). He seems to hope that this lack of authorial comment will, in turn, undermine the presence of the thinking self in his audiences. As he explained in a 1963 interview, when the people who come to exhibitions "don't have to think . . . they just sort of see the things and they like them and they understand them easier" (*IBYM*, 32).

All the while, this state of maximal receptivity and minimal memory produces a massive collection of sound, a huge accumulation of cassette tapes. The medium specificity of the audiotape, the way the cassettes' materiality and logic shapes the perceptions that are stored in them, along with the form of the tapes themselves, constitute the basic contours of this open-ended collection. Instead of being ordered by chronological sequence, these sounds are ordered as a group of likenesses within a collection. The existence of this collection allowed Warhol, even when he did not have his "wife" with him, to think about sounds as entering into a collection with all the other sounds (an instance of which I examine below).

Warhol appeared to seek as many recording devices as possible so that he could, in effect, mediate each of his senses through likeness-generating recorder-collectors. He had taken some sixty-six thousand photographs

46 Stadler, "Tape Recorder," 440.

47 This is how Henry Geldzahler describes a lesson he absorbed from Warhol, as recounted in *POPism*, 16.

48 Stadler, "Tape Recorder," 438.

by the time he died, many during his last fifteen years, with the small SLR camera he carried most of the time.[49] The variety and everydayness of these photographs makes it clear that he recorded scenes of even minor visual interest almost everywhere he went, as if he were trying to live a maximally photographically mediated life (a pursuit that has become much more common in the era of the smart phone and image-based social media). And if we think of the cardboard box as itself a medium, a way of storing a particular kind of information, then we might think of the 612 Time Capsules, the boxes Warhol filled mainly with pieces of paper that passed through his hands, as a particular way to store experiences of touching, holding, and otherwise interacting with the surfaces of things through such activities as reading, writing, and drawing.[50] They were also, it seems, a way to store anything that he wanted to be able to collect but for which there was not an existing collection. The Time Capsules vary in content; one, for example, was reserved for items connected to his mother, including her clothes. Some contain source material, others original drawings. One contains a number of newspaper clippings covering the debate about censorship and pornography (relevant to the censorship of his *Blue Movie*), while another holds a collection of hundreds of cover pages of the *New York News* and *New York Post* (a not infrequent subject of his photographs as well).

By establishing a particular protocol for his mode of perceiving and encountering the world, Warhol's perfumes, cassette tapes, photographs, and Time Capsules all keep him connected to and caring about—*liking*—the world, because they allow him to reorder the world and his memory of it in terms of likenesses. At least in the case of the audiotapes, this reordering also seems to have been attractive to the persons *being* taped:

> Nothing was ever a problem again, because a problem just meant a good tape, and when a problem transforms itself into a good tape it's not a problem any more. An interesting problem was an interesting tape. Everybody knew that and performed for the tape. You couldn't tell which problems

49 The figure is cited by Ludger Derenthal in "Andy Warhol, Photographic Tradition and Zeitgeist," *Andy Warhol Photography*, 33–39.

50 John Smith: "Reportedly, the earliest Time Capsules are a result of Warhol's 1974 move from his studio at 33 Union Square West to a new space at 860 Broadway. After completing the move, Warhol recognized that these simple, inexpensive cardboard boxes were an efficient and economical method for dealing with the daily flood of correspondence, magazines and newspapers, gifts, photographs, business records, collectibles and ephemera that passed through his hands" (Smith and Wrbican, *Time Capsule 21*, 11). See also Warhol's reflections on space and storage in *Phil*, 144–45, including this: "What you should do is get a box for a month, and drop everything in it and at the end of the month lock it up. Then date it and send it over to Jersey. You should try to keep track of it, but if you can't and you lose it, that's fine, because it's one less thing to think about, another load off your mind. . . . now I just drop everything into the same-size brown cardboard boxes that have a color patch on the side for the month of the year."

> were real and which problems were exaggerated for the tape. Better yet, the people telling you the problems couldn't decide any more if they were really having the problems or if they were just performing. (*Phil*, 26)

In what might also be a gloss of the reparative effects of what is sometimes called "camp," Warhol here explains how his tape recorder had a powerful antidepressive effect on performers.[51] When a "problem" (one of Warhol's standard euphemisms for nonnormative sexual practices or attractions) is transformed into a tape "it's not a problem any more." Like many of Warhol's films (as David James points out), his tape-recording "makes performance inevitable" and "constitutes being as performance."[52] As it becomes "performance," other people get interested in it, and the person with the problem may also become interested in it and even "have fun with it." What had been alienating or depressing becomes a source of a connection to other people. "Better yet," as problems are pluralized, publicized, and shared, their ontological status changes; it becomes difficult to tell the difference between "just performing" and "really having the problems."[53] In moving from the realm of the isolated, private individual, the interior or alienated space of emotional problems, into a common, "unreal" place where it dwells alongside all the other tapes, the problem becomes something both shareable and imitable, and thereby loses its depressing "reality." This trick—creating magic spheres of problem-erasing similitude into which he could invite other people—was one of Warhol's main ways to create a sense of queer group existence and belonging. It was a way to generate more "liking" encounters around him. As such, for the shy Warhol, it was also an important technique for managing (potentially awkward or embarrassing) social interactions more generally, including ones that might involve sexual attraction.

"Doing a cock book"

As the example of his tape recorder suggests, the collector's approach to daily experience structured more than Warhol's experience of objects. Warhol

51 In *Mother Camp: Female Impersonators in America* (Chicago: University of Chicago Press, 1972), Esther Newton writes, "Camp humor is a system of laughing at one's incongruous position instead of crying. That is, the humor does not cover up, it transforms" (109).
52 David James, *Allegories of Cinema* (Princeton, NJ: Princeton University Press, 1989), 69.
53 On Warhol's approach to the relation between sound and publicity, see Stadler, "Tape Recorder": "The flurry of sonically engaged work that Warhol took up in the mid-1960s suggests that, for him, human sound fundamentally tended toward expansion and publicity, and evaded containment and privacy; sounds made by people carried this quality whether they issued from the concealed circuitry of a loudspeaker cabinet or from the insides of 'Talkers'—the quality to which Jean-Luc Nancy alludes when he calls sound 'methexic' (that is, having to do with participation, sharing, or contagion)" (428).

was also "a people collector."[54] This collecting took a variety of forms. For instance, "During this period [1969] I took thousands of Polaroids of genitals. Whenever somebody came up to the Factory, no matter how straight-looking he was, I'd ask him to take his pants off so I could photograph his cock and balls. It was surprising who'd let me and who wouldn't" (*POP*, 294).[55] In the 1970s he continued and expanded his photography of male genitals to include images of men having sex, some of which became the basis for two series of paintings, prints, and drawings—Torsos and Sex Parts.[56] In these instances, the camera, and later painting and "art" as such, were props that gave Warhol an excuse to ask men to drop their pants for him and that permitted them to do so.[57] Earlier in his life, the sketch pad had done the trick. To be sure, being drawn and being photographed each alter "the rhythm of perception and experience" in their own striking way, for model and artist alike. But in each instance, by way of a repetitive, accumulative pattern, Warhol was able to assemble large collections of images of male genitalia. Nathan Gluck recalls that "Andy had this great passion for drawing people's cocks," and he remembers seeing "pads and pads and pads" of cock drawings in Warhol's apartment in the 1950s.[58] Ted Carey remembers

54 Gerard Malanga, quoted in *The Velvet Years: Warhol's Factory 1965–67* (New York: Thunder's Mouth Press, 1995), 45.

55 Mario Amaya and Ultra Violet also recall this practice. Amaya said, "In '68 or '69, he was doing Polaroid shots of all his friends' penises. He asked me if I could expose myself and he did a Polaroid shot" (*Edie*, 216). Ultra Violet writes, "Especially to the boys, Andy says, 'Bend down. I'd like to Polaroid your ass.' The kids are either embarrassed or amused. They have never had such an open proposition. If they are embarrassed they are shown Polaroids of other kids." Ultra Violet (Isabelle Collin Dufresne), *Famous for 15 Minutes: My Years with Andy Warhol* (New York: Avon Books, 1988), 157. While it seems unlikely that Warhol, Amaya, and Ultra Violet would have invented this story, neither the Andy Warhol Foundation nor the Andy Warhol Museum can confirm the existence of these Polaroids. Sally King-Nero, executive editor of the *Andy Warhol Catalogue Raisonné* at the Warhol Foundation for the Visual Arts, writes that "there are only roughly 200 Polaroids in the collection with a film date of 1969, and the subject matter varies considerably. It is not until 1972, when Polaroid introduced the SX-70 Land camera, replacing the wet peel-apart development process with dry films able to develop in light, that a real spike in Warhol's Polaroid productivity occurs. Even in 1972, there are few examples of male genitals in the collection. It is not until 1977, when Warhol begins to work on the 'Torso' series, that the number of Polaroids of genitals reaches the 'thousands' mark" (email communication, January 22, 2010). Matt Wrbican, archivist at the Andy Warhol Museum, notes that these Polaroids, or some of them, may be found in one of the yet unarchived Time Capsules.

56 See Bob Colacello's recollections of these series in *Holy Terror*, esp. 337–38. Some of these images are reproduced in *Andy Warhol Nudes* (New York: Robert Miller Gallery, 1995) and *Andy Warhol Piss and Sex Paintings and Drawings* (New York: Gagosian Gallery, 2002).

57 When Colacello complained about Warhol leaving the prints from these sessions all over the office, wondering what other people in the office might think, Warhol replied, "Just tell them it's *art* Bob. They're landscapes" (*Holy Terror*, 337).

58 Gluck continues: "They're drawings of the penis, the balls and everything, and there'd be a little heart on them or tied with a little ribbon. And they're—if he still has them—they're in pads just sitting around. . . . every time he got to know somebody, even as a friend some-

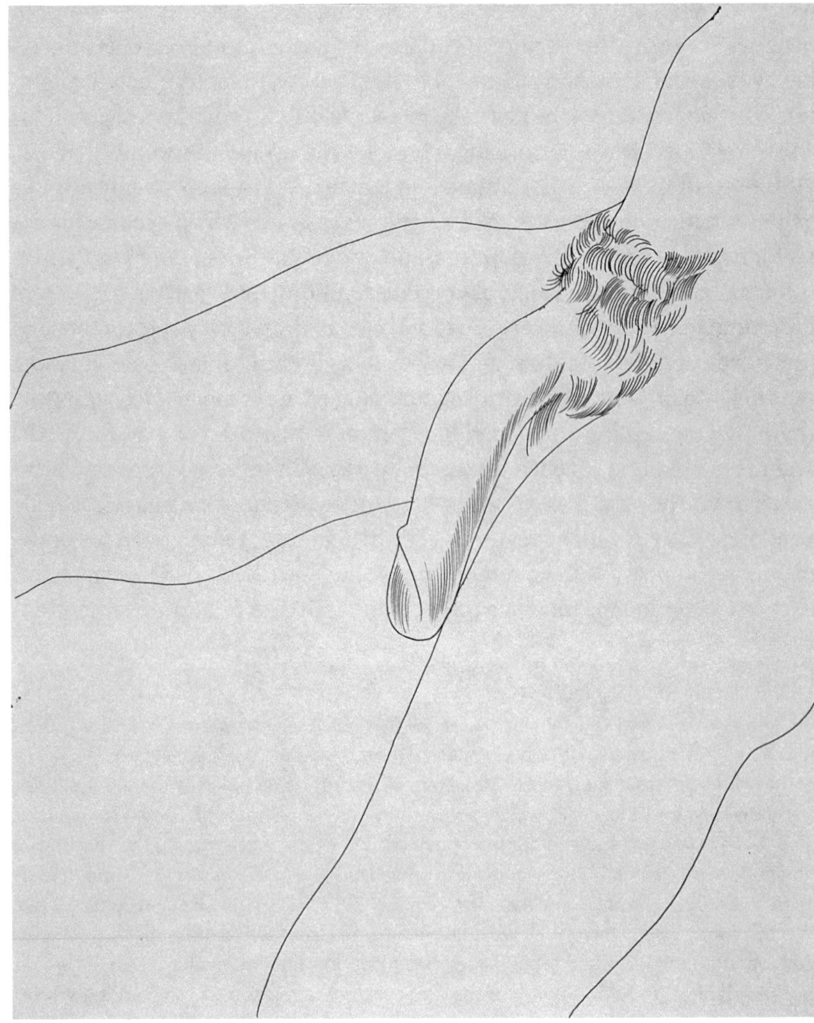

1.5 Andy Warhol, untitled (seated male nude torso), ca.1956. Black ballpoint on white paper, 17⅛ × 14 inches. © 2016 Andy Warhol Foundation for the Visual Arts/Artists Rights Society (ARS), New York.

how Warhol would go about soliciting models: "Like if he met somebody at a party or something, and he thought they were fascinating or interesting,

times, he'd say " Let me draw your cock." Smith: "And then they would volunteer?" Gluck: "Yeah. They'd drop their pants, and Andy would make a drawing. That was it. And then he'd say, 'thank you'" (Smith, *Conversations*, 62–63). See also, in the same compilation, Robert Fleischer's comments: "He said he was going to do what he called his *Boy Book*, and he wanted all of us to pose nude, and we did. There were loads of us" (114). Other accounts of these drawings include Mario Amaya's (in *Edie*, 216) and Dick Banks's (quoted in Scherman and Dalton, *Pop*, 32). For a brilliant reading of his early Dick Tracy painting in relation to these (dick-tracing) drawings from the 1950s, see Moon, "Screen Memories."

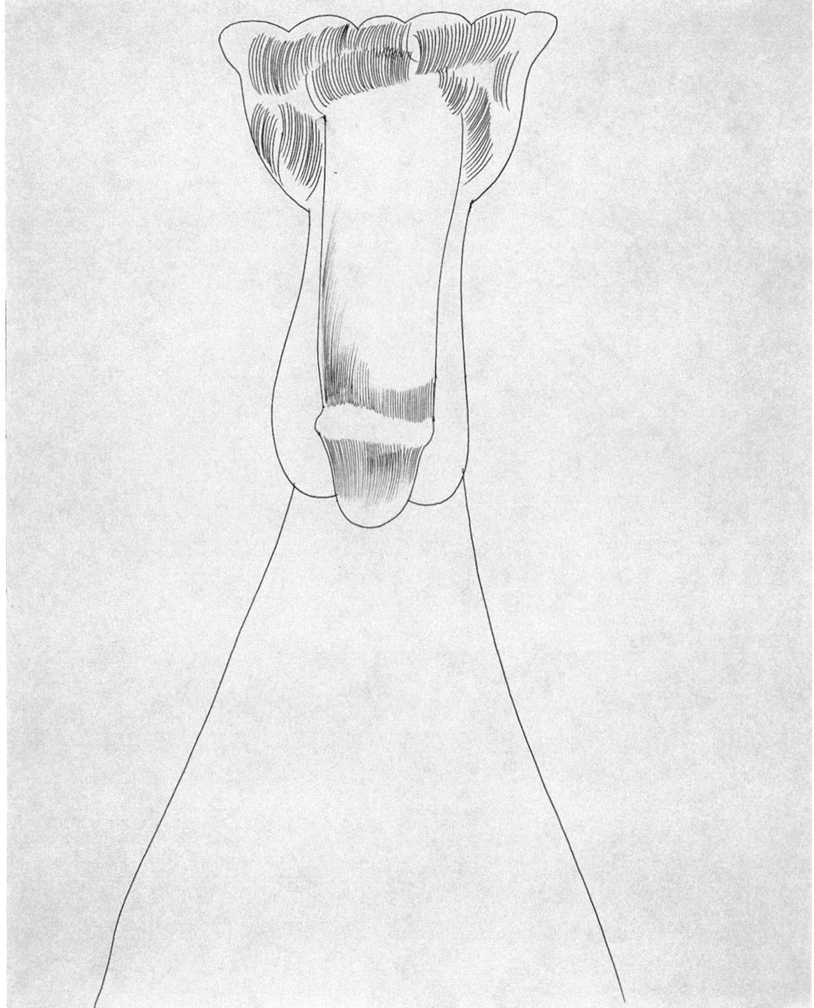

1.6 Andy Warhol, untitled (standing male nude torso), ca.1956. Black ballpoint on white paper, 17⅛ × 14 inches. © 2016 Andy Warhol Foundation for the Visual Arts/Artists Rights Society (ARS), New York.

he'd say, 'Oh, ah, let me draw your cock. I'm doing a cock book.' And surprising enough, most people were flattered when asked to be drawn. So he had no trouble getting people to draw, and he did a lot of beautiful drawings."[59]

Although the invitation to model as a mode of seduction was not new to Warhol, the additional enticement of becoming part of a collection, one of many, rather than the one, special beauty is distinctly Warholian. For the men being drawn or photographed, entering into the artist's collection allowed them to see themselves—or more precisely, their genitals—becoming

59 Cited in Smith, *Conversations*, 94.

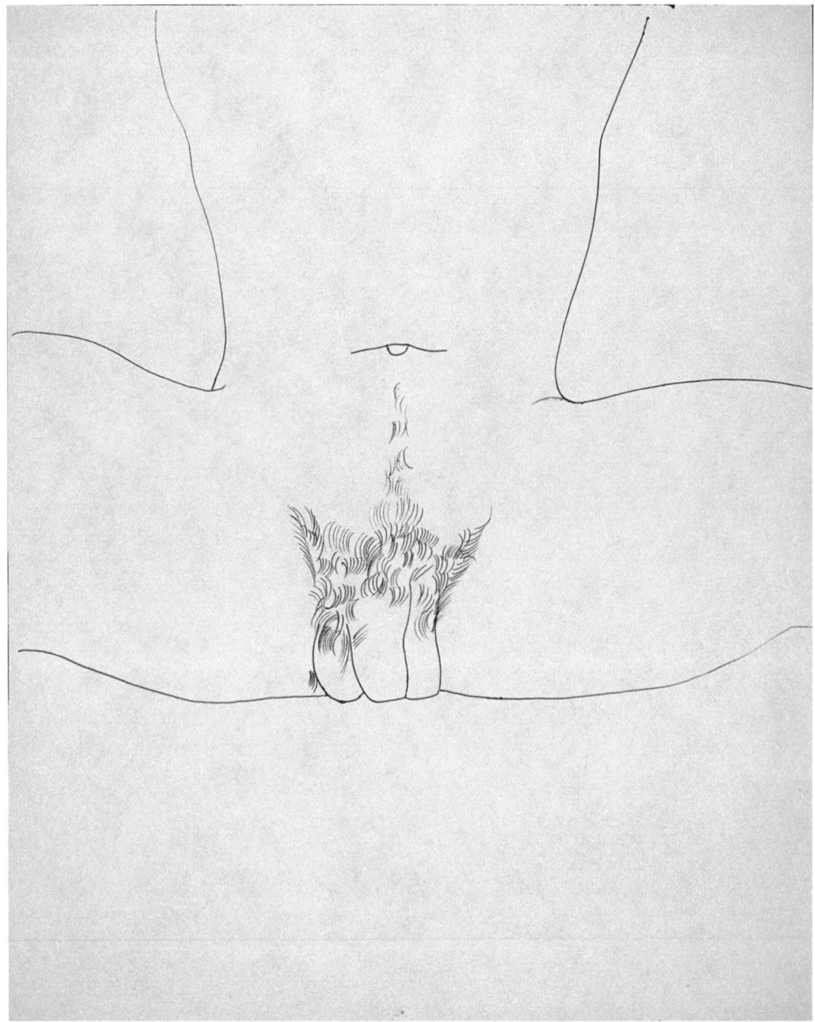

1.7 Andy Warhol, untitled (seated male nude torso), ca.1956–1957. Black ballpoint on manila paper, 16⅞ × 13⅞ inches. © 2016 Andy Warhol Foundation for the Visual Arts/ Artists Rights Society (ARS), New York.

"a Warhol," and thereby to be initiated into a special realm of similars, at once identified with Warhol and liked by him. They become "wanted men," a being-wanted constituted, as Richard Meyer put it, "collectively rather than monogamously."[60] At this moment of transition, these men, wanted in their being-similar and similar in their being-wanted, become like-beings, resemblers. By way of this Warholian "identity game," as their cocks were

60 Meyer, "Warhol's Clones," in *Negotiating Lesbian and Gay Subjects*, ed. Monica Dorenkamp and Richard Henke, 93–122 (New York: Routledge, 1995), esp. 97–98.

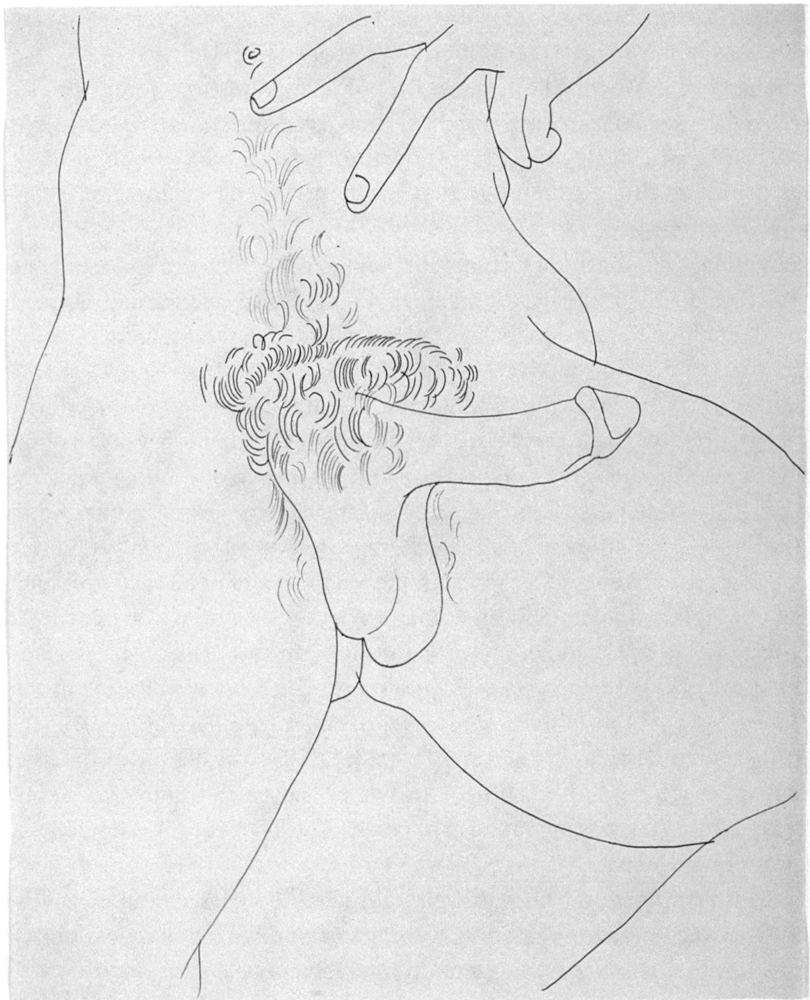

1.8 Andy Warhol, untitled (reclining nude torso), ca. 1957. Black ballpoint on manila paper, 16⅞ × 13¾ inches. © 2016 Andy Warhol Foundation for the Visual Arts/Artists Rights Society (ARS), New York.

initiated into this common space of belonging and becoming, where they could mingle with all the other cocks in Warhol's ever expanding collection, the men Warhol photographed and drew were momentarily freed from the requirements of everyday, "straight" identity. This may not only have enticed them to drop their pants but permitted them to experience their own surprising attractions or excitements as they did so.

The creation of a collection here is certainly a way for Warhol to embolden himself—"no matter how straight looking" the potential model was—where he might otherwise be shy. In this way, we could say that the collection establishes the conditions of possibility for Warhol to like cock. This liking (as

I noted in the introduction) is distinct from what is usually called desire. Whereas desire suggests lack, Warhol likes precisely what he already has, and has lots of. He can like acquiring new drawings or photos—and the "sitters" can enjoy being photographed or drawn into the collection—precisely because he already has a collection of them. This is an erotic economy based on already having, on nonutilitarian accumulation, not on identity, difference, or absence.

Warhol's emphasis on likeness and on the collection as a space of commonality does not mean, however, that singularity is unvalued. Indeed, the field of similarity established by the collected creates a uniquely ideal site for appreciating specificity. Ultra Violet (Isabelle Dufresne) describes Warhol's interest in his photo collection. "He has an extensive collection of photographs of naked people. He delights in the fact that every organ of the body varies immensely in shape, form and color from one individual to the next. Just as one torso or one face tells a different story from another, so, to Andy, one penis or one ass tells a different story from another."[61] Outside of the space of likeness—as, for example, on the pages of an academic journal or scholarly monograph—the image of a penis signifies first of all as "a penis," that is, not as something else. But alongside other images of penises, the specificity, the "story," of each one emerges. In other words (as Jean-Luc Nancy, Michael Hardt and Antonio Negri, and others have argued), specificity or singularity, as distinct from what we might call "identity," emerges only in a such fields of likeness.[62] In Warhol's cock collections we have a queer erotic economy operating in a society of similarities and singularities: the more the merrier.

This economy matched up well with what Douglas Crimp calls "the ethos of gay liberation regarding the expansion of affectional possibility," an ethos that was not centered on the monogamous couple and that welcomed the possibility of "a great variety of forms of affectional and sexual relationships."[63] Within this affective world, "coupling was newly seen not as a 'happily ever after' compact, but as an in-the-moment union for sharing pleasure. . . . Pleasure was its own reward." Similarly, Warhol's liking was not instrumentalized toward love or the happy couple, it was valuable in itself, disattached from "identity" or even "personhood."[64]

61 Ultra Violet, *Famous for 15 Minutes*, 157.

62 "No singularity can exist or be conceived on its own, but instead both its existence and definition necessarily derive from its relations with the other singularities that constitute society." Hardt and Negri, *Commonwealth* (Cambridge, MA: Harvard University Press, 2000), 338. On the relation between singularity and the common, see also Cesare Cesarino and Negri, *In Praise of the Common: A Conversation on Philosophy and Politics*, esp. 82–83, 126–27. Nancy also emphasizes the necessary relation between singularity and plurality in *Inoperative Community* and *Being Singular Plural*.

63 Crimp, "Disss-co," 15, and in Takemoto, "Melancholia of AIDS," 86.

64 While distinct, Warhol's liking has correspondences with the "sociability" Leo Bersani describes in "Sociability and Cruising."

"Part of the movie, too"

In a less obvious way, the Screen Tests also originate in a homoerotic context. As Callie Angell documents, the first Screen Tests were filmed for the series *The Thirteen Most Beautiful Boys*, inspired by the New York Police Department's *Thirteen Most Wanted* pamphlet, which had also been the basis for Warhol's censored *Thirteen Most Wanted Men* mural at the 1964 world's fair.[65] This replacement of a juridical with a homoerotic "wanting" not only plays with and points up the fact that sexual "wanting" of men by men was then criminalized, as Richard Meyer has argued in his important reading of *Thirteen Most Wanted Men* and its censorship.[66] It also exemplifies Warhol's persistent capacity for finding sites where his own liking could poach on existing modes of attention and interest, even, or especially, if those modes needed to be translated into another social or medial context, or perverted by a prurient point of view.[67]

The *Thirteen Most Beautiful Boys* films generated a companion series, *Thirteen Most Beautiful Women*, each of which came to include many more than thirteen members, suggesting that the initial premise of the exclusivity of a limited series was not taken especially seriously by Warhol, even if it appealed to his sitters.[68] Moreover, as he remarks in his *Philosophy*, he had a principled opposition to singling out some beauties as opposed to others, remarking that "I've never met a person that I couldn't call a beauty" and "If everybody's not a beauty then nobody is."[69] And as with Warhol's collecting more generally, once he got going, he found it difficult to stop. He ended up producing 472 of these individual short portrait films between 1964 and 1966, filming a range of poets, artists, writers, actors, critics, filmmakers,

65 For a discussion of this series (and a reproduction of the cover of the pamphlet from the Warhol archives), see Angell's indispensable *Andy Warhol Screen Tests: The Films of Andy Warhol Catalogue Raisonné*, vol. 1 (New York: Abrams, 2006), 244–45.

66 "The title of the mural—initially known as *Thirteen Most Wanted Men* but often referred to more simply, as the *Most Wanted Men*—turns on a double entendre: it is not only that these men are wanted by the FBI, but that the very act of 'wanting men' constitutes a form of criminality if the wanter is also male, if, say, the wanter is Warhol" (Meyer, "Warhol's Clones," 98).

67 "Rather than the 'Thirteen Most Wanted Men,' what you should really do is *The Thirteen Most Beautiful Boys*, and *The Thirteen Most Beautiful Girls*, and that's what everybody would like. This is Andy's overt reasoning; this is how he would talk to you." Billy Name, interviewed by Mirra Bank Brockman, December 17, 1991, Andy Warhol Foundation; cited by Angell, *Andy Warhol Screen Tests*, 244.

68 In these series, there are forty-two Screen Tests of thirty-five men, and forty-seven Screen Tests of thirty different women. Ibid., 243–59.

69 *Phil*, 61, 62. The full passage is pertinent: "For a year once it was in all the magazines that my next movie was going to be *The Beauties*. The publicity for it was great, but then I could never decide who should be in it. If everybody's not a beauty, then nobody is, so I didn't want to imply that the kids in *The Beauties* were beauties but the kids in my other movies weren't so I had to back out on the basis of the title. It was all wrong."

musicians, dancers, models, speed freaks, opera queens, Harvard students, hustlers, wealthy art collectors, art dealers, a few celebrities, and various of his friends, collaborators, and assistants.[70]

As the project expanded in scope, it may have also been attractive to Warhol as an aid in a task that he found particularly challenging: representing the Factory and the people who passed through it. In *POPism*, Warhol remarks that journalists often were puzzled in their attempts to write about the Factory and that he was no help because "I never knew what was going on myself" (*POP*, 130). His description of one particular effort to apprehend the Factory during the summer of 1966 can give us a sense of how the Screen Tests may have helped to represent the Factory as a space and as a collectivity:

> The Factory felt more strange to me than ever that summer. I loved it, I thrived there, but the atmosphere was totally impenetrable—even when you were in the middle of it, you didn't know what was going on.
>
> The air didn't really move. I would sit in a corner for hours, watching people come and go and stay, not moving myself, trying to get a complete idea, but everything stayed fragmentary; I never knew what was really happening. I'd sit there and listen to every sound: the freight elevator moving in the shaft, the sound of the grate opening and closing when people got in and went out, the steady traffic all the way downstairs on 47th Street, the projector running, a camera shutter clicking, a magazine page turning, somebody lighting a match, the colored sheets of gelatin and sheets of silver paper moving when the fan hit them, the high school typists hitting a key every couple of seconds, the scissors shearing as Paul cut out E.P.I. [Exploding Plastic Inevitable] clippings and pasted them into scrapbooks, the water running over the prints in Billy's darkroom, the timer going off, the dryer operating, someone trying to make the toilet work, men having sex in the back room, girls closing compacts and makeup cases. The mixture of the mechanical sounds and the people sounds made everything seem unreal and if you heard a projector going while you were watching somebody, you felt that they must be a part of the movie, too. (*POP*, 171–72)

Warhol's efforts to get a "complete idea" of the Factory by "watching people come and go" are thwarted by its "impenetrable" atmosphere. His response is deceptively simple: in imitation of his "wife," he shifts his mode of perception from watching to let-everything-in listening. By opening himself to an indiscriminate, machine-like collection of sounds, he transforms a welter of fragments into a medium-based series. By creating this common space

70 For detailed information about the Screen Tests, including who is depicted in each test and how they knew Warhol or came to the Factory, see Angell, *Andy Warhol Screen Tests*.

to bring together all of the activities taking place in the Factory and perceive them in relation to each other, Warhol gets around the representational difficulty of getting a "complete idea." Within the space of the collection, "the people sounds" and "the mechanical sounds" mix together in way that puts everything in the atmosphere of the "unreal," outside the field of the everyday "real" where things are identifiable, fixable, and locatable.

For Warhol, "unreal" was another word for something one could imagine as being like other things, including oneself. One could imagine imitating the evidently unreal; the obviously artificial does not exclude improper ways of being from joining it. (This was a reason he preferred the "wrong" person for a part: "no person is ever completely right for any part, because a part is a role is never real"; *Phil*, 83). Gathering the phenomena in the Factory into a sound collection was a way to order the otherwise impenetrable atmosphere into a set of likable things. "Unreal" or "artificial" in this sense also generally means more moving, more affectively compelling, and thus—like the compelling and moving representation of emotion in Hollywood movies—more "real."[71] Like the trip around his townhouse to peer in at his collections, then, Warhol's listing of every-sound-in-the-Factory reattunes him to similarity and its production. In this now common space of sound *semblables*, activities that might in other contexts be singled out for attack, such as "men having sex in the back room," merge into the group without requiring special identification. At the same time, as part of what defines the collection of things-heard-at-the Factory, the singularity of this sound forms part of the "magic circle" in relation to which all the other sounds acquire their own significance.

Having thus altered the rhythm of his perception, Warhol can then "see" the visual realm from the point of view of this newly engaging "unreal" sound collection. Sound is not located and perspectival in the way vision is; it suffuses the Factory with its ambience, so that "if you heard a projector going while you were watching somebody, you felt that they must be a part of the movie, too," even or especially if the person you were looking at was not being filmed at all.

The Screen Tests are an essential part of this overall strategy; after all, Warhol can relate to everyone in the Factory as if they were "part of the

71 For instance, in a discussion of his viewing of his twenty-five-hour film **** in 1967, Warhol writes, "Seeing it all together that night somehow made it seem more real to me (I mean, more *un*real, which was actually more real) than it had when it was happening" (*POP*, 251). The film, which collected the reels of film Warhol had shot over the past year, translated his experiences into the "unreal" field of cinematic mediation, out of the ("real") means-ends rationality of everyday life, with its obligations and demands, anxieties and desires, its need to be a person with a verifiable identity. Only there are the defenses policing the mimetic faculty relaxed, and affects from the past (including those from the event being shown on the film) can finally travel along the paths of similarity they need to make it out into the world, enabling them to become "real."

movie, too," only if it is in fact the case that he is constantly filming people. The Screen Tests were a remarkably effective collecting technique; without the need for a scenario or a cast, they gave Warhol a pretext for asking anyone at all if they wanted to be filmed. Like his cock book or audiotapes, the Screen Tests transfer the Factory's residents and visitors out of the everyday realm of identity into a specific cinematic world where their participation in an assembly of likenesses is quite easy to apprehend, laid out for contemplation as such in an almost pedagogical fashion.

In this instance, the similarity is established not only by the nature of the medium and the three-minute reels on which each Test was recorded, but by the specific formal principles shaping them. As Callie Angell notes, the Screen Tests were based on standard forms of photo portraiture, like the ID photo, and followed a set of basic rules: The camera should be stationary, the background plain, the subjects well-lit and centered. Sitters should remain face forward, stay as still as possible, and refrain from talking, smiling, or even blinking for the three minutes it takes the reel to finish.[72]

This means that most (though by no means all) of the Screen Tests capture faces trying to stay motionless or at least maintain a pose. Everyone responds differently to the situation (some disregarding Warhol's directions entirely). Usually, since they are trying to be still, as if for a photograph, one can discern an effort to make the face signify in some way, to project a coherent character: Lou Reed is cool, Jane Holzer glamorous and amused; others look bored or stoned or intimidatingly serious. In the Screen Tests, we see people trying to maintain for three minutes the "picture face" one sometimes makes for a photograph. Although we may study a photograph over and over, turning a momentary look into a site of extended contemplation (in one of the central tensions and attractions of photography), that look is not often subjected to being maintained—while being observed—durationally. Indeed, one does not often have to hold such faces for more than a few seconds (though one may think of early photographs with their long exposure times or the moment at the end of newscasts where reporters try to hold their faces until the camera cuts away). In the Screen Tests, we witness a sitter left alone with this unexpected demand.

Predictably, this presents certain difficulties. It can be hard to prevent one's ever-shifting affect from registering on the face, the "prime organ of affect."[73] And there is plenty to affect one in this scene; for starters, one

72 Angell, *Andy Warhol Screen Tests*, 14. As Angell points out, the later Screen Tests were sometimes more experimental, less rule bound, some involving movement on the part of the sitter, or camera movement including close-ups. Some of these were projected behind the Velvet Underground during the famous "Exploding Plastic Inevitable." On the use of film in the EPI, see Branden Joseph, "'My Mind Split Open': Andy Warhol's Exploding Plastic Inevitable," *Grey Room*, no. 8 (Summer 2002), 80–107.

73 The phrase is Tomkins's; see *Affect, Imagery, Consciousness*, vol. 1 of *Affect, Imagery, Consciousness; The Complete Edition* (New York: Springer, 2008), chap. 7, "The Primary Site of the Affects: The Face."

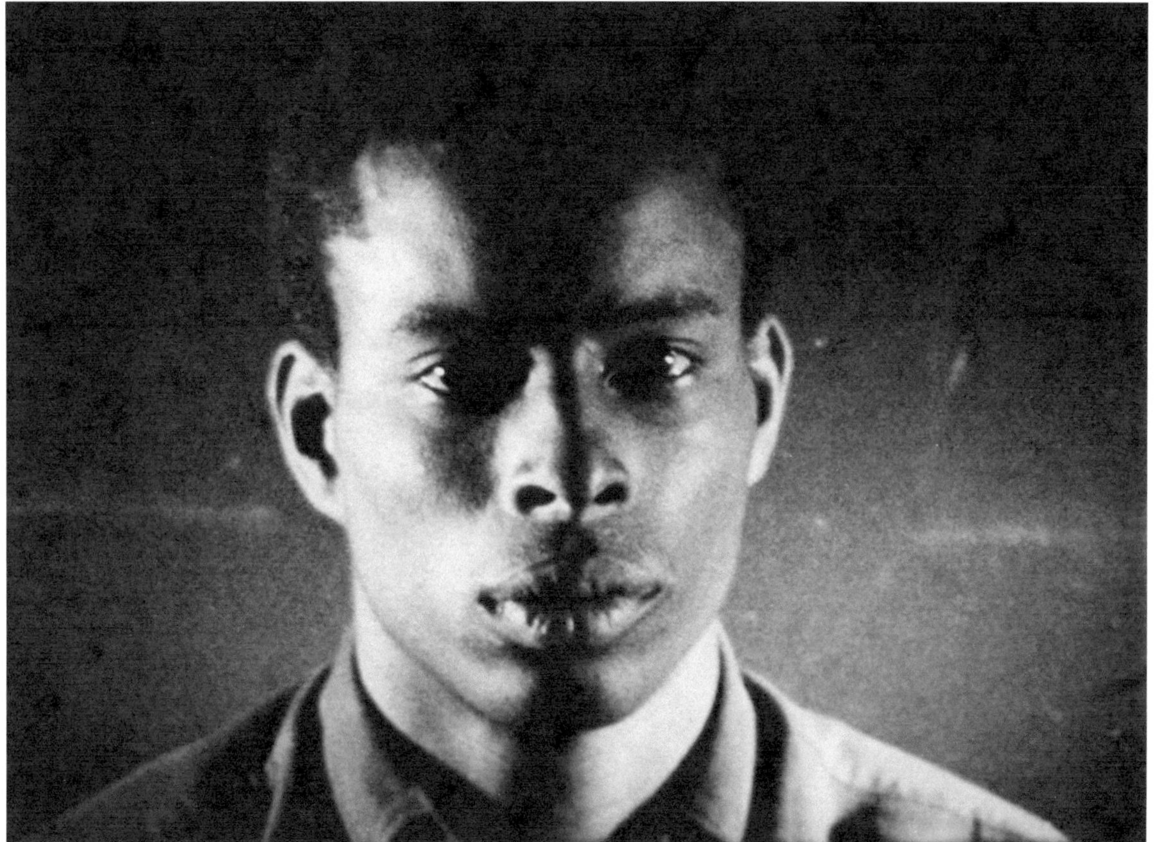

1.9 Andy Warhol, *Screen Test: Rufus Collins* [ST61], 1964. 16mm film, black and white, silent, 4.3 minutes at 16 frames per second. © 2016 The Andy Warhol Museum, a museum of Carnegie Institute.

may be surprised by the task of holding a single expression over time. Then there may be the nervousness associated with being filmed, the discomfort of being under the lights, or the excitement of being in the orbit of a famous artist. It is a situation, as David James notes, not unlike "that of psychoanalysis; the camera is the silent analyst who has abandoned the subject to the necessity of his fantastic self-projection."[74]

In any case, no person succeeds in keeping her or his face entirely still for three minutes. At the very least, the eyes usually blink. Other parts of the face may also start to move: muscles twitch, eyelids quiver, lips are licked, and occasionally the whole face relaxes or falls out of its pose into laughter or a scrunching up or a quick shake as the sitter tires or loses focus and seeks to "clear" the face before resetting. In one spectacular test, Ann Buchanan manages not to blink. We see, maybe, just the faintest of trembles around

74 David James, "Andy Warhol: The Producer as Author," in *Allegories of Cinema*, 58–84, 69.

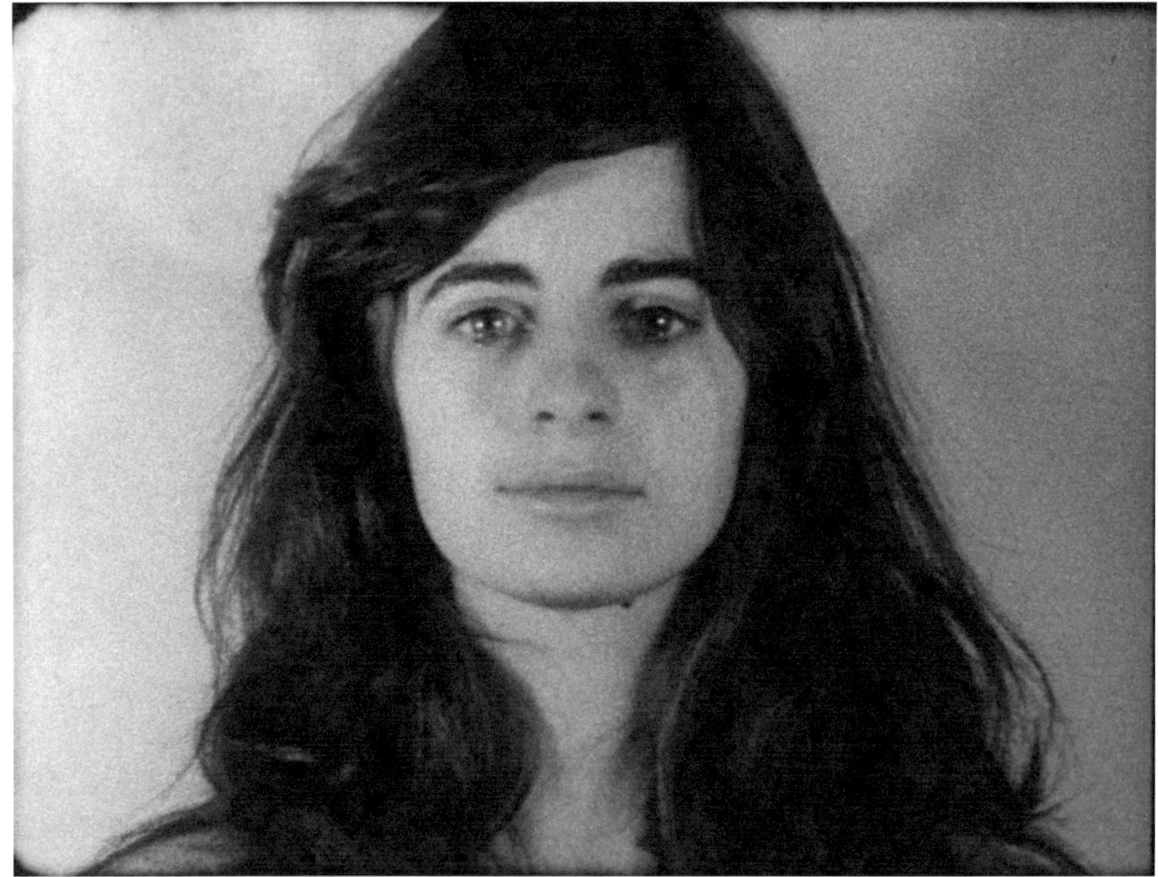

1.10 Andy Warhol, *Screen Test: Ann Buchanan* [ST33], 1964. 16mm film, black and white, silent, 4.5 minutes at 16 frames per second. © 2016 The Andy Warhol Museum, a museum of Carnegie Institute.

her eyes until, about halfway through, tears begin to well and then stream down her face. Even when one is determined and able to hold a pose, the face is physiologically incapable of it, even for this relatively short duration.

Thus, the Screen Tests are dramas not only of self-presentation, but of self-disintegration. What they dramatize above all is the singular way each sitter fails to hold onto an identity, the way each person comes together and falls apart. How does each sitter deal with the failure to keep a coherent face together? Overall, in their display of faces composing and uncomposing, the Screen Tests present the self as a series of imperfect imitations, an accumulation of shifting likenesses, performed over time, one after the other.[75]

75 The Screen Test series called *Six Months* illustrates this idea even more concretely. The idea was to shoot daily Tests of Warhol's boyfriend at the time, Philip Fagan, thereby registering the passage of time. However, they broke up after three months, so the project is truncated. Like a celebrity silkscreen, *Six Months* multiplies Fagan, not through paint

In effect, Warhol has created a situation in which everyone can succeed in failing, and become a star of their own out-take. Like so much of his work, Warhol's Screen Tests sing "vivas to those who have fail'd."[76] On a formal level, they present a collectivity based on an inevitable, common, but varied failure to follow the given rules and maintain an identity.

Here, as elsewhere in Warhol's work, failure is something to share. Warhol observed that when you are on a date, waiting in line for a movie and "never getting in is the most exciting, but after that waiting to get in is the most exciting" (*Phil*, 115). This is because "you've shared a complete experience." Usually the seriality of the line (as in Sartre's famous example of people waiting for the bus) distinguishes and isolates those in line from each other even as it makes them the same, inasmuch as they all "are" their place in line and are thus "not themselves."[77] But waiting and failing dissolves the sequential ordering of the line and turns the homogenizing isolation into a "whole experience" to share. The Screen Tests allegorize the experience of being in a line where *everyone* fails to get in, or at least stays waiting long enough to make apparent their commonality with everyone else in line (as in Vladimir Sorokin's great novel *The Queue*). Warhol seemed to see the Factory as a place where such failures could bring one together with a group of others who failed to properly fit into their assigned "stock roles."[78] The Factory was a place where a series of failed subjects could experience their misfitting together; the Screen Tests help Warhol imagine this togetherness as one he could belong to.[79]

---

smudges or blurred edges but through changes in lighting, hairstyle, and pose. What emerges is a series of likenesses of a single person, highlighting this sense of the "individual" subject also as a collection, one who does not contain multitudes but is himself multitudinous. At the same time it creates a certain "star effect," as if Fagan were Elvis or Marilyn, a reproduction of his many star roles, or of the different versions of him that various fans have incorporated. The series also suggests that for Warhol the principle of liking being based on a collection of likenesses extends to the "individual" person as well. See Angell, *Andy Warhol Screen Tests*, 217–42.

76 Walt Whitman, "Song of Myself," in *Portable Walt Whitman*, 21.

77 Jean-Paul Sartre, *The Critique of Dialectical Reason* (New York: Verso, 2004), 256–69.

78 I am referring to the passage in *POPism* (discussed in the introduction) where Warhol reflected on the aggressive attacks on homosexuality directed at the Factory and speculated that it was not homosexuality as such that was being attacked so much as the way gays in the Factory were "strong enough to say you were different and actually have fun with it" instead of being "hypocritical and covert" (222–23). Such attacks, Warhol thought, indicated a lack of care for "all the miserable people in the world who just can't fit into stock roles."

79 Marx famously laments that while a class (in this case, the small peasants) may be formed by group of persons who live in similar conditions and share a set of economic interests (interests opposed to those of another group of persons), such a class may have no way of communicating among themselves and representing themselves to themselves, and may therefore have no awareness that their interests are shared by others, which makes it impossible for the class to defend those interests. "They cannot represent

The mode of collecting Warhol practices in the Screen Tests does the work of representing the collectivity of alienated misfits who assembled at the Factory without attempting to stand in or "speak for" them.[80] He does not reduce an essentially diverse or plural group to a unity, "the people" or "the nation," or to an undifferentiated "masses." Warhol preserves singularity and multiplicity, indeed, actively seeks and emphasizes it. He represents in the Screen Tests a "plurality which persists as such," Paolo Virno's gloss for "the multitude," the very plurality of which can make representation and togetherness a challenge.[81] We might say, to borrow from Jean-Luc Nancy, that the Screen Tests present a collective of "singulars singularly together, where the togetherness is neither the sum, nor the incorporation, nor the 'society,' nor the 'community.' The togetherness of singularities is singularity 'itself.' It 'assembles' them insofar as it spaces them; they are 'linked' insofar as they are not unified."[82] Warhol noted that singularity flourished at the Factory, which "brought out strange things in people. By 'strange' I don't necessarily mean 'wild! uninhibited!' I mean atypical—it could even bring out, say, a puritanism that a person didn't know he had" (*POP*, 130).[83]

* * *

The Screen Tests not only represent a particular mode of togetherness, composed by the correspondences created by failures to fit and to be. They

---

themselves, they must be represented." *The Eighteenth Brumaire of Louis Bonaparte* (New York: International Publishers, 1963), 123–24. For Lenin (as he argues in *What Is to Be Done*), the way to move this "class-in-itself," one that is not conscious of itself and is thus without agency, to a "class for itself," a self-conscious class capable of acting in its interest, is by way of the party, where political professionals do the work of representing the working class to itself from outside the space of economic struggle, by way of the newspaper, above all.

80 Gayatri Spivak, "Can the Subaltern Speak?," in *Marxism and the Interpretation of Culture*, ed. Cary Nelson and Lawrence Grossberg (Urbana: University of Illinois Press, 1988), 271–313. See also her *Critique of Postcolonial Reason* (Cambridge, MA: Harvard University Press, 1999), esp. 244–76. Spivak emphasizes the difference between two senses of "representation" that may be easily conflated—representation as "speaking for," as in politics, and representation as "re-presentation," or "portraiture," as in art or philosophy. Where we have one word, German has two: *vertreten* ("represent" in the first, political sense) and *darstellen* ("re-present" in the second, aesthetic sense).

81 See Virno, *A Grammar of the Multitude* (New York: Semiotext(e), 2004), 31.

82 Nancy, *Being Singular Plural*, 33.

83 For anecdotal accounts of the Factory atmosphere, see especially the interviews in *The Velvet Years*, accompanied by photographs by Stephen Shore and text by Lynne Tillman. For instance, Pat Hartley: "It actually seemed like a world of consenting adults, which the outside world didn't seem to be" (58). Or Maureen Tucker: "The reason I liked Andy so much was I never felt out of place in the Factory, even though, given my personality at the time, I should have felt very out of place" (71). Or Sterling Morrison: "There was always this feeling that something incredible was going to happen, something really exciting or fun or new. . . . As shown in the pictures, there's this tension, always this potential" (89).

also invite viewers into the mode of belonging the series as a whole constitutes, by way of the aesthetic experience they proffer. By teaching us how to like and be like, the Tests initiate us into this group of likenesses. They do this, in part, by shifting us out of our habitual ways of looking at faces.

In the way that they encourage sustained, close gazing at another's face, the Screen Tests recall an infant's mode of looking. One of the first things one may realize in watching a Screen Test is how rarely, as adults, we spend even four uninterrupted minutes freely, openly, gazing at another's more or less stationary face. Such interocular gazing is the very mark of the closest intimacy; only when in love, or about to fight, or on drugs (as Warhol notes about kids on acid at the Easter Sunday Central Park Be-In[84]) are persons likely to engage in this kind of looking. However, for infants, as Daniel Stern notes, "the face is the most attractive and fascinating object that exists."[85] Consequently, as infants, the time we spend looking at faces, proportionally, is greater than at any other time in our lives. Indeed, because infant vision is involuntarily attracted to precisely the visual elements that compose the face, this looking, which can go on for long periods, is a kind of "obligatory attention."

One potential effect of such durational looking, Stern suggests, is a split between the focus of vision and the focus of attention.[86] That is, after looking at the same spot for a few moments, one's *attention* tends to drift away from that spot even as one's eyes remained focused on it. As our attention and focus split off from one another, visual distortions are produced. We are all familiar with this phenomenon: stare at a spot on the wall, a leaf, a word on the page, for long enough and it starts to shift and shimmer, the space around it collapses and folds, colors seem to hover in and out of existence at the edges.[87] The Screen Tests (like other of Warhol's minimal films, and, in a different way, his double-screen films) promote this split between vision and attention and its hallucinatory side effects, effects that are heightened by the frequent use of lighting to produce high contrasts in the contours of the face, and the fact that the films were filmed at sound speed (24 frames per second) but shown at silent speed (16 fps), which makes the movements of the face seem slightly "off" or "unreal."[88]

In mimicking the durational attention to a face characteristic of infant looking, the Screen Tests eliminate the essential feature of that looking, its

84 "They could stand there staring at each other for hours without moving" (*POP*, 207).

85 Stern, *Diary of a Baby* (New York: Basic Books, 1990, 1998), 47.

86 Ibid., 17–22.

87 Because this hallucinatory effect is a basic feature of infant vision, for infants "there are no 'dead' inanimate objects out there . . . only different forces at play" (ibid., 21).

88 On the use of lighting to produce hallucinatory effects also see Joseph, "My Mind Split Open," and Homay King, "Stroboscopic: Warhol and the Exploding Plastic Inevitable," and Tan Lin, "Disco, Cybernetics, and the Migration of Warhol's Shadows into Computation," both in *Criticism* 56, no. 3 (Summer 2014; Warhol special issue).

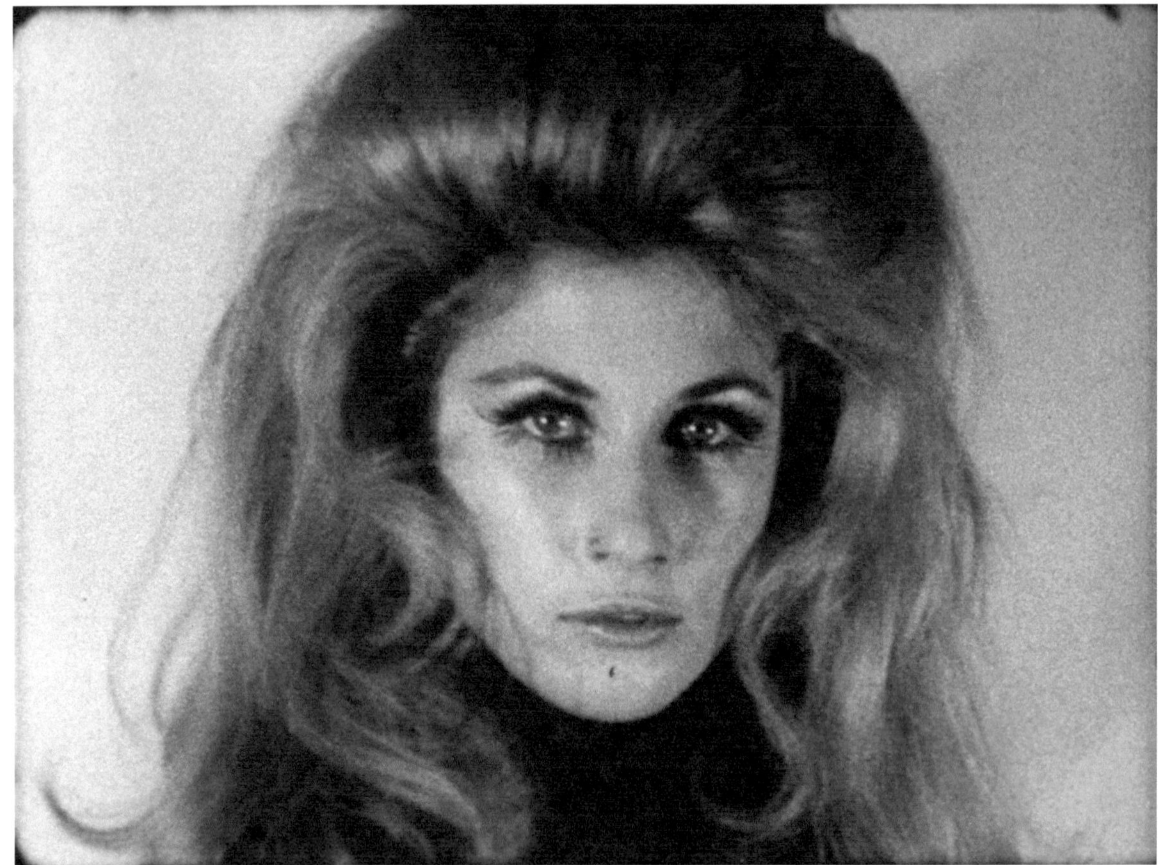

1.11 Andy Warhol, *Screen Test: Jane Holzer* [ST142], 1964. 16mm film, black and white, silent, 4.5 minutes at 16 frames per second. © 2016 The Andy Warhol Museum, a museum of Carnegie Institute.

mutuality, the communication and attunement that occurs between the faces of infants and their caretakers. Yet, paradoxically, it is precisely this subtraction of the possibility of response that makes the experience compelling, indeed infantlike. Only because the other's face is not mimetically open to us can we be mimetically open to it. For it is only minus the concern with the other's reaction to us, when we are free from any number of everyday face-looking habits, that we can engage in the sustained, dreamy, emotionally open, intensely interested looking that characterizes infant experience. We do not need to look with sympathy or smile in return at the friend, nor must we look away with a yawn or shy distraction if caught looking at a stranger. Perhaps most significantly, we are free to *not* seek to see in the eyes and expressions of the other signs of our own being liked or loved or recognized or desired. Nor, for that matter, do we need to keep a composed face, or indeed to be or have an identity at all. We are returned to an unself-conscious state,

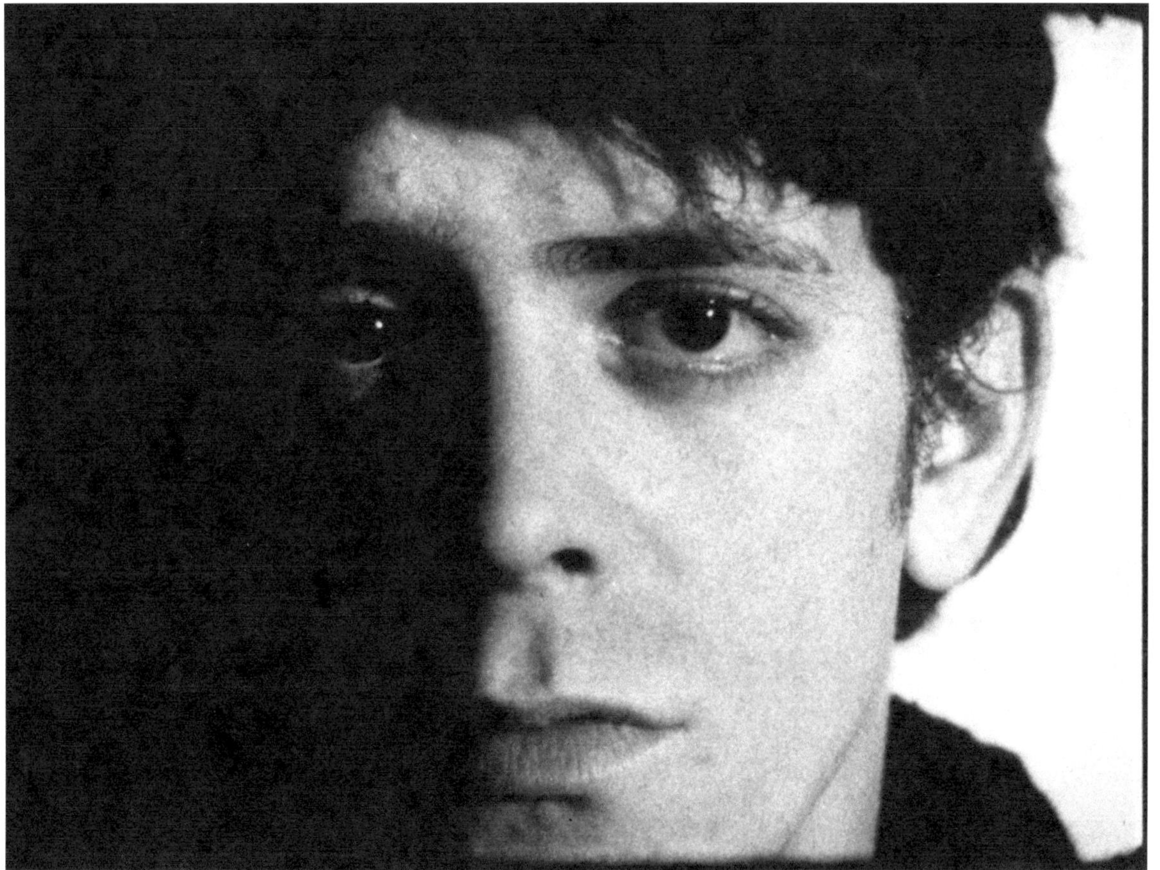

1.12 Andy Warhol, *Screen Test: Lou Reed* [ST263], 1966. 16mm film, black and white, silent, 4.3 minutes at 16 frames per second. © 2016 The Andy Warhol Museum, a museum of Carnegie Institute

where we might forget to "act grown up" and set aside the need to police our capacity and impulse for being alike. In so doing, we are actually returned to that mode of attunement where, as Merleau-Ponty remarks, "I live in the facial expression of the other, as I feel him living in mine."[89]

In this instance (because their faces are not responding to ours and because they disappear at the end of the film), we cannot feel Freddy Herko or Rufus Collins or Ann Buchanan or Allen Ginsberg living in our facial expressions. But in a departure from everyday experience, we wish that we could. Moreover, we have this experience in relation to a face whose own status as a singular collection of likenesses is being dramatized. If, as Vittorio Gallese suggests, perceiving the movement in another's face results in an internal,

89 Maurice Merleau-Ponty, "The Child's Relation with Others," in *The Primacy of Perception*, ed. James M. Edie (Evanston: Northwestern University Press, 1964), 96–155, 146.

embodied simulation of it, then when we watch the Screen Tests we simulate, or co-experience, our own loss of identity.[90] And we become aware, instead—at least for a moment—of ourselves as accumulations of likenesses.

In the Screen Tests, then, we are recalled to the pleasures and confusions of being-like and at the same time reminded of their absence. We get up from the experience of watching a collection of ten Screen Tests dazzled but also a bit dazed, in a perceptual world distorted by resemblances, wondering where and how we might have this experience not only with a filmed face but with other persons in our everyday lives, and why we do not. We find ourselves in the mood for being-like. Perhaps, to this end, we will have picked up Warhol's trick for relating to the people he saw as if they "were in the movie, too," and then may wish we were, as well.

90 See Vittorio Gallese, "The Manifold Nature of Interpersonal Relations: The Quest for a Common Mechanism," in *Neuroscience of Social Interaction*, ed. Christopher D. Frith and Daniel M. Wolpert (New York: Oxford University Press, 2004), 159–82, and "The 'Shared Manifold' Hypothesis: From Mirror Neurons to Empathy," *Journal of Consciousness Studies* 8, nos. 5–7 (2001): 33–50.

2: Art Machine

The reason I'm painting this way is that I want to be a machine, and I feel whatever I do and do machine-like is what I want to do. **Andy Warhol**, "What Is Pop Art?"

The idea becomes a machine that makes the art.
Sol LeWitt, "Paragraphs on Conceptual Art"[1]

One machine is always coupled with another.
Gilles Deleuze and Felix Guattari, *Anti-Oedipus*[2]

Given their differences—in style, sensibility, aesthetic ideology, and artistic practices—it is rather remarkable that in the 1960s both Andy Warhol and Sol LeWitt, paradigms of the Pop Artist and Conceptual Artist respectively, shared the desire to model their artistic practices on the machine. What made the machine so attractive as an object of imitation?

Perhaps the easiest answer is that being a machine was a way *not* to be an abstract expressionist. The rhetoric of the machine was ready-made for the aesthetic-ideological work of negating the perceived humanism and romanticism of abstract expressionism because it aggressively references the rationalized and alienating mode of labor that had been for most of the century the opposite of "art." Imitating the machine enabled LeWitt and Warhol to change their art historical referent from abstract expressionism toward "noncomposition," an anti-art tradition that can be traced back to

1 "Paragraphs on Conceptual Art," in *Sol LeWitt: Critical Texts*, ed. Adachiara Zevi (Rome: I Libri di AEIOU). This chapter is a much-revised version of an essay I wrote for Nicholas Baume's *Sol LeWitt: Incomplete Open Cubes*, Wadsworth Atheneum (Cambridge, MA: MIT Press, 2001). Many thanks to Nicholas for inviting me to the write the essay, to Carol LeWitt for her numerous hospitalities and assistances, and to Sol LeWitt for several illuminating conversations about his work.

2 Gilles Deleuze and Felix Guattari, *Anti-Oedipus: Capitalism and Schizophrenia* (New York: Penguin, 1977).

Duchamp and the Russian avant-garde. The noncompositional task involves finding an ordering principle for one's art or literature that depends as little as possible (ideally, not at all) on subjective choice. A pregiven system—a machine—produces the artwork in a way that erases one's own subjectivity and individuality.[3]

Artists' baldly proclaimed and widely publicized embrace of the machine in the 1960s carried with it the danger of appearing to affirm postwar industrial society and the new forms of labor, organization, mass culture, and the commodity that characterized it. If everyday life, the argument would go, has *already* turned us into machines, as workers and as consumers, then art should help us reconnect with what is human and creative, not underscore our subjection to the mechanical. The notion of person-as-machine conjures up images of workers on the assembly line. As Marx put it, "In handicrafts and manufacture, the worker makes use of a tool; in the factory, the machine makes use of him. . . . In the factory we have a lifeless mechanism which is independent of the workers, who are incorporated into it as living appendages."[4] And modern designers of the factory did, in fact, think of the human body as a machine. In his influential 1911 study, *The Principles of Scientific Management*, F. W. Taylor argued that a radical increase in the efficiency of work processes could be achieved by conducting rigorous time and motion studies of each part of the labor process. Once the most efficient bodily movements were determined, they would establish a standard that the "scientific manager" could teach and enforce.[5] Henry Ford implemented and expanded Taylor's insights in his automobile factories, more or less institutionalizing the assembly line and the repetitive motions it required from workers as the basis of modern industrial production.

However, it is worth remembering that before the 1960s, the contexts in which it seemed possible to bring the machine into art-making included the explicitly anticapitalist ones of Soviet constructivism and the Bauhaus. In those movements, the artist took the machine out of the Taylorized, Fordist factory and put it in the context of art in an attempt to put the machine to other uses, including explicitly affective ones. The Soviet poet Vladimir Mayakovsky, for example, could speak of his "machine-parts" in proclaiming, "I myself feel like a Soviet factory, manufacturing happiness."[6] The

3 On "noncomposition," see Yves-Alain Bois's forthcoming *The Limit of Almost: Non-Composition, Entropy and Other Erasures of Subjectivity in 20th Century Art*, his "Les Annees Supports/Surfaces," *Artforum* 37, no. 4 (December 1988), and Howard Singerman, "The Effects of Non-Composition," in *La Part de l'Oeil* (Brussels, 2000).

4 Karl Marx, *Capital: A Critique of Political Economy*, vol. 1, trans. Ben Fowkes (New York: Penguin Books, 1976), 548.

5 *The Principles of Scientific Management* (New York: Norton, 1967). Also see David Harvey on the Taylorist and Fordist projects in *The Condition of Postmodernity* (Cambridge: Basil Blackwell, 1989).

6 In the 1925 poem "Back Home!" ("Domoy"), in *The Bedbug and Selected Poetry*, trans. Max Hayward and George Reavey (Bloomington: Indiana University Press, 1975), 186–

constructivist reconceptualization of the role of the artist along technological lines was part of an effort to figure out how the artist could play a role in the creation of a noncapitalist modernity. In her study of the "machine in the studio" Caroline Jones makes the case that those political motivations had more or less evaporated by the 1960s when artists like Frank Stella, Warhol, and Robert Smithson started not only to represent the machine but to imitate it.[7] While it does seem clear, as Jones writes, that "postwar industrial capitalism inhabited the consciousness" of these artists and "motivated the making of their art,"[8] this does not necessarily imply simple affirmation of postwar industrial/consumer capitalism's particular use of the machine and mechanization. Indeed, both LeWitt and Warhol, in their distinct imitations of the machine, are involved in efforts to transform, distort, and reimagine the human-machine interface.

The advantages of examining Warhol and LeWitt together here are several. The juxtaposition puts each into a different context and thus helps to render both newly unfamiliar. While Warhol and LeWitt are each interested in the machine in their own idiosyncratic way, by looking at these two ways of seeing the world in relation to each other, we can better appreciate not only their singularity but also the historical situation they share. What is the historical mood in which the aesthetic experience offered to viewers in the work of Warhol and LeWitt is attractive?

My claim here is that the idea of the machine provides a site through which Warhol and LeWitt are able to mediate—to represent and transform, to reproduce and allegorize—two related historical processes. The first, mentioned above, is the Taylorization of labor: the treatment of the human body as a machine, an instrument, in order to increase its efficiency in the context of industrial labor. This instrumentalization of the body was, of course, not limited to the factory context and was broadly perceived in the postwar period to have penetrated many areas of American life, including

---

87. Also see Christina Lodder, *Constructivism* (New Haven, CT: Yale University Press, 1983), and Maria Gough, *The Artist as Producer: Russian Constructivism in Revolution* (Berkeley: University of California, 2005).

7 Jones (*Machine in the Studio*, 55) makes a helpful distinction between iconic and performative referencing of the mechanical. The representation is iconic, she writes, in "an image, figure, or representation that is somehow indexed to technology, to the industrial order or to the machine." The performative is defined as "a mode of production that aspires to, or structurally resembles, an industrial process, and/or a self-presentation on the part of the artist that implies a collaboratively generated technological solution or mechanistic goal." Jones argues that while the machine as icon is a widely deployed trope in modernist works of art, the attempt to model one's compositional practices on the machine distinguishes postwar American artists like Stella, Warhol, and Smithson from those that preceded them. "American artists of the 1960s effected a union of the iconic and performative, attempting to offer a kind of sublimity in the both the technological look, and the quasi-industrial production of their art."

8 Ibid., 359.

the life of the professional-managerial class, as well as the realms of leisure and consumption. Increasingly, it was understood to organize emotional life as well.

The second process is what the German sociologist Niklas Luhmann has called the "differentiation of society." By this he means (and here I simplify) the division of society into autonomous subsystems, each of which has its own logic and function: civil society, law, medicine, the economy, art, school, and so on.[9] We might call this development the systematization of the lifeworld, but a systematization that works not according to a single logic but to multiple, system-specific logics. To live in this world requires not only that we learn the internal logic and procedures of multiple systems but that we learn to negotiate among them as well.

A system, Luhmann writes, operates by reducing "infinite to finite information loads." It achieves this through a form of "functional simplification . . . a reduction of complexity that can be constructed and realized even though the world and the society where this takes place is unknown."[10] I propose that we understand the "machine" in both LeWitt and Warhol to refer, among other things, to this moment of "functional simplification." "Systems theory," Luhmann writes, "supplanted the classical model of a whole made out of parts and relations between parts with a model emphasizing the difference between systems and environments."[11] Because a system views everything else—the "environment"—only on the terms relevant to the system, it is monologic. Or, as Deleuze and Guattari have put it, in speaking of corporeal systems: "Doubtless each organ-machine interprets the entire world from the point of view of its own flux, from the point of view of the energy that flows from it: the eye interprets everything—speaking, understanding, shitting, fucking—in terms of seeing."[12] Because the reason for the system's coming into being is precisely to cope with an environment, to simplify it and make it manageable, all systems are always interacting with other ones. By definition, although the system is totalizing and monologic in its own space, it is never singular: "one machine is always coupled with another . . . a connection with another machine is always established, along a transverse path, so that one machine interrupts the current of the other or 'sees' its own current interrupted."[13]

On a societal level, "functional differentiation," Luhmann writes, "leads to a condition in which the genesis of problems and the solution to problems fall asunder. Problems can no longer be solved by the system that produces

9 Luhmann, *The Differentiation of Society*, trans. Stephen Holmes and Charles Larmore (New York: Columbia University Press, 1982).

10 Luhmann, "Modernity in Contemporary Society," in *Observations on Modernity* (Stanford, CA: Stanford University Press, 1998), 1, 6. For one take on Luhmann's theory of modernity, see Fredric Jameson, *A Singular Modernity* (New York: Verso, 2002), 88–94.

11 *Differentiation of Society*, 230.

12 Deleuze and Guattari, *Anti-Oedipus*, 6.

13 Ibid.

them. They have to be transferred to the system that is best equipped and specialized to solve them."[14] Each subsystem has to be ready to deal with problems generated out of its sphere, even though, as we know, they often are not. In any case, life is less and less determined by local contexts, as the local system context—whether art, the family, the city, psychiatry, the school system, or the legal system—is always responding to problems produced elsewhere. While each system has increased "autonomy"—an ability to apply "specific rules and procedures to special problems"—it also has decreased "autarchy," that is, less and less authority outside of its own subsystem, and less of an ability to decide *what* problems it will deal with.[15] The increased autonomy can produce a false sense of confidence in the efficaciousness of its own operations. Modernism could be seen as the recurring moment of misrecognition whereby each system operates as if its autonomy means that it can and should solve the world's problems. Modernist legal theory, economics, international relations (think of the League of Nations), linguistics (the invention of Esperanto), and of course literature and art—all are colored with a such a redemptive strain.

There is a strong tradition wherein art is understood as a space that can redeem, repair, or at least offer a temporary hiding place (for artist and viewer) from a depressing world, from that thing in the world which one wants to escape: capitalism, means-ends rationality, reification, misogyny, homophobia, racism, or another oppressive social force. One critique of the idea of autonomous art has been that it is essentially compensatory, and therefore affirmative of the order of things.[16] That "art develops its own strategies to satisfy needs that originate in other realms of social interaction" was seen as preventing people from trying to actually change these other realms of social interaction.[17] It was against this idea of art as a separate sphere that the historical avant-garde—the Russian futurists, Dada, and surrealism—reacted.[18] The idea was that if you destroyed art, then all those creative energies that were being wasted in the sphere of art would be released into the world. Hence the avant-garde slogan "Art into Life."

As a rejoinder to the avant-gardiste desire to sublate art into life, Luhmann might point out that there are not just two systems, "art" and "life," but multiple systems, and dissolving one opposition does not overthrow the entire aggregate. Indeed, the differentiation of society makes opposition dif-

14 Luhmann, *Differentiation of Society*, 249.

15 Ibid.

16 This is the argument made by Herbert Marcuse in "The Affirmative Character of Culture," in *Negations: Essays in Critical Theory* (Boston: Beacon Press, 1968), 88–133.

17 Jochen Schulte-Sasse, "Afterword: Can the Imagination Be Mimetic under Conditions of Modernity?" in Luiz Costa Lima, *Control of the Imaginary: Reason and Imagination in Modern Times* (Minneapolis: University of Minnesota Press, 1988), 215.

18 The classic formulation of this argument can be found in Peter Bürger, *The Theory of the Avant-garde*, trans. Michael Shaw (Minneapolis: University of Minnesota Press, 1984). The term "historical avant-garde" is Bürger's.

ficult: inasmuch as we are always seeing the world from within a system at any given time, it is impossible to have a total picture of all the systems. This is a major distinction from the whole-parts model of society; here, there is no holistic logic, no unified system organizing the systems. This means that there is inevitably a contradiction between "a phenomenological description of the life of an individual and a more properly structural model of the conditions of existence of that experience" because that overall structural model is impossible to attain.[19] This contradiction between the experience of everyday life and the possibility of describing the transpersonal, historical forces that make that experience possible has become endemic. As such, it constitutes a basic problem for *any* attempt to represent the world. LeWitt and Warhol offer quite different responses to the problem created by this contradiction, but they are both, I argue, preoccupied with it. The attractions of their art as well as the significance of their differences make more sense when we presume that the world structured by what Luhmann calls "functional differentiation" is their context.

It is widely recognized that Warhol's Pop represents a move away from autonomous art.[20] For Warhol, there is not going to be any redemption going on in any one system, art included. Instead, he ceaselessly focuses on moments of interface or connection between systems (the art world, the artist's studio, cinema, advertising, mass culture), to increase his own capacities for affecting and being affected by the world and to show us how we might do so as well. In his art, Warhol reproduces the experience of negotiating between different social systems by setting up the transfer of an object of perception produced by one systemic logic—usually a medium—to another. So, for instance, photographic images are transposed onto a painted canvas by way a technology associated with mass printing in Warhol's silkscreen paintings; a video recording playing on a television monitor is viewed through the medium of 16-millimeter film (in *Outer and Inner Space*); or a series of tape-recorded conversations are typewritten by various volunteers to make *A: A Novel*. My claim is that such "transactions of context" (I. A. Richards's definition of metaphor) produce creative mistranslations that reorient our perception toward similarities and correspondences. Such a reorientation, I have been arguing, is Warhol's principal tactic for getting in the mood to like things.

19 Fredric Jameson, *Postmodernism, or the Cultural Logic of Late Capital* (Durham, NC: Duke University Press, 1990), 410.

20 No one has examined the nature and consequences of Warhol's shift in this regard more intelligently than Benjamin Buchloh, who writes, for instance, "Warhol's work sang the swansong of a fundamental dialectic of the avant-garde in the twentieth century: between an artistic culture with its discursive conventions, genres, and institutional spaces, and the incessantly expanding and encroaching forms of proto-totalitarian consumption. Any such differentiation between the production and perception of an artistic object and an object of industrial consumption could not be maintained any longer (a condition obviously celebrated by Warhol's children, Koons and Murakami)" ("Drawing Blanks," 13). See also his important "Andy Warhol's One-Dimensional Art."

Where Warhol is interested in this moment of system coupling or system interface as a way to produce similarities and stimulate our perception of them, LeWitt is concerned with the nominalistic pleasures of systematicity as such; his systems-based wall drawings and serial works reproduce in an abstracted form the moment of "functional simplification," that "reduction of complexity that can be constructed and realized even though the world and the society where this takes place is unknown."[21] Within the aesthetic experience itself, LeWitt restages the above-mentioned contradiction between everyday experience and a structural model of the conditions of possibility of that experience. This aesthetic experience is characterized by a tension between the visual perception of his work and the cognitive comprehension of the structural concept organizing it. Much (although of course not all) of LeWitt's work dramatizes this difference between *comprehension* and *perception*. LeWitt thereby takes the contradiction produced by autonomous, *competing* systems (that preclude a view of the totality of systems), abstracts it into an aesthetic feeling, and encompasses this feeling itself within a system. In *Variations on Incomplete Open Cubes*, LeWitt duplicates and defamiliarizes the social fact of this contradiction and at the same time shows us what the resolution of this contradiction would feel like, since the total organizing concept is there, even if it is in tension with its own material manifestation. This move takes on additional critical force, I contend, inasmuch as mass culture and the commodity present the world as if everyday life is more or less in harmony with the social order as a whole, as if the particular is always happily made meaningful by the universal. If LeWitt's work interrupts this illusion of harmony between the particular with the general, it has a more utopian side as well, reproducing as an abstract feeling what Luhmann argues is the best we can hope for: to engage imaginatively and creatively with the possibilities of combination between different systems. This is what Luhmann calls "the unity of the imaginary space of [a system's] own combinatory potentials."[22] After all, "and all of its combinations" is one of LeWitt's favorite ways to build a system.

"Liking things is like being a machine"

> Children's play is everywhere permeated by mimetic modes of behavior, and its realm is by no means limited to what one person can imitate in another. The child plays at being not only a shopkeeper or teacher but also a windmill or a train.
>
> **Walter Benjamin**, "Doctrine of the Similar"[23]

Warhol's often-cited statement that he "want[s] to be a machine" has a simplicity of diction that belies the number of symbolic strands and social

21 Luhmann, "Modernity," 6.
22 Ibid., 10.
23 *SW2*, 694.

desires and anxieties it catches up. To begin with (as I suggested above), it provocatively departs from dominant ideologies of artistic imagination, composition, and creativity while appearing to affirm Max Weber's "iron cage" of complete rationalization and to welcome consumer capitalism's replacement of human feeling and imagination with automatic, standardized behaviors and patterns of mind. But more than anything else, Warhol's assertion has been taken to refer to what Branden Joseph calls his "intention to render himself an affectless and uncaring machine."[24] This personal disinclination or incapacity to have feelings or be affected is usually seen to extend to his works, which are thereby understood as illustrations of an effort to achieve emotional distance from the world. But then how do we account for Warhol's observation that *liking* is machine-like? Isn't liking an affect, perhaps even a way of caring in a world where "it would be so much easier not to care"?[25]

In his 1963 interview with Gene Swenson, Warhol clearly associates being a machine with liking and being alike. He follows his assertion that "everybody looks alike and acts alike, and we're getting more and more that way" by stating that "I think everybody should be a machine. I think everybody should like everybody." So, "liking things is like being a machine?" Swenson asks. "Yes," Warhol answers, "because you do the same thing every time. You do it over and over again" (*IBYM*, 16). Warhol elaborates this repetitive quality of liking later in the interview when he says that he painted Campbell's soup cans because "I used to have the same lunch every day, for twenty years, I guess, the same thing over and over again" (18): the seriality of his paintings is an imitation of his repetitive liking.[26] As habitual, repetitive practices of interest and attention, the paintings are themselves a way of "liking things." In this sense, as Swenson remarked, "The paintings and boxes of Warhol *are* feelings, as much as paint in Abstract Expressionist painting is paint."[27]

Warhol's everyday consumption of Campbell's soup appears to be a perfect mirror of its mass production, as if Warhol has shaped his liking to match the ongoing seriality of the assembly line. "I like to be doing the same thing over again," he said in an interview with Edward Lucie-Smith.[28] However, I

24 "The Play of Repetition, Andy Warhol's *Sleep*," *Grey Room*, no. 19 (Spring 2005), 22–53, 31. Although I disagree with Joseph on this point, I find him to be one of Warhol's smartest and most careful readers.

25 Slate, "USA Artists," in *IBYM*, 81; Berg, "True Story," in *IBYM*, 96.

26 In this, Warhol's series of can "portraits" (exhibited at the Ferus Gallery in Los Angeles in 1962) resemble On Kawara's date paintings; like a diary, they affirm his daily, habitual consumption: today, like everyday, I ate a can of Campbell's soup.

27 Flier for the exhibition *The Personality of the Artist*, Stable Gallery (April 21–May 9, 1964), Warhol Archives.

28 Lucie-Smith, "Conversations with Artists," 8. Elsewhere, Warhol underscores this commitment to everyday repetition, while still leaving room for the possibility of surprise: "Either once only, or every day. If you do something once its exciting, and if you do it everyday its exciting. . . . nothing in between is as good as once or everyday" (*Phil*, 166).

do not think that for Warhol the imbrication of liking with mass production and consumption implies that liking is therefore debased, or somehow not a feeling. ("I like everybody, so that's affectionate."[29]) Instead, I think Warhol understands liking, like affect as such, to be *already* essentially machine-like. In its tendency toward automatic or habitual repetitive actions, its independence of operation, its autonomous systemic logic, the complexity of its interlocking parts, and its ability to interface with other machines, "liking things is like being a machine."[30] This may contradict commonsense understandings of affect and emotion as the most human thing about humans, what a robot or android would have the most trouble imitating (like the character Data in *Star Trek: The Next Generation*, for instance). But in his overall understanding of affect as machine-like, Warhol is generally in step with a number of influential twentieth-century theories of affect and feeling, from William James, Pavlov, and Freud forward.[31] In fact, as Mark Seltzer has shown, the mechanical nature of feelings has been a central strand in the modern preoccupation with the logic and erotics of "the body in machine culture."[32]

Warhol's sense of the body and of feelings as mechanical resonated in a different way with then-contemporary research in cybernetics, which saw the human organism as a complex set of interacting systems. This strand of cybernetic thinking influenced the affect theorist Silvan Tomkins, who argued for treating the affects as a "motivation system" or "assembly," one that inevitably interacts ("coassembles") with but is nonetheless distinct from the drives, from the "motoric system," and from perception and memory and other elements of "cognition" such as belief, thought, and choice. Like visual perception or the reasoning mind, Tomkins proposed, the affects constitute a system with their own irreducible internal logic.[33]

29 Lucie-Smith, "Conversations with Artists," 17.

30 Warhol often refers to the human body in mechanical terms, remarking, for instance, that "the machinery is always going. Even when you sleep" (*Phil*, 96). This is a point also highlighted in paintings such as *Where Is Your Rupture* [1] (*CR* no. 002), or *Male Genital Diagram* (*CR* no. 075) that reproduce diagrams of the body.

31 For instance, as I observed above, although it is the death drive (or repetition compulsion) that has gotten the most attention as being repetitive and mechanical, Freud also observes that affective attachment to objects tends toward a mechanical repetition analogous to processes of printing and reprinting. On the brain as a physical machine, see, for instance, William James, *Principles of Psychology* (Cambridge, MA: Harvard University Press, 1983), 19, 143; cited in Mark Seltzer, *Bodies and Machines* (New York: Routledge, 1992), 104. Seltzer's fascinating analysis of what he calls the "body-machine complex" (mainly in late nineteenth- and early twentieth-century American literature) establishes another tradition in which to view Warhol's preoccupation with the machine and his desire for what Seltzer calls "intimacy with machines."

32 *Bodies and Machines*, 21.

33 For an overview of Tomkins's theory, see his "What Are Affects," in Sedgwick and Frank, *Shame and Its Sisters*, 33–74, and, in the same volume, Sedgwick and Frank's "Shame in the Cybernetic Fold: Reading Silvan Tomkins." Also see Tomkins, "The Quest for Primary Motives: Biography and Autobiography of an Idea," in *Exploring Affect: The*

As a system with its own operating procedures, affect is predictably susceptible to manipulation by any number of forces, such as advertising, amphetamines, or aesthetic activity. And liking, as the most basic of affective responses, involving an elemental attraction toward a stimulus, may be especially susceptible. As experiments by Robert Zajonc and other psychologists have shown, "mere exposure," even beneath the level of conscious recognition, is enough to substantially affect our liking, increasing our willingness to approach (rather than avoid) and pay attention to something.[34] Warhol sought to use whatever tricks he could to position his machine of liking, what Jonathan Haidt called the "like-o-meter," at its highest possible setting.[35] In this sense, Warhol's imitation of the machine was not at all an effort to *escape* from feeling or to be uncaring. Instead, it was an attempt to increase his capacity for liking, and thereby to exert agency over feelings he may have sometimes wanted to avoid but knew he could not.[36] If advertising and mass culture can manipulate us into liking or not liking things, Warhol seems to be saying, why can't we influence our own liking?

Above all, for Warhol (as I have been arguing), "being a machine" represented an attempt to manipulate his like-o-meter by stimulating what Benjamin called the mimetic faculty (the human capacity for perceiving and producing similarities as distinct from identities or samenesses), which has its own affinity for the machine.[37] For Benjamin, the child's imitation of machines like windmills and trains indicates mimetic vitality; children are willing to imitate anything, across differences later policed, with little respect for what constitutes a proper or improper object of imitation.[38] In fact,

Selected Writings of Silvan S. Tomkins, ed. E. Virginia Demos, 27–63 (Cambridge: Cambridge University Press, 1995). Rosalind Picard's lucid *Affective Computing* (Cambridge, MA: MIT Press, 1997) examines the attempt to theorize and create computers with affects.

34 Zajonc, "Feeling and Thinking." Based on experimental evidence, Zajonc makes a strong case for the primacy and basicness of affect, arguing that "affective reactions to a stimulus may be acquired by virtue of experience with that stimulus even if not accompanied by such an elementary cold cognitive process as conscious recognition" (163).

35 Haidt, *Happiness Hypothesis*, 26–27.

36 This exchange with Lucie-Smith ("Conversations with Artists," 15) seems particularly telling:

ELS: Do you believe in feelings and emotions?
AW: Um, well no I don't, but I have them. I wish . . . I wish I didn't.
ELS: What you'd like to get rid of them altogether would you?
AW: er . . . it would be a good idea, yea
ELS: why, do you think you'd be happier? But happiness is a feeling, too, isn't it?
AW: er, well, no just . . . just you know, just a feeling of doing the right . . . you know, just getting by.

37 See my discussion of mimetic faculty in the introduction.

38 This receptivity is realized in multiple ways. Summarizing Benjamin, Miriam Hansen writes that children "practice an inventive reception of this world of things in their modes of collecting and organizing objects, in particular discarded ones, thus producing a host

children's mimetic impulses may be drawn to the repetitive motions of machines (the rhythm of a train's chugga-chugga-choo-choo or the windmill's spinning) inasmuch as mimetic behavior is itself machine-like, in "repeating" a model by forming its behavior in relation to it but also in its automatic and autonomic operation.

Indeed, it has long been observed that children seem to be propelled by an automatic, involuntary compulsion to be-like.[39] This is why Plato worried about poetry in *The Republic* (that foundational expression of anxieties about mimesis): children cannot help imitating what they perceive. Socrates describes the child as a malleable "thing" that "assimilates itself to the model whose stamp anyone wishes to give to it."[40] While children are presented here as tender and "plastic," the metaphor of assimilation suggests that they are not merely passive; they are *ready*, even driven, to liken themselves, and this is what makes them so moldable.[41] Children are imitation machines. While this tendency to be shaped and changed by imitation is most intense for children, Socrates worries that the tendency persists into adulthood, where the irresistibly mimetic quality of reading may lead even the virtuous man into improper practices of self-likening. To read Achilles's grief-filled speech in *The Iliad* entails "acting like" (*homoia poiein*) Achilles in grief.[42] And when we engage in these imaginative acts, Socrates asserts, we "get a taste for the being from its imitation," and such tastes can lead to habits of being, especially if they are repeated.[43] Mimesis, in this understanding, involves an ontological openness: at the moment of imitating something or

---

of bewildering and hidden correspondences, tropes of creative miscognition" (*Cinema and Experience*, 150).

39 See Seltzer on children as machine-like workers, especially his reading of Jack London's story "The Apostate," originally subtitled "A Parable of Child Labor" (*Bodies and Machines*, 13–17).

40 *The Republic of Plato*, trans. Allan Bloom (New York: Basic Books, 1968), 54 (377a). The full quote: "Don't you know that the beginning is the most important part of every work and that this is especially so with anything young and tender? For at that stage it's most plastic, and each thing assimilates itself to the model whose stamp anyone wishes to give to it." What is translated here as "model" is the Greek *tupoi*, which may also translated as "mold" or "image." On this passage and on model as *tupoi*, see Stephen Halliwell, *Aesthetics of Mimesis* (Princeton, NJ: Princeton University Press, 2002), 51–53.

41 This metaphor is also used at *Republic*, 396d–e.

42 Ibid., 2.377e–378a. In an environment such as Plato's, where, as Stephen Halliwell notes, reading aloud and reciting poetry were the norm, reading does "effectively make the 'reader' into a kind of performer." Indeed, for Plato, "reading dramatic poetry is always a kind of dramatic acting" (Halliwell, *Aesthetics of Mimesis*, 51–53). Plato does not seem to limit his mimetic understanding of reading to actual performances, though they remain a key point of reference.

43 "Don't you know," he warns, that "imitations, if they are practiced continually from youth onwards, become established as habits and nature, in body and sounds and in thought" (*Republic*, 395c).

someone else, one actually becomes someone else. And because acting like somebody else is how we get to be who we are, and since the ideal republic needs the right kinds of subjects for the different roles in a polis structured by a strict division of labor, mimesis must be tightly controlled. Plato thus offers an early articulation of a deep-seated anxiety about mimetic comportment and its ungovernability, one that led to a taboo on "uncontrolled mimesis" that Adorno and Horkheimer argue is foundational for Western "civilization" as such.[44]

Like Plato, both Benjamin and Warhol see mimetic perception and behavior as a basic mode of apprehension of and interaction with the world, one especially fundamental to aesthetic experience, with directly subject-shaping and hence political consequences. But, in contrast to Plato, Benjamin and Warhol make the case for *more* mimetic behavior, which would be less policed and less subject to means-ends rationality, as a way to facilitate an empowering, collectively experienced, childlike affective receptivity and engagement with the world. Like Benjamin, Warhol sees new modes of mass production, and technological reproduction in particular, as resources for lubricating the mimetic machine; they both "envision a regeneration of affect by means of mechanically produced images."[45] Like Plato, Benjamin and Warhol understand that mimetic processes beget mimetic behaviors.[46] Warhol sought to replicate such processes in his works in several different ways, first of all in his painting.

Indeed, it is worth emphasizing that Warhol's painting practice (and not his personal emotional life) was the primary context for his assertion that he wanted to be a machine. Asked by Swenson if he aims to "turn art history upside down" with his silkscreen technique, Warhol replies, "No. The reason I'm painting this way is that I want to be a machine, and I feel that

44 In *Dialectic of Enlightenment* (ed. Gunzelin Schmid Noerr, trans. Edmund Jephcott [Stanford, CA: Stanford University Press, 2002]) they write, "Civilization replaced the organic adaptation to otherness, mimetic behavior proper, firstly, in the magical phase, with the organized manipulation of mimesis, and finally, in the historical phase, with rational praxis, work. Uncontrolled mimesis is proscribed. . . . Those blinded by civilization have contact with their own tabooed mimetic traits only through certain gestures and forms of behavior they encounter in others, as isolated, shameful residues in their rationalized environment. What repels them as alien is all too familiar" (148–49). On the mimetic in Adorno and Horkheimer, see Joseph Litvak, *The Un-Americans: Jews, The Blacklist and Stoolpigeon Culture* (Durham, NC: Duke University Press, 2009), and Shierry Weber Nicholson, *Exact Imagination, Late Work: On Adorno's Aesthetics* (Cambridge, MA: MIT Press, 1999).

45 Miriam Hansen writes that Benjamin sees "the possibility of countering the alienation of the human sensorium with the same means and media that are part of the technological proliferation of shock anaesthetics-aestheticization" (*Cinema and Experience*, 153). I discuss this point in the introduction.

46 Which is why, as I noted earlier, Benjamin argues that mimetic behavior is stimulated "less by demonstrating found similarities than by replicating the processes which generate such similarities" (*SW2*, 694).

whatever I do and do machine-like is what I want to do." Warhol explains in *POPism* that he started silkscreening late in 1962 because "the rubber-stamp method I'd been using to repeat images suddenly seemed too home-made." By contrast, "with silkscreening, you pick a photograph, blow it up, transfer it in glue onto silk, and then roll ink across it so the ink goes through the silk but not through the glue. That way you get the same image, slightly different, each time. It was all so simple—quick and chancy. I was thrilled with it" (*POP*, 22). The silkscreens allowed Warhol to print an image based on a photographic model "over and over," while eliminating ("homemade") traces of the author's hand. Moreover, by painting with silkscreens, Warhol replaced what had been thought of as a quintessential product of the human hand with an impersonal, autonomous mechanism that in principle could be used by anybody. "I think it would be so great," Warhol said, "if more people took up silk screens so that no one would know whether my picture was mine or somebody else's" (*IBYM*, 17). Mechanical and anonymous, capable of quantity and repetition: in these ways, the silkscreen method achieved the "assembly line effect" Warhol wanted.

As I noted in the introduction, perhaps the most important element of this effect, however, was similarity as such. Unlike the rubber stamps, stencils, and tracings Warhol used in his earliest Pop paintings, the the messier silkscreen process produced "mistakes," images that were noticeably non-identical. Warhol emphasized this "slightly different" similar, especially in the paintings he made right after he started using the screens, such as the "heads" of stars like Natalie Wood, Troy Donahue, Warren Beatty, and Marilyn Monroe.[47] In some of his earliest pop paintings from 1961 (such as *Make Him Want You*, *Little King*, *Nancy*, *Storm Door*, and *$199 Television*), Warhol had produced messiness with drips, areas of hand-painted or drawn canvas. As he moved to using stencils and stamps in order to produce serial images, as with the Campbell's Soup Cans, the paintings become cleaner (see figure 0.2). The turn to silkscreens then allowed him to print from the same model over and over, and at the same time to produce a mechanical, apparently nonintentional, noncomposed "chancy" variation, as a by-product of the silkscreening process itself. This was especially true if the screening was done quickly, which might lead to leftover ink caking on the bottom of the screens, irregular seepage through the screens, or screens placed imprecisely and inconsistently on the canvas. In this way, the silkscreens were a machine for producing likenesses whose form announced their affiliation with the machine, a pedagogical reminder of the machine's capacity for producing similarity.

Before Warhol found the silkscreen technique, one can see him searching

47 "My first experiments with screens were heads of Troy Donahue and Warren Beatty, and then when Marilyn Monroe happened to die that month, I got the idea to make screens of her beautiful face—the first Marilyns" (*POP*, 22).

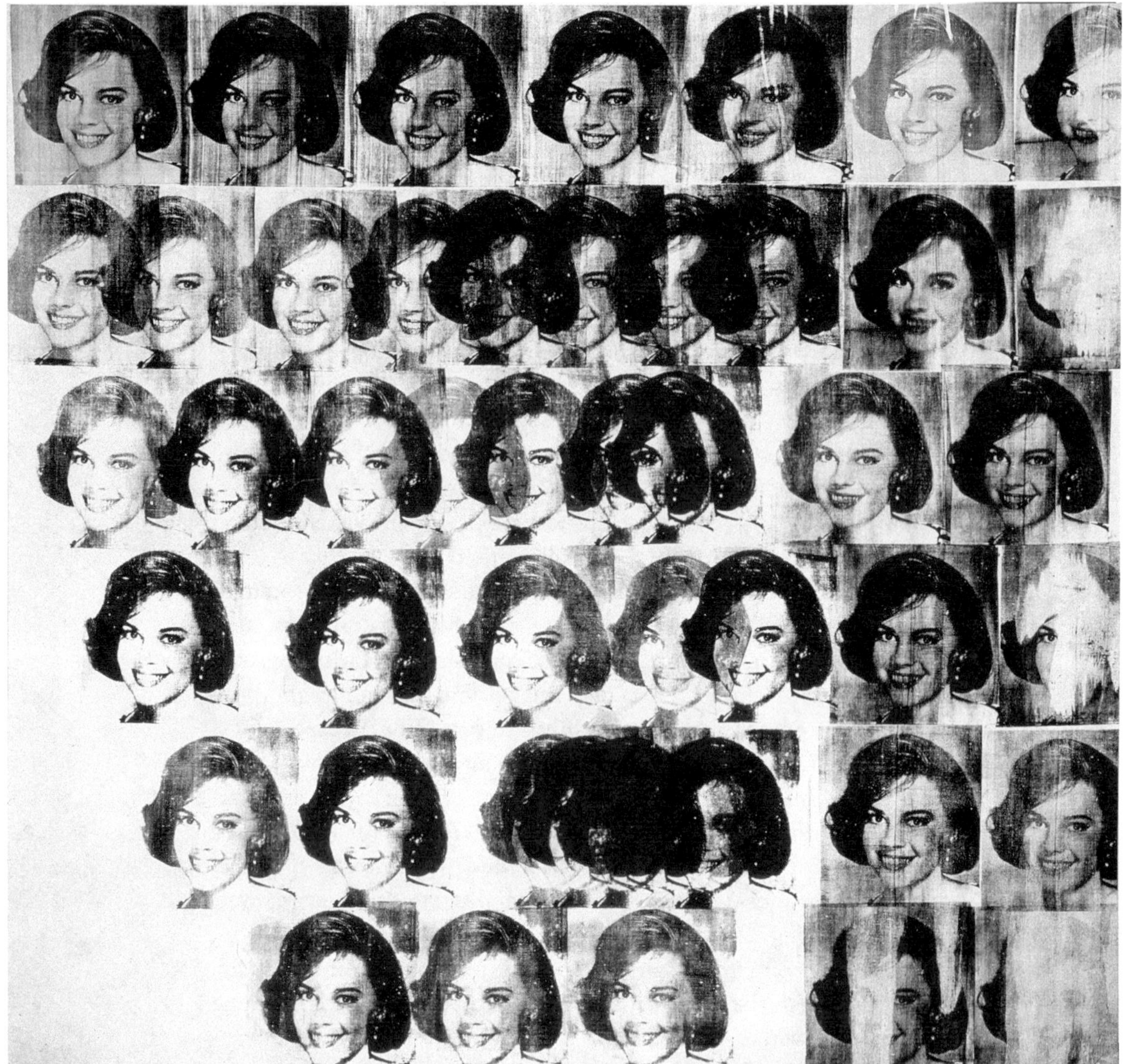

2.1 Andy Warhol, *Natalie Wood*, 1962. Silkscreen ink on linen, 83 × 89⅛ inches. © 2016 Andy Warhol Foundation for the Visual Arts/Artists Rights Society (ARS), New York.

for ways to paint more like a machine. Some of his pre-silkscreen paintings, such as the Dance Diagram and Do It Yourself paintings—two series from 1962 that appropriate mass-produced instructions for "creative" activity—seem to have that search as their topic; as such, they serve as apt allegories for his efforts to imitate the machine more generally. The seven Dance Diagram paintings appropriate diagrams (from two books published by the Dance Guild in 1956) that offer to teach readers ballroom dances such as the Fox Trot, Lindy, and Charleston by mapping out a sequence of steps using gendered Left and Right shoe markings. Warhol enlarged the diagrams by

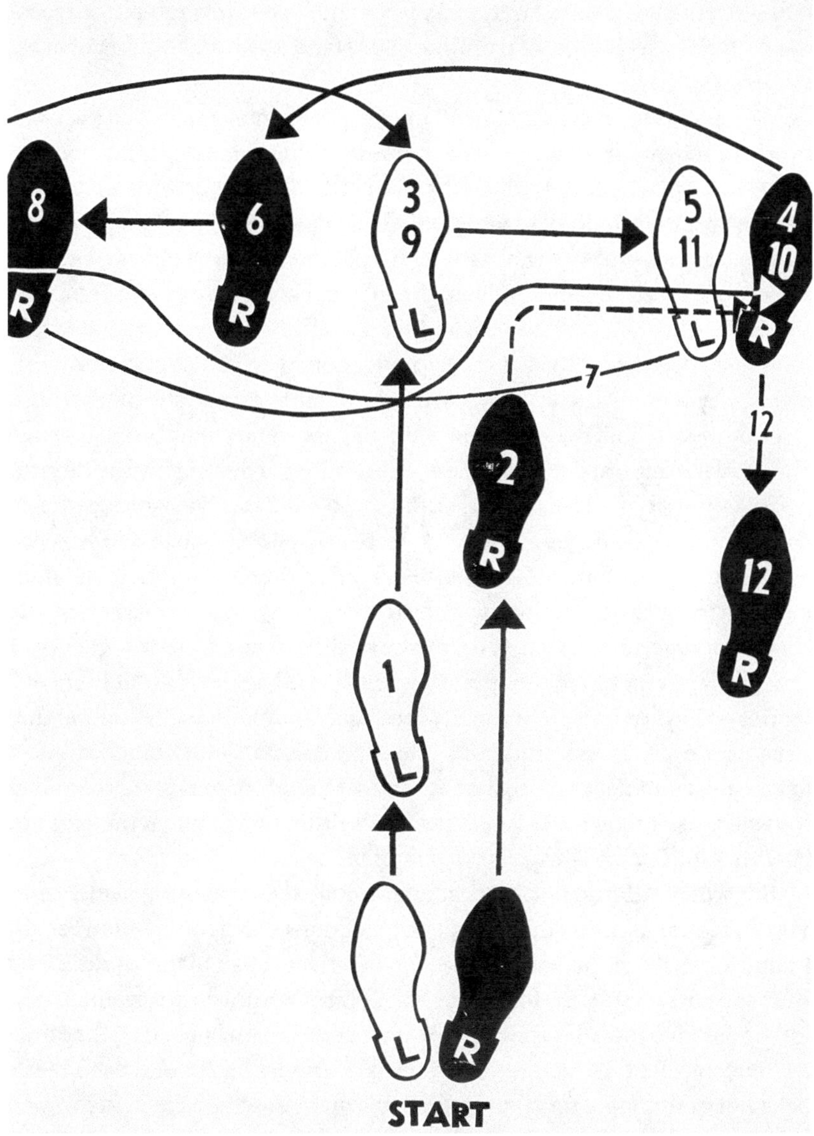

2.2 Andy Warhol, *Dance Diagram* [2] (*Fox Trot: "The Double Twinkle–Man"*), 1962. Casein and pencil on linen, 71½ × 51¾ inches. © 2016 Andy Warhol Foundation for the Visual Arts/Artists Rights Society (ARS), New York.

projecting them from an opaque projector onto a canvas.[48] The paintings were displayed horizontally on low platforms just off the floor, directly inviting viewers to imagine moving their feet through the charted steps. As Ro-

48 According to Neil Printz, the images were first traced in pencil (which is still visible in one work, cat.72, *Fox Trot: "The Right Turn–Man"*), then painted, with the help of pencil outlines and masking tape (still present on that same painting). *CR1*, 78.

salind Krauss has pointed out, this placement also subtly referenced Jackson Pollock's preference for painting while standing on and leaning over his canvases.[49]

By conjoining an activity linked to pleasurable movement and sociability with a schematized, mechanical mimesis, these paintings recall the Taylorist rationalization and schematization of bodily movements that made standardized assembly-line labor possible. What is usually thought of as a passionate, expressive, social activity has, in the Dance Diagrams, become a mass-produced scheme. Indeed, the dance diagrams *seem* to offer a paradigmatic illustration of Adorno and Horkheimer's observation that in late capitalism "entertainment is the prolongation of work." While entertainment, they write, "is sought by those who want to escape the mechanized labor process so that they can cope with it again . . . mechanization has such power over leisure and its happiness, determines so thoroughly the fabrication of entertainment commodities, that the off-duty worker can experience nothing but after-images of the work process itself." So habituated have we become to the "automated sequence of standardized tasks" that any non-mechanized activity is too demanding to be relaxing. In such a situation, the content of entertainment is less important than its machine-like quality of standardized repetition; the spectator "must need no thoughts of his own." Work and leisure come to mutually reinforce the automatic repetition that structures each. In this situation, "pleasure congeals into boredom since, to be amusement, it must cost no effort and therefore moves strictly along the well-worn grooves of association."[50] Neither independent thought nor idiosyncratic feeling is anywhere promoted.

But where Adorno and Horkheimer might see depressing evidence of the total rationalization of life in dance diagrams or a paint-by-number kit, I think Warhol sees new ways of being affectively open to the world. To be sure, such preset systems for the organization of leisure do not promote critical or creative thought; they openly encourage a mechanical (rather than an "uncontrolled") imitation. But I think Warhol, like Plato, sees mimetic behavior as fundamentally uncontrollable and unpredictable in the ways it affects and alters people—which is precisely why Socrates argued for banning it from the ideal republic.

In Plato, the prohibition of uncontrolled mimesis corresponds to a

49 "The tacky image of the middle-aged rake trying to learn the rumba from the Arthur Murray instructor in a mass-cultural fantasy of Everyman his own Fred Astaire rises from these schematic renderings of dance steps lifted from the ads carried by supermarket magazines. But as footprint finds its way to canvas, its new context carries other resonances, and we seem to hear Pollock's famously defiant, 'I'd rather stand on my painting,' the possible double meaning of which *Time* magazine rushed to exploit in its well publicized sneer at Pollock's technique: 'All it says, in effect, is that Jack the Dripper, 44, still stands on his work'" (Krauss, *Optical Unconscious*, 275).

50 Horkheimer and Adorno, *Dialectic of Enlightenment*, 109.

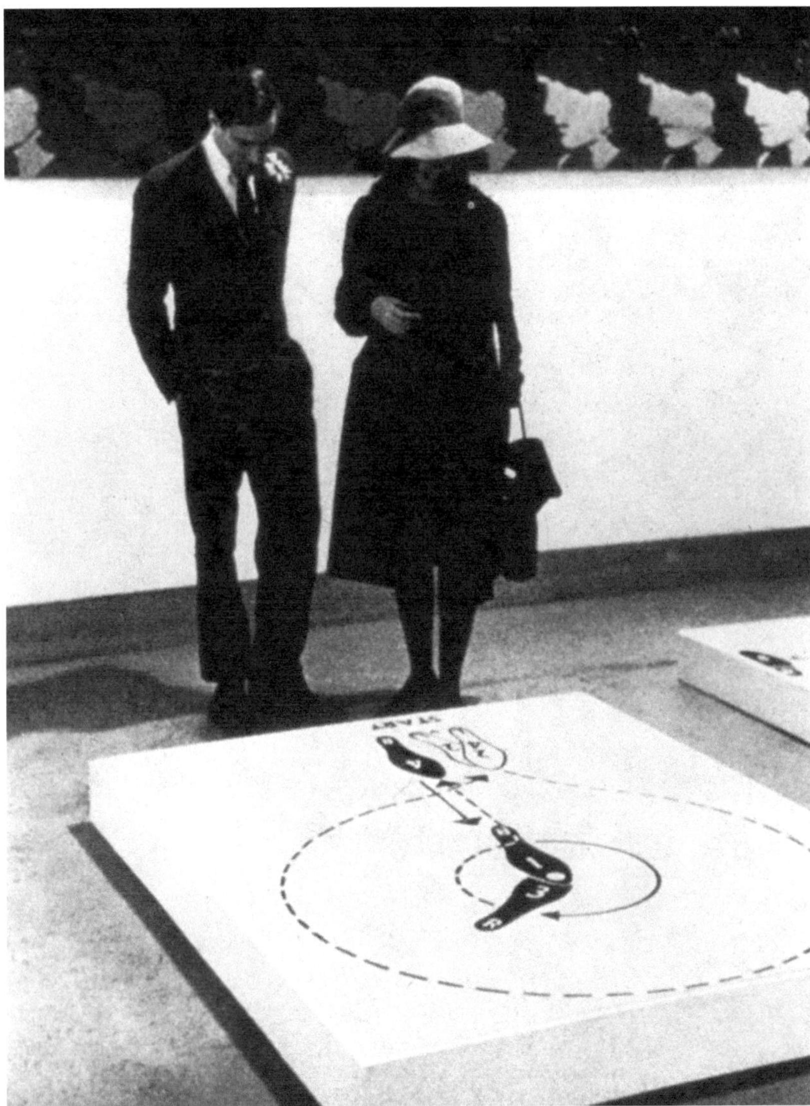

2.3 *The Atmosphere of '64*, installation view, Institute of Contemporary Art, University of Pennsylvania, April 17–June 1, 1964.

prioritization of reasoned thought. Like Plato, Warhol saw "thinking" and mimetic openness as competing forces, and thus he sought to calm or distract the "thinking" mind. The "consciousness," which (as Benjamin argued) may keep potentially disruptive or traumatic experiences at bay (while also controlling mimetic comportment), may make it difficult to "get lost" in things like sex or love:

> The best love is not-to-think-about-it love. Some people can have sex and really let their minds go blank and fill up with the sex; other people can never

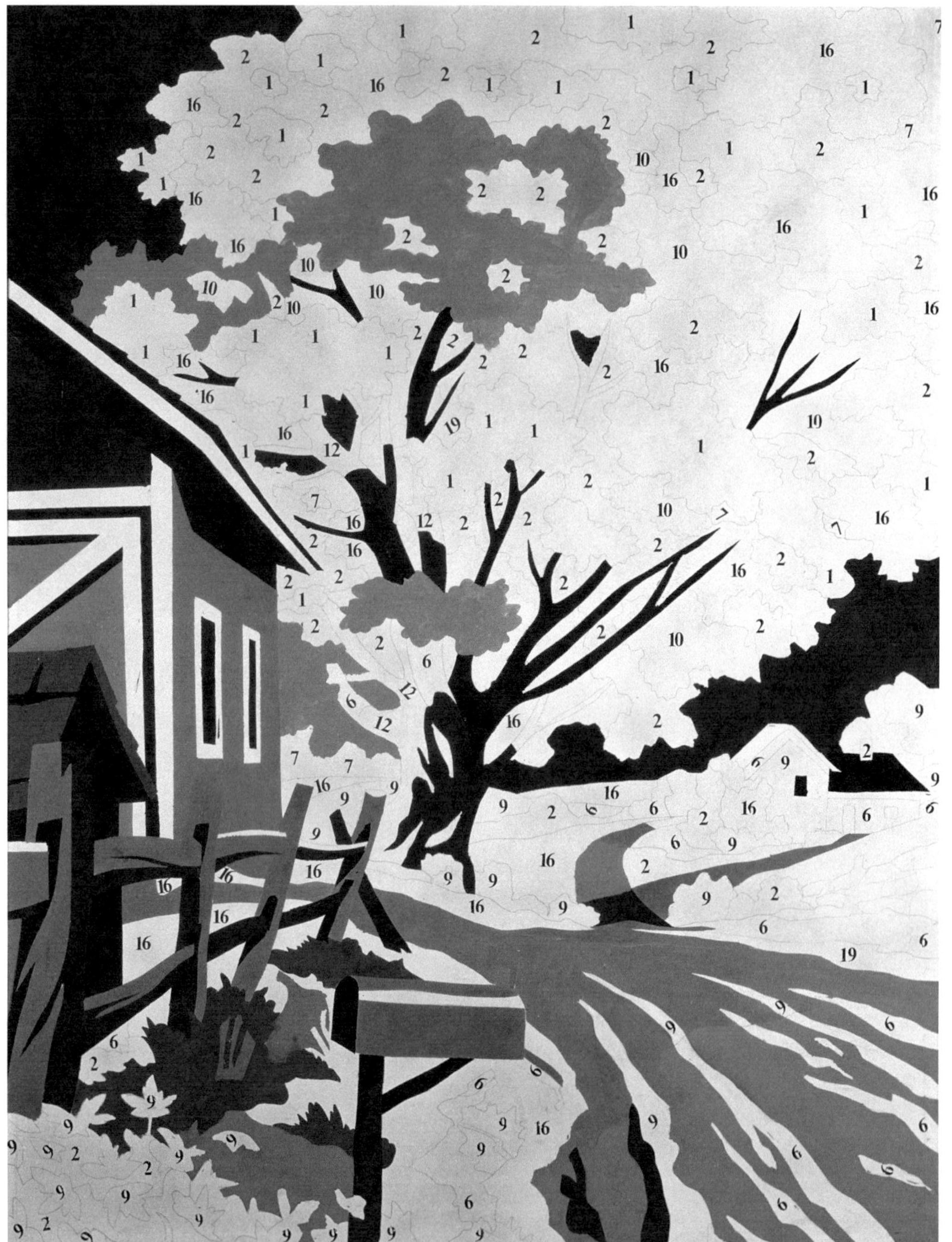

2.4 Andy Warhol, *Do It Yourself (Landscape)*, 1962. Acrylic, pencil, and Letraset on linen, 69¾ × 54⅛ inches. © 2016 Andy Warhol Foundation for the Visual Arts/Artists Rights Society (ARS), New York.

> let their minds go blank and fill up with the sex, so while they're having the sex, they're thinking, "Can this really be me? Am I really doing this? This is very strange. Five minutes ago I wasn't doing this. In a little while I won't be doing it. What would mom say? How did people ever think of doing this? So the first type of person—the type that can let their mind go blank and fill up with sex and not-think-about-it—is better off. The other type has to find something else to relax with and get lost in. (*Phil*, 48–49)

Being able "not-to-think-about-it" does not imply an absence of affect so much as a state of relaxation, receptivity, and openness, the condition of possibility for enjoyment. Thus, when Warhol writes that "the more you look at the same exact thing, the more the meaning goes away, and the better and emptier you feel" (*POP*, 50), I think he is referring not to the negation of feeling (as is sometimes assumed) but to the way the absence of meaning quiets the thinking, choosing, remembering, judging mind.[51] Feeling "emptier" is also feeling "better" because it means that one can be "filled up" with things like sex, love, talking, dancing, or painting.[52] If, as Deleuze (explaining Spinoza) put it, "what a body can do corresponds to the nature and limits of its power to be affected," then this power (as Michael Hardt wrote) "in turn depends on the qualities of the affects that 'fill' it."[53] Warhol's aesthetic practices were centrally concerned with finding something to "relax with" so that he could be "filled up" by the right affects.

So when Warhol says he wants to be a machine, one thing he aspires to is the avoidance of choice and thinking (though not the avoidance of work) in his painting practice, precisely as a way to be more receptive, to paint what he likes and like what he paints. "When I have to think about it, I know the picture is wrong," he wrote. "My instinct about painting says, 'If you don't think about it, its right.' As soon as you have to decide and choose, it's wrong. And the more you decide about, the more wrong it gets" (*Phil*, 149). Thus, Warhol used images that were already on his mind (and better yet, on everybody's mind), things he already liked, whether because of daily habit (Campbell's Soup Cans) or media exposure (Marilyns, Tunafish Disaster, Race Riots, Jackies). Sometimes he avoided choosing and thinking by asking other people what to paint (Dollar Bills).[54] Painting on commission was another tactic for liking without deciding.[55] Of course, *this* liking entails the fee

51 In another interview from the fall of 1963, Warhol says that people who come to see Pop exhibitions "don't have to think." They "just sort of see the things and they like them and they understand them easier" (*IBYM*, 32).

52 See discussion of the tape recorder as Warhol's wife in chapter 1.

53 Deleuze, "What a Body Can Do," in *Expressionism in Philosophy: Spinoza*; 218; Hardt, "Power to Be Affected," 217.

54 "I was never embarrassed about asking someone, literally, 'What should I paint?' because Pop comes from the outside, and how is asking someone for ideas any different from looking for them in a magazine?" (*POP*, 16).

55 When Lucie-Smith asked him how he chose who to paint, Warhol answered, "I paint anybody. Anybody that asks me. . . . that's the only way. Well, I like it. I like everybody. So

required to commission the portrait. But as with the *Village Voice* classified ad he took out in 1966 offering to "endorse with my name any of the following: clothing, AC-DC, cigarettes, small tapes, sound equipment, ROCK 'N' ROLL RECORDS, anything, film, and film equipment, Food, Helium, Whips, MONEY," so too with his commissioned portraits—Warhol is not himself involved in thinking or choosing what to paint. Someone else tells him what to like and pays him for the service. His like-o-meter set on high, Warhol is ready to like anything or anybody.

In their representation of instructions that one could follow without thinking or choosing, that one could "get lost in," the Dance Diagram and Do It Yourself paintings present models for Warhol's aesthetic practices more generally (which may be one reason he exhibited them frequently in the early 1960s). The Dance Diagrams, in particular, seem to offer a lesson in the advantages of machine-like imitation for increasing one's capacity for liking, first of all because the diagrams make use of the body's ability to move automatically according to a preset system, not to enable efficient wage labor but to teach a paradigmatically social activity, oriented toward connecting and corresponding with others. Furthermore, although the diagrams are themselves standardized, this does not mean that the mimetic comportment they promote will be uniform, controlled, or predictable. Learning to dance changes what the body can do, altering its capacity for affecting and being affected.[56] Who knows how one's habitus will be shifted and what forms of affiliation will become newly possible by adding the "double twinkle" step of the Fox Trot to one's bodily skill set?

Not only do the dance diagrams offer to change one's capacity for affecting and being affected, giving one access to new modes of social engagement, they do so by way of experiences and feelings that are themselves shared. In their "commonist" offer to teach anyone to dance, the dance diagrams literalize widely experienced modes of attachment to mass culture: they appeal to the fan who wants to "look and act like" the stars. We know that Warhol was one such fan (and thus unlikely to look down on the

---

I don't really . . . decide, you know, whether I like them or not. I really like everybody" ("Conversations with Artists," 1).

56 In fact, a given system or rules provides an occasion for us to attend with particular attention to "mistakes" or "variations." Just as the semantic structures of language allow affective intensity to enter at the level of enunciation, glottal pressure, or rhythm, or the givenness of letter forms allows handwriting's particularities to communicate particular vitalities and idiosyncrasies, so too the choreographic syntax of a given dance provides a structure within which particular variations can stand out. The oomph added to a particular thrust of the hips, the extra bounce added to a jump, the particular shape given to the sway of the shoulders—these signify precisely inasmuch as they add something extra to a given scheme. As such, they may also function as points of affective engagement and communication. On dance, habitus, affect, and "kinesthetic sensation," I learned a lot from Carrie Noland's brilliant *Agency and Embodiment: Performing Gestures/Producing Culture* (Cambridge, MA: Harvard University Press, 2009).

diagrams as "tacky" or "kitsch," as some critics have suggested.[57]) For instance, Warhol said (probably referring to his childhood admiration for Shirley Temple), "I never wanted to be a painter; I wanted to be a tap dancer" (*IBYM*, 89).[58] In fact, his Dance Diagrams might have shared their title with a painting he made in 1948 called *I Like Dance*, which was, as Douglas Crimp points out, one stop on a fairly constant and long-standing affection for and artistic interest in dance and dancers.[59] It need hardly be added that during this period (1940s to 1960s), as Gavin Butt notes, the attachment to dance and to dancing was especially widely shared among boys and men who were or would become identified as "homosexual."[60] Thus, as Butt writes, "in some respects one might say that via *Dance Diagram*, Warhol metaphorically steps into Pollock's shoes, and in the process he replaces the action painters solemn dance around his prone canvas with the mincing clumsy footwork of the Hollywood obsessed sissy-boy."[61] That is, in referring to the desire to learn to dance like a star, the Dance Diagrams not only invoke a widely shared mimetic attachment to mass culture, but a particularly queer one. They represent—and invite viewers to join—a group of what Butt calls "queer dancer types."

Fans' shared imitation of the same set of stars produces a world where "everybody looks alike and acts alike," itself the condition of possibility for Warhol's optimistic call for everybody to like everybody.[62] Thus, for Warhol, *contra* Adorno and Horkheimer (and many of Warhol's critics), mechanized, repetitive mass culture was compelling not as a degraded mode of experience that had to be redeemed, but as an underappreciated source of common feeling and shared mimetic experience, precisely inasmuch as it pro-

57 Krauss, recall, sees in the diagrams the "tacky image of the middle-aged rake trying to learn the rumba from the Arthur Murray instructor" (*Optical Unconscious*, 275), which she and Yve-Alain Bois call "kitsch content" that was referenced but transformed in Warhol's painting of it. Bois and Krauss, *Formless: A User's Guide* (New York: Zone Books, 1997), 102.

58 Along with Shirley Temple (whose tap dancing he admired), Warhol made efforts to be like Truman Capote, Edie Sedgwick, and Diana Vreeland (whom he called "the most copied woman in the world"), among others. See *Exposures*, where he writes, "I love Diana Vreeland because she's the most copied woman in the world. She's like a Campbell's soup can. Everywhere I go I see people who look like Diana Vreeland" (63). On Warhol's imitation of Capote, see Printz, "Other Voices Other Rooms."

59 See Crimp, *Our Kind of Movie*, 112–13, for a brief survey of Warhol's interest in dance, which included his membership in the mostly female dance club while he was at Carnegie Tech, numerous drawings of dancers, Screen Tests of dancers such as Lucinda Childs and Freddy Herko, and his film of Paul Swan, the subject of Crimp's beautiful "Most Beautiful" chapter.

60 "The dancer—along with certain other professional figures such as actors, hairdressers, and window dressers—were readily suggestive of male homosexuality" (Butt, *Between You and Me*, 121).

61 Ibid., 122.

62 *IBYM*, 16–20. On stardom and imitation see introduction and chapter 4.

vided standardized objects of affective attachment and imitation. ("Think of all the James Deans and what it means.") Precisely *because* they are standardized the dance diagrams can be shared, and their commonality—the fact that others are also learning the same dance, for similar reasons—is, in turn, an essential element of their appeal. They present a way to "relax with" others.

Whether one is learning from a diagram, a teacher, or the silver screen, mastering a complex ballroom dance involves a series of repeated efforts at copying a model, with inevitable mistakes along the way. In their repeated but distinct copies of a model, Warhol's celebrity silkscreens seem to document such an effort, especially when he is painting people who performed famous dances, like Natalie Wood, fresh off her singing-and-dancing star turn as Maria in the film version of *West Side Story* ("I feel pretty and witty and gay"). The varied, unevenly printed faces scattered across the canvas, with a tight cluster of overlaid images near the middle of the canvas's bottom, suggests a basic inconsistency across the varied attempts to imitate the star model, offering an object lesson in the collective, but also singular (and similar), quality of each act of imitation.[63]

The irregularity of the images also suggests that even when the looks and moves of stars have been incorporated at the level of habit, we do not become the stars we imitate. Indeed we imitate them "over and over" precisely inasmuch as we are not them. Mimesis may involve becoming something else, as Plato worried, but that something else is distinct from the model one imitates. As Warhol notes in his discussion of "all the James Deans," our fandom (indeed our very subjectivity) is constituted by a melancholic imitation of what we did not get and cannot be.[64] But such mimetic failures, of constant interest to Warhol (from the good "bad actors" he promoted to "all the miserable people in the world who just can't fit into stock roles"), are successful insofar as they also make all us imitators alike. And like the sometimes lighter, sometimes darker, sometimes obscure and layered images of Wood in Warhol's painting, we become alike as imitators not just in the way we do manage to look like our models ("all the James Deans," all the Marilyns, and so on), but inasmuch as we fail to be them. Like the varied likenesses of stars sharing the spaces of Warhol's canvases, we are not alone in our aspirational, inconsistent copying.

Taking Advantage of Static

Like his serial celebrity silkscreens, the Dance Diagram and Do It Yourself paintings point toward the unpredictability inherent in any mimetic act,

63 Representing a different register of celebrity, and a different kind of dancing, Warhol's 1962 paintings of Merce Cunningham in a series of poses from his dance *Antic Meet* remind viewers of the repetition involved in professional performance too.
64 See introduction.

the way that even the most schematic copying (as in the paint-by-numbers kits Warhol replicates and paints in the latter series) produces idiosyncratic "mistakes." We all know that different people following a given paint-by-number scheme will not produce identical paintings; not only will basic formal characteristics like brushstrokes and paint density be different from painting to painting, but one might paint outside the lines, use differently "wrong" colors, or fail to color in all the spaces.[65] These paintings, like the Dance Diagrams, draw our attention to the fact that the particularities and tendencies of different bodies and their mimetic capabilities mean that even when based on the same scheme or model, each imitation (even from the "same" body at different moments) will be distinct, altering the model in its own specific way.

On a basic level, mimetic acts change what they imitate because they involve mediation. Imitation involves translating some information from one medium into another. Whether it is the human voice or body, ink printed on paper, paint on canvas, the telephone, TV, a window, or celluloid or magnetic tape, each medium has its own systemic logic, its own way of "letting in" information and processing it. As Friedrich Kittler notes, "To transfer messages from one medium to another always involves reshaping them to conform to new standards and materials."[66] Yet, at the same time, as Marshall McLuhan put it, "All media are active metaphors in their power to translate experience into new forms."[67] Like metaphors, translations from one medium to another articulate similarities across shifts in material, context, and system.

So even as a work such as Dance Diagrams directs our attention to the mediated unpredictability of mimetic acts, it also highlights the mimetic *skill* involved in translating from one medium (the arrows and footprints and dotted lines of the diagram) into another (the kinesthetic lexicon of the moving body). Try it yourself; it takes a minute to read the diagram and figure out how to move your feet to correspond to the "L" and "R" feet on the canvas.[68] This interface between media and the senses (from seeing the printed diagram to moving one's body) tests and exercises one's "gift for producing similarities," which is, after all, one of dance's "oldest functions," as Walter Benjamin notes (*SW2*, 720). In dance, a body might correspond

65 In *Do It Yourself (Seascape)* (*CR* no. 195), Warhol responds to the paint-by-numbers directions by *over*-imitating, copying the whole scheme, including the numbers to paint-by, which are painted over the filled-in colors. He thereby openly and excessively embraces the machine-like quality of the exercise, while suggesting that once initiated, mimetic behavior may not know where to stop.

66 Kittler, *Discourse Networks 1800/1900* (Stanford, CA: Stanford University Press, 1990), 265.

67 McLuhan, *Understanding Media* (1964; Cambridge: MIT Press, 1994), 57.

68 See, for instance, the photographs on the Whitney Museum website of schoolteachers learning to dance the Fox Trot from one of the diagrams. http://whitney.org/Education/EducationBlog/DoingTheFoxTrot (accessed July 31, 2015).

its movement to the rhythm and intensity of music, the movements of other bodies, or things less obviously like a body, such as jewels or a season. Such nonobvious imitations, ones that may cross between senses or media, involve what Benjamin calls "nonsensuous" similarities (which he also saw, for instance, in astrology's perception of a similarity between a moment of birth and the constellation of the stars). By moving across a gap that necessarily alters what is being mimed, such mimetic acts also emphasize the power of the human capacity to perceive and produce similarities.

Such an emphasis may be particularly attractive and valuable because the perception of such similarities is essential to the sharing of affective states by way of "affect attunement." Infant psychologist Daniel Stern argues that the infant's capacity for relationality and engagement depends upon the parent's ability to engage in such attunement, which parents accomplish by performing "some behavior that is not a strict imitation but nonetheless corresponds in some way to the infant's overt behavior," So, for example, in one instance, "the intensity level and duration of the girl's voice is matched by the mother's body movements." In another, "features of a boy's arm movements are matched by features of the mother's voice,"[69] That is, the mother engages in an activity that is not identical to the infant's but is like it, a likeness made by way of a translation between modes or senses, from sound to movement or vice versa, by way of "amodal" characteristics such as intensity, shape, or rhythm (which Stern elsewhere calls "vitality affects"). In this way, Stern writes, "what is matched is not the other person's behavior per se, but rather some aspect of the behavior that reflects the persons' feeling state." This nonidentical match is what communicates the common affective experience. "The capacities for identifying cross-modal equivalences [what Benjamin called the mimetic faculty] that make for a perceptually unified world are the same capacities that permit the mother and the infant to engage in affect attunement to achieve affective intersubjectivity."[70]

Warhol's work returns over and over to the (machine-like) human capacity for perceiving and producing cross-modal imitations, reminding us that the value of this capacity is not its accuracy or identity but its facility for acts that are (as Stern puts it) "not a strict imitation but nonetheless correspond in some way." It is only by way of such correspondences that we might be aware that others have what Whitman called "the like / out of the like feel-

69 Daniel Stern, *The Interpersonal World of the Infant: A View from Psychoanalysis and Developmental Psychology* (New York: Basic Books, 1985), 139, 141.

70 Ibid., 156. One of the most surprising aspects of the interactions Stern observed was that, while the infant took no apparent notice of attunement behaviors on the part of the mother, when the mother abruptly stopped these behaviors or acted in way that was noncorresponding, through mismatches of intensity or rhythm, the infants interrupted their activities, often displaying confusion or uncertainty. Without the sharing of an affect, the infant stops engagement in a behavior because she or he is not sure how to continue, as if affects require a plural existence, a sense of their imitability, to come into being at all.

ings."[71] And in the proliferation of machines for storing and transmitting information, Warhol found a vast resource for this project.

One of Warhol's main devices for stimulating and exercising our capacity for perceiving similarities across difference was the transposition of idioms, sensations, and information from one medium to another. This device, as both Callie Angell and Wayne Koestenbaum observe, runs through his body of work with remarkable consistency.[72] The sometimes unexpected effect of the reshaping demanded by each medium was the point of the transfer.

So, for instance (as I noted above), Warhol's paintings use photographic images and imitate photography in their mode of production. Photographs are translated into silkscreens, which are then used (like photographic negatives) to print images onto painted canvases.[73] This rough, sometimes messy printing loses the precision of the photograph printed on proper photographic paper, even as it recalls the dotted halftone printing one sees in newspapers and magazines. Having the photographic image in the "wrong" place draws attention to photographic mediation as such, and the way it has always already distorted information in some way. At the same time, it draws attention to the mediatedness of painting. Especially when the image is repeated, the silkscreened photographs highlight the surface of the canvas and its paintedness in a way that detracts from its capacity to effectively "represent" a space or objects (Marilyn, a car crash, an electric chair, a shadow) like a good "realistic" painting would. In terms of the standards of the given media, the result is neither a good photograph nor a good painting.

With other formal elements, too, Warhol has borrowed idioms from other media. Colors and paints are often recognizably nonpainterly, instead referencing product design, cosmetics, advertisement, or interior decoration. Some paintings are sized like billboards or movie screens.[74] Similarly, War-

71 "Live Oak with Moss," 208.

72 Angell writes that the Screen Tests, like much of Warhol's work, involve a "formal transposition of idioms from one medium to another"(*Screen Tests*, 14). Koestenbaum makes a similar observation: "Warhol's game throughout his career was to transpose sensation from one medium to another—to turn a photograph into a painting by silkscreening it; to transform a movie into a sculpture by filming motionless objects and individuals" (*Andy Warhol*, 133–34).

73 Gerard Malanga is particularly emphatic about the constant, if varying, role of photography as model and reference point in the silkscreens. He notes, for instance, that the large Elvis paintings were explicitly "trying to duplicate a photographic effect" (Smith, *Conversations*, 167).

74 See David Batchelor, *Chromophobia* (London: Reaktion, 2000), on color in the painting of the 1960s, which I discuss in chapter 4. In many early screens, Warhol has enlarged the image, approaching billboard or cinematic scale, a goal he was explicitly aiming for in a series of Flowers and Electric Chairs (*CR*, cat. nos. 2031–2055) prepared for his 1968 exhibition in Stockholm; see *CR3* 02B, 344–65. Printz writes, "Unlike prior surveys of Warhol's work in Philadelphia and Boston in 1966, the Stockholm exhibition was planned as an alternative to a conventional retrospective. Its principal premise was to demonstrate the relationship between Warhol's paintings and his films. Warhol made

hol remarked that "in my early films, I wanted to 'paint' in a new medium" (*IBYM*, 186). He did so by filming a "moving picture still-life of the Empire State Building" or "moving picture portraits," as in *Eat* or *Henry Geldzahler* or the Screen Tests. By calling the latter "stillies," Warhol and his friends indicated the way these "movies" imitated the stillness of photographs or painted portraits.[75] Trying to make one medium like another often drew out the ways a given medium fails to accurately capture, store, or transmit information. Warhol's transpositions were a way to draw attention to those failures as themselves productive of surprising and pleasing correspondences.

As Warhol said of the video equipment Norelco lent him in 1965, "We like to take advantage of static" (*IBYM*, 76). For Warhol, the most "weird" and "fascinating" thing about recordings made with the new video machine (which he started using a few months before Nam Jun Paik) were the odd distortions, moiré patterns, and vertical slides they included, distortions that were even more visible if they were then mediated by film, as Warhol did in *Outer and Inner Space* (1965).[76] Likewise, as Gustavus Stadler points out, the tape recorder was attractive as a companion and model in part because it is a poor listener; "it doesn't make many choices about what is more and less important as it listens; it can't very effectively separate sounds to create the impression of space. It is easily overloaded with incoming sonic information . . . including the drone of the recorder itself."[77] Indeed, the "bad tape" became a kind of general metaphor for Warhol of the pleasingly inaccurate mediation.

Warhol saw the possibility for such mistranslations anywhere one machine was joined with another, which is to say pretty much everywhere. In his work, at every stage, from production to display and circulation, Warhol sought out opportunities to exploit the moments of interface between different systems for processing or storing information. Thus, he viewed the people he worked with as themselves a kind of transmission medium that he might draw into his project of system mistranslation. In his *Philosophy*

---

two new bodies of work for the exhibition, both based on the earlier subjects *Electric Chairs* and *Flowers*, but enlarged to the scale of images projected on a movie screen which were screened in the same gallery as the paintings" (*CR3*, 345). Most overtly, his serial repetition of the images borrows an idiom from mass production and consumption.

75 Adding another, subtler system shift, these early silent films were shot at sound speed (24 frames per second) but projected at silent speed (16 fps). See Angell, *Screen Tests*, 14. See also my discussions of the Screen Tests in chapter 1.

76 When you film (or photograph) a video image on a television, it brings to the fore noise in the image (connected to its refresh rate) that the human eye misses. As the "KODAK Scientific Imaging Products" brochure explains, "Because images on a television or computer screen are formed line-by-line by a rapidly moving electron beam, you can obtain a complete picture of the screen only if the camera shutter speed is slow enough to allow the moving beam to complete its scan" (http://www.skepticfiles.org/cowtext/comput~1/photoscn.htm, accessed August 3, 2015).

77 Stadler, "Tape Recorder," 440.

he remarked, "Something that I look for in an associate is a certain amount of misunderstanding of what I'm trying to do. Not a fundamental misunderstanding; just minor misunderstandings here and there. When someone doesn't quite completely understand what you want from them, or when the tape is bad, or when their own fantasies start coming through, I often wind up liking what comes out of it all better than I liked my original idea" (*Phil*, 99). In fact, Warhol would often give a fairly vague description of his "original idea" (which was usually his own appropriation of an idea from somewhere else) so that people would have to introduce their "own fantasies" to interpret the idea and translate it into an action of some kind. For instance, he would ask Ron Tavel to produce a script that was "simple and plastic and white" (*POP*, 91), which seemed to be based on his wish to imitate what he liked in the film *The Carpetbaggers*. And like the game of "telephone," the more transmissions you add, the more distorted the "message" becomes:

> If you take what the first person who misunderstood you did, and you give that to someone else and tell them to make it more like how they know you would want it, that's good too. If people never misunderstand you, and if they do everything exactly the way you tell them to, they're just transmitters of your ideas, and you get bored with that. But when you work with people who misunderstand you, instead of getting *transmissions*, you get *transmutations*, and that's much more interesting in the long run. (*Phil*, 99)

The static involved in the chain of misunderstanding here produces automatic, noncomposed, and nonintentional imaginative miscognitions—transmutations—which is what Warhol sought to produce in his work as a general principle.

Although Warhol is interested in the particular procedures and logics that each medium imposes on its material (what we might call each medium's "own fantasies"), the point would seem not to be an assertion of medium specificity so much as something like what Miriam Hansen (commenting on Siegfried Kracauer) called a "configuration of intermedial relations in which the unstable specificity of one medium works to cite and interrogate the other."[78] Warhol liked his media unstable and leaky ("low" rather than "high" fidelity), and always already "citing" and remediating each other.[79]

This is attractive not only because it thematizes and stimulates our capacity for seeing and producing similarities across difference. But also, in transposing idioms and information from one medium or sensory realm to another, Warhol's work focuses our attention on the interface between dis-

78 Hansen, *Cinema and Experience*, 23.

79 See Stadler, "Tape Recorder," on the discourse of fidelity and its application to both marriage and sound reproduction. On the medium as itself, by definition, always remediating other media, see Jay David Bolter and Richard Grusin, *Remediation: Understanding New Media* (Cambridge, MA: MIT Press, 2000).

tinct systems, each with its own rules for differentiating between "inside" and "outside" and its own mechanisms for processing and producing information. Thus, to come back to this chapter's overarching argument: Warhol's staging of interfaces between different media, with their own machine-like systemic logics and procedures, is appealing in part because it mediates a world defined by what Luhmann called functional differentiation. This is a world in which "problems can no longer be solved by the system that produces them. They have to be transferred to the system that is best equipped and specialized to solve them. There is, on the level of subsystems, less autarchy and self-sufficiency but higher autonomy in applying specific rules and procedures to special problems."[80] On a mundane level, we are all familiar with this differentiation, since everyday life requires that we move back and forth between such systems. We may work at jobs located within a particular professional or social system, with its own autonomous "rules and procedures" but with frustratingly little autarchy in determining what problems we must apply these rules and procedures to. For instance, the public education system (as is widely observed) seems increasingly to be held responsible for problems created by poverty. As we negotiate within and between systems—on hold with the health insurance company trying to get our prescriptions filled or walking by the abandoned houses "owned" by banks while homeless people sleep on the street—we may wonder which problems are actually being transferred to the system "best equipped to solve them."

Warhol may be said to compensate for the lack of system autarchy and the difficulties it produces by using his artwork to stage the transfer of problems from one system to another. The effect, however, is not to produce a *better* match between problems and system (so that problems really do find their way to the system that can solve them) but to highlight the fact of problematic problem transfer in itself and to show how the correspondences and likenesses that the mistranslations and errors of transfer inevitably produce may in fact *increase* one's capacity for liking and being alike. And this system-interface-produced increase may itself solve some problems (such as being stigmatized for not properly fitting into one's role, or feeling alienated from the world or depressed by it). Thus, rather than limit system interfaces or control them in order to make them more successful, Warhol sought to de-instrumentalize and proliferate them.

This was a strategy for encouraging connectedness and openness. As Brian Massumi put it, "What you can do, your potential, is defined by your connectedness, the way you're connected and how intensely, not your ability to separate off and decide by yourself."[81] For Warhol, being a machine was about joining with other machines to make assemblages, thereby expanding one's capacity for affecting and being affected, an ability, as Michael Hardt

80 Luhmann, *Differentiation of Society*, 249.
81 Zournazi, "Navigating Movements."

writes, to "register and feel [the world's] diverse powers" by increasing one's ability to receive, transmit, and correspond.[82] "But to do that," Massumi notes, "you have to abdicate your own self-interest up to a point, and this opens you to risk. You have to place yourself not in a position but in the middle, in a fairly indeterminate, fairly vague situation, where things meet at the edges and pass into each other."[83] Doing things in a machine-like way means being in the middle—a medium—at the points of interface and transmutation.

Being at the point of interface between different medial system logics, its risks and pleasures, is the overt topic of *Outer and Inner Space*, where Warhol made use of the video equipment and the static it afforded in a formally and affectively powerful portrait of Edie Sedgwick. Warhol first videotaped Sedgwick in profile, while she was talking to someone offscreen, looking up slightly. He then filmed two 33-minute reels of her sitting in front of that videotaped image of herself playing on a monitor, so that it often appears she is talking into her own ear. The two reels were then projected on two screens so that the viewer sees four images of Sedgwick in a complex spatial and temporal arrangement. As she sits there talking, while listening to her prior self talking behind her, she is at times made visibly nervous, unnerved and embarrassed by the experience of listening to her own taped voice. Callie Angell suggests that the title refers not only to the vividly apparent disjuncture between her "outer beauty and inner turmoil" but also to the "two very different spaces of representation occupied by the video/television medium and by film."[84] That is, in addition to dramatizing Sedgwick's relation to being filmed (like Warhol's other portrait films), *Outer and Inner Space* records her reaction to being in the presence of her videotaped self.

In the background, the video image looks flat and very clearly mediated, especially as it warps and stretches and dissolves the image of Sedgwick's head. By contrast, the filmed face is expressively shadowy and emotionally present to the viewer. This, of course, dramatizes the significance of mediation: these are two different Edies. Overall, the depiction of Edie's experience of reacting to her own mediation does not come off as a call for Edie to learn to accept herself or somehow be more authentic or more comfortable with herself. Instead, the film seems to encourage one to learn how to like—or even be dazzled by—one's inevitable mediated self-alienations, which Edie evidently struggles with here. (Perhaps, we wonder, if she could *see* how obviously mediated and artificial her electronic visage appears, instead of just hearing it, she would find the sound of her voice less uncomfortable.) But in

82 Hardt, "Power to Be Affected," 216.

83 Zournazi, "Navigating Movements."

84 "Andy Warhol: Outer and Inner Space," in *From Stills to Motion and Back Again: Texts on Andy Warhol's Screen Tests and Outer and Inner Space* (North Vancouver, BC: Presentation House Gallery, 2003), 14. For an account of the spatial logic of the film, see Crimp, *Our Kind of Movie*, 77, 79.

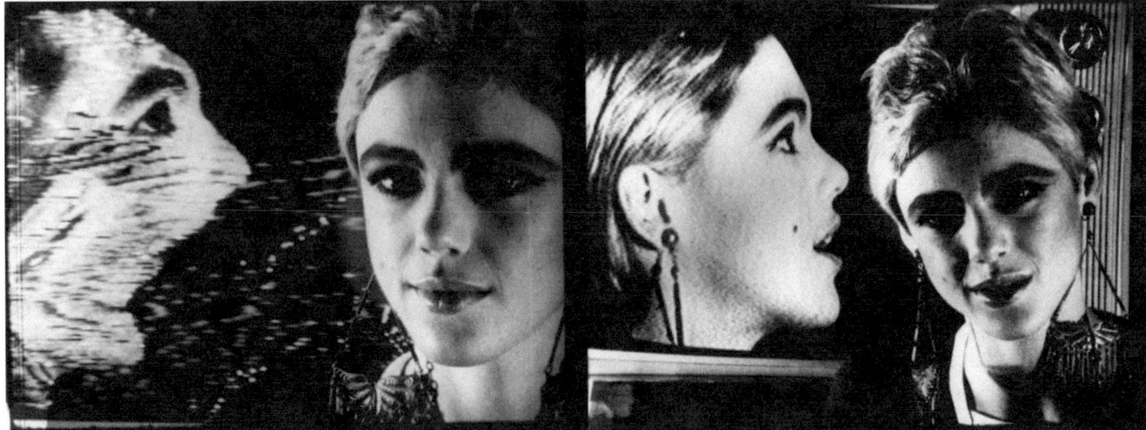

2.5 Andy Warhol, *Outer and Inner Space*, 1965. 16mm film, black and white, sound, 66 minutes or 33 minutes in double screen. © 2016 The Andy Warhol Museum, a museum of Carnegie Institute.

one stunning sequence, we get a sense of how her mediated self-alienation might be differently experienced. The video Edie sneezes, startling Edie in the foreground, who flinches. "I can do that anytime," she says on the monitor.[85] "Could you tell if that was a real sneeze?" the videotaped background Edie continues, and then this Edie sneezes again, demonstrating her talent for *making* herself sneeze, for tricking her body into a paradigmatically autonomic, involuntary, "machine-like" behavior (which was also the subject of one of the very first films, Edison's 1893–1894 kinetoscope *Fred Ott's Sneeze*).[86] At this point, reminded of her machinic-mimetic talent for simulation, Edie (in the foreground) imitates her video self and sneezes. As we witness this rapid, exciting flurry of sneezes, the different Edies become a little confused, as imitation and similarity moves back and forth between media, from past to present, background to foreground. Wait, which Edie sneezed first? Did her sneeze cause her (and which her?) to sneeze? Are these real sneezes? Which Edie is which? As she simulates her simulation, a self-estranging self-mediation becomes a dazzling spectacle for us. For her it appears to become a resource for disclosing a pleasing artifice, over which

85 The difficult-to-hear dialogue has been transcribed in *From Stills to Motion*, 27–39; the sneeze passage appears on 36–37.

86 On *Fred Ott's Sneeze*, see Jonathan Auerbach, *Body Shots: Early Cinema's Incarnations* (Berkeley: University of California Press, 2007), and Linda Williams, *Hard Core: Power, Pleasure, and the "Frenzy of the Visible"* (Berkeley: University of California Press, 1989), 51–52, 63–64. Williams observes the similarities between the convulsions of the sneeze and the convulsions of "ecstasy," which may have motivated initial interest in having Edison film a female model sneezing. Edie's capacity to voluntarily produce this usually involuntary reflexive behavior corresponds to Warhol's own efforts to exert agency over his capacity to like.

one might, moreover, exert some control. With the real fake sneeze Edie manipulates the machinery to increase her body's capacities for affecting and being affected. And as she does so, her mood seems to lift, if only for a moment.

Warhol's excitement about the imminent arrival of the video equipment from Norelco is an intermittent topic of the first chapter of *A: A Novel*, a book transcribed from recordings made on his Norelco tape recorder ("Norelco projects," J. Hoberman suggests). It was clearly a moment of excitement about the possibility of using media to produce the "good mistakes" that he liked.[87] In *A*, tape recording the amphetamine-infused conversations of Ondine and others and then turning these tapes into written text by way of the typewriter amplified the mistakes of the tape recorder by subjecting them to the human ears of typists and the errors their hands made as they typed. (Complicating matters further, Warhol and Billy Linich added more errors at the editing stage, as Lucy Mulroney has shown.[88]) The "right" words are replaced by words that sound or look like them (or both). Callas becomes calls, callous Callas.[89] Shit sometimes becomes sit. The transcription errors both repeat and amplify the frequent mishearings and repetition and punning and wordplay and operatic slides into French or Italian that already characterize the speech in *A*. Like a dream, *A* is structured by patterns of concealed similarities that affects use to transport themselves out of the unconscious. But it reads like somebody else's dream, filled with the correspondences and substitutions that somebody else's affects needed to find their way out. In an effort to make sense from the disorienting effect such a text can produce, one starts to read for similarities, to guess at or presume them. For instance, when Ondine is talking about Warhol's "heart on," one reads it as a mistranscription of "hard on" (66). But then, one wonders if it might not be a mistranscription at all but Ondine's pun or Warhol's (or someone else's) coinage. Or is it my "own fantasies coming through," what Warhol called the "prurience" that "is part of the machine," that "keeps you happy" and "keeps you running" (*IBYM*, 189)? To be sure, the constant, detailed descriptions of various sexual encounters and fantasies in *A* certainly does "appeal to prurient interests." But then, whether the "mistake" is the typists, or Ondine's, or mine, like a good metaphor it asks one to consider the connection between affective attachment (heart-on) and sexual arousal (hard-on).

Such metaphorical transactions of context can be found and productively considered in many of Warhol's works. The transpositions in two great bodies of work from the 1970s suggest Warhol's persistent interest in bringing into painting idioms and information from queer social spaces, in an effort not only to make painting a little sexier but to remind us of the

87 Warhol refers to his "same good mistakes" in *Phil*, 114.

88 Lucy Mulroney, "Editing Andy Warhol," *Grey Room*, no. 46 (Winter 2012), 46–71.

89 *A: A Novel*, 265. See Craig Dworkin on the interest of this particular shift, in "Whereof One Cannot Speak," *Grey Room*, no. 21 (Fall 2005), 46–69 (for Callas/callous, 54–55).

limits of painting and the institutional space of "art." In his abstract Oxidation Paintings, piss replaces paint as the agent of color, and copper-treated canvases take the place of the sexually aroused men Warhol may have observed receiving golden showers in "sex pits" like "the Anvil, the Toilet, the Mineshaft, the Cave, the Eagle's Nest, the Strap, Crisco Disco."[90] As with the Dance Diagrams, the Oxidation Paintings reference the floor as a space of composition, and it is a floor that might be a site of pleasurable social interaction. Another effort to bring together dancing and painting can be found in his ambient, room-filling, "disco décor" *Shadows*. As Tan Lin has shown, in this work Warhol transposes the digital on-off effects of the strobe light into the analog space of painting.[91] In appearing to ask how painting might make a space and a mood for dancing, Warhol returns to the project of the Dance Diagram paintings.

In the Dance Diagrams, Warhol invites the viewer to be a point of mimetic, mediated contact. Formally, he repeats (in the paintings) the intermedial quality of learning to dance from a diagram by taking the diagram from the print medium of the book and translating it into paint on canvas. Then, he places the painting on the floor, like a sculpture, but a sculpture that is also a dance floor. From printed book to projection to (traced) painting to sculpture to dance floor, the series of metaphorical "transactions of context" creates the work's particular aesthetic effect. Even though it is paint on canvas and is likely to be encountered among other paintings in a gallery, it does not solicit a disembodied gaze through the painting's frame into a representation *of* something. Nor, although it draws our attention to the painting's surface, does it do so in order to focus on the paint-on-canvasness of it (as Clement Greenberg famously argued was the value of modernist painting). Instead, the paintings seem to frame a space for mimetic bodily movement. One is directly reminded of one's own body, especially one's feet (a body part of considerable interest to Warhol).[92] Can I learn the double

90 Warhol lists these places in the section on "downtown" in *Andy Warhol's Exposures*, 235.

91 Warhol writes that "someone asks me if they were art and I said no. You see, the opening party had disco. I guess that makes them disco décor." "Painter Hangs Own Paintings," *New York* 12, no. 6 (February 5, 1979); reprinted in *Warhol Shadows* (Houston: Menil Foundation, 1979), n.p. In "Disco, Cybernetics, and the Migration of Warhol's Shadows into Computation," Tan Lin makes brilliant use of Friedrich Kittler's distinction between storage, transmission, and computation media to "argue that Shadows is not principally a storage mechanism like film, photography, or painting, and although it manifests characteristics of a transmission mechanism like a mirror or television (it bears a passing relation to Screen Tests and celebrity portraits), it resembles a system designed to perform calculations endemic to what John Johnston terms the 'translation of any medium into any other through the digitalization of all information'" (484).

92 Artistically, of course, Warhol drew many feet (including a series of drawings in the 1950s) and shoes (from I Miller ads to Diamond Dust drag queen shoes). See Mandy Merck, "Figuring Out Andy Warhol," in Doyle, Flatley, and Muñoz, *Pop Out*. John Giorno

twinkle step right here? To the extent that the footprints just off the floor seem to invite one to step into them, the paintings may not only ask viewers to associate Warhol with the figure of the dancer, as Gavin Butt argues, but also remind them of their own potential as dancers, or as "dancer types."

But if the Dance Diagram paintings are invitations to dance, they are invitations that cannot actually be answered by the viewer without stepping on the painting. They thus solicit an activity that they simultaneously discourage—they are "the right thing in the wrong space and the wrong thing in the right space."[93] They remind one of the degree to which the context of "art" itself, including the space of the gallery (where dancing on the paintings is definitely not allowed), polices mimetic comportment. By implication, we are encouraged to "do it yourself," to transpose the mimetic activity solicited by the painting into some other context, or to change the art context so that different things can happen *there*. The painting sets up a chain of transpositions (or, to use a different vocabulary, a machinic assemblage) to which the viewer may add her or himself.[94] If viewers make mistakes in managing that translation into another context by way of their own bodies and their feelings and fantasies, all the better.

Contradiction

The artists who succumb to ideology are precisely those who conceal this contradiction instead of assimilating it into the consciousness of their own production.

Max Horkheimer and Theodor Adorno, "The Culture Industry"[95]

Like Warhol, Sol LeWitt borrows the affective force of his work from the fact that we live in a world in which "life is determined less and less by local

---

recalls, "One thing led to another and he was kissing and licking my shoes. I had always heard he was a foot fetishist, all those years designing shoe ads for Henri Bendel and Bonwit Teller. There was Andy Warhol on his hands and knees, licking my shoes with his little red tongue. Too good to be believed! I thought with a rush, 'He's sucking my shoes!' It was hot" (*You Got to Burn to Shine*, 131–32).

93 "I like to be the right thing in the wrong space and the wrong thing in the right space. But when you hit one of the two, people turn the lights out on you, or spit on you, or write bad reviews of you, or beat you up, or mug you, or say you're 'climbing.' But usually being the right thing in the wrong space and the wrong thing in the right space is worth it, because something funny always happens. Believe me, because I've made a career out of being the right thing in the wrong space and the wrong thing in the right space. That's one thing I really do know about"(*Phil*, 158).

94 This is the language of Deleuze and Guattari, especially in *Anti-Oedipus*. See Gerald Raunig's examination of such machinic assemblages in *A Thousand Machines* (New York: Semiotex(e), 2010). The machine, he writes, "is not limited to managing and striating entities closed off to one another, but opens to other machines and, together with them, moves machinic assemblages" (33).

95 "The Culture Industry: Enlightenment as Mass Deception," in *Dialectic of Enlightenment*, 127.

contexts," a world defined by the need for transition and translation between different systemic logics. But where Warhol is interested in creative mistranslations between systems, LeWitt's work, as I mentioned earlier, replicates—in the serial works as well as many of the wall drawings—the more nominalistic pleasure of reducing "infinite to finite information loads" by bringing the viewer into the world of a readily graspable systemic logic. LeWitt's work brings what Luhmann called the "unity of the imaginary space of combinatory potentials" *inside* the system. "Variation" and "combination" are two of LeWitt's favorite tropes, two of his most reliable ways to build systems. However, in works as various as *Variations of Incomplete Open Cubes* and *All Combinations of Arcs from Corners and Sides; Straight Lines, Not-Straight-Lines and Broken Lines*, LeWitt brings the combinatory impulse, the generation of variations, into the work in a completely abstracted way, not directly referable to any social context. This gives the viewer a kind of abstract affective map of the combinatory experience. In this map, variation and combination always appear in relation to a total concept, a concept with which, however, variation is always also in a kind of tension. If being a machine for Warhol is about coupling with other machines, for LeWitt it is about duplicating for the viewer one element of life in a machine-like world. This element is the experience of a contradiction between the conceptual grasp of a total system and the particular perceptual experience of it.

Where for Warhol being a machine increases our powers to affect and be affected, inasmuch as it reminds us how to like, LeWitt sees his artwork as explicitly *affectless*. Indeed, he sees the avoidance of emotional expression as a major advantage of the conceptual approach. "Conceptual art is made to engage the mind of the viewer rather than his eye or emotions. . . . It is the objective of the artist who is concerned with conceptual art to make his work conceptually interesting to the spectator, and therefore he would want it to become emotionally dry."[96] This does not mean that LeWitt's work is not in some way about emotion; expression is not the only way to represent an emotion. LeWitt's work is "about" emotion and subjectivity precisely inasmuch as it negates these things.[97] As Adorno has put it, "There is no

96 LeWitt, "Paragraphs on Conceptual Art," 78.

97 Of course, the desire to combat romanticism and expressionism is one of the major strands of twentieth-century art, a desire perhaps most famously expressed in T. S. Eliot's assertion "Poetry is not a turning loose of emotion, but an escape from emotion; it is not the expression of personality, but an escape from personality. But of course only those who have personality and emotions know what it means to escape from those things" ("Tradition and the Individual Talent," in *Selected Prose*, 43). This last sentence makes it clear that poetry is still about emotion to the precise extent that it negates it. The unstated implication is that it is only in a world where one wants to escape from the emotions of everyday life—where those emotions are unpleasant—that this poetic gesture is attractive. For Eliot, this is a universal human condition—one *always* wants to escape from and transform emotion and personality in the realm of art. This is what makes life worth living. Of course, the universality of art-as-escape has been widely

art that does not contain in itself as an element, negated, what it repulses. If it is more than mere indifference, the Kantian 'without interest' must be shadowed by the wildest interest, and there is much to be said for the idea that the dignity of artworks depends on the intensity of the interest from which they are wrested."[98] We can see the nature of the interest from which LeWittian disinterest is wrested by examining the specific quality of the aesthetic experience LeWitt's work offers.

* * *

In 1967, relatively early in LeWitt's career, artist and critic Mel Bochner provided an aptly prescient characterization of the aesthetic experience LeWitt's work produces: "When one encounters a LeWitt, although an order is immediately intuited, how to apprehend or penetrate it is nowhere revealed. Instead one is overwhelmed with a mass of data—lines, joints, angles. By controlling so rigidly the conception of the work, never adjusting it to any predetermined ideas of how a work of art should look, LeWitt arrives at a unique perceptual breakdown of conceptual order into visual chaos."[99] Although Bochner was speaking of LeWitt's early serial structures (*Serial Project Set A* is his primary example), I think the characterization holds true for many of the wall drawings as well. These are also often organized by a simple schema that is easily graspable conceptually—*Vertical Lines, Not Straight, Not Touching*, or *Ten thousand Lines, One Inch Long, Evenly Spaced on Six Walls Each of Differing Area*, for example—but perceptually overwhelming in their size and scope. The experience of a gap between apprehension (the sensory perception of the material object) and comprehension (the cognition of the total system organizing that material) would seem to be a recurring theme in LeWitt's art. As Tan Lin has argued, the effect bears a family resemblance to the optical illusion, where the mind imposes an underlying order that is contradicted by visual experience, leading you to see something that is not there.[100] LeWitt's work operates like an *unraveled* optical illusion.[101] Here, visual experience and cognitive comprehension are collapsed but then held apart. This generates the effect not of illusion (where we see something that

---

challenged in twentieth-century art, not least by avant-garde movements like surrealism, Dada, and constructivism, which sought to explode the creative energies to be found in "art into life." (Indeed, one might read even Eliot's own poetry as a critique of art-as-escape.) However, even if art is always about negation, the *particular* emotions that are worth escaping at a particular moment are widely variable and historically specific.

98 Adorno, *Aesthetic Theory*, 11.

99 Bochner, "Serial Art, Systems, Solipsism," in *Minimal Art: A Critical Anthology*, ed. Gregory Battcock (New York: Dutton, 1968), 101.

100 "This Is a Novel or a Stopwatch," in *Elsewhere*, ed. Mary Ceruti (New York: Sculpture Center, 2000).

101 I am thinking of Foucault's argument about Magritte's work, which, Foucault argues, functions like an "unraveled calligram" (*This Is Not a Pipe*).

2.6 Sol LeWitt, *Wall Drawing No. 46 (Vertical Lines, not straight, not touching, uniformly dispersed with maximum density, covering the entire surface of the wall)* (detail), 1970. Black pencil. The LeWitt collection, Chester, Connecticut. © 2016 The LeWitt Estate/ Artists Rights Society (ARS), New York.

is not there) so much as of allegory (where representation operates across a gap). As I discuss below, the overall effect is one of surprise; viewing LeWitt's art, one is frequently surprised that such a simple concept could produce such an overwhelming visual experience.

Often, LeWitt's art actively assists the intuition of an overall order with language: *Lines Not Straight Not Touching*, *Five Cubes on 25 Squares*, *10,000 Lines Five Inches Long*, and of course *Variations of Incomplete Open Cubes*, our primary topic here. If the title is insufficient or if one has not read it, LeWitt often provides a smaller, visually graspable version of the work. In the case of the large wall drawings, this takes the form of a smaller schematic drawing that accompanies the work. Or with the *Variations*, there is the overall schematic drawing. Which is to say: while LeWitt's work is often confusing, not to say stupefying on the local level, it generally provides easy access to the system from which this perceptual experience has been generated.

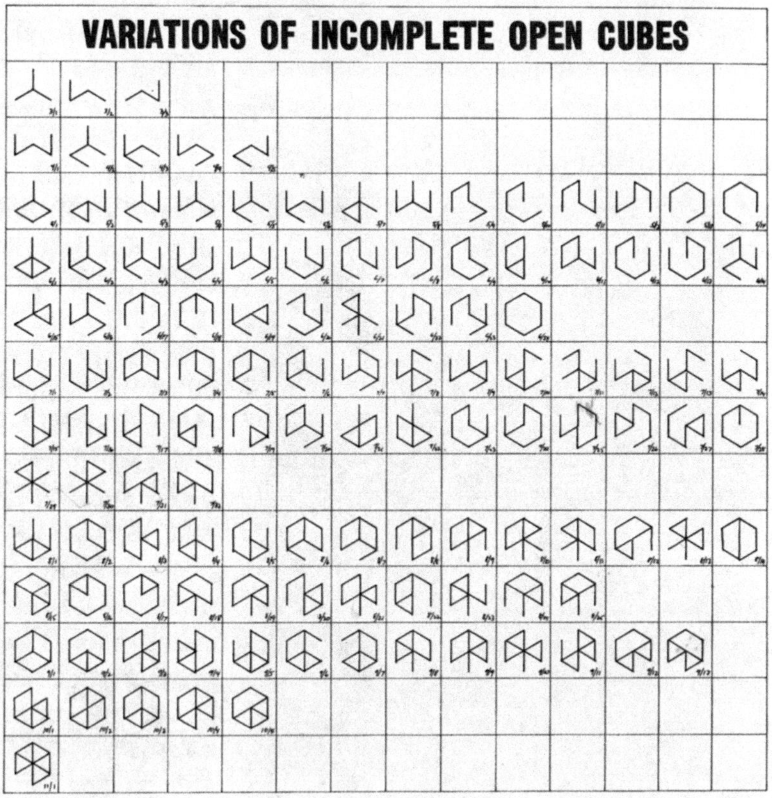

VARIATIONS OF INCOMPLETE OPEN CUBES

2.7 Sol LeWitt, *Schematic Drawing for Incomplete Open Cubes*, 1974. From printed four-page announcement for the exhibition *Wall Drawings and Sculptures: The Location of Six Geometric Figures/Variations of Incomplete Open Cubes*, John Weber Gallery, New York, October–November 1974. The Lewitt Collection, Chester Connecticut. © 2016 The LeWitt Estate/Artists Rights Society (ARS), New York.

Part of the brilliance of *Variations of Incomplete Open Cubes* is its achievement of a particular, and particularly maximized, tension between perception and conception. The tension can be seen in the difficulty of executing the project. LeWitt writes that "although at first I thought it was not a complex project, this piece provided more problems than anticipated."[102] The concept was straightforward: a series constituted by all the possible variations of an open cube that was not complete. "The series started with three-part pieces because a cube implies three dimensions and, of course, ends with one eleven-part piece (one bar removed)."[103] The difficulty lay in the task of figuring out all of the variations without duplicating them. Rotation here is the key formal problem since the same cube rotated often

102 "Commentaries," in *Sol LeWitt*, ed. Alicia Legg (New York: Museum of Modern Art, 1978), 81.
103 Ibid.

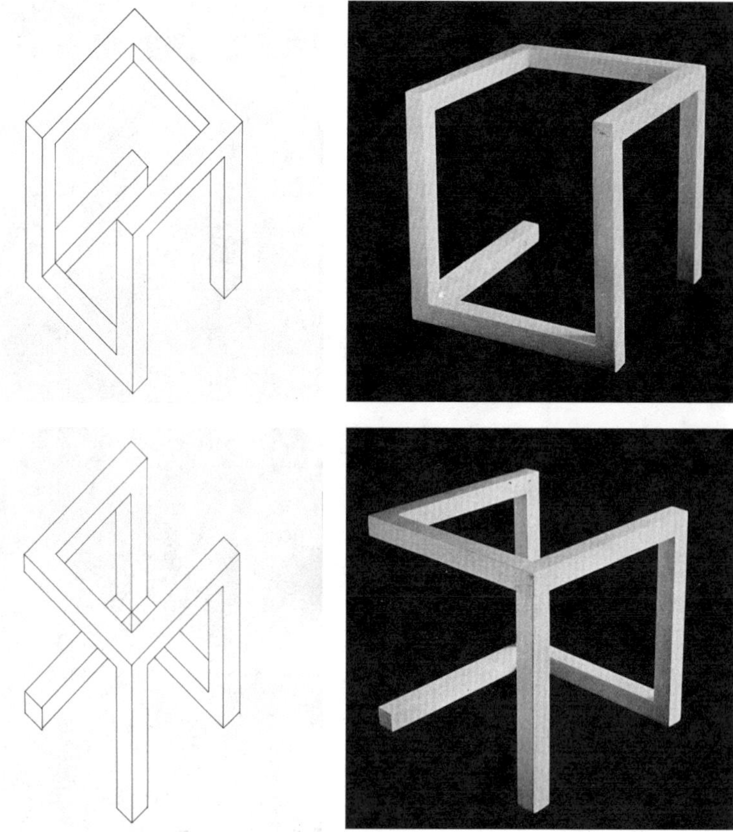

2.8 Sol LeWitt, *Incomplete Open Cubes*, 1974. Artist's book, 122 pages. John Weber Gallery (New York), 1974. Author's collection. © 2016 The LeWitt Estate/Artists Rights Society (ARS), New York.

appears to be a different cube. In fact, despite LeWitt's persistent efforts, as the working drawings suggest, LeWitt discovered that rotating the incomplete cubes in one's head or in two dimensions proved to be impossible. "You can't construct the cubes in your mind, I find it impossible," LeWitt said. "I can't do it, and no one I know can do it."[104] LeWitt found that it was absolutely necessary to make models—at first from pipe cleaners and paperclips—to figure it out.

The perceptual difficulty of the *Incomplete Open Cubes* may be related to the tendency to perceive the incomplete open cube in terms of the complete cube. In other words, it is not that we complete the cube imaginatively in our head, but that a set of sometimes misleading perceptual truths about the complete open cube seems to infiltrate our perception of the incomplete ones. For example, it is surprising how difficult it is to move between two and three dimensions with the incomplete cubes. Because the complete cube looks the same from any angle, one is not prepared for the fact that,

104 LeWitt, in conversation with author and Nicholas Baume, August 9, 2000.

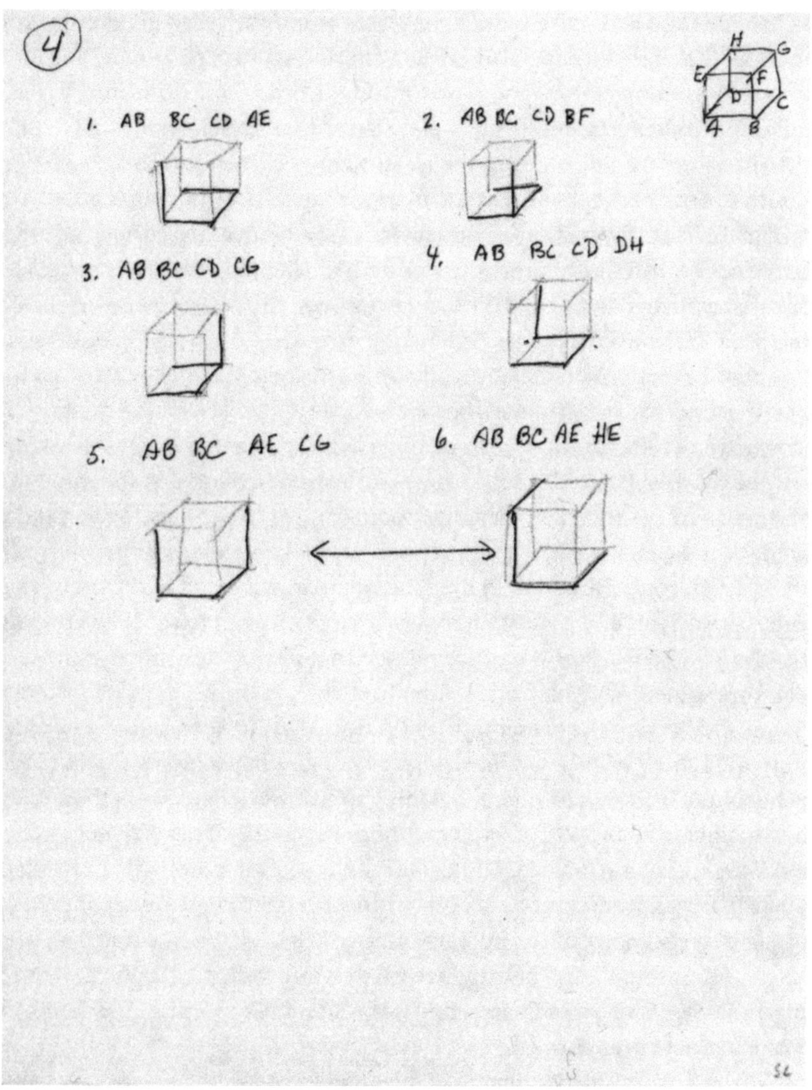

2.9 Sol LeWitt, working drawing for *Incomplete Open Cubes (Alphabetical)*, 1973–1974. Ink and pencil on paper, 11 × 8½ inches. The LeWitt Collection, Chester, Connecticut. © 2016 The LeWitt Estate/Artists Rights Society (ARS), New York.

when drawn two-dimensionally or photographed, the cube looks completely different depending on the angle it is seen from. Look, for example, at 8-12 and 8-13 in the artist's book or in the photographic composite: it is not, I think, immediately apparent that the two cubes, if presented from a different angle, are mirror images. The expectation of symmetry misguides us. Or as Nicholas Baume notes: "The difference between a mirror image, which is not identical, and a repetition rotated so that it appears to be different, is often difficult to discern."[105] In short, the complete cube is so easy

105 "The Music of Forgetting," in Baume, *Sol LeWitt: Incomplete Open Cubes*, 24.

to perceive and recognize immediately that one is surprised not only by the number of incomplete open cubes but by the difficulty of perceiving and distinguishing among them. The viewer intuits an order but, as Bochner wrote, it is quite difficult to apprehend: "one is overwhelmed with a mass of data."

The layout of the cubes in the schematic drawings and in the smaller three-dimensional version seem to increase the difficulty of perception. Although LeWitt may insist that *any* layout is strictly speaking correct (so long as the cubes with same number of elements are kept together) it is nonetheless instructive to notice the difference between the working drawings and the final schematic drawings. When one examines the working drawings, one can see that LeWitt usually works with a system that makes it as easy as possible to discern differences between cubes and to see where duplicates are generated. For example, in a working drawing where LeWitt is working out the four-part variations, the three-part base is oriented in the same direction from cube to cube, making it quite simple to see how the variation works. One can see easily and precisely how each cube is different from the previous one. However, in the schematic drawing and in the book, the cubes are oriented in a way that makes it more difficult to see the variation from cube to cube. The bases are rotated in different directions; mirrored pairs are sometimes established, sometimes not. In the selection of systems themselves and in the presentation of the art, LeWitt seems to have a definite preference toward emphasizing the tension between perception and conception. It should be noted that this gap is at work not only in the smallest version, where all 122 incomplete cubes (each 2⅝ × 2⅝ × 2⅝ inches) are exhibited as a single piece, but also in the book, the schematic drawings, and the largest versions (40 × 40 × 40 inches). With the larger cubes, the space between generality and particularity is held open inasmuch as you know there is a totality, but the size—and worldwide distribution—of the object prevents one from perceiving it through the object itself; one has to make a leap to the concept.

While LeWitt's art emphasizes the gap between the perception of the object and the comprehension of the concept that produced it, the viewer can always bridge the gap. In this sense, the LeWittian aesthetic experience echoes the Kantian sublime, where an initial moment of being overwhelmed is followed by a moment of containment and representation of that which was formerly overwhelming because of its sheer size or its unimaginable force.[106] The experience of LeWitt's work—in a work like the cube series or

106 Kant's examples are mostly from nature—mountains, the Milky Way, a huge sea storm. The classic art historical representation of the sublime would be those Turner paintings of a very small boat in a huge sea, or the paintings by the Hudson River School of small people in the midst of an immense valley or mountain setting. Here is Kant's description of the phenomenon: "[What happens is that] our imagination strives to progress towards infinity, while our reason demands absolute totality as a real idea, and so [the imagination,] our power of estimating the magnitude of things in the world of sense,

in a wall drawing such as *Lines Not Straight Not Touching*—is distinguished from the Kantian sublime by the fact that it is not the infinite and unrepresentable that overwhelms one at first (as in the sublime) but rather a large finite number. Here, we do not have the romantic experience of triumph as the power of our mind defeats the terror of being overwhelmed. Rather, we are momentarily stupefied by a mass of perceptual data that remains in tension with a relatively simple conceptual schema that organizes that data. The experience is more like what Sianne Ngai has called the "*stuplime*": "in experiencing the sublime one confronts the infinite and elemental; in stuplimity, one confronts the machine or system, the taxonomy or vast combinatory, of which one is a part."[107] The sublime pretends to be universal and transcendental; the stuplime is more modest, but also more directly relevant to the social experience of modernity and modernization.

The relation that LeWitt establishes with the processes of modernization is that of a homeopathic negation. In order to neutralize them, LeWitt incorporates elements of the industrial process into both the production and the aesthetic experience of the artwork. Like Warhol, LeWitt references and mimics the industrial work process. In LeWitt's famous formulation, "When an artist uses a conceptual form of art, it means that all of the planning and decisions are made beforehand and the execution is a perfunctory affair. The idea becomes a machine that makes the art." The idea is a "machine" in the sense that it works automatically, without any subjective input. "To work with a plan that is preset is one way of avoiding subjectivity."[108] The planning and execution are as rigorously divided as in a factory where the workers have neither time nor liberty to plan or think creatively about their task. The labor of producing the object itself involves technical skill but no creativity, taste, or subjective decisions. This of course is the structure of rationalized labor, which is alienating precisely to the extent that the worker's subjectivity is unrecognized in the work process and, indeed, is destroyed as it forces the worker to become, as Marx argued, an "appendage of the machine."

LeWitt's conceptual approach is designed to duplicate a similar division of labor between planning and execution. In the production of the serial struc-

---

is inadequate to that idea. Yet this inadequacy itself is the arousal in us of the feeling that we have within us a supersensible power; and what is absolutely large is not an object of sense, but is the use that judgment makes use naturally of certain objects so as to [arouse] this (feeling), and in contrast with that any other use is small. Hence what is to be called sublime is not the object, but the attunement that the intellect [gets] through a certain presentation that occupies reflective judgment. . . . *Sublime is what even to be able to think proves that the mind has a power surpassing any standard of sense.*" *Critique of Judgment*, trans. Pluhar, 106 (Pluhar's emphasis).

107 Sianne Ngai, "Stuplimity: Boredom and Shock in 20th Century Aesthetics," *Postmodern Culture* 10, no. 2 (January 2000): 14.

108 LeWitt, "Paragraphs," 79.

tures and the wall drawings alike, LeWitt willingly embraces the moment of being worked mechanistically, following an automatic course according to a preset logic. But, in mimicking the industrial production process, he recreates it, "distorted in the state of similarity."[109] Where the rationalized work process is designed to maximize efficiency and predictability, LeWitt champions the "irrational thought," for it is the "irrational thought," when followed "absolutely and logically," that can produce "new experience."[110] Irrational ideas are precisely those that are unpredictable, wasteful, and "purposeless." In LeWitt's work the division of labor is a technique for producing surprise, in a manner, moreover, that is highly inefficient: "The artist cannot imagine his art, and cannot perceive it until it is complete."[111] The point of the compositional division of labor is to enable a moment of surprise, the surprise of perception unanticipated by and in tension with the conception. And as one can see in the working drawings for the *Incomplete Open Cubes*, when one decides in advance to follow an idea "absolutely and logically," it can entail unexpected amounts of labor. Hence, LeWitt can say that he is "always surprised and never really surprised": always surprised in the sense that one never can predict the nature of the perceptual experience from the concept, and never surprised in the sense that this gap or rupture between concept and perception can be adopted as a general rule.[112]

In essence, LeWitt dissevers the process of rationalization from rationality. He redirects the basic principles of the Fordist factory—systematic simplification (the reduction of "infinite to finite information loads") and the treatment of the human body as a systemic machine. Like Warhol, LeWitt reappropriates a mode of operation from the world of industrial capital and distorts it, defamiliarizes it, and puts it to a different use. His work is a kind of lesson in the way that systematicity and mechanicity—which at times seem wholly in service to means-ends rationality and the efficient production of predictable and hence profitable commodities—can be used to produce surprises. These surprises, I will now argue, are pleasurable precisely to the extent that they homeopathically neutralize elements of an everyday life defined by "functional differentiation."

* * *

The negotiation between perception on a local level and the total system that organizes that perception is not unlike the individual's experience of urban space. This is especially true in an urban space like Manhattan, where the grid system—in its conceptual totality—that we keep in our head allows us to negotiate city space even when we do not know where we are by way of

109 Benjamin, "Image of Proust," *SW2*, 240.

110 LeWitt, "Sentences on Conceptual Art," in *LeWitt: Critical Texts*, 88.

111 Ibid., 89.

112 Sol LeWitt, public discussion with Gary Garrels and Andrea Miller-Keller, San Francisco Museum of Modern Art, February 19, 2000.

experiential knowledge or visual recognition. In a place like Manhattan, the finiteness of the grid, inscribed on an island with definitive edges, means it is not an infinite space within which we are locating ourselves. As in LeWitt's systems, there is predictable, systemic variation within a large but finite totality. As a shorthand for this ability to have an image in our minds of the city we are negotiating, an image that gives us a sense of direction and location, Fredric Jameson, borrowing from Kevin Lynch's influential *Image of the City*, uses the term "cognitive mapping."[113] We might distinguish, however, as Lynch does, between a city in which one locates oneself according to the anonymous grid and one in which monuments, nodes, boundaries, and landmarks facilitate "the construction or reconstruction of an articulated ensemble which can be retained in memory and which the individual subject can map and remap along the moments of mobile, alternative trajectories."[114] The difference is that the grid requires little or no perceptual, experiential knowledge of the place: with the grid there is a gap between the total structure organizing the space and the perceptual experience of it. In a nongrid city like Boston, with points of reference like the Charles River, Boston Common, and Boston Harbor, one acquires a cognitive map of the city through repetitive experience of it. The grid, we might say, is a system developed for organizing large, finite bodies of information; in New York, it serves to reduce extraordinary information loads. Lynch emphasizes the emotional effects of our ability to produce a cognitive map. Insofar as an image of the total system in which one is located is crucial to establishing confidence in one's ability to live in the world—to see friends, go to concerts, go out to dinner, get to the train station—the lack of such an image can produce a sense of anxiety, loneliness, and alienation. LeWitt's *Incomplete Open Cubes* series at once references this moment of alienation and resolves it; it reproduces the difficulty of acquiring a cognitive map as well as the pleasures of having one.

We begin to see the social significance of LeWitt's conceptual approach when we recognize that it is not only for cities that cognitive maps are helpful. We need and desire cognitive maps of social space as well, of the social structures, systems, and institutions we negotiate on a daily basis. Such a map's function is "to enable a situational representation on the part of the individual subject to that vaster and properly unrepresentable totality which is the ensemble of society's structures as a whole."[115] We are speaking, then, of particular mode of ideology, one way of representing our "imaginary relationship to real conditions of existence" (in Althusser's classic formulation).[116] In social space, as in city space, one requires a cognitive map

113 *The Image of the City* (Cambridge, MA: MIT Press, 1960). Lynch's examples are Boston (nongrid) and Jersey City (grid).

114 Jameson, *Postmodernism*, 51.

115 Ibid., 51.

116 Louis Althusser, "Ideology and Ideological State Apparatuses," in *Lenin and Philosophy* (New York: Monthly Review Press, 1971).

to have a sense of agency. Here too, the lack of a map can produce a sense of anxiety, isolation, and immobility. Modernization could be seen as a process that continually widens the gap between individual experience and the systems that structure and enable that experience. If colonialism meant that the truth of life in the metropolis was in some way determined in and by the colonies—far from a local context—then globalization has made the gap even more substantial.[117] Today, the systems that constitute our lives and on which we rely in innumerable ways are even more diffuse, multiple, and distant. The complex operations of the computer on which I am writing this book, and of the global economies that enabled its production and made it affordable to me—these I could maybe comprehend if I now devoted my life to the task. But neither I nor anyone else can comprehend in their totality the aggregate of orders and systems that structures our daily life.

In such a context, the function of ideology is to pretend that the universal context in which daily life is to be understood is in fact accessible, there at hand, or that there is not really much *to* understand. Often, as we all know, it is consumption itself that promises to assuage one's anxieties and place one's life in an understandable and meaningful context. And such pleasures are hard to resist. But the fact that my computer was assembled in China, the wage that workers were paid to assemble it, the fact that these wages are kept low by practices actively supported by my government—these and many other considerations are nowhere to be found in the consumption context. There is no profit to be found in encouraging me to think about these problems. On the contrary, these are facts that lead to protest. These are the sorts of things being talked about by the people challenging the World Bank and the IMF in Seattle and Prague in the 1990s; by the Occupy movement in its effort to give voice to the 99%; by the Greek leaders and people as they attempt to resist what their former finance minister Yanis Varoufakis called the minotaur, the neoliberal imperative that the banks must be paid.

In an influential essay, Adorno and Horkheimer argue that the function of mass culture is to make the world seem instantly comprehensible in terms that are already available in order to make consumption easy and self-affirming and to prevent critical thought:

> Even during their leisure time, consumers must orient themselves according to the unity of production. The active contribution which Kantian schematism still expected of subjects—that they should, from the first, relate sen-

117 Jameson writes that colonialism would constitute a pivotal moment in that history, the moment when "the truth of [daily] experience no longer coincides with the place in which it takes place. The truth of that limited daily experience of London lies, rather, in India or Jamaica or Hong Kong; it is bound up with the whole colonial system of the British Empire that determines the very quality of the individual's subjective life. Yet those structural coordinates are no longer accessible to immediate lived experience and are often not even conceptualizable for most people" (*Postmodernism*, 411).

> suous multiplicity to fundamental concepts—is denied to the subject by industry. It purveys schematism as its first service to the customer. According to Kantian schematism, a secret mechanism within the psyche preformed immediate data to fit them into the system of pure reason. That secret has now been unraveled. . . . there is nothing left to classify, since the classification has already been preempted by the schematism of production.[118]

Even if I do not agree with their sense of the total domination of mass culture, to the exclusion of any possible resistance on the part of the consumer, I reference Adorno and Horkheimer here because they offer what I take to be a more or less received notion regarding mass culture's dominant paradigm. They are speaking of the way that Hollywood films and popular music are standardized into completely predictable forms. The ending of the movie, the length and pace of the sitcom, the placement of the chorus in a song, all follow forms that we know instantly because they correspond to preset formulas. There is nothing left for the consumer to classify. Extensive market research and focus groups mean that mass culture offers us what we want before we have even thought to want it. In this formulation, the mass-cultural text produces no tension with any universal since it inevitably matches up with it exactly. In order to be attractive, easy to view, and recognizable, mass culture must work, as Adorno and Horkheimer put it elsewhere, in the "worn grooves of association." Above all, the consumer must never be surprised or confused.

In this world, LeWitt's work constitutes a stoppage and an interruption. This is the reason that the surprise his work produces is pleasurable. In our everyday lives, we all experience the difficulty of matching up our daily experience with an understanding of the structures that make that experience possible. Adorno and Horkheimer argue, I think rightly, that one of the primary functions of mass culture is to disavow this difficulty. In contrast to this everyday world, LeWitt offers us the chance to experience this contradiction between the general and the particular, and what a relief it is to find a place to experience that set of feelings. But LeWitt also offers us a feeling for what it might be like if the overall principle organizing perceptual experience *could* be understood, if we as viewers had the power—as we always do in a LeWitt work—to think about the perceptual and the conceptual in relation to each other, even if that relationship is contradictory or paradoxical.

Here we can see the social significance of what Rosalind Krauss called LeWitt's "absurd nominalism." LeWitt's work is nominalist insofar as it resists the forms of universality already present in the world—namely the universality of universal equivalence. But he does not reject the universal outright; rather, he homeopathically incorporates "the universal" as a kind

118 "The Culture Industry: Enlightenment as Mass Deception," in *Dialectic of Enlightenment*, 98.

of empty signifier into his art in the form of the idea that is the machine that creates the art. Adorno argues that a nominalist art is the only art that can resist the forces of the commodity and mass culture that he wrote about with Horkheimer. As Jameson explains:

> Nominalism here dissociates the remnant of lived immediacy itself from its "universal," which has now become the universal equivalence and abstraction of the commodity form: the work of art, however, stubbornly holds on to both, in order to preserve the truth of their contradiction. . . . The commodity form, then, is to the situation of nominalism as the false universal to the bereft particular: the former's empty abstraction determines a heterogeneity of isolated data—whether in the world or the self—that can no longer be made to *mean*, if one understands "meaning" in the traditional way as the subsumption of a particular under a general."[119]

To bring this notion of nominalism to the *Incomplete Open Cubes* series, we might say that in that work, the "lived immediacy" of the cubes is dissociated from the total concept of the series as a whole, but the concept is still there across a gap, preserving "the truth of their contradiction." LeWitt's work reproduces the desire for and experience of a universal, but in a way that marks the discontinuity between his system and the systems at work in the everyday lifeworld. In this sense, LeWitt's is an avowedly false universality, quite different from the ideological false universality of mass culture, which pretends to be real. In this sense, it is mass culture that produces the optical illusion and LeWitt who unravels it. LeWitt's systems are like props designed to generate the *feeling* of pleasure one gets from a group of objects organized by a total system. While refusing to give in to the universal equivalence embodied in the commodity form, LeWitt's work nonetheless holds out the possibility of a total system. Here again, LeWitt's systems resemble but distort the commodity system. Instead of producing equivalences, they produce *variation*. And LeWitt's variations resist exchange; they resist an abstraction that would make them equivalent with each other.

Where Warhol's art is about liking and being alike—groups formed though likeness—LeWitt's is about group affinities formed through variation in relation to a system. This principle can be seen best in the *Incomplete Open Cubes* series. Each of the 122 incomplete cubes is unique, different from each of the others in a predetermined way. This makes LeWitt's seriality also about "likeness," though in a way distinct from Warhol's. Here, likeness is achieved through a shared lack. What the cubes all share is their incompletion, their falling short of cubeness. All lack the same thing, but each in a different specific way. And like Freud's melancholic, each incomplete cube

119 Fredric Jameson, *Late Modernism: Adorno, or The Persistence of the Dialectic* (New York: Verso, 1990), 168.

has introjected its loss; it cannot help but signify its lost cube. However—and here is one of the sources of the pleasure of the piece—the cubes are not alone in their loss; indeed, it is *loss* that brings them together. Brought together by what they are missing, they form a kind of diasporic community. In an abstracted way, LeWitt's work reproduces the feeling of belonging to a melancholic community, a feeling of affiliation arising from shared negation. This is a form of affiliation that can support collective opposition, and as such it may be especially apt for the present historical moment. Thus the attraction, the emotional-historical force motivating us to give in to the idea-machine that produces the work: By letting the idea be the "machine that makes the art," LeWitt is able to produce art that helps us to remember not only what it feels like to be aware of the machines that order our everyday lives. *Variations of Incomplete Open Cubes* reminds us also that the alienation that is an inevitable effect of being part of the machine-assemblage can be transformed into the basis of affiliation, and perhaps collective opposition.

Adorno once remarked that "the feelings provoked by artworks are real and to this extent extra-aesthetic."[120] He was writing of the fact that it is through their affective impact that artworks exceed themselves, contradicting their own apparent disinterestedness and autonomy. One might make the case that, inasmuch as affects need situations and objects to come into existence, artworks allow affects to come into existence in forms that otherwise might not exist. This is the locus of their political importance. While LeWitt and Warhol have quite different strategies for bringing unexpected affects into existence, being machine-like is for both of them a means of reorienting us in relation to our affects, providing us with alternative maps of our affective worlds. The paradox at the center of both of their projects is that the negation of subjectivity achieved through the imitation of the machine does not increase our alienation; instead it rescues us from our isolation by reminding us to notice the ways in which the very forces alienating us may make us alike and teach us how to become alike.

120 Adorno, *Aesthetic Theory*, 269.

3: Allegories of Boredom

A work needs only to be interesting. **Donald Judd**, "Specific Objects"[1]

[Pop Art] is liking things. **Andy Warhol**, "What Is Pop Art?"[2]

Allegory consists in the withdrawal of self-sufficiency of meaning from a given representation. **Fredric Jameson**, *Brecht and Method*[3]

Despite their significant differences, Andy Warhol and Donald Judd held similar ideas about the kind of aesthetic experience they hoped to create with their work. Each sought to solicit from his audience and produce for himself an apparently mundane form of emotional attachment, which Judd called "interest" and Warhol "liking." In doing so, they happily ignored loftier (and more widely recognized and respected) artistic goals such as the creation of beauty or sublimity, the representation of reality, or the expression of the artist's complex inner feelings or unique interpretation of the world. Moreover, each seemed to feel that the only art that could create an emotionally resonant aesthetic experience was one that was maximally emptied of subjective or expressive intent. As Alex Potts wrote (speaking of Judd, but just as accurately describing Warhol's work), "A situation has been reached where it is felt that any intensified bodily or libidinal charge will be

1 "Specific Objects," in *Donald Judd: Complete Writings 1959–1975* (Halifax: Press of the Nova Scotia College of Art and Design, 1975),184. An earlier version of this chapter was written for Ann Goldstein's *A Minimal Future: Art as Object 1958–1968*, exh. cat., Los Angeles Museum of Contemporary Art (Cambridge, MA: MIT Press, 2004). Many thanks to Ann for the invitation and to Marianne Stockebrand and Stefan Boddeker for being such gracious and generous hosts at the Chinati Foundation in Marfa; Stefan's knowledge and kind shepherding were especially appreciated. Mary Leclere, whose conversation and company in Marfa was very welcome, also offered helpful feedback on my thoughts about Judd.
2 *IBYM*, 16.
3 *Brecht and Method* (London: Verso, 1998), 122.

blocked if these qualities are seen to be objectified in the work."[4] In other words, for Judd and Warhol the only affecting art was one that appeared to be affectless.

When Warhol and Judd first started showing their art in galleries in the early 1960s, "the purging of authorial feeling and demonstrable intention," as James Meyer put it, "was poorly received by viewers steeped in the aesthetics of abstract expressionism, who insisted that a work of art was by definition the handmade product of a subjective self."[5] The distinctions that would later seem so significant and obvious—Judd's emphasis on nonreferentiality and construction versus Warhol's mimetic appropriation, Judd's apparent distance from consumer culture and Warhol's proximity to it, Judd's butch intellectuality and Warhol's fey naïveté—were less visible than what Judd and Warhol shared: the turn toward a "cool," noncomposed, affectless art to which "meaning" was difficult to attribute. I am interested in focusing on this moment of commonality between Judd and Warhol in order to consider the nature of the historical situation to which they are both responding. My aim is to examine what is at stake in their differences by determining the logics and limits of the field of contestation that they share.[6]

In proposing a different idea about what art is and does, Judd's "interesting" and Warhol's "liking" each also suggests a new understanding of the problem to which art is responding. By seeking to produce affect without representing it, they neatly reversed the model that had held for abstract expressionism and for modernism more broadly. There, the paintings were understood to be representing an emotional truth that had been repressed by the "manufactured bonhomie of the white collar workplace and the willed optimism of the culture promoted by advertising,"[7] but the critical voice that championed them was one that engaged with the paintings through a Kantian "disinterest." In other words, art should *represent* emotion but not

4 Potts, *The Sculptural Imagination* (New Haven, CT: Yale University Press, 2000), 305.

5 As Meyer recounts in *Minimalism: Art and Polemics in the Sixties* (New Haven, CT: Yale University Press, 2001): "During the spring of 1963 there was no 'minimalism' that could be opposed to 'pop.' Pop itself was hardly an established venture as the heterogeneous Janis [Gallery] show and numerous debates around this work suggested. As Larry Poons later recalled, during the early sixties 'there weren't any distinctions made between the abstractions of, say, Stella and Lichtenstein and Warhol's work. . . . For a moment everything existed on the same walls and it was fine'" (45).

6 A secondary goal is to render the overarching and sometimes misleading terms "Pop" and "minimalism" less familiar, enabling us to see differences within, as well as connections between, the two movements. The artists themselves had very different relations to the terms most often used to describe their work. Where Warhol more or less embraced "Pop," Judd repeatedly rejected the term "minimalism" and his placement under its rubric. He felt himself to have more in common with artists such as Claes Oldenburg, John Chamberlain, Yayoi Kusama, and Lee Bontecou than with other "minimalists" like Robert Morris.

7 Jackson Lears, *Fables of Abundance: A Cultural History of Advertising in America* (New York: Basic Books, 1994), 363.

solicit it. It was this space of disinterestedness that gave the beholder the necessary distance to have insights about emotions that were otherwise too immediate in their domination of one's everyday life. As I noted in chapter 2, the disinterested moment of aesthetic experience and judgment may be attractive precisely inasmuch as it is "shadowed by the wildest interest" from which the artwork is wrested.[8]

What then to do with an art that reverses this model and seeks the beholder's interest while representing no emotion? If, as Adorno suggests, art always contains an element of what it repulses, then we might hypothesize that Juddian interest and Warholian liking are attractive precisely inasmuch as the world from which they spring is characterized by an anaesthetizing boredom. Like Baudelaire, who faced an audience seized by *Ennui*, that "*monstre delicat*" who would "willingly make rubble of the earth / And swallow up creation in a yawn,"[9] so too Judd and Warhol seem to be responding to a world in which it is difficult to be interested in anything at all, in which, as Warhol said, "it would be so much easier not to care" (*IBYM*, 96). Judd and Warhol replace the dialectic between interest and disinterest with the one between interest and boredom.

There was a lot of anxiety about boredom in the 1950s and early 1960s. In books such as C. Wright Mills's *White Collar*, David Riesman's *The Lonely Crowd*, and William Whyte's *The Organization Man*, the increasing power of large, impersonal institutions—corporations, government bureaucracies, mass universities, the military establishment, the mass media—in structuring work and leisure alike was adduced as a source of a disabling sense of dissociation, especially among the new white middle classes.[10] And white-collar workers had it no worse than their wives, Betty Friedan argued in *The Feminine Mystique*, since the "endless, monotonous, unrewarding" nature of the housewife's work, combined with her social isolation and lack of avenues for individual expression, turns her into "an anonymous biological robot in a docile mass."[11]

In such accounts, everybody shared the experience of a mass culture that treated them as passive recipients of "mechanically vivified experiences," giving both parts to play in the "scheme for pre-scheduled mass emotions."[12] In promising to distract us from our boredom (enforcing the idea that boredom is something horrible to be avoided), while never surprising us, entertainment perpetuates the boredom that is supposedly being

8 Adorno, *Aesthetic Theory*, 11.

9 Charles Baudelaire, "To the Reader," in *The Flowers of Evil*, trans. Stanley Kunitz (New York: New Directions, 1955).

10 In addition to the books from the 1950s, see the cultural histories by Wilfred McClay, *The Masterless: Self and Society in Modern America* (Chapel Hill: University of North Carolina Press, 1994), and Brick, *Age of Contradiction*.

11 *The Feminine Mystique* (New York: Dell, 1963), 296.

12 C. Wright Mills, *White Collar* (New York: Oxford University Press, 1956), 333.

relieved. Moreover, in supporting the simple idea that "work" and "life" are things from which one needs escape, "leisure" activities naturalize the bindingness and inescapability of the nature of work and the economic system on which it depends. Thinking about the society in which we live becomes that-from-which-we-must-be-distracted. In comparison to entertainment, politics becomes "dull and threadbare."[13] Thus, despite a widespread sense of alienation, Mills writes, "there were no plain targets of revolt; and the cold metropolitan manner had so entered the soul of overpowered men that they were made completely private and blasé, deep down and for good."[14]

In his social history of melancholy, Wolf Lepenies argues that boredom typically appears as a collective phenomenon in classes that, for one reason or another, feel a lack of political agency, which means that boredom contains within it a readiness and desire for social transformation.[15] Thus Baudelaire could write of converting a disillusioned *ennui* into *spleen*, an active interest in and anger about the losses one suffered and a sense of urgency about the need to redress them *right now*. The success of the civil rights movement in interesting and mobilizing people toward political action, and the subsequent explosion in the 1960s of social movements and countercultures, testifies to the desire and readiness for transformation that lay nascent within the boredom that writers like Friedan and Mills decried.

In creating affectless works, Warhol and Judd also presumed that there were affects in their audiences just waiting to find a space in which they could appear. If, as Siegfried Kracauer wrote, the problem is that "even if one perhaps isn't interested in the world, the world itself is much too interested for one to find the peace and quiet necessary to be as thoroughly bored with the world as it ultimately deserves,"[16] then Judd's and Warhol's task was to create work that did *not* promise to distract, nor claim to represent authentic feelings (like abstract expressionism), in order to create a space in which otherwise obscured or repressed affects could come into being.

Thus, what Warhol called "the cold 'no comment'" look (*POP*, 7) marked a departure from advertising images that "would have feelings, they would have a style . . . the process of doing work in commercial art was machine-like, but the attitude had feeling to it" (*IBYM*, 18). Unlike advertisements, which generally strive to associate a product with a specific emotional experience, Judd's and Warhol's work sought not to produce a *specific* affective response so much as to clear the space for *any* affect to occur. This was a tactic cham-

13 For Mills, political life was perhaps the most serious casualty of the new mass media, insofar as political concerns are squeezed into "formulas which are repeated and repeated," the main function of which is to "divert from the explicitly political" (ibid., 336).

14 Ibid., 329.

15 Lepenies, *Melancholy and Society* (Cambridge, MA: Harvard University Press, 1992), esp. 50–62.

16 Kracauer, "Boredom," in *The Mass Ornament*, trans. and ed. Thomas Y. Levin (Cambridge, MA: Harvard University Press, 1995), 332.

pioned by Yippie activist Abbie Hoffman, who wrote in *Revolution for the Hell of It*, "Blank space, the interrupted statement, the unsolved puzzle, they are all involving. . . . Blank space is the transmission of information whereby the viewer has an opportunity to become involved as a participant."[17] The strategy is also not unlike the one employed by the psychoanalyst, who strives to facilitate perspective on one's own emotional life so that one can become interested in the mechanisms of one's own transferences. Bringing this transference into existence was best achieved, Freud thought, by displaying in therapy a "calm quiet attentiveness," and appearing "impenetrable to the patient, and, like a mirror, reflect[ing] nothing but what is shown to him."[18]

By mimicking the lack of affect one might feel toward the everyday world of things and images (as against the overcharged emotionality that characterizes the mode of address of that world itself), Judd and Warhol's work awakens the basic boredom that the everyday life of late capital "deserves." Martin Heidegger might have written that Warhol and Judd were trying to awaken boredom not just as a passing feeling to be ignored or avoided, but as a fundamental mode of attunement, a basic mood or *Stimmung* of their historical moment.[19] This "profound" boredom tells us something about our shared situation; it discloses the degree to which channels of affective engagement and connection are absent or blocked. The particular affects that might arise in this mood are thus themselves a kind of social datum, inasmuch as the feelings that might come into being are precisely ones that have otherwise been unable to find a place or an object where they might attach.

At the level of aesthetic experience, this more fundamental boredom also feels different from what we usually call "boredom." It is not characterized by impatience for time to pass, nor is it the self-disavowing, deadening, depressive *Ennui* of Baudelaire's "To the Reader." Instead, it is an opening, a transitional state in which one's capacities for affecting and being affected have been increased, and where one might be surprised by the tendencies of one's perception, feeling, and attention. (Adam Phillips: "We can think of boredom as a defense against waiting, which is, at one remove, the acknowledgement of the possibility of desire."[20]) If "sleep is the apogee of physical

17 *Revolution for the Hell of It* (New York: Pocket Books, 1968/1970), 83–86; passage reprinted in *Cultural Resistance Reader*, ed. Stephen Duncombe, 328–30 (New York: Verso, 2002).

18 "Recommendations for Physicians on the Psychoanalytic Method of Treatment (1912)," in *Therapy and Technique*, ed. Philip Rieff (New York: Collier Books, 1963), 117–26 (quotes, 118, 124).

19 See Heidegger on boredom as a fundamental *Stimmung* in *Fundamental Concepts of Metaphysics*, esp. 132–59. See also Giorgio Agamben's comments on Heidegger on boredom in *The Open: Man and Animal* (Stanford, CA: Stanford University Press, 2004), esp. 63–70.

20 "On Being Bored," in *On Kissing, Tickling and Being Bored: Psychoanalytic Essays on the Unexamined Life* (Cambridge, MA: Harvard University Press, 1993), 68–78, 76.

relaxation," Walter Benjamin writes in "The Storyteller," then "boredom is the apogee of mental relaxation." In such a state, one's defenses against being affected have been lowered, which is why Benjamin saw there "the dream bird that hatches the egg of experience."[21] In what follows, I will examine Judd's and Warhol's efforts to produce settings in which this "dream bird" might come to nest, a task that was trickier than it might seem since, as Benjamin notes, the "slightest rustling" drives the bird away.

The Opposition to Interest

Literalist work is often condemned—when it is condemned—for being boring. A tougher charge would be that it is merely interesting.

Michael Fried, "Art and Objecthood"

The question of interest and its validity as an aesthetic goal occupies a central place in the most famous and influential essay on minimalism, Michael Fried's antiminimalist jeremiad "Art and Objecthood." There Fried assailed "literalism" (his name for minimalism) for, among other things, its abdication of all standards of aesthetic value. As the peak of his demonstration of minimalism's corrupt and corrupting relativism, Fried cites Judd's suggestion that "a work needs only to be interesting," contrasting it with the "conviction" of a work's quality that (in his view) real modernist work inspires. "For Judd, as for literalist sensibility generally, all that matters is whether or not a given work is able to elicit and sustain (his) interest."[22] For Fried, interest is a low aesthetic standard that facilitates a thoroughgoing degradation of the autonomy of art (and especially painting). Interest is the kind of feeling one has everyday; there is nothing to distinguish it as "aesthetic," nothing to separate it out from life. Moreover, it has no *telos* other than its own continuation, duration itself. The experience of interest, Fried wrote, was "endless the way a road might be, if it were circular, for example."[23]

For Fried, the goal of interest also implies a dubious solicitation of the beholder. Like theater (Fried's central charge against minimalism), the work exists for an audience; its ontology includes the beholder. Fried writes (citing Robert Morris), "Whereas in previous art 'what is to be had from the work is located strictly within it,' the experience of literalist art is of an object in a situation—one that, virtually by definition, includes the beholder."[24] Rather than take the beholder into a different world brought into existence by the work, the work addresses and enters into the world of the beholder.

21 "The Storyteller," in *Walter Benjamin: Selected Writings*, vol. 3, ed. Howard Eiland and Michael W. Jennings (Cambridge, MA: Harvard University Press, 2002), 149.

22 Michael Fried, "Art and Objecthood," in *Art and Objecthood* (Chicago: University of Chicago Press, 1998), 164–65.

23 Ibid., 166.

24 Ibid., 153.

This means that the boundaries between "art" and "life" become murky, the critical distance of the viewer is effaced, and there is no longer any clear standard or tradition in relation to which the work might be judged because it is not exactly clear what object is being judged.

In contrast, for Fried, modernist painters are motivated by something more ambitious—the conviction that the quality of one's work can compare with the best offered by the tradition of that particular art form.[25] To experience this art, to "get" it, one has to be able to believe that "at every moment the work itself" could be "wholly manifest," to believe in its ability to elevate us into a state outside of time, a place of world-renewing and redeeming "presentness." The work's ability to inspire this sense of "conviction" (which is only possible if there can be no doubt about the basis on which it is to be judged) is the condition of possibility for its reception. We get our clearest sense of the value of this experience (which is, despite Fried's own conviction, somewhat obscure) in the final lines of the essay: "I want to call attention to the utter pervasiveness—the virtual universality—of the sensibility or mode of being that I have characterized as corrupted or perverted by theater. We are all literalists most of our lives. Presentness is grace."[26] In these final lines, the compensatory and redemptive quality of Fried's defense of art becomes fully explicit: art is valuable inasmuch as it allows an escape from the literalism of everyday life. What becomes clear here is that the persuasiveness of Fried's argument rests entirely on our agreement that the world we live in is in fact characterized by "literality" and theatricality, something Fried presents as self-evident (and thus not requiring explanation). Thus, his argument presupposes an idea about modernity (as characterized by "literality") that he nowhere elaborates or theorizes.

The fundamental aesthetic reorientation of the 1960s starts to look less like an abandonment of value and more like an attempt to rethink what value is when we consider these developments in relation to the experience of a change in the nature of everyday life and not only in relation to the internal conversations of art history. It is not difficult to see, for example, how new technologies of reproduction, and the challenges made to art by the forms of mass culture that these technologies enabled, constituted an important historical context not just for Judd but for art in the 1960s more generally. The increasing importance of the image, its proliferation in everyday life, its commodification, and its use in advertising changed how people related to all forms of two-dimensional representation. In fact, we might say that

25 This implies a deep knowledge of and engagement with tradition, as exemplified in T. S. Eliot's "Tradition and the Individual Talent." Fried insists that the question of quality can only be decided in relation to the tradition in a specific medium. Part of the problem with minimalist "theatricality" was that it was between media or, as Judd put it in the opening sentence of "Specific Objects," "neither painting nor sculpture." See Fried, "Art and Objecthood," 164.

26 Ibid., 168.

it is not literalness and duration that has become pervasive so much as our confrontation by images defined by their reproducibility and multiplicity and the instantaneity with which they demand to be read. The images we see every day (of the Coca-Cola logo, the Marlboro man, the busty blond in a tight shirt) work by signal, they run in what Adorno and Horkheimer called the "worn grooves of association." They are icons, the meaning of which we always know in advance, and as such do not require interpretation.[27] Despite its conceptual distance from the experience of consumption, Fried's celebration of presentness and disdain for duration nonetheless corresponds with it. Fried's critical energies should have been directed not toward minimalism but toward the historical forces to which minimalism was responding.

Many critics have argued that Fried is incorrect in his evaluation of minimalism but more or less accurate in the terms he proposes for understanding it, in particular regarding its "theatricality."[28] Thus, minimalism is valued, for example, for the way that it can put the viewing body itself on stage, giving us a heightened awareness of our own modes of perception. I will argue, however, not only against Fried's evaluation of minimalism but also against his terms, at least for thinking about Judd's work. Fried's misrecognition of the nature of his own allergy to minimalism also distorts the terms with which he evaluates it. I do not think concepts such as theatricality or the abdication of value or the promotion of endless repetition help us understand how Judd promotes an aesthetic experience that attempts to intervene in the very modernity of which Fried seems unaware. Not only does Judd have a different understanding of the world in which both he and Fried live, but he is (unlike Fried) open to the possibility that art should be in conversation with the broader social context and that its value might be determined by the nature of that conversation.[29] For Judd, the medium of this conversation is the affect of interest.

27 The styles of Pollock and Rothko were themselves being appropriated as instantly readable signals of American high culture and sophistication in American cold war propaganda, advertising, and fashion shoots. See Lears, *Fables of Abundance*, esp. 366–67, and the now classic Serge Guilbaut, *How New York Stole the Idea of Modern Art*, trans. Arthur Goldhammer (Chicago: University of Chicago Press, 1983). That speed was an important feature of emergent consumer culture in the United States is also evidenced, for example, by the invention of "fast food," which we might date to the opening of Ray Kroc's first McDonald's franchise in 1955.

28 For Hal Foster, for example, the "fundamental reorientation" inaugurated by minimalism is that "the viewer, refused the safe, sovereign space of formal art, is cast back on the here and now; and rather than scan the surface of a work for a topographical mapping of the properties of the medium, he or she is prompted to explore the perceptual consequences of a particular intervention in a given state." "The Crux of Minimalism," in *The Return of the Real* (Cambridge, MA: MIT Press, 1996), 38.

29 "The experience of another time and society, which is tenuous since so little is known, can nevertheless, almost uniquely, be gained through art" (Judd, *Complete Writings*, 33).

Polarity

Obviously, what you feel and what things are aren't the same.

Donald Judd, "Jackson Pollock"[30]

Unsurprisingly, Judd was less than sanguine about Fried's attack on him. Given the well-known and foundational place occupied by the notion of interest and interestedness in modern aesthetics and twentieth-century theories of affect, of which Fried should have known, it must be admitted that Judd had a point. In an interview with James Meyer, Judd referred to the notion of interest developed by the American philosopher Ralph Barton Perry, a follower of William James.[31] For Perry, interest was the *sole* source of value: "That which is an object of interest is *eo ipso* invested with value."[32] Value cannot exist outside of interest. As Silvan Tomkins puts it, "There is no human competence which can be achieved in the absence of a sustaining interest, and the development of cognitive competence is peculiarly vulnerable to anomie . . . to think, as to engage in any other human activity, one must care, one must be excited, must be continually rewarded."[33] This is not an object-centered theory of value, but one that was concerned to understand *how* people attribute value to things, how interest is produced and sustained. Judd did not want to obviate the question of value so much as redefine it in a way that seemed more relevant to the current situation, one in which the production of interest presented itself as a real task.[34]

For Judd, the key to producing interest was what he called "polarity," a concept that may be illustrated by his reading of Claes Oldenburg.[35] He takes the example of Oldenburg's large floppy hamburger. The primary trick, according to Judd, is that "Oldenburg . . . made the emotive form, with him basic and biopsychological, the same as the shape of an object."[36] Oldenburg brings two things into collision. On the one hand, there is the essentially corporeal, fleshy feeling that is generated by the latex-filled painted

30 "Jackson Pollock," in *Complete Writings*, 195.

31 Meyer, *Minimalism*, 140.

32 Ralph Barton Perry, *General Theory of Value: Its Meaning and Basic Principles Construed in Terms of Interest* (New York: Longmans, Green and Company, 1926), 115.

33 In Sedgwick and Frank, *Shame and Its Sisters*, 77. Tomkins emphasizes that not only sustained cognitive activity requires a particular active and sustainable interest, but even basic drives such as hunger and sexual desire can be suppressed if there is insufficient interest to support them.

34 On the logic of interest and its status as an aesthetic category, see Sianne Ngai's important chapter "Merely Interesting," in *Our Aesthetic Categories* (published after I first composed this essay, but speaking directly to its concerns).

35 For a different reading of the place of polarity in Judd's work, see Richard Schiff, "Donald Judd: Fast Thinking," in *Donald Judd: Late Work* (New York: Pace Wildenstein, 2000), 4–23.

36 Judd, "Specific Objects," 188.

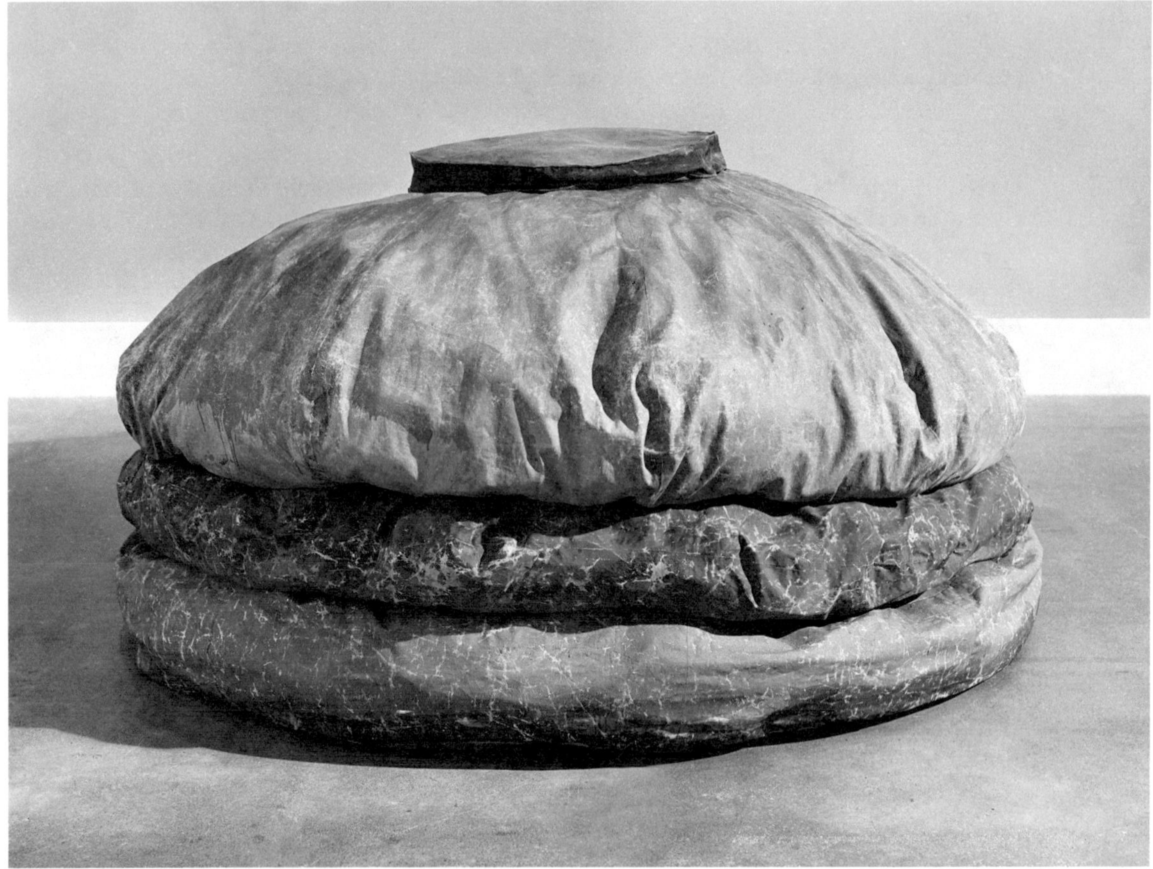

3.1 Claes Oldenburg, *Floor Burger*, 1962. Canvas filled with foam rubber and cardboard boxes, painted with latex and Liquitex, 52 inches high; 84 inches diameter. Art Gallery of Ontario, Toronto, Purchase 1967. © 1962 Claes Oldenburg.

canvas, *bodiliness* rather than a body.[37] On the other hand, there is what we see literally represented—and that is a hamburger and bun: the emotive form has become the same as the shape of an object. Here, the emotion and the perception, which we tend to think of as fitting together, push away from each other, setting up an internal polarity. (As Judd says, "Obviously, what you feel and what things are aren't the same.") The contrast defamiliarizes

37 Judd's reading of Oldenburg's large light switch is more specific about the "emotive form" at work: "The whole switch seems to be like breasts but doesn't resemble them and isn't descriptive, even abstractedly. There aren't two breasts, just two nipples. The two switches don't seem like two breasts. As nipples though, they are far too large for the chest. . . . The form is whole and simple and has no discrete parts. The two switches aren't separate from the rectangle; the three physically separable parts don't, visually, add up to the whole. They're made as a whole. They're the same material and it bulges and sags the same throughout." "Claes Oldenburg," in Judd, *Complete Writings*, 193.

both the emotion and the perception. In fact, Judd makes the case that the feelings attached to the emotive form (bodiliness in this case) cannot come into existence as such—they need a form, a shuttle, as it were, on which they can ride into the world.[38]

Just as the patient needs a therapist onto whom s/he can "transfer" feelings from some past relationship, so too these emotions need an object through which they can come into existence. In the case of analysis, the perception of some similarity between a person from your past (a parent, for example) and the therapist is what is needed to allow the transfer to take place. The similarity can be quite minimal (the structural position of authoritative interlocutor is often enough); it is as if the emotions are waiting for a similarity to appear on which they can ride. They cannot be represented as such; for Judd they "disappear when you try to make them into imaginable visual or tactile forms."

The special force of Oldenburg's work is generated out of the fact that it is a hamburger, the quintessential fast food, that gives a corporeally rooted emotion a way to occur. In doing so, Oldenburg has reversed the "usual anthropomorphism" wherein "the appearance of human feelings in things that are inanimate or not human usually [occurs] as if those feelings are the essential nature of the thing described."[39] In a perversion of T. S. Eliot's famous "objective correlative," instead of providing a way to objectify an emotion that is appropriate to it, that allows us to substitute that thing for the emotion, in Oldenburg (*par* Judd) the trick is to stimulate an emotion precisely in a spot where it will be in tension with the representation.[40] The nature of that tension will be the truth content of the work.

Polarity is a way to conceptualize, not the expression of emotions, but a kind of scene for their appearance, one in which we can see the emotion's distinctness from that which expresses it. Oldenburg, in Judd's reading, objectifies our emotions in a form that estranges us from them for a moment. Judd too is interested in producing this kind of a productive self-estrangement from our emotions. And, as Walter Benjamin argued (in relation to Baudelaire), self-estrangement is "the decisively new ferment that enters the *taedium vitae* and turns it into *spleen*."[41] To convert boredom into interest, one needs first to become alienated from oneself, to gain some de-

38 "The sense of objects occurs with forms that are near some simple, basic, profound forms you feel. These disappear when you try to make them into imaginable visual or tactile forms. The reference to objects gives them a way to occur. The reference and the basic form as one thing is Oldenburg's main idea" (ibid., 192).

39 Ibid., 191.

40 Eliot: "The only way of expressing emotion in the form of art is by finding an 'objective correlative'; in other words, a set of objects, a situation, a chain of events which shall be the formula for that particular emotion; such that when the external facts, which must terminate in a sensual experience, are given, the emotion is immediately evoked" ("Hamlet," in *Selected Prose*, 48).

41 Benjamin, "Central Park," *SW4*, 163.

familiarizing distance on one's own emotional life. Judd's "specific object" is essentially a technology for the production of such a self-estrangement.

"The Language of Things"

Radicalized, what is called reification probes for the language of things. It narrows the distance to the idea of that nature that extirpates the primacy of human meaning. Emphatically modern art breaks out of the sphere of the portrayal of emotions and is transformed into the expression of what no significative language can achieve.

Theodor Adorno, *Aesthetic Theory*[42]

Judd's objects aspire to the condition of natural beauty. This goal is suggested in his work in several ways. For example, he often organizes his objects using the Fibonacci series, in which each number is the sum of the two previous numbers (1, 1, 2, 3, 5, 8, etc)—a sequence also found in natural things like pinecones, spiral shells, and the spacing of flower petals. Also, like a mountain range, tree, or waterfall, Judd's works demand one's physical presence in order to apprehend them; they do not lend themselves to reproduction. Because Judd's objects always produce multiple and variable images, any single view and the photographic image it might produce is always radically partial.[43] Furthermore, the frequent use of translucent and reflective material means that what one sees also varies with the quality of light present, and thus in cases where the work is displayed in natural light (always Judd's preference) what one sees also depends on the season, weather, and time of day.

Judd's "wall stacks" with the Plexiglas tops and bottoms (one of the examples Judd himself frequently mentions) provide good examples of the variability and complexity of the visual experiences offered by his work. When one faces a wall stack at a distance of approximately twenty feet, for example, one sees a row of shiny metal rectangles that seem to float in the air in front of the wall, a sense that is amplified by the glowing light that renders the wall to either side a light yellow (or orange or pink). As one moves closer or walks to the side, the cantilever from the wall becomes apparent, as does the nature of the construction of the shelflike boxes themselves. From very close, one can look through the Plexiglas inside the work and see the internal seams, the width of the material, how the different pieces are

42 *Aesthetic Theory*, 60.

43 Judd notes: "I'm also interested in what might be called black areas, or just plain areas, and what is seen obliquely, like the stack with the Plexiglas top and bottom. When viewed frontally the sides are seen obliquely, so the color and the plane and the face are somewhat obscure compared to the front. It's the other way around when seeing the side. In most of my pieces, there are no front or sides—it depends on the viewing position of the observer." "Don Judd: An Interview with John Coplans," in *don judd*, ed. John Coplans (Pasadena, CA: Pasadena Art Museum, 1971), 36.

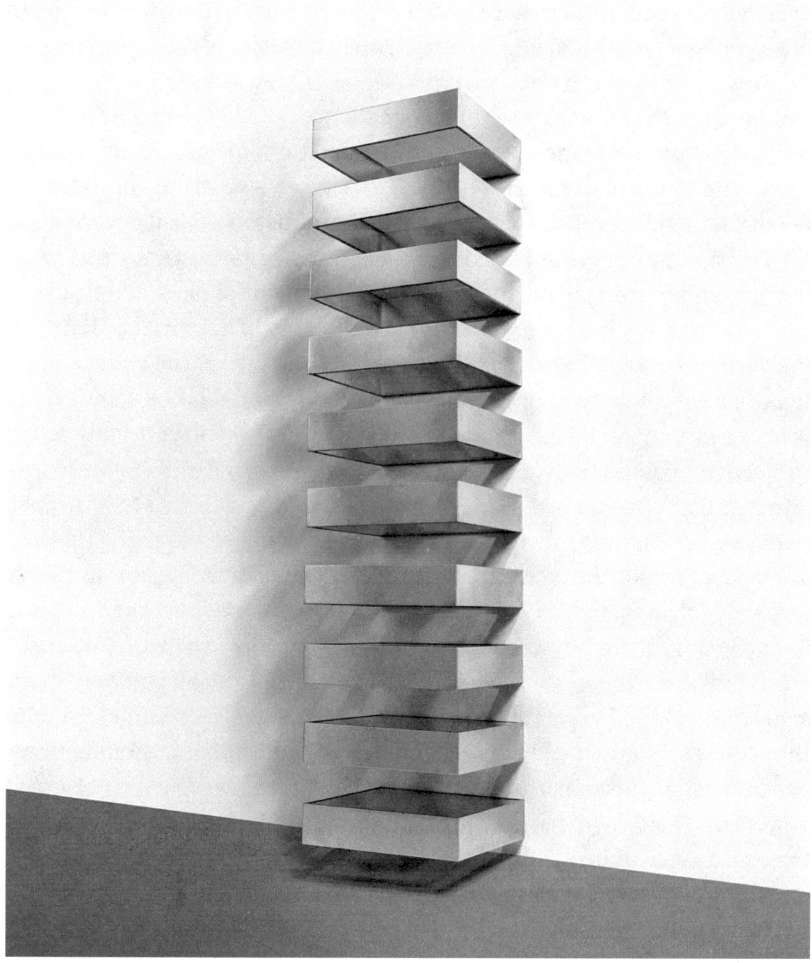

3.2 Donald Judd, untitled (DSS 120), 1968. Stainless steel and yellow Plexiglas; 10 units, each 9 × 40 × 31 inches. Private collection/Bridgeman Images. © 2016 Judd Foundation/ Artists Rights Society (ARS), New York.

joined. Up close one also begins to notice the complicated views established interior to the column formed by the work. Light that has filtered already through one piece of Plexiglas casts a different light onto the piece of Plexiglas below it than does the natural light alone, so that the Plexiglas itself appears to be multicolored.[44] With this work, as with much of Judd's work,

44 Like a film still, any photo of Judd's work represents a single moment in a work whose value and ontology lies in its duration. This is not to say that Judd's works do not make excellent, beautiful photographs—the plays of light and shadow, sharp edges, and bright hues invite the photographic eye. But, inasmuch as the point is to experience the visual complexity produced by movement around the work, a photograph substitutes a view that is fundamentally incompatible with that experience. Such a photographic image presents a view the human eye never really had.

every view seems to reference its own incompleteness, its own proximity to other, oblique views that may be surprisingly distinct.

This is one aspect of the visual complexity of Judd's objects, which, when combined with the work's significatory silence, produces an aesthetic experience akin to the one we associate with natural beauty. That is, Judd's works attempt to refuse to mean, allude, or express, but at the same time offer surprisingly complex, even internally contradictory, visual experiences.

The significatory silence is the result of Judd's rigorous efforts to avoid "composing," probably the most distinctive element of his aesthetic ideology. Noncomposition for Judd meant avoiding the hierarchical ordering of the parts of an object, such that, for example, there are central and marginal figures, foreground and background. This hierarchical relation among parts is where figuration, the invitation to interpretation, and the attribution of a subjectivity behind the work sneak in. It is nearly impossible to avoid this effect in painting, since, as Judd wrote, "Anything on a surface has space behind it."[45] Painting, in other words, is about giving you a feeling that you are seeing through the painting into a space; inasmuch as "a painting always has a model on its outside," it "is always a window."[46] Thus, like Gertrude Stein, who "made innumerable efforts to make words write without sense" but found that "there is no such thing as putting [words] together without sense," Judd "tried to get rid of spatial illusionism, but . . . couldn't."[47] While three dimensions helped to relieve the window-effect that Judd sometimes called "spatial illusionism," a hierarchical relation between parts remained a problem. This is the basis of Judd's critique of Mark di Suvero: "A beam thrusts, a piece of iron follows a gesture; together they form a naturalistic and anthropomorphic image. The space corresponds."[48]

In a modern update of the biblical prohibition on graven images, Judd's task was to produce an object that gave one nothing to latch onto in order to make guesses about what the artist might be saying or feeling.[49] At the beginning, achieving the effect of noncomposition proved to be quite difficult. Speaking of one of his early pieces, a red plywood box with a recessed semicircular trough across the top, Judd noted that "I did a great deal of juggling to make it uncomposed. I spent a lot of time determining where the trough should be on top of the box, having to do with it not being in any particular or obvious spot. . . . I wanted to get rid of all the extraneous meanings—

45 Judd, "Specific Objects," 182.

46 Gilles Deleuze, *The Fold: Leibniz and the Baroque*, trans. Tom Conley (Minneapolis: University of Minnesota Press, 1993), 27.

47 Stein, in "A Transatlantic Interview 1946," in *A Primer for the Gradual Understanding of Gertrude Stein*, ed. Robert Bartlett Haas (Los Angeles: Black Sparrow Press, 1973), 18 (describing experiments that led to the writing of *Tender Buttons*); Judd, "Interview with John Coplans," 21.

48 Judd, "Specific Objects," 183.

49 "It's not conceived part by part, it's done in one shot. The progressions made it possible to use an asymmetrical arrangement, yet to have some sort of order not involved in composition" ("Interview with John Coplans," 41).

connections to things that didn't mean anything to the art."[50] Later decisions were motivated by a similar desire to avoid the appearance of mystery or ambiguity as much as possible, to avoid elements that might invite "reading in." For example, the move from plywood to factory-fabricated metal and Plexiglas removed traces of the artist's hand. Likewise, in order to disclose the nature of the material that he was working with as much as possible he would do things like recess the top of a box to make visible the thickness of the material, or use Plexiglas to open up the interior of constructions so that they were not hidden. Seriality ("one thing after another") and instantly recognizable geometric forms became Judd's main strategies for avoiding the appearance of hierarchical relations between parts.

Like Leibniz's *monad*, the Juddian object offers no windows "through which anything could come in or out" but at the same time contains the surrounding world by reflecting and refracting it.[51] That there is no representation going on in Judd's works does not mean there is not a lot to see. Indeed, with Judd's works it is not always possible to determine *what* it is that you are seeing, even as oblique angles and refracted, colored light beckon one to explore what is there. One frequently gets the sense that there "appears to be more than what is literally there."[52] In the slightly glowing floating rectangles of the wall stacks, or the boxes with colored or reflective interiors that seem bigger than the shiny metal that encases them, we are often confronted with visual information that seems to exceed or contradict the rigorously noncomposed object before us.

This surprising visual information is often presented in oblique or apparently marginal spaces or surfaces. One might examine, for example, the space *between* the horizontal wall boxes. At first these spaces seem empty. But in keeping with Judd's refusal to hierarchize—to allow any element of the work to be background, empty space, or part of a figure—one finds in this space a beguiling set of reflections. There is one set of reflections on the external surface of the Plexiglas and another *inside* the box. The two cannot be seen at the same time, since one has to refocus one's eyes to shift from one to the other. The interior reflection redoubles the space between the boxes. One sees reflected a stripe of wall the same width as the gap between the boxes. But upon close examination, the reflections do not match up with the adjacent brick wall, so the reflection must be coming from somewhere else. The "outside" of the work is represented—in a confusing, distorted way—as an effect of reflective and refractive relations "inside" the work. The work thereby performs its own internal differences, its nonidentity with itself as an object of perception.

By not "meaning," avoiding composition and thereby discouraging the beholder from attributing a subjectivity to the work, Judd's objects are freed

50 Ibid., 32.

51 G. W. Leibniz, "Monadology," in *Leibniz: Philosophical Texts*, trans. Richard Francks and R. S. Woolhouse (Oxford: Oxford University Press, 1998), 268.

52 Adorno, *Aesthetic Theory*, 71.

from the burden of identity: it is not so much that we see them "in themselves" as that we see the impossibility of seeing them in themselves; we see that there is no object in-itself available to perception. This is perhaps what Robert Smithson called the "uncanny materiality" he saw in Judd's works.[53] Such an uncanny lack of self-identity is usually reserved only for "nature."

Adorno argues that "natural beauty is the trace of the nonidentical in things under the spell of universal identity."[54] The trace of nonidentity is an escape from the mutually reinforcing logic of identity and universal exchangeability that governs everyday life. In this logic, everything—land, cows, square meters of sheltered space, diamonds, organically grown arugula, human labor, shoes—must be available for abstraction into the universal exchangeability of money. The flip side of universal exchangeability is self-identity or genuineness: exchange demands that there be a measurable, specifiable, knowable "thing" to be exchanged. Thus, Adorno is as suspicious of the genuine as he is of universal exchangeability itself:

> The discovery of genuineness as a last bulwark of individualistic ethics is a reflection of industrial mass production. Only when countless standardized commodities project, for the sake of profit, the illusion of being unique, does the idea take shape, as their antithesis, yet in keeping with the same criteria, that the non-reproducible is the truly genuine.[55]

That which announces its internal contradictoriness for the same reason resists this logic. Perhaps it would be more precise to say that we hold onto the thought of an outside of reification by reserving a setting for perception that is neither "genuine" nor subjected to the "spell of universal identity" but that resists both in its ambient, nonidentifiable quality. Thus, "nature" does not offer its visual pleasures to the objectifying (identificatory) gaze of the person who has made the trip to a famous site in order to gaze at beauty ("oh, this is beautiful!") but only to a relaxed, unconscious apperception in which we attain a state of "free-floating attention," the affective state Freud suggested for the analyst, which is also how Adam Phillips describes "boredom." Juddian "interest" requires just such a boredom.

Judd's *100 Aluminum Boxes* (1982–1986) vividly dramatize the aesthetic effects most characteristic of his work more generally. The boxes are permanently installed in Marfa, Texas, in two former Army artillery sheds. There are forty-eight boxes in one room and fifty-two in the other, arranged in long rows on the floor. Each box has been altered in some way: a side missing,

53 Robert Smithson, "Donald Judd (1965)," in *Donald Judd: Early Fabricated Work* (New York: Pace Wildenstein, 1998), 15. See also Rosalind Krauss's "The Uncanny Materiality," in the same volume.

54 Adorno, *Aesthetic Theory*, 73.

55 Adorno, *Minima Moralia*, 155.

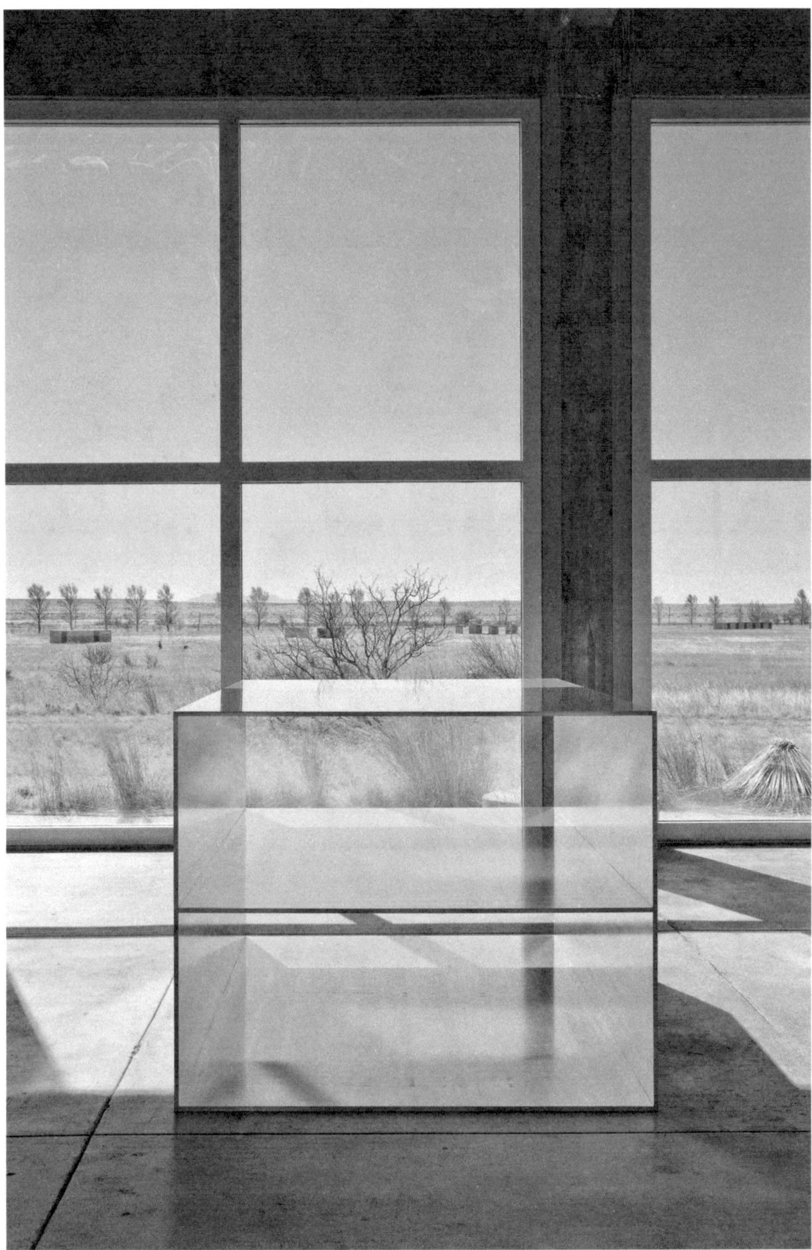

3.3 Donald Judd, untitled (100 untitled works in mill aluminum) (detail), 1982–1986. Aluminum; 100 units, each 41 × 51 × 72 inches. Collection Chinati Foundation, Marfa, TX. Photograph: Douglas Tuck. © 2016 Judd Foundation/Artists Rights Society (ARS), New York.

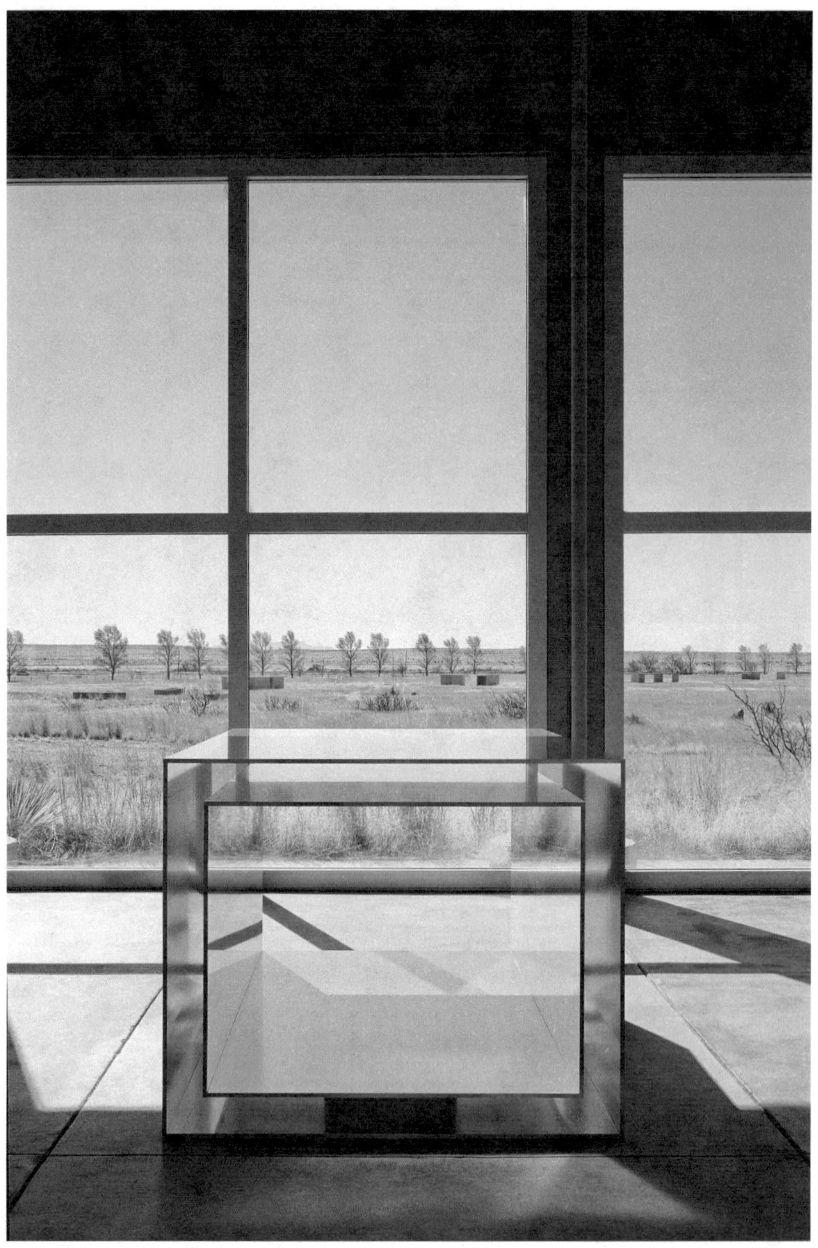

3.4 Donald Judd, untitled (100 untitled works in mill aluminum) (detail), 1982–1986. Aluminum; 100 units, each 41 × 51 × 72 inches. Collection Chinati Foundation, Marfa, TX. Photograph: Douglas Tuck. © 2016 Judd Foundation/Artists Rights Society (ARS), New York.

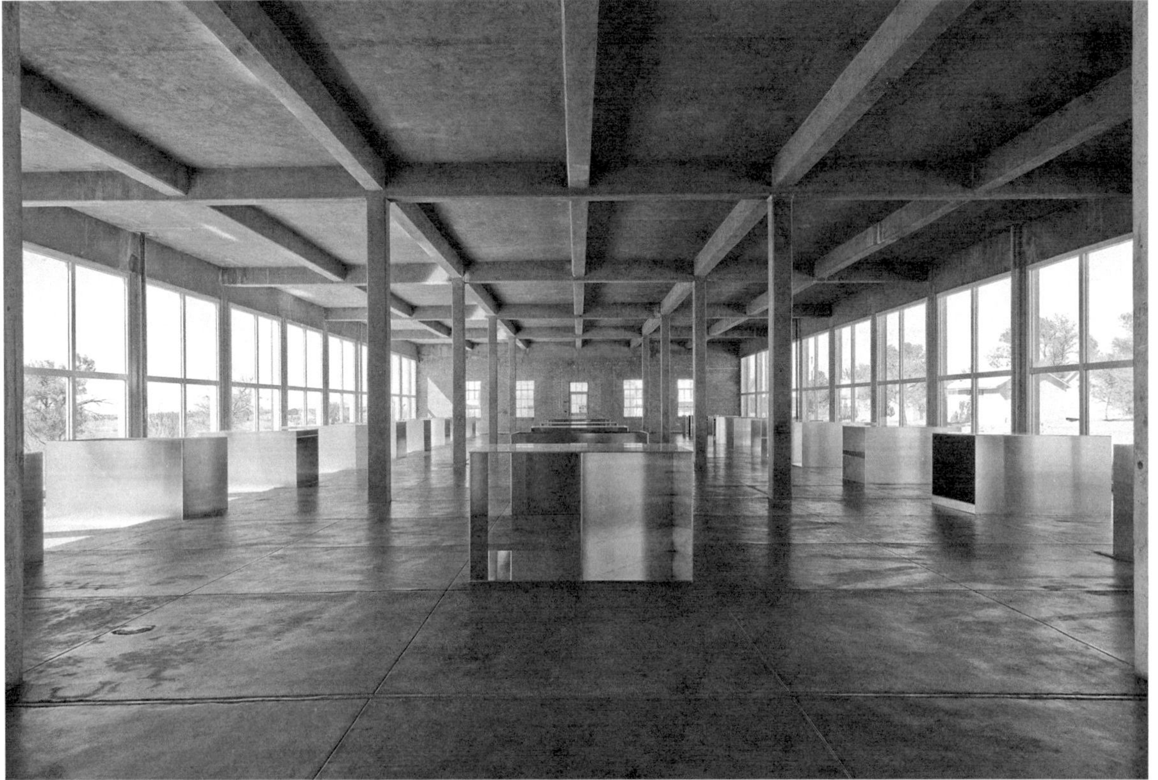

3.5 Donald Judd, untitled (100 untitled works in mill aluminum) (detail), 1982–1986. Aluminum; 100 units, each 41 × 51 × 72 inches. Collection Chinati Foundation, Marfa, TX. Photograph: Douglas Tuck. © 2016 Judd Foundation/Artists Rights Society (ARS), New York.

the top recessed, the sides taken off and another box put inside, diagonals running from one edge to another.

In the *Aluminum Boxes*, as in the horizontal wall boxes with the Plexiglas sides, an internal fold reflects something outside of the object as an effect of the folding itself so that what we see when we look at the box is much more than the box itself—such as the surrounding landscapes—yet at the same time nothing but the box. The visual experience is an effect of an internal refraction or fold, much like the camera obscura or the eye itself.

This produces a couple of effects. Extraordinary specificity of views is accompanied by apparently infinite variability, replacing the identity-difference binary with a expansive field of similarities. The movement of one's own eye is matched at every point by a new and different view, setting up a mimetic relay between your eye and the eyelike aperture made by the fold in the box. This effect is redoubled by the fact that in trying to figure out how what it is that you see there got to be reflected there, one finds oneself trying to imagine one's eyes at various points inside the box:

What would I see from there? Where is the light coming from? What are the relevant angles? For a moment we see the world from the point of view of the box, and even if the effort does not fully succeed, a mimetic relationship is enacted. The box is not a window through which we see another reality, but itself an eye (which mimes our own even as it operates according to another systemic logic), which teaches us to see a different world in flashes of mimetic apperception.

Thus, if Judd's objects aspire to the condition of natural beauty, it is important to add that this "nature" is not ours. Smithson suggested this in comparing one of Judd's works to a "giant crystal from another planet."[56] Rather than represent reality from a distance, Judd has cut it open like a surgeon and implanted a natural object from a nature that is not ours. Or perhaps it is *we* who have been dropped into a landscape that does not exist. This is a mode of sheer artifice to which neither painting nor theater aspires. It is closer to film, which also aspires to give us a feeling for a natural world that does not exist. (Perhaps this is why other planets have from the very beginning been a privileged *mise en scene* of film.)

In Judd's alternate world, the places of nature and modernization in the artwork are reorganized. In the landscape painting or still life, for example, nature is a raw material for the artwork, just as it is for industrial modernity. Realistic depictions of nature offer us windows onto that distant nature, which remains an object for our subjectivity. Judd's works, on the other hand, take the seemingly unspectacular stuff of industrial modernity as raw material.[57] With this material he produces objects that do not imitate nature but nevertheless end up resembling it in their rigorous silence and perceptual-experiential complexity. In fact, Judd's own practice as an artist mimes the total control and factory production that characterize the modern domination of nature. Judd's objects are no less refined, precise, and washed clean of any human trace than any factory product—they are paragons of a machine aesthetic. If the very function of the commodity form (in the trademark or brand name, for example) is to hide the labor that went into the object and gave it value, "so as not to reveal that the one who sells it did not in fact make it, but rather appropriated to himself the labor that went into it," then Judd has made the work of art into an absolute commodity.[58] Inasmuch as the effacement of the subjectivity of its maker is the goal of Judd's noncomposition, it is also a perfection of the commodity form, a carefully prepared and controlled intensification of the reification of human labor.

56 The work is question is Judd's "pink Plexiglas box." Smithson, "The Crystal Land (1966)," in *Donald Judd: Early Fabricated Works*, 16.

57 Plexiglas is a brilliant choice here for many reasons, not least because it is one of the first plastics after Bakelite to receive wide industrial, military, and everyday uses. Plastic, of course, is one of the enduring symbols of the falseness of consumer culture, even becoming a synonym for fakeness itself.

58 Adorno, *In Search of Wagner*, trans. Rodney Livingstone (London: Verso, 1981), 82–83.

One of the many ironies here is the way that it is precisely the imposition of a strict order on the materials and the attempt to erase traces of the human hand in them that allow their material substance—their "obduracy," Judd called it—to come into existence as such.[59] Judd radicalizes reification, excising all traces of subjectivity in an object that appears to be of no use to anyone. Only thereby does he allow us to listen to what we might call "the language of things." And like factory workers conversing, gossiping, or complaining on the assembly line, even as they are dominated by a totalizing order, these things—Judd's materials—preserve their own quiet language. They carry on secret conversations with the world around them, murmuring with the echoes of Plexiglas jukebox windows, car parts, cutlery, and shiny metal turnstiles. The colors are more gregarious, looking at us with familiar eyes: we all know red, yellow, and orange personally, even intimately. Judd's materials surprise us like crumbs of *madeleine*. They do not provoke full-fledged Proustian "involuntary memories" so much as they animate shards of affect from the collective history of everyday life.

By so starkly framing his objects as unmeaningful and nonexpressive and then stimulating these secret feelings that can only be apprehended passively, as it were, Judd seems to be reminding us of the value of this relaxed attitude toward the world. The thrill of this reminder is that our mimetic capacities are reawakened, if only for a moment, within an artistic space governed precisely by the principle of the rational, mechanical ordering. Briefly, we have an experience in a world that does not exist, and in so doing, we gain a momentary glimpse of the finitude of our own subjectivities. Only then can the closedness of our monadic subjectivity be glimpsed and felt. Even if the reawakening of the mimetic faculty that has occurred in relation to Judd's objects cannot easily be translated back into the world, at least we can have an affective relation to our inability to be affectively open to the world. We can mourn the absence of our connection to the world around us.

Put differently, in Judd's specific objects we become interested in our own reification. And inasmuch as we are allowed to step back from our reification for a moment, or witness the process of reification turned inside out, we can consider the ways in which this reification is shared, how it too dwells in a field of similarities.

* * *

Of course, even as Judd exemplifies a paradigm of noncompositional art, his example—not entirely intentionally—also demonstrates its limits. This

59 "Materials vary greatly and are simply materials—formica, aluminum, cold-rolled steel, Plexiglas, red and common brass, and so forth. They are specific. If they are used directly, they are more specific. Also, they are usually aggressive. There is an objectivity to the obdurate identity of a material" (Judd, "Specific Objects," 187).

is because, despite Judd's avowed desire to make his artworks about nothing but themselves, the fact remains that they are immediately recognizable as "Judds." Even the erasure of one's own authorship can be recuperated by the art market as an authorial gesture like any other. Only a completely anonymous art would escape this fate, and then one could not be a functioning (i.e., moneymaking) artist in the art world. In order to operate on the art market, the artist must submit to the iron rule of self-identity, ultimately guaranteed by the (unique, individual) person of the artist her- or himself. Like any other commodity-producing entity, the artist must guarantee brand recognizability and authenticity; Judd cannot help but produce one "Judd" after another. Thus, even though the works as such are obstinate in their refusal to represent, express, signify, or refer, in order to be exchanged, they must borrow an identity from Judd. Inevitably (as in this very chapter), Judd's works are talked about in terms of the arc of his career, his development as an artist, the coherence of his various works as an *oeuvre*, the going rate for a good Judd at auction, and so on.

Judd found his need to comply with the rules of the market distasteful, and he tried to insist that it was not his intention to create commodities; it was just how he happened to make his living: "My work and the work of my contemporaries that I acquired was not made to be property. It's simply art."[60] There is more than a little bit of what used to be called "bad faith" here, and I suspect Judd knows it. It is, of course, not so simple to separate "business" from "art," but Judd clearly (and understandably) resents his own reification, and I suspect that this difficulty accounts in part for his vituperative attacks on the commercialism and careerism of Warhol, who irritated everyone by avowing what everyone else was trying desperately to sweep under the rug: that artists, as a condition for being artists, are also always advertisers and businesspeople, selling, moreover, mainly to the richest, most privileged capitalist class. If many artists, Judd included, could not bear to avow this, they nonetheless often allegorized it in their work. By contrast, Warhol embraced it, but in so doing he perverted the business of art, scandalously proclaiming: "being good in business is the most fascinating kind of art . . . Business Art. Art Business. The Business Art Business" (*Phil*, 92). For Warhol, this was not "giving in" to business; for him, "art" was bigger than "business"; the world of business, like advertising, movies, publicity, and so on was just more material.

In its own way, Warhol's Pop was a totalizing practice. It was a way of seeing that sought to transform—even replace—the entire world, by liking it or by learning how to be bored by it, which was, for Warhol, ultimately the same thing. For Warhol, as for Judd, a boredom that allowed one to experience the artwork as ambience and thus also as self-nonidentical, was the condition of possibility for affecting and being affected by something.

60 Judd, *Complete Writings*, 9.

Looking Out a Window

For the housewife, despite the films which are supposed to integrate her still further, the dark of the cinema grants a refuge in which she can spend a few unsupervised hours, just as once, when there were still dwellings and evening repose, she could sit gazing out of the window.

Max Horkheimer and Theodor Adorno, "The Culture Industry"[61]

Everyone and everything is interesting. Years ago, people used to sit looking out of their windows at the street. . . . they would stay for hours without being bored although nothing much was going on. This is my favorite theme in moviemaking—just watching something happening for two hours or so. **Andy Warhol**[62]

Where Donald Judd could at least defend his prioritization of interest with a respectable philosophical discourse on the topic, for Warhol's often repeated assertions that Pop Art "is liking things," and that one of the things that he "liked" was "being bored," no intellectual pedigree was offered and for the most part none found. Warhol's assertions were taken (and usually still are) to be a sign of his naïve or cynical affirmation of mass culture, advertising, the commodity, and consumer society. Yet in some ways, Warhol's ambitions were greater than Judd's. If, like Judd, Warhol produced works that would be affectless but interesting, he also saw his artwork as a way to help him and teach others how to see the world so that "*everyone* and *everything* is interesting" (*IBYM*, 187; my emphases). He saw a particular mode of boredom as one way to get people in the mood for a maximal affective receptivity. On a formal level, repetition (in his paintings) and duration (in his films) were two ways to create aesthetic experiences that might bring this boredom into being.

Here, I want to consider how Warhol's early minimal films, especially *Sleep* and *Empire*, encourage a kind of durational looking at something long enough that "the meaning goes away" (*IBYM*, 95), at which point other things can happen. When he first started making movies, Warhol's longtime assistant and friend Billy Linich remembers, "He got a tripod and just put the camera on the tripod and said, 'We're going to find out what the camera does first.' . . . He wanted to be relaxed about the whole thing and to stop trying to come up with ideas. Just relax and learn more about the camera and see how it works."[63] Warhol's early films—which he described as "one scene with one star performing a very simple function" (*IBYM*, 186)—allowed him to explore "what the camera does," and the ways in which it sees a different world than the human eye.

The relaxation Linich saw in Warhol's approach to filming corresponds

61 "Culture Industry," 111.

62 Quoted in "Andy Warhol, MovieMan: 'It's Hard to Be Your Own Script,'" interview by Leticia Kent, *Vogue*, March 1, 1970; reprinted in *IBYM*, 187.

63 *Unseen Warhol*, ed. John O'Connor and Benjamin Liu (New York: Rizzoli, 1996), 40.

to Warhol's view of the value of his films for viewers. Of course, audiences often objected to the films as boring: looking at different extended shots of parts of John Giorno's sleeping body, the Empire State Building, Henry Geldzahler sitting, or Robert Indiana eating a mushroom certainly disrupted audience expectations for "entertainment." But Warhol defended them and the experience they presented to viewers by reminding us that "years ago, people used to sit looking out of their windows at the street. . . . they would stay for hours without being bored although nothing much was going on" (*IBYM*, 187). In fact, looking out the window seems for Warhol to have been an enduring image of relaxation (perhaps even of something like happiness) in which liking and enjoyment came easily. "When you just sit and look out a window, that's enjoyable" (*IBYM*, 168). In such a state, anything at all could hold one's visual interest. Warhol notes of the "creative people" living in the East Village in the early 1960s (such as his friend James Waring, and at an earlier moment Warhol himself) that they "weren't hustling work, they weren't 'upwardly mobile,' they were happy just to drift around the streets looking at everything, enjoying everything—Ratner's, Gem's Spa, Polish restaurants, junk stores, dry goods stores—maybe go home and write in a diary about what they'd enjoyed that day or choreograph something they'd gotten an idea about" (*POP*, 52). This relaxed mode of enjoyment, what he called "just watching something happening for two hours or so" was, Warhol said, his "favorite theme in movie making" (*IBYM*, 187).

That is, like Adorno and Horkheimer, Warhol sees in film the survival and transformation of a older structure of feeling, one that supported looking out the window as a regular, relaxing experience. For Adorno and Horkheimer, the image of the beleaguered housewife seeking a moment of peace and quiet in the movie theater is meant to indicate at once the extent of the rationalization of everyday life (from which the darkness of the theater is the only place one can find refuge) and the poverty of the aesthetic experience Hollywood has to offer (providing nothing more rewarding than a momentary freedom from being "supervised"). In the dark theater one can look—it hardly matters at what—without the anxiety produced by the need to be aware of one's identity; one can forget the need to *be* a self.

In his films, Warhol enthusiastically promoted and prioritized the housewife-ish experience of relaxed looking. But where Adorno and Horkheimer saw it as an accidental side effect of the cinematic experience, Warhol saw it as a positive task that required setting aside the formal patterns of the culture industry and the viewing habits those forms created. Because they had plots that instrumentalized one's looking—one wants to know how it *ends*—Hollywood movies made it difficult to look relaxedly. "I don't think plot is important," Warhol would say. "If you see a movie, say, of two people talking, you can watch it over and over again without being bored. You get involved—you miss things—you come back to it—you see new things. But you can't see the same movie over again if it has a plot because you already know the ending" (*IBYM*, 187). Television was similarly problematic. The "most popular action shows on TV" follow a preset formula in which the details change but the basic forms and experiences themselves do not vary ("the same plots and the same shots and the same cuts over and over again"). Indeed, that is the point: one consumes entertainment in order to receive a particular and predictable emotional experience. For Warhol, watching the "exact same thing," on the other hand, is more likely to produce an *unexpected* experience, precisely inasmuch as it stops demanding our attention.[64] That is one reason why "the less something has to say the more perfect it is" (*IBYM*, 91).

But, as Warhol remarked about not wanting to sit and watch *Sleep* himself, "Sometimes I like to be bored, and sometimes I don't—it depends what kind of mood I'm in. Everyone knows how it is, some days you can sit and look out the window for hours and hours and some days you can't sit still for a single second" (*POP*, 50). The question was how to get in the right mood to be this kind of relaxed-bored. Drugs could help (depending on the drugs). But also, in themselves, Warhol's minimal films teach us how to be bored. That is, if one *can* manage just to sit still for at least the first few minutes, Warhol's films are themselves machines for putting one in such a mood.

* * *

Sleep was Warhol's first movie concept. Even before he had a camera, he was talking about making an eight-hour film of someone sleeping. Both Warhol and John Giorno suggest that the idea came to Warhol at a party at Wynn Chamberlain's house in Old Lyme, Connecticut, where Warhol stayed up watching Giorno sleep one night (on which, more shortly). But the film is not a continuous representation of Giorno sleeping for eight hours. As Callie Angell notes, "Warhol's efforts to complete his 8 hour film as planned were greatly complicated by the limitations of his equipment," which only shot four-minute reels, which were time-consuming to change, especially for the novice filmmaker.[65] Because Warhol could not get a long single shot, or a series of continuous shots, as Branden Joseph details in his careful anal-

64 The full passage is one of Warhol's best known: "I've been quoted a lot as saying 'I like boring things.' Well, I said it and I meant it. But that doesn't mean I'm not bored by them. Of course, what I think is boring must not be the same as what other people think is, since I could never stand to watch all the most popular action shows on TV, because they're essentially the same plots and the same shots and the same cuts over and over again. Apparently, most people love watching the same basic thing, as long as the details are different. But I'm just the opposite; if I'm going to sit and watch the same thing I saw the night before, I don't want it to be essentially the same—I want it to be *exactly* the same. Because the more you look at the same exact thing, the more the meaning goes away, and the better and emptier you feel" (*POP*, 50).

65 For an account of the making of the film, see Angell, *Films of Andy Warhol Part II* (New York: Whitney Museum of American Art, 1994).

ysis, the final film is five hours and twenty-one minutes long, made up of "twenty-two separate close-ups of Giorno's body, multiply printed and then spliced together into variously repeating sequences."[66] The overall visual effect of the resulting film is complex, in part because the different close-ups give us highly directed, sometimes abstract or even confusing looks at Giorno's sleeping body.

Like *Eat* (a film of Robert Indiana eating a mushroom), *Henry Geldzahler* (a two-hour film of his curator friend sitting on the couch), or *Empire* (an eight-hour film of the Empire State Building), *Sleep* had a simple concept. These concepts, however, were in tension with what Juan Suárez calls "the intricacy of their textures and internal movement, which makes actual description nearly impossible and turns them indeed into works that can *only* be experienced."[67] Along similar lines, Angell writes that "to actually watch *Sleep* is to discover a work whose physical presence—meditative, beautiful, yet complexly structured, achronological, and endlessly repetitious—is significantly at odds with the simplicity of its conception."[68] This complex aesthetic experience distorts perception and affectivity in several ways.

As a very long silent, black-and-white film in which there is neither plot nor spectacle, and which makes no effort to capture or hold audience attention, the film egregiously disappoints any expectation we might have for a movie and disrupts what Parker Tyler calls the habits formed by "the theater seat itself."[69] It's not, as Andrew Uroskie observes, that films of this length were unprecedented—he discusses Erich von Stroheim's *Greed* and Abel Gance's *Napoleon*—but that, unlike these earlier films, *Sleep* made no effort to retain its viewers' attention. Some audience members at early screenings were very angry.[70] To be sure, after several minutes, or less, of

66 Joseph, "Play of Repetition," 28.

67 Suárez, "Warhol's 1960s Films," 634.

68 Angell, *Films Part II*, 10. After *Sleep*, Warhol abandoned editing almost entirely for a few years, and he never again edited as much as he did in *Sleep*. Angell, Joseph, and Andrew Uroskie all note the similarities to John Cage's 1963 performance of Erik Satie's *Vexations*, which Warhol attended after he had shot but before he had edited the footage. This 18-hour, 40-minute concert comprises an 80-second piece of music being repeated 840 times by a changing roster of pianists. As Uroskie notes, "In both works, an extreme reduction of incident, repeated over an extended duration, resulted in a phenomenologically charged perceptual situation. Minor variations struck with novel resonance; in the absence of variation, the viewer was thrown back on herself, on her own act of spectatorship." Uroskie, *Expanded Cinema and Postwar Art* (Chicago: University of Chicago Press, 2014), 46.

69 Tyler writes, in what remains one of the best essays on Warhol's films: "Film-seeing implies the most passive psychological state of all the visual arts because the theater seat itself is habit forming, and because while watching plays, on the contrary, one shares a certain tension with the live performers." "Dragtime and Drugtime, or, Film a la Warhol," *Evergreen Review* 11, no. 46 (1967); reprinted in O'Pray, *Film Factory*, 97.

70 Angell and Uroskie recount this anger, reported in Jonas Mekas, "Movie Journal," *Village Voice*, July 2, 1964. Mike Getz, the theater manager at a 1964 screening in Los

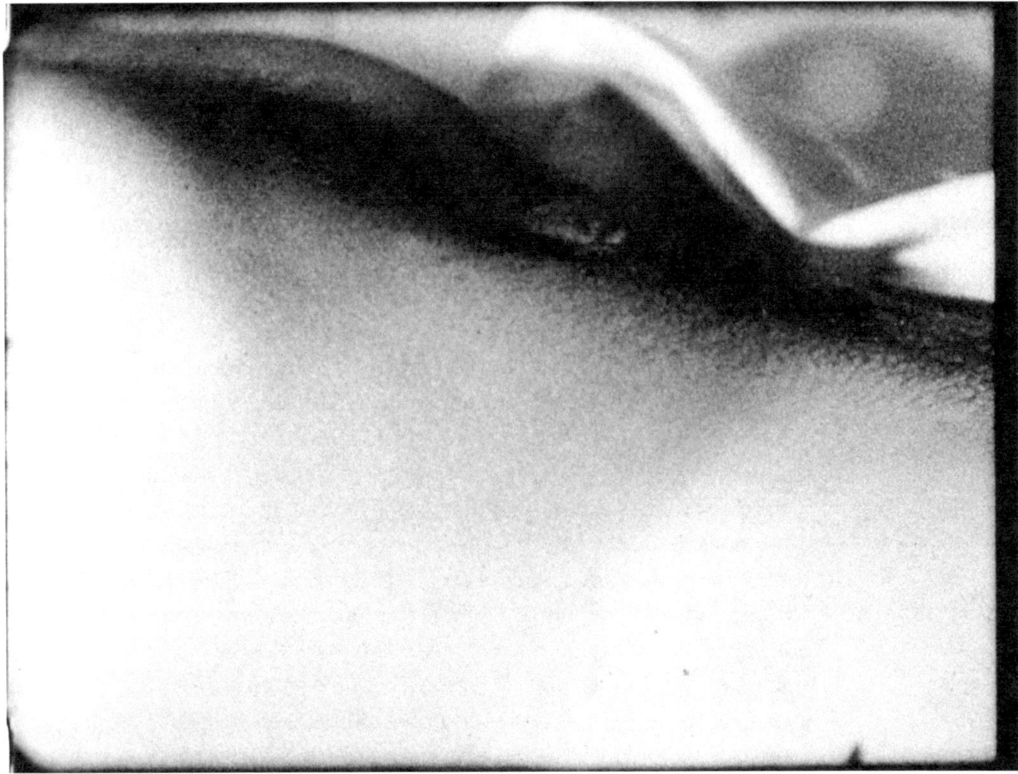

3.6 Andy Warhol, *Sleep*, 1963. 16mm film, black and white, silent, 5 hours 21 minutes at 16 frames per second. Reel 1, Shot A. © The Andy Warhol Museum, a museum of Carnegie Institute.

looking at the same shot of Giorno's torso, with his bellybutton rising and falling slowly, one begins to get antsy. One looks at the time; impatience rises. Our usual modes of paying attention and being interested do not work here. How much time has passed now? Can I possibly do this for five more hours? The mood of impatience might intensify into positive annoyance with the sense that one is being duped or "cheated." One has paid one's

Angeles, described how people started to leave after fifteen minutes, with those who remained growing more and more restless and agitated. Getz wrote in a letter to Mekas, "One red-faced guy very agitated, says I have 30 seconds to give him his money back or he'll run into theatre and start a 'lynch riot.' 'We'll all come out here and lynch you, buddy!!'" He recalled how he was "forced to give out free passes, and how one woman later called to inform him that she had been forced to leave early, fearing imminent violence" (Uroskie, *Expanded Cinema*, 46). Angell suggests that this anger *might* have been because viewers were expecting a continuous shot of someone sleeping for eight hours (which remains a remarkably consistent incorrect description of the film). But I suspect it was, and remains, because the film so thoroughly and unapologetically disrupts our moviegoing habits, even for those accustomed to difficult avant-garde films.

money and set aside this highly impractical block of time—how is this experience in any sense "worth" it?

So the first thing *Sleep* does is force one to reflect on one's own viewing habits and expectations. One must make the most basic value judgments about the film: Will I stay in my seat and continue to watch it? Can I like this? Will I open myself to being affected by the film? Even if one leaves in anger at the tedium to which one has been exposed, the disruption of viewing habits has made one aware of them.

But if one makes it past this initial phase of impatience, annoyance, or anger, and can relax a little, one's mood shifts. Having given up on being entertained, and having decided to set aside the time, one is lulled, by *Sleep*'s rhythms, into a different temporality, with altered perceptual possibilities. "The pulse beat of the spectator's available interest," Tyler suggests, becomes attuned to the "pulse beat of the camera and the respiration of a sleeping man." As one allows one's liking to be guided by the rhythms of the film, one comes to occupy a boredom distinct from the impatience of waiting for the time to pass or annoyance at an object that fails to attract or hold one's attention. As Heidegger put it, "Being left empty here is no longer the absence of a particular satisfaction." Instead, this boredom—the one, produced by a significatory absence, that left Warhol feeling "better and emptier"—creates a neutral space of openness and potentiality. It accomplishes a dramatic leveling effect, which "makes everything of equally great and equally little worth"; by first experiencing nothing as interesting, everything becomes interesting.[71] Emptiness becomes a readiness to be filled. "When people go to a show today they're never involved any more," Warhol observed. "A movie like *Sleep* gets them involved again. They get involved with themselves and they create their own entertainment" (*IBYM*, 168). What may first appear to be the familiar boredom produced by what Uroskie calls the "extreme reduction of incident" turns out to produce instead a "phenomenologically charged perceptual situation" that gets the viewer "involved again," and in several ways.[72]

First, just as looking out the window may permit the transference of the emotional comfort of being at home to one's view of the street, and thus help one's emotions to be transferred onto objects in one's visual field (sometimes called daydreaming), so the otherworldliness of film permits "an unconsciously penetrated space [to be] substituted for a space consciously explored by the eye."[73] As we look at this "breathing painting," "feel[ing] the shapes with [our] eyes" (*IBYM*, 95), the rules of perception themselves

71 Heidegger, *Fundamental Concepts*, 139, 137.

72 Uroskie, *Expanded Cinema*, 46.

73 Walter Benjamin, "The Work of Art in the Age of Its Technological Reproducibility," in *Walter Benjamin Selected Writings*, vol. 3 (Cambridge, MA: Harvard University Press, 2002), 236.

seem to bend; the images lose their identity.[74] As we might dream about how clouds are "rows and flows of angel hair," "feather canyons," or "ice cream castles in the air" (as Joni Mitchell has it), so too the shadowy nooks and white planes of flesh, the patterns of light and dark formed by Giorno's body and the sheets around it, start to look like other things. We may also get lost for a while in the squiggling worms of film grain, what Suárez describes as the "quiver that both composes and dissolves the image."[75] Combined with the hallucinatory effects of the infant-like split between focus (where one's eyes are looking) and attention (where one's mind is) mentioned in chapter 1, we find ourselves in an altered sensory condition, one in which Giorno's body is freed from the need to "be itself."

Warhol acknowledges the hallucinatory quality durational looking can take on in his observations of the 1967 "be-in":

> The Easter Sunday be-in in Central Park was incredible; thousands of kids handing you flowers, burning incense, smoking grass, taking acid, passing drugs around right out in the open, taking their clothes off and rolling around on the ground, painting their bodies and faces with Day-Glo, doing Far East–type chants, playing with their toys—balloons and pinwheels and sheriff's badges and Frisbees. They could stand there staring at each other for hours without moving. As I said before, that had always fascinated me, the way people could sit by a window or on a porch all day and look out and never be bored, but then if they went to a movie or play, they suddenly objected to being bored. I always felt that a very slow film could be just as interesting as a porch-sit if you thought about it the same way. And now all these kids on acid were demonstrating the exact same thing. (*POP*, 207)

To the same degree that he was impressed with the flexibility and variability of the mood of the kids at the be-in, Warhol was genuinely puzzled that people "objected to being bored" at his movies. But the kids demonstrating that it was still possible to be so perceptually receptive and relaxed, even if drugs were helping, gave him hope that audiences could learn to like his "very slow" films.

Parker Tyler also turns to the sensory-altering experience of drugs in elaborating the temporal experience promoted by Warhol's films. He argues

74 Ronald Tavel remarks that for Warhol, film "was closer to painting, to what I think of as a 'breathing painting,' than for other filmmakers. With Andy it really was s slightly moving painting, and every slight movement fascinated him." Tavel, interviewed by Matt Wrbican, May 10, 1997; quoted in Scherman and Dalton, *Pop*, 181. Parker Tyler puts it a little differently, and perhaps less generously: "A sort of hypnotism emanates from the screen so that you begin to feel rather like a rabbit being fascinated by a snake" ("Dragtime," 97).

75 Suárez, "Warhol's 1960s Films," 635.

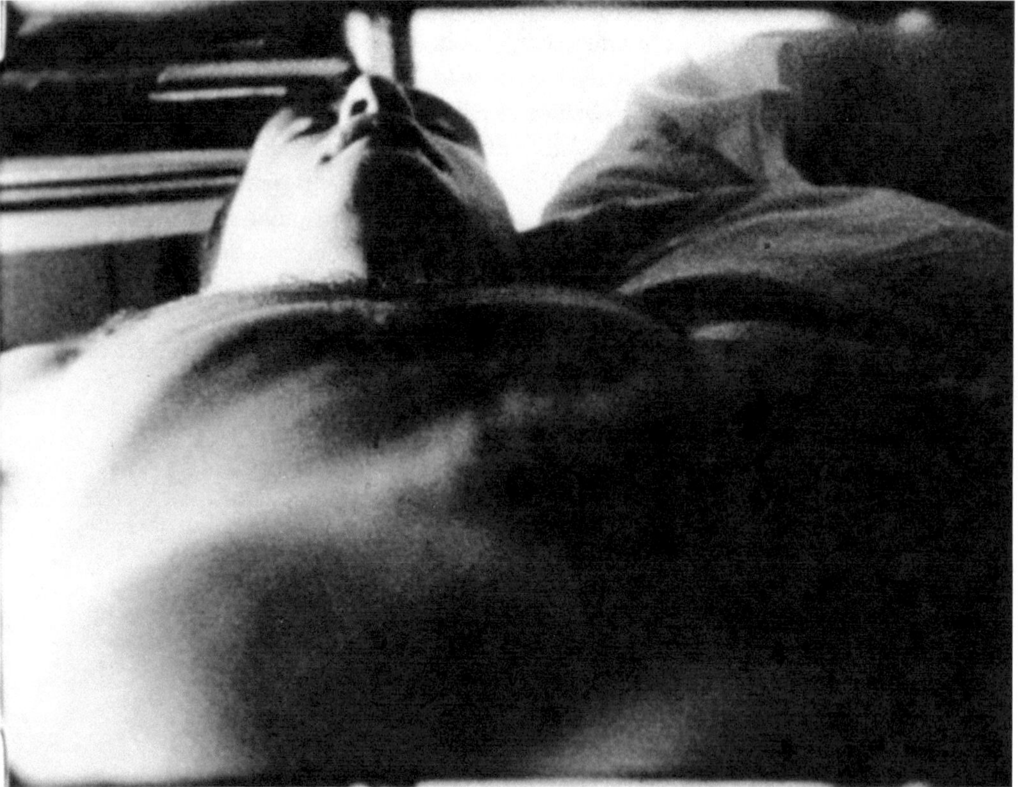

3.7 Andy Warhol, *Sleep*, 1963. 16mm film, black and white, silent, 5 hours 21 minutes at 16 frames per second. Reel 1, shot B. © The Andy Warhol Museum, a museum of Carnegie Institute

that what seems at first to be a dragging out of time ("dragtime"), a perverse and even cruel imposition of boredom, turns out to entail a simulation of the peculiar enhancement of sensation facilitated by certain drugs. Just as marijuana can make the simple event of a cat crossing the room into a marvelous and fascinating occurrence, "the anti-heroic film marathons he calls *Sleep*, *Eat*, *Haircut*, *Kiss*, and *Empire* can be conceived by dedicated audiences as if they were drugtime—that is, as inexplicable wonders of eventfulness."[76] This eventfulness is created not just by the hallucinatory effects of the film but by the way it alters the rhythms of one's perception. In the opening minutes of the film, one settles in to some way or ways of liking being bored by this image of Giorno's gently moving, fleshily indented belly, and then after forty minutes or so, with no warning whatsoever—the image changes! The surprising affective force of this cut can be quite a joy, a real "wonder of eventfulness." When I saw *Sleep* in Moscow in 2001, at the first cut the entire audience of several hundred people erupted in cheers. This is

76 Tyler, "Dragtime," 103.

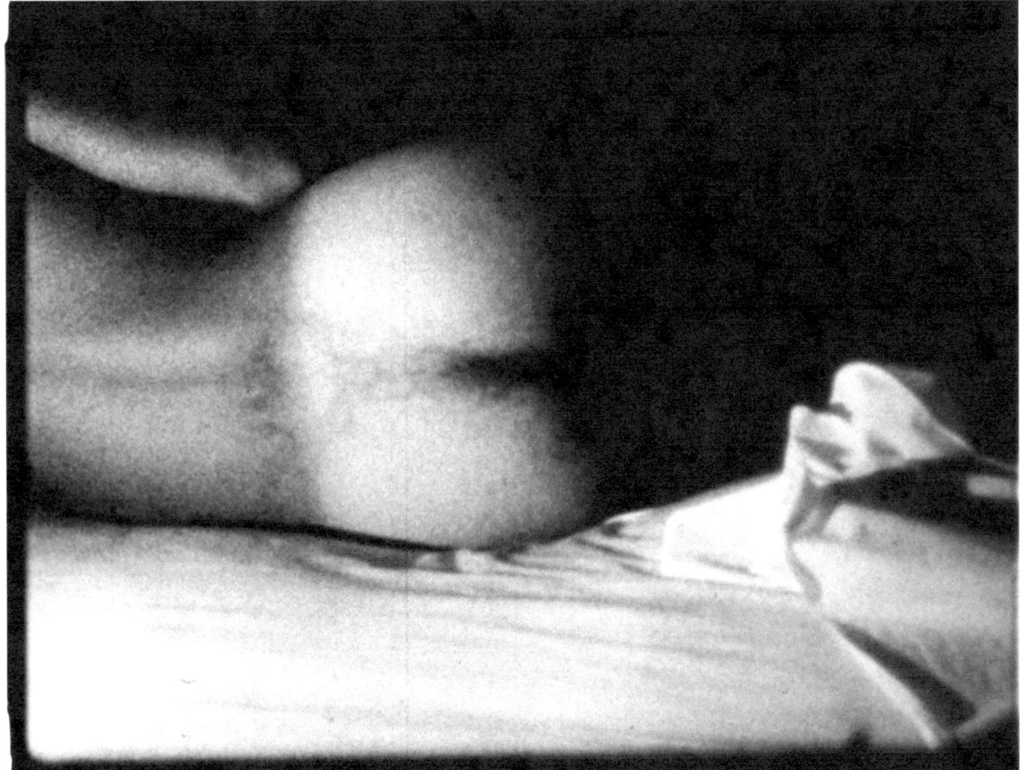

3.8. Andy Warhol, *Sleep*, 1963. 16mm film, black and white, silent, 5 hours 21 minutes at 16 frames per second. Reel 2, shot H. © The Andy Warhol Museum, a museum of Carnegie Institute.

heightened perception, for sure, as well as an increased capacity for being affected. Within this new, highly sensitive mode of viewing, each of Giorno's movements is a major event, as many viewers have noted.[77] As one occupies this loose, relaxed, receptive habitus, one senses that one could be interested in just about anything if one looks at it long enough. One also realizes that one's mood has been shifted into what Ernst Bloch calls "anticipatory illumination," if we can think of anticipation as also relaxed. What next?

One might, for instance, also be aroused by the film. There certainly is time for that. Although *Sleep*'s tone is more intimate than pornographic, Giorno's body is handsome, and we are treated to long shots of his ass, the top of his ass crack, his armpits, his jawline, his hips, and his hairy stomach

77 Patrick Smith: "I can still remember that when [the sleeper, John] Giorno made the slightest movement, I was startled" (*Andy Warhol's Art and Films* [Ann Arbor: UMI Research Press, 1981], 155; brackets in source). David Bourdon: "Suddenly, the performer blinks or swallows, and the involuntary action becomes in this context a highly dramatic event, as climactic as the burning of Atlanta in *Gone with the Wind*" (*Warhol*, 178; cited in Joseph, "Play of Repetition," 26).

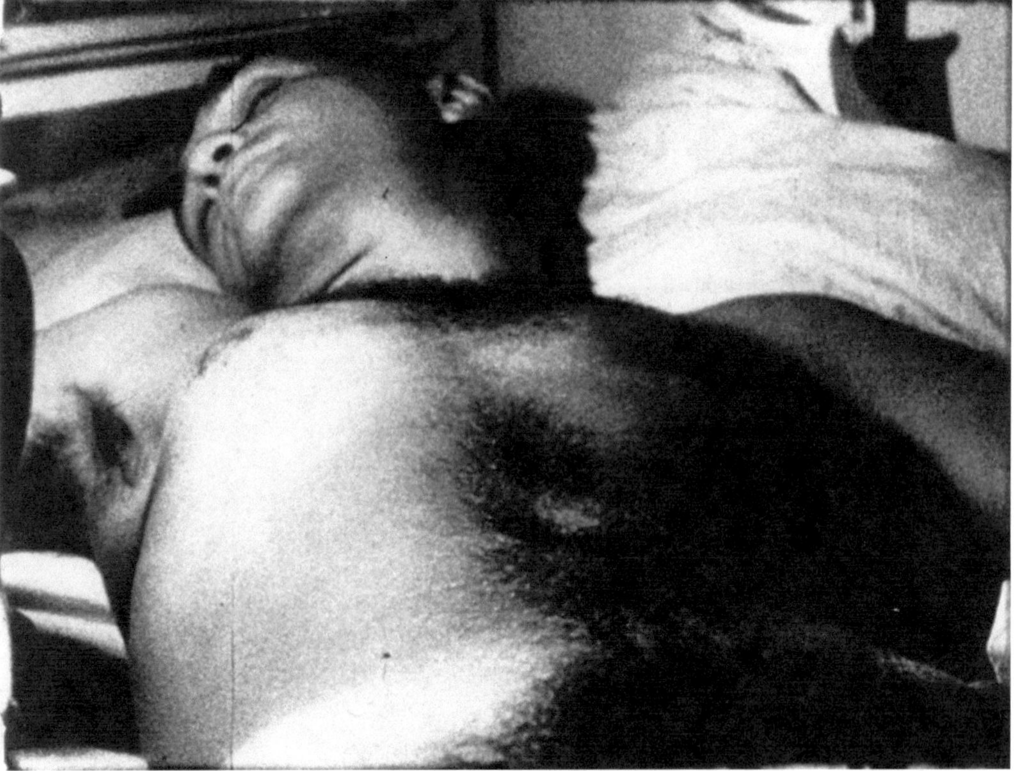

3.9 Andy Warhol, *Sleep*, 1963. 16mm film, black and white, silent, 5 hours 21 minutes at 16 frames per second. Reel 3, shot L. © The Andy Warhol Museum, a museum of Carnegie Institute.

interrupted by the soft indentation of his belly button. "I made my first films using, for several hours, just one actor on the screen doing the same thing: eating or sleeping or smoking. I did this because usually people just go to the movies to see only the star, to eat him up, so here at last is a chance to look only at the star for as long as you like, no matter what he does and to eat him up all you want to" (*IBYM*, 90). In the film's longest repeated shot, for around an hour and half, we see Giorno "from just above the groin, sleeping on his back," as Joseph puts it.[78] That is, our longest view is the one might have of Giorno if we looked up at his face while fellating him, an act, incidentally, that Giorno describes Warhol performing on him with enthusiasm and skill.[79]

78 The "third and fourth reels each contain only a single shot, which repeats throughout their entire duration. Reel three consists of twenty one-hundred-foot rolls of film depicting Giorno, from just above the groin, sleeping on his back" (Joseph, "Play of Repetition," 31).

79 "He was really good at it. He had a soft succulent mouth, quivering fingers, and a deep throat" (Giorno, *You Got To Burn To Shine*, 144).

Turned on or not, one becomes unusually attuned to one's own presence in the theater as a spectator, which itself leads to several effects, including the activation of the theatrical site itself.[80] Warhol again: "My first films using the stationary objects were also made to help the audiences become acquainted with themselves. Usually, when you go to the movies you sit in a fantasy world, but when you see something that disturbs you, you get more involved with the people next to you" (*IBYM*, 92). One might turn to others to figure out how to relate to the film, as if seeking confirmation of one's own experience. Inasmuch as one is having an unfamiliar experience that disrupts one's habits, one starts to wonder if other people are also noticing those crazy squiggles of grain, or if they saw that surprisingly short shot of an underarm, or if that dark area is shadow or hair, or if one's aesthetic reactions are completely idiosyncratic. It is difficult *not* to wonder how other people are relating to this experience, to "share and confirm these feelings in public."[81] Part of the energy behind the eruption into applause at *Sleep*'s first cut that time in Moscow, I think, stems from this impulse to affirm and create a *sensus communis*.

Having turned to ask one's neighbor about her or his experience of the film, one might begin to talk about other things too. The film thus acts as a shared and shareable experience—you know at least *one* thing that you now have in common with the people around you—and so promotes a certain conviviality and sociality (even if it is the conviviality of shared annoyance or discomfort). To support this sociality, and perhaps to suggest the possibility of its being connected to other, broader audiences and groups, Warhol reports that early screenings sometimes included a radio playing.[82] Because the film did not demand attention, it was possible to come and go or even to "walk around and dance and sing" (*IBYM*, 41). "You could do more things watching my movies than with other kinds of movies: you could eat and drink and smoke and cough and look away and then look back and they'd still be there. It's not the ideal movie, its just my kind of movie" (*IBYM*, 92). Like many of his other works (such as the Dance Diagrams, discussed in chapter 2), *Sleep* encourages us to turn away from the works themselves and

80 As Uroskie observes, "*Sleep*'s radical duration, far from remaining a formal feature of the work, must rather be understood as a transformation of the theatrical site" (*Expanded Cinema*, 48).

81 Ngai, *Our Aesthetic Categories*, 44. See her discussion of the sociality of judgment, the way aesthetic judgment (especially of something as "interesting") implies and requires the presence of other people (esp. 44–47, 113–15).

82 Warhol: "The first time we showed it (*Sleep*), we had a radio on in the theater. Instead of recording a sound track, we just put a radio next to it and everyday put on a new station. And if a person was bored with the movie, he could just listen to the radio. People listen to radios" (*IBYM*, 165). Angell confirms Warhol's report, adding that these screenings were at the Gramercy Arts Theater in 1964 and recalling that Rauschenberg's *Broadcast* had put a radio behind its canvas and Ken Jacobs' *Blond Cobra* (1963) had called for a live radio to be played two times during the film (*Films Part II*, 11).

remember to like other people. More importantly, they put us in the mood to do so. "People always have a better time, have more fun together than watching what is on the screen," he remarked years later about the experience of these early films (*IBYM*, 225).

Of course, it is important that we experience the particular aesthetic effects of *Sleep* in relation to images of John Giorno's sleeping body. That is, we relax into daydreamy boredom in relation to the image of relaxation as such; the film thematizes the experience it solicits. In this way, it seems quite directly to be preparing the space for us to consider sleep, as such. What feelings might we have about sleep? To begin with, as we look at this resplendent model of relaxation, we are certainly aware that we are *not* sleeping, that we are not occupying a bed but a theater seat. In order to watch someone sleeping, after all, one must be awake. It may occur to us, as Adam Phillips writes, that sleep, which is "one of our most intimate and essential activities . . . can only be known about from someone else." We are never present to our own sleep; at best we feel ourselves falling asleep, or are aware of having been asleep as we begin to wake up. But as such, in itself, sleep is a desire "that we can only experience in, and as, anticipation."[83]

As we consider this particular sleeping body and sleep more generally, we are returned to the initial situation for the film's making, which was the contrast between Warhol's wakefulness and Giorno's impressive sleep. The party at which Warhol was inspired to make the film took place at Chamberlain's country house. "There were never enough beds," Warhol remarked, "but most of the guests didn't sleep anyway" (*POP*, 32–33). This was because everyone was on amphetamines, including Warhol, who "started taking a fourth of a diet pill a day (Obetrol) that winter after I saw a picture of myself in a magazine where I looked really fat" (*POP*, 33). That night at Chamberlain's, Giorno reports, he woke to find Warhol in the bed next to him, "his head propped up on his arm, wide-eyed from speed, looking at me."[84] Warhol observes that "seeing everybody so up all the time made me think that sleep was becoming pretty obsolete, so I decided I'd better quickly do a movie of a person sleeping" (*POP*, 33).

Warhol definitely saw how increased wakefulness could produce value. Even the quarter pill of Obetrol he was taking "was enough to give you that wired, happy go-go-go feeling in your stomach that made you want to work-work-work." And since it gave him more time, it allowed him to take advantage of the fact that there were "so many things to do," which may have itself been "because there was more awake time for them to happen in (since so many people were on amphetamine)" (*POP*, 32–33).[85] Amphet-

83 Phillips, "On Sleep," *Threepenny Review*, no. 109 (Spring 2007).

84 Giorno, *You Got To Burn To Shine*, 144.

85 Later in *POPism*, Warhol writes: "As I've said, amphetamine was the big drug in New York in the sixties because there was so much to do that everybody was living double-time or they'd miss half of what was going on. There was never a minute around the clock

amines expanded the time available for activity and gave people the desire and capacity to fill it, making a new collective mood. "Everybody was feeling the acceleration" (*POP*, 194).

Although sleep has not yet "become obsolete," Warhol identified a vulnerability that contemporary capitalism is getting better at exploiting. As Jonathan Crary has observed in *24/7: Late Capitalism and the Ends of Sleep*, our capacity for sleep is under active assault, and from various quarters. From the point of view of capital, sleep is a negative space, a limit to expansion. How does one extract value from the sleeping body? It cannot work, or generate value by liking a Facebook post or opening an app or viewing an advertisement (or by generating *Matrix*-like battery power). Yet sleep, and the sleeping body, remains highly vulnerable. (Crary reminds us that Thomas Hobbes saw the protection of the sleeping body from attack and injury to be one of the chief functions of the state.) By demanding our waking attention all the more aggressively, and stimulating our nervous systems at every opportunity, contemporary capitalism challenges our capacities to fall asleep and stay asleep, which itself requires a range of highly profitable pharmacological solutions.[86]

In the face of the threat posed by productive and enjoyable stimulation, Warhol aimed to celebrate the positive capacity for sleep as something to be valued and appreciated as such. Like Aristotle, who, as Alexei Penzin notes, saw sleep as a potential, the ground of our existence, Warhol presents sleep not just as absence, as that from which one should be awakened, but as an activity with its own quality and beauty. "It's just John sleeping for eight hours. His nose and his mouth. His chest breathing. Occasionally he moves. His face. Oh, it's so beautiful" (*IBYM*, 25). *Sleep* is an ode to Giorno's ability to be asleep. In recording Giorno's breathing, pulsing, turning body, it focuses our attention on "respiration and circulation," which Jean-Luc Nancy calls the "only processes that belong to sleep."[87] In this, Warhol seems to have been inspired not just by Giorno's talent for sleep, but also by his devotion to

where you couldn't be at some kind of a party. It's amazing how little you want to sleep when there's something to do. ('Remember how we never went to bed?' somebody said to me in '69, nostalgic already for the '65–'67 era. And it really was a whole era, those two years)" (194).

86 In this context, sleep *can* produce value. Where sleep is disturbed in order to extract value from it, Alexei Penzin writes, "Sleep as an act of non-communication and non-productivity is a powerful form of exodus from a society, which is based on communication and production." Penzin suggests that sleep apnea, involuntary disruptions of breathing during sleep, may be the sleep disorder characteristic to post-Fordism. "It is a secret illness," hidden and obscure, thus requiring expensive tests to diagnose and an expensive apparatus to treat. "The Only Place to Hide? The Art and Politics of Sleep in Cognitive Capitalism," Alexei Penzin in conversation with Maria Chekhonadsikh, in *The Psychopathologies of Cognitive Capitalism: Part Two*, ed. Warren Neidich (Berlin: Archive Books, 2013), 221–44, 240, 232.

87 Nancy, *The Fall of Sleep* (New York: Fordham University Press, 2009), 29.

it. "I loved to sleep," Giorno writes. "I slept all the time, twelve hours a day, every day. It was the only place that felt good: complete oblivion, resting in a warm dream world, taking refuge in the lower realms."[88] For Giorno, sleep is what Penzin calls a "singular state of being" with its own "productive, constitutive forces."[89] And yet, this singular state is, as Phillips puts it, "not something we can grasp, but only something we can receive."[90] Among the many effects of watching *Sleep*, we may also be reminded that being affected, in the most general sense, like liking itself, is not something we can decide to do. Instead, it is a politically and historically situated event we can only prepare for, and, like sleep, anticipate and receive.

* * *

Although Warhol compared the experience of watching a long film like *Sleep* to looking out the window, this was an aesthetic goal he more precisely achieved with *Empire*. Where *Sleep* is made up of a sequence of multiple, short shots edited together, *Empire* offers a single, stationary view of the Empire State Building, from about 8 p.m. to 2:30 a.m. Its projection at 16 instead of 24 frames per second accounts for the difference between the time of its filming and its eight-hour, five-minute projection time.[91] Imitating the painting-as-window famously proposed by Leon Battista Alberti in the fifteenth century, Warhol's "moving picture still-life of the Empire State Building" (in which "the light changes but the object remains stationary") is literally filmed through a window on the forty-first floor of the Time-Life Building in Rockefeller Center.[92] In its imitation of the paradigmatically painterly view through the window, *Empire* directly addresses his wish to "'paint' in a new medium" (*IBYM*, 186). As with *Sleep*, although the film is usually understood as a conceptual work—what is important is the *idea* of an eight-hour movie of the Empire State Building—one finds that the movie

88 Giorno, *You Got To Burn To Shine*, 136.

89 Penzin, "100 Notes–100 / 100 Notizen–100 Gedanken, No. 87: Rex Exsomnis: Sleep and Subjectivity in Capitalist Modernity/Rex Exsomnis: Schlaf und Subjektivität in der kapitalistischen Moderne," *dOCUMENTA (13)* (Ostfildern: Hatje Catnz, 2012), 12, and "Art and Politics of Sleep," 224.

90 Phillips, "On Sleep," n.p.

91 For details on the filming, equipment, and timing, see Callie Angell's indispensable essay and "Guide to EMPIRE," which charts the events in the film, in *Films, Part II*, 15–18. The film—shot using a rented, tripod-mounted Auricon camera that took 1,200-foot film magazines (approximately 33 minutes projected at 24 fps, or 48 minutes at 16 fps)—comprises ten reels. Also see Angell's overview essay "Andy Warhol, Filmmaker," in *The Andy Warhol Museum* (Pittsburgh: Andy Warhol Museum), 1994.

92 On Alberti's proposition that the painter regard the frame of the painting as a window, see Anne Friedberg, *The Virtual Window: From Alberti to Microsoft* (Cambridge, MA: MIT Press, 2006), 1, 26–39. The window also appears as a subject in several of Warhol's early paintings. The topic of windows and/as mediation in Warhol's work is worthy of further treatment.

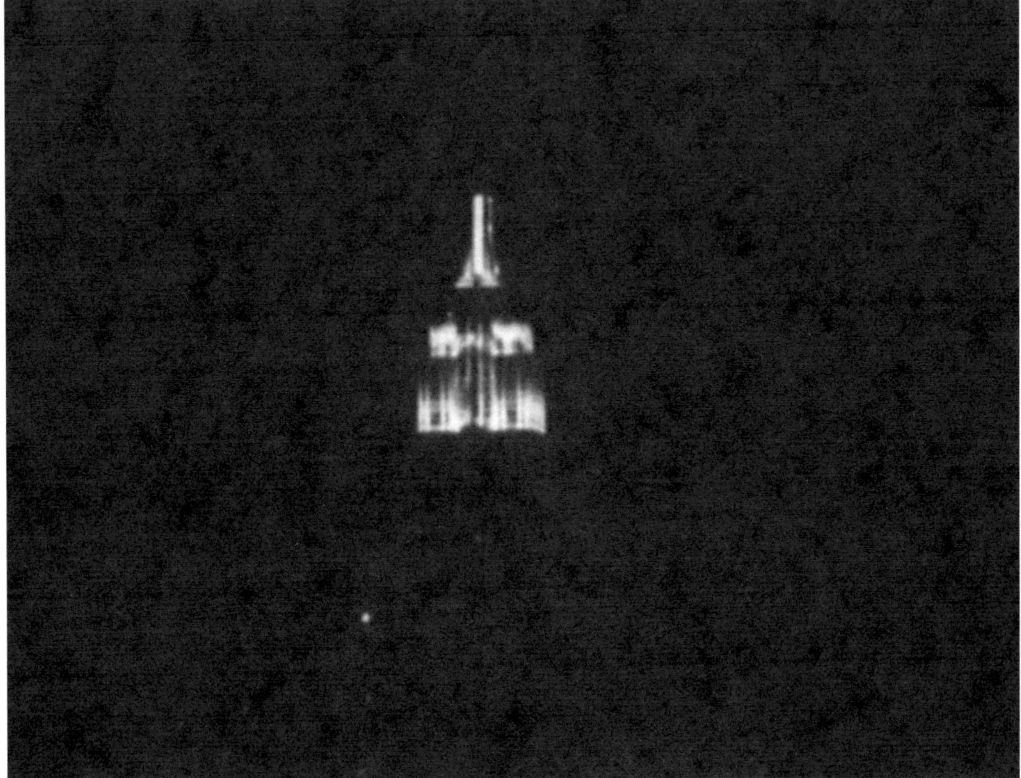

3.10 Andy Warhol, *Empire*, 1964. 16mm film, black and white, silent, 8 hours 5 minutes at 16 frames per second. © The Andy Warhol Museum, a museum of Carnegie Institute.

offers a powerful aesthetic experience. At least in part this is because any image, when looked at long enough, loses its meaning and identity, and any durational experience of such a length tends to separate itself out from the means-ends logic of everyday life in which time is money. (Who has eight hours—a full working day—to watch a "very slow" movie?) But *Empire* also compellingly exploits and allegorizes the otherworldly space of filmic representation itself.

As Callie Angell notes, "the most dramatic events in Empire are events of light."[93] The opening frames of the film are entirely white. If one cannot hear the projector running, or see the beam of light it sends through a dark theater, it can be hard to discern whether the film has really started. Then, slowly, as the screen gets darker by small, barely noticeable increments, a faint image of the Empire State Building shimmers into view, as if emerging from a heavy fog.[94] We "see the architecture's shape, then its form, then its details," Douglas Crimp writes. We are also seeing a representation of a

93 *Films, Part II*, 16.
94 Indeed, Gregory Battcock thought that it *was* emerging from a heavy fog. See "Four Films by Andy Warhol," in O'Pray, *Film Factory*, 42–53, 44.

sunset, but one "distorted in the state of similarity."[95] By filming with Tri-X negative stock pushed to ASA 1000 and with the lens aperture wide open, Warhol reverses the usual relation between light and visibility: here, the disappearance of the sun enables the building to come into the light. Like Judd's specific objects, Warhol's film produces a hallucinatory, illusionary effect, as an effect of the material itself. Like Judd, Warhol drops us into a world of otherworldly natural beauty.

After the sunset, the building settles into clear view for a few minutes. Then, in a sudden flash, the floodlights (which had been installed a few months earlier for the New York World's Fair) go on, and by the end of that first reel we "see no architectural details or forms or shapes that are not solely configured as light."[96] As the meaning quite definitely "goes away," another period of discomfort or disorientation is likely to set in. Even more assuredly than with *Sleep*, the screen image is indifferent to us. There is no cut from one shot to another to bring the audience together in applause. We *do* see brief ghostly reflections of Jonas Mekas, Warhol, and John Palmer in the window at the beginning of reels (5, 7, and 10 respectively), reflections produced by the lights in the office where they were filming, which remained on for a few seconds after the reels had been changed. Other than that, and the occasional flashing light, there are no "details" to keep track of, no sequential, narrative logic other than the passage of time itself. As one stares, or spaces out, the split between attention and focus tends to produce the visual effects I noted earlier, and the Empire State Building stops being the Empire State Building. In his wonderfully precise description of the film and the viewing experience it creates, Crimp notes that "what I found happened most was that the perspective of the building kept reversing itself, so that instead of a solid contour I seemed to be looking at a hollowed-out volume, as if I were seeing a cutaway of interior space."[97] This hallucinatory de-identification allows likenesses to float to the surface of perception like magic bubbles from the springs of one's unconscious. So, for Callie Angell, the image made by the floodlights "suggest[ed] at various times . . . a rocket ship, a hypodermic needle, a heavenly cathedral, or a broad paintbrush that had been dipped in white paint and placed on the surface of a dark gray canvas."[98] For his part, Warhol liked to say that "*Empire* is a—uh—pornographic movie. When the light goes on in the Empire State Building, it's supposed to represent . . ." (*IBYM*, 186). Perhaps we all get the Empire State Building we deserve.

Like Warhol's other minimal films, *Empire* changes one's sense of time, but without the respiration, bodily turns, or editing rhythm that guides us in *Sleep*. Instead, one only has the pulse of the projector itself, which inevi-

95 Benjamin, "Image of Proust," *SW2*, 240.

96 Crimp, *Our Kind of Movie*, 137.

97 See "Epilogue: Warhol's Time," in Crimp, *Our Kind of Movie*, 137–45, 140.

98 Angell, *Films Part II*, 16.

tably also becomes a focus of attention and reflection as the film continues. Following Warhol's own assertion that the point of the film was to "see time go by," both Crimp and Pamela Lee examine the film's production of a particular Warholian filmic time.[99] The movie starts with a paradigmatic temporal marker—the sun going down—altered by the film medium. Then, a bit later, one may notice that the lights occasionally flashing on a building in the background (the Metropolitan Life Insurance Company Tower) are a clock, marking time every 15 minutes like a church bell, with a series of flashes correponding to the hour as the hour turns. Because the projection speed is slower than the recording speed (rendering the clock in the background "inaccurate"), clock-time is "literally" slowed down, which serves to underscore the degree to which the rhythm of our perception and affective attunement has also entered a different, slower Warholian time.

As I noted in chapter 1, the Screen Tests show us that we can be brought into this slower rhythm and distinct mode of apprehension (without drugs) even in four minutes, which turns out to be already quite a bit longer than we are accustomed to directing our gaze at a face, even a filmed one. It is not that we are unaccustomed to seeing intensive expressive movements appear on the reflective background of the face in the standard close-up: someone breaking into a smile, the eyebrow rising, the tear welling. These are moments when a part of the face moves, departing from the unity of the whole, registering a moment of transformation, of being affected. But for the most part, even though they include these micromovements, Warhol's Screen Tests are not what Deleuze calls affection-images; instead, they chart the disintegration of the face. As I observed earlier, although Ann Buchanan manages not to blink for the duration of her Screen Test, keeping as still as one could possibly imagine, her eyes reach their physiological limit and begin to produce lubricating tears, which well at the corner of her eyes and then start to stream down her face. These tears do not quite register as signs of emotion, since her face has already become a mildly hallucinatory set of patterns of light and shadow. Just as a word you have stared at for too long stops looking like a word and instead becomes a strange assemblage of lines and shapes, the faces in the Screen Tests often stop signifying as faces: "faciality traits themselves finally elude the organization of the face," as Deleuze and Guattari write, "freckles dashing toward the horizon, hair carried off by the wind, eyes you traverse instead of seeing yourself in or gazing into those glum face to face encounters between signifying subjectivities."[100] And as the face you look at stops being a signifying subjectivity, so does yours.

99 See Crimp, "Epilogue"; Lee, *Chronophobia: On Time in the Art of the 1960s* (Cambridge, MA: MIT Press, 2004), 83–88. Warhol's statement is quoted by David Bourdon (citing a 1968 lecture in Minneapolis), in *Warhol* (New York: Abrams, 1989), 188.

100 Deleuze and Guattari, *A Thousand Plateaus*, trans. Brian Massumi (Minneapolis: University of Minnesota Press, 1987), 171.

With all of Warhol's minimal films, I have found, Warholian time and the hallucinatory visual effects and receptive, relaxed, bored mood that goes with it may persist as one leaves the theater. One leaves the theater to enter a "world in which everything that happens" has begun to appear "not in identical but in similar guise, opaquely similar to itself."[101] Because our way of seeing the objects of our perception has left them newly de-identified and de-reified, one is ready to be "dazzled" by the world, and not only by the "modern" commodities that were Pop's overt topic, but by everyday ambient objects like the skyline, the streetlights, the statue in the park, or the stones and concrete beneath one's feet. For a little while at least, everything seems to be obscurely if amazingly imitating itself.

Unearthly

If . . . one has . . . the sort of patience specific to legitimate boredom, then one experiences a kind of bliss that is almost unearthly. A landscape appears in which colourful peacocks strut about, and images of people suffused with soul come into view. And look—your own soul is likewise swelling, and in ecstasy you name what you have always lacked: the great *passion*. Were this passion—which shimmers like a comet—to descend, were it to envelop you, the others and the world—oh, then boredom would come to an end, and everything that exists would be . . .

Siegfried Kracauer, "Boredom"[102]

For Warhol and Judd both, affectlessness functioned as an aesthetic strategy that encourages affective openness and involvement inasmuch as it de-identifies the objects of perception in a way that makes them available for transferences of affect from (and then to) various quarters of everyday life. The relaxed, bored state that Judd's and Warhol's work may bring into being functions as a kind of transitional state, a mood in which affects can emerge from viewers that might otherwise find no place to do so. The promise of the work of both is that a patient experience of boredom (such as Kracauer evokes in this section's epigraph) will allow unexpected and unpredictable passion—even "bliss"—to emerge. Such a boredom (to shift to the language of Spinoza and Deleuze) is joyful, inasmuch as it increases one's powers of affecting and being affected.

The strategy of affectlessness makes sense only in a specific situation, one in which people experience difficulty being affectively involved because they have withdrawn from a world that makes too many aggressive emotional demands on them. Warhol found it "hard to care" in part because, as I have observed, there was too much to care about: the ever-increasing violence of warfare, which by the 1950s had reached the point where the an-

101 Benjamin, "Image of Proust," *SW2*, 239.
102 "Boredom," 334.

nihilation of the human life as such had become a possibility; the automatic, repetitive, sensorially demanding quality of work and consumption alike; the scale and size of city space and the masses of people one encounters there; and the number of other lives and deaths and sufferings one comes into contact with via the "news." In such environments, the finer antennae of our mimetic faculties are dulled; we lose our ability to notice similarities and to make them. Inasmuch as affects appear according to a mimetic logic, this loss decreases our agency in relation to our affects.

Both Judd and Warhol seek to give us more agency in relation to our affective lives by making our affects available to us in the carefully framed environments of their work, environments that resemble our everyday life enough to allow our affects to be transferred from there, but are "unearthly" enough to defamiliarize those affects. Judd's specific objects allow us to consider how our shared reification causes us to resemble each other; Warhol's durational films encourage a kind of affective zero-degree of relaxation and openness while they de-identify our objects of perception, including our "selves." In these ways, Judd and Warhol share an opposition to universal fungibility and to the illusion of the "genuine" that it produces as a distracting side effect.

It is worth emphasizing that Judd's and Warhol's insistence on similarity and nonidentity as keys to our capacity to affect and be affected are not promotions of homogeneity. Like metaphors, the strategies Judd and Warhol employ do not erase the difference between things that resemble each other but instead reassert their specificity. In part, this is because things that resemble each other require no intervening abstraction to be in relation—they cannot be made to *equal* each other. That both Judd and Warhol knew they were themselves subject to the application of universal standards of value—whether provided by the art market or by art critics—only made the assertion of resemblance more attractive. Thus, it is in an effort to promote a metaphorical "transaction of contexts" that I here juxtapose Judd and Warhol in my own attempt to mimic and perpetuate the production of similarities I have argued are central to their aesthetic projects.

4: Skin Problems

"If someone asked me, 'What's your problem?' I'd have to say, 'Skin.'"

The Philosophy of Andy Warhol[1]

With its production of and reliance on reified categories of racial difference and its use of them to promote *dislike*, Jim Crow racism would seem the very paradigm of what Warhol's Pop dedication to liking and likeness sought to oppose. Indeed, I see Warhol's insistence, in the interview with Gene Swenson in the fall of 1963, that people were becoming "more and more" alike and his avowed desire that "everybody should like everybody" partly as responses to the civil rights movement and the racist reaction to it, which had reached a certain peak of violence (and news coverage) that summer.[2] A turning point in the civil rights movement, the summer of 1963 ended with Martin Luther King Jr.'s "I Have A Dream" speech at the August 28 March on Washington, and then, on September 15, the bombing of the 16th Street Baptist Church in Birmingham, Alabama. Throughout the season, broad media coverage directed public attention toward police violence against protesters across the South, especially in Birmingham, home of notorious police chief "Bull" Connor. Photos from one such confrontation, published in the May 17 issue of *Life* magazine, served as the source material for Warhol's Race Riot paintings, produced shortly thereafter. My contention here is that Warhol's conception of Pop and the centrality of liking and likeness to it is fundamentally inflected by the racist and antiracist politics of the early

1 *Phil*, 8.

2 That summer also saw the assassination of civil rights leader Medgar Evers (on June 20) and the deaths of many other civil rights activists and leaders. By the end of the year, "the Southern Regional Council estimated that there had been 930 protests in 115 cities in the 11 Southern states, with more than 20,000 arrests, at least 35 bombings, and 10 deaths that were directly related to racial protests." Fred Powledge, *Free at Last? The Civil Rights Movement and the People Who Made It* (New York: Harper Perennial, 1991), 523.

1960s, which were on vivid display in the summer of 1963 and in Warhol's Race Riot paintings.

Not only in the Race Riot canvases, but throughout Warhol's career, one can discern a preoccupation with the color line, that boundary separating—and joining—"white" and "black" that W. E. B. Du Bois, in 1903, presciently and famously called "the problem of the Twentieth Century,"[3] even though the relative lack of critical work on the topic might give one a different impression.[4] From the 1960 proto-Pop drawing of a *Journal American* newspaper with the headline "Woman Stabs Rev. King in Harlem" to the 1983 works reproducing newspaper coverage of the death of graffiti artist Michael Stewart while in police custody, we see Warhol's interest in the mass publicity of violence against black persons, especially as it is connected to the struggle for civil rights.[5] In other works, Warhol drew attention to crossings of the color line, as in his 1963 film *Kiss*, which features a kiss between an African American man and a white woman (Rufus Collins and Naomi Levine), at a time when kisses had yet to cross the color line in Hollywood film. His collaborations with Jean-Michel Basquiat in 1985 and 1986 represent the color line and its crossings in a range of implicit and explicit ways (as José Esteban Muñoz's important essay shows), not least by putting on public display their

3 Du Bois, *The Souls of Black Folk* (New York: Everyman's Library, 1993), 5. He repeats the observation on 37.

4 Exceptions include Anne Wagner, "Warhol Paints History, or Race in America" *Representations*, no. 55 (Summer 1996); Eve Kosofsky Sedgwick, "Queer Performativity: Warhol's Shyness/Warhol's Whiteness" (134–43) and José Esteban Muñoz, "Famous and Dandy Like B. 'n' Andy: Race, Pop and Basquiat" (144–79), both in in Doyle, Flatley, and Muñoz, *Pop Out*; and Taro Nettleton, "White-on-White: The Overbearing Whiteness of Warhol's Being," *Art Journal* 62, no. 1 (Spring 2003): 15–23.

5 On the 1960 drawing, *Journal American*, see Neil Printz, "Painting Death in America," in *Andy Warhol Death and Disasters*, 11–22, 12. Stewart comes up in the *Diaries* in connection to Keith Haring, who was Stewart's friend: "Keith was ranting and raving about this black graffiti artist that's in the papers now because the police killed him—Michael Stewart. And Keith said that he's been arrested four times, but that because he looks normal they just sort of call him a fairy and let him go. But this kid that was killed, he had that Jean Michel look—dreadlocks" (*Diaries*, Thursday, September 29, 1983, 533). See also Molly Donovan, "Where's Warhol? Triangulating Warhol in the Headlines," in *Warhol Headlines*, exh. cat., ed. Donovan (Washington, DC: National Gallery of Art, 2011), 19: "Daily News (Artist Could Have Been Choked) (pl. 58) and Daily News (Gimbels Anniversary Sale) (pl. 59) again paired advertising—for the Gimbels department store—and news: of the death of twenty-five-year-old graffiti artist Michael Stewart, reportedly at the hands of police. Warhol's reason for making a painting of this particular page likely related to the disturbing story about Stewart, a friend of Warhol's friend and fellow artist Keith Haring. The work draws our attention to the strikingly, but not surprisingly, diminutive space allotted to the story of an individual's wrongful death relative to the large department store ad alongside it. In the latter painting, the silkscreen process registers such a degree of slippage that, except for the headline, the article's text is mostly illegible. Warhol also silkscreened this news page onto Mylar, crumpled it, then flattened it out to make a new work (pl. 60)."

friendship and collaboration as such.[6] Warhol's abiding interest in fame and wealth, especially movie star celebrity, meant that his star portraits largely reproduced Hollywood's bias toward whiteness, as Taro Nettleton has pointed out.[7] Yet, in portraits of figures such as Bobby Short, Russell Means, Muhammed Ali, O. J. Simpson, Diana Ross, Grace Jones, Aretha Franklin, Michael Jackson, Prince, his friend and collaborator Basquiat, and, in a different register of celebrity, Mao Tse Tung, Warhol presents a compelling visual archive of nonwhite fame, and of how the processes of racialization and celebrity work therein. His 1975 Ladies and Gentlemen series, which I discuss below, provocatively addresses the relation between racial and sexual visibility and self-presentation in its 268 paintings of black and Latino drag queens. Rufus Collins, Dorothy Dean, and Mario Montez (who also appeared in Jack Smith's *Flaming Creatures* and *Normal Love*) are recurring figures in his films. As Warhol's films continue to be preserved and enjoy more publicity, it has become increasingly clear that Montez was one of the most significant and compelling queer performers of the era, as work by Callie Angell, Douglas Crimp, José Muñoz, Marc Siegel, and others demonstrates.[8] And as Frances Negron-Muntaner has shown, in Warhol's engagement with figures such as Montez, Holly Woodlawn, and Basquiat, we see a significant Puerto Rican presence in his work.[9] I mention this large body of material, which I cannot fully cover here, to call attention to Warhol's recurring thematic focus on racism, the color line, and the representation of nonwhite persons—a compelling feature of his work that deserves more critical treatment than it has so far received.

My focus here is more specific. I am concerned with Warhol's various formal strategies for producing and emphasizing likenesses that were them-

6 Muñoz, "Famous and Dandy."

7 Nettleton argues that Warhol saw whiteness as both "a requirement for inclusion" in the mass public sphere, and as "an impossible ideal" ("White-on-White," 18). Yet, he suggests, "despite Warhol's understanding of the complex and problematic function of whiteness in the process of becoming public, the chromatic consistency of his portraits' subjects suggests a failure to critically engage such issues" (23).

8 Montez appeared in Warhol's *Batman Dracula, Mario Banana, Mario Montez Dances, Harlot, Screen Test No. 2, Camp, More Milk Yvette, Hedy, Chelsea Girls, Bufferin Commercial*, and *Ari and Mario*. For an excellent biographical sketch, see Angell, *Andy Warhol Screen Tests*: "As Warhol film star, Montez became one of the first transvestite actors to gain mainstream recognition" (134). For brilliant, close readings of Montez in Warhol's films, see Crimp, *Our Kind of Movie*, esp. the chapters "Mario Montez, for Shame" and "Coming Together to Stay Apart." Also see *Criticism* 56, no. 2 (Spring 2014; Jack Smith special issue), especially José Esteban Muñoz, "Wise Latinas" (in part about *Screen Test No. 2*), and Marc Siegel, "The Return of Mario Montez," and Siegel's chapter on Montez's performance in *Harlot* in *A Gossip of Images* (Durham, NC: Duke University Press, 2017).

9 Frances Negron-Muntaner, *Boricua Pop: Puerto Ricans and the Latinization of American Culture* (New York: NYU Press, 2004), esp. chaps. 4 ("From Puerto Rico With *Trash*: Holly Woodlawn's *Low Life in High Heels*") and 5 ("The Writing on the Wall: The Life and Passion of Jean-Michel Basquiat").

selves, at the same time, reflections on how we come to know, see, feel, and experience racial difference. In the Race Riots, the early celebrity silkscreens, the Ladies and Gentlemen series, and his collaborations with Basquiat, I see Warhol addressing the mediation of skin and skin color as a kind of "racial technology" (to borrow from Jennifer Gonzalez, Beth Coleman, and Wendy Chun), a way of creating racial difference as a relation, an "encounter that enables certain actions and bars others."[10]

Throughout his career, I think Warhol was guided in his response to reified notions of racial sameness and difference by a desire to display the possibilities of being alike across the color line, as a way to promote different, possibly nonracist, forms of affective engagement and attachment. This was not an attempt to "transcend race" or negate the reality of the color line. Instead, in its attention to the way the color line polices imitation and affection, barring some relations and enabling others, his work lay bare some of the mechanisms through which "race" comes into being, helping to defamiliarize the workings of the color line in a way that may allow viewers to become newly or differently aware of how they feel or experience or come to know "race." In the spectatorial and performative practices of nonwhite drag queens in particular, I think Warhol saw how one might (as Chun puts it) "make race do different things."[11]

* * *

Warhol appears to indicate his sensitivity to the significance of the mediation of skin and skin color in his comments about his own well-known skin problems, which gave him an odd and unattractively white skin, frequently noted in physical descriptions by friends and acquaintances. "That's what struck me," David Bowie remarked: "He's the wrong color. This man is the wrong color to be a human being."[12] In *The Philosophy of Andy Warhol*, Warhol writes, "I lost all my pigment when I was 8 years old." One biographer guesses that he suffered from vitiligo, a condition that causes skin depigmentation, producing patches of unnatural-looking whiteness.[13] In addi-

10 Chun, "Introduction: Race and/as Technology; or, How to Do Things to Race," *Camera Obscura* 24, no. 1 (2009): 7–34, 23. In the same issue, see Gonzalez, "The Face and the Public: Race, Secrecy, and Digital Art Practice" (37–60), and Coleman, "Race as Technology" (177–207). See also Gonzalez, "Morphologies: Race as Visual Technology," in *Only Skin Deep: Changing Visions of the American Self*, ed. Coco Fusco and Brian Wallis (New York: International Center of Photography, 2003), 379–93.

11 Chun, "Race and/as Technology," 28.

12 "Beat Godfather Meets Glitter Mainman: William Burroughs Say Hello to David Bowie" (interview by Craig Copetas), *Rolling Stone*, February 28, 1974; reprinted in *David Bowie: The Last Interview and Other Conversations* (Brooklyn: Melville House, 2016), 31–53, 49.

13 See Scherman and Dalton, *Pop*, 7. Also see Ivan Karp's remarks on the "incredible whiteness of his complexion" (72).

tion, his nose was frequently covered in pimply red splotches (probably from what dermatologists call rosacea), to the extent that even his family called him "Andy the red nosed Warhola" (*Phil*, 63–64). And throughout his life he suffered from acne. While techniques for dealing with his various skin problems improved as Warhol got older (and had more money), his skin required daily treatment.

At the beginning of his *Philosophy*, Warhol recounts his morning skin-care routine. Sitting at the mirror, he applies alcohol and then "the flesh-colored acne-pimple medication that doesn't resemble any human flesh I've ever seen, though it does come pretty close to mine" (9). While registering the nonhuman quality of the "flesh-colored" cream, Warhol also mockingly notes the abnormal normality of his own skin: unlike that of anyone he has seen, *his* skin actually resembles the color of the medication. That this normative, commodified flesh color is not desirable becomes even more clear as Warhol describes his skin's odd appearance: "the chalky, puckish mask"; "the pale, soft-spoken, magical presence, the skin and bones"; "the albino-chalk skin. Parchmentlike. Reptilian. Almost blue"; "the long bony arms, so white they look bleached"; "the graying lips" (10). This "wasted pallor," veering to blue or gray, appears either to have been produced by some whitening process (chalky, bleached) or to be nonhuman altogether (parchmentlike, reptilian).[14] It is unnatural, excessive, and, above all, unattractive.[15] It was a "problem," one that required management, not unlike his queerness.

Eve Sedgwick suggests that the sense of shame attaching to Warhol's "problems" functioned as a source of transformational, experimental energy for him, and that various of Warhol's modes of self-presentation and artistic practices were at the same time either tactics for managing his multiply spoiled identity or intimately related to them.[16] Indeed, I think there is much to be gained in seeing Warhol's Pop, and its commitment to liking and likeness, as an archive of various, and variously appropriable, strategies for managing stigma.

That Warhol felt marked by his peculiar skin does not mean, of course, that he did not benefit from its whiteness; unattractive and oddly white skin

14 Warhol refers several times in his *Diaries* to his sense of being marked by his weird, unattractive appearance. Also see *POP*, 199–200, for Silver George's description of Warhol while impersonating Warhol on the phone, also discussed by Sedgwick in "Warhol's Shyness/Warhol's Whiteness," esp. 135–39.

15 "In its very allegorical excessiveness," Sedgwick notes, it "resists being normalized or universalized" ("Warhol's Shyness/Warhol's Whiteness," 139).

16 I'm borrowing here from Sedgwick: "The subtitle of any truly queer . . . politics will be the same as the one that Erving Goffman gave to his book [*Stigma: Notes on the Management of Spoiled Identity*] . . . more than its management: its experimental, creative, performative force." "Queer Performativity: Henry James's *Art of the Novel*," 4. See also Crimp, "Mario Montez, for Shame," for a reading of *Screen Test No.2* (and Warhol's films more generally) in relation to Sedgwick's work on queer shame (*Our Kind of Movie*, 20–37).

did not, after all, subject him to racism. Warhol could and did operate in the explicitly and implicitly "whites only" spaces that shaped his world. Nor did his own skin problems bring him to a particularly sophisticated or coherent personal analysis of race or racism, as various racist (and antiracist) remarks in the *Diaries*, for instance, indicate. Rather, my proposition here is that Warhol was interested in skin *as* a problem, as something one might be alienated from and stigmatized by, which attuned him to the artificiality and mediatedness of our seeing of skin in general. He was very attentive to the representation of skin, and to the technologies and techniques available for changing how skin looks. In his portrait practice, this meant that he was sympathetic to all manner of beauty tricks, especially concerning how he depicted (posed, accessorized, made-up, lit, photographed, painted) a sitter's skin, as he strove to give sitters the look they wanted.[17] Warhol's interest in the problematicity and mediatedness of skin and skin color may be one reason why his work is a keen register of the racial technologies of his historical moment.

One of these racial technologies is the aesthetic opposition between black and white, as it takes form in the print medium especially. Warhol's work directs our attention to the importance of this opposition, and of color more generally, in turning skin into "race." Particularly in his early paintings and films—including the Race Riots but also the serial celebrity portraits and Screen Tests, for instance—Warhol explores the function of this aesthetic opposition between black and white in shaping our capacity to engage what Deleuze and Guattari call the "faciality machine," the systemic logic through which we come to apprehend and recognize a face.[18]

17 About his portrait practice, Bob Colacello remarked, "What Andy did to the negative was more like plastic surgery, though the end result was magical: beasts turned into beauties. He simply took scissors and snipped out double chins, bumps in noses, bags under eyes, the shadows of pimples, the blackness of beards. His most elderly clients were left, like Marilyn, like Elvis, with eyes, nostrils, lips and jaw lines" (*Holy Terror*, 89). Warhol writes, 'When I did my self portrait, I left all the pimples out because you always should" (*Phil*, 62). Regarding his anxiety about representing skin and skin color, see Warhol's comments in the *Diaries* about Diana Ross's *Interview* cover (not made by Warhol): "Diana didn't say she liked her cover and I just know it's because it made her look too black" (*Diaries*, September 21, 1978, 171). Later, when he was working on her portrait, he noted, " I painted some backgrounds for the Diana Ross portrait—I wonder what color I should make her—I wonder if she wants to be black or white" (August 11, 1981, 400).
18 For Deleuze and Guattari, the opposition between black and white is essential to faciality itself. In *A Thousand Plateaus*, they describe the faciality machine in the following way: "Signifiance is never without a white wall upon which it inscribes its signs and redundancies. Subjectification is never without a black hole in which it lodges its consciousness, passion, and redundancies"; the face is this "white wall/black hole system" (167). In *Cinema 1: The Movement Image*, trans. Hugh Tomlinson and Barbara Habberjam (Minneapolis: University of Minnesota Press, 1989), Deleuze puts it slightly differently, emphasizing the two poles as a "receptive immobile surface, receptive plate of inscription, impassive suspense . . . a reflecting and reflected unity" (87), on which an intensive series of micromovements can take place. In each formulation, the opposition between

In other words, Warhol's work encourages us to consider the functions of color in the region of prosopopoeia, the trope "that ascribes face, name, or voice to the absent, inanimate, or dead; it means literally to give or create a face or person, to person-ify."[19] Inasmuch as the fight against white supremacy in the United States across the twentieth century has been concerned to create and represent an African American personhood that is recognized by the legal and governmental apparatus of the United States, where such personhood had previously been denied, this trope of personification, of fame and shame alike, has been central to antiracist representational politics and to the mass-mediated apprehension of it. The logics of prosopopoeia, the medium of face intelligibility, are on ample and evocative display in the Race Riot paintings, an examination of which shows not only how racial technologies are at work in the print medium but also how such technologies—and their use and apprehension by audiences—affect and guide the experience of spectatorship more generally.

"Very Black + White"

Plese [*sic*] make contrasts very black + white.

Andy Warhol, note to his silkscreen maker on the Race Riot source image

In the summer of 1963 Warhol began a series of paintings based on three photographs taken by Charles Moore and published in *Life* magazine on May 17, 1963, as part of its coverage of demonstrations in Birmingham, Alabama.[20] The images dramatize the violence and force necessary to enforce

white and black is central; indeed Deleuze and Guattari write that the faciality machine is fundamentally racializing: "The face is not a universal. It is not even that of the white man; it is White Man himself with his broad white cheeks and the black hole of his eyes" (*Thousand Plateaus*, 176). Racism, then, "operates by the determination of degrees of deviance in relation to the White-Man face" (178). In this context, Deleuze and Guattari call for a "dismantling of the face": "Here, the program, the slogan, of schizoanalysis is: Find your black holes and white walls, know them, know your faces; it is the only way you will be able to dismantle them and draw your lines of flight" (188). Warhol offers multiple assistances in this project.

19 Flatley, "Warhol Gives Good Face," 106. In this essay, I argue that "many of Warhol's persistent interests—portraiture, celebrity, consumption, pornography, and disasters—can be usefully understood together in terms of prosopopoiea." Borrowing from Paul de Man, I note that, as the trope that creates the fiction of the voice beyond the grave, prosopopoeia has a double-movement: "the giving of face, to the extent that it must presuppose an absence, always also entails a de-facing," producing "anonymity as it enables recognition" and failing to "distinguish between the dead and the living" (106). In a real sense, the posthumous portrait (as in Warhol's portrait of Marilyn) is the ideal one, and being recognized can feel self-affirming to the precise extent that it is, at the same time, self-negating. See de Man, "Autobiography as De-facement," in *The Rhetoric of Romanticism* (New York: Columbia University Press, 1984).

20 "For many viewers today, almost the entirety of the civil rights movement is captured, quite literally, in the photographs of Birmingham 1963." Leigh Raiford, *Imprisoned in*

the color line by focusing our attention on three white policemen, who, with girded hips and strained arms, direct German shepherds to attack a black demonstrator at the center of the frame. In the final, and largest, photo in the spread, the man is under attack from two sides, a black dog's teeth tugging on his back pocket as he appears to be pulling his torn sleeve away from another dog, whose white teeth are bared and threatening. Like the man at the photo's center, viewers of this last photo are also faced by one of the dogs, which is captured in vibrant and compelling detail. The last image, where the dog, unaggressive in that moment, faces the photographer, seems to draw attention to the dog as an affecting agent in its own right, indeed as a being forced to occupy the volatile, violent space between black and white throughout white supremacy's history in the United States.[21] The "Race Riot" title (of unclear origin, like many of Warhol's painting titles) is misleading here, since what we see is not a riot but the organized white supremacist violence of the state, carried out by white policemen, against an unarmed, nonviolent citizen.[22]

For Warhol's paintings, the three images from the *Life* spread were enlarged to produce 30-inch screens, which were then used to print black images on four large canvases with differently colored grounds (red or pink, mustard, mauve, white). Each of the paintings features distinct and significant variations in the ordering, placement, and cropping of the images, in background treatment, and in the density and quality of black silkscreen ink. Roughly a year later, in 1964, Warhol used just one of the images to produce ten "Little Race Riots."[23] *Mustard Race Riot* is a diptych, featuring

---

A Luminous Glare: Photography and the African American Freedom Struggle (Chapel Hill: University of North Carolina Press, 2011), 2. Moore, a staff photographer for the *Birmingham Advertiser*, took many of the most famous photographs of the movement. See Michael S. Dunham, *Powerful Days: The Civil Rights Photography of Charles Moore* (Tuscaloosa: University of Alabama Press, 1991). On the taking of these photographs in particular, see Martin Berger, *Seeing through Race: A Reinterpretation of Civil Rights Photography* (Berkeley: University of California Press, 2011), esp. 50–53.

21 On dogs and the history of white supremacy in the United State, see Berger, *Seeing through Race*, 65. As Berger notes, the image of slaves being hunted by tracking dogs appears throughout nineteenth-century print and visual culture, including, famously, in Stowe's *Uncle Tom's Cabin* and Douglass's *The Life and Times of Frederick Douglass*. For a fascinating analysis of Warhol's persistent interest in nonhuman animals, see Anthony Grudin, "Warhol's Animal Life," *Criticism* 56, no. 3 (Summer 2014; Warhol special issue).

22 In the "What Is Pop Art?" interview, Warhol referred to them as "the dogs in Birmingham" (*IBYM*, 18). In notes to himself, he referred to the *Mustard Race Riot* as the "tan negro painting" or as "Mongomerty [*sic*] negro dog"; in the 1965 Philadelphia ICA catalog it is titled *Selma*. See Printz on the titling of this painting (*CR1*, 380, 383), which appears to have been supplied by someone at the Sonnabend Gallery.

23 The pink and mustard-colored Little Race Riot paintings were exhibited in numerous gallery and museum shows through the 1960s and 1970s. The mauve one is categorized as "present location unknown" in the *Catalogue Raisonné*, and the white painting appears to have gone directly into storage, not receiving public exhibition until after Warhol's death. Where, in the earlier works, variations in ordering, cropping, background treat-

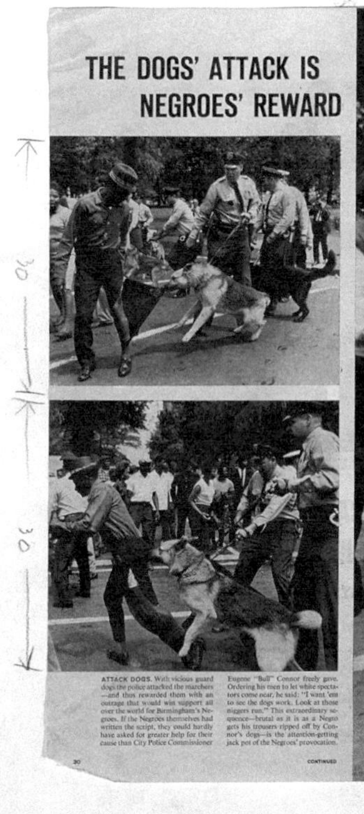

THE DOGS' ATTACK IS NEGROES' REWARD

ATTACK DOGS. With vicious guard dogs the police attacked the marchers—and thus rewarded them with an outrage that would win support all over the world for Birmingham's Negroes. If the Negroes themselves had written the script, they could hardly have asked for greater help for their cause than City Police Commissioner Eugene "Bull" Connor freely gave. Ordering his men to let white spectators come near, he said: "I want 'em to see the dogs work. Look at those niggers run." This extraordinary sequence—brutal as it is as a Negro gets his trousers ripped off by Connor's dogs—is the attention-getting jack pot of the Negroes' provocation.

30

CONTINUED

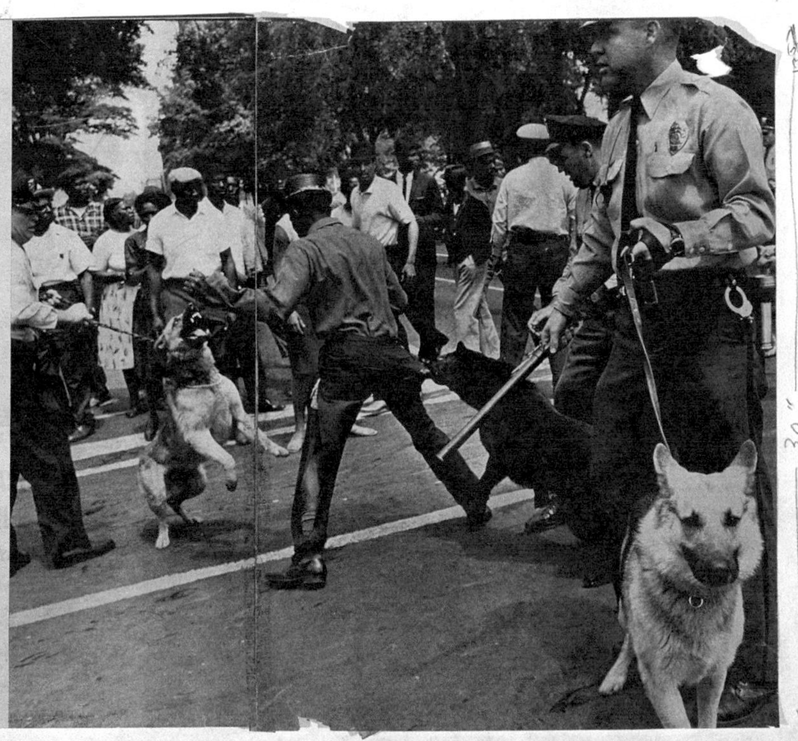

4.1 Andy Warhol, collage ("The Dogs' Attack Is Negroes' Reward," from *Life* magazine, May 17, 1963; photographs by Charles Moore), source for Warhol's Race Riot series, 1963. Newsprint clipping, graphite, tape, and gouache on heavyweight paper, 20 × 22½ inches. The Andy Warhol Museum, Pittsburgh; Founding Collection, contribution of the Andy Warhol Foundation for the Visual Arts.

a monochrome canvas, which Warhol referred to as a "blank," alongside the screen-printed one.[24] Like the other Death and Disaster paintings, the Race

---

ment, and density and quality of ink might be read as compositional, even expressive, in ways that suggest various interpretive possibilities, the Little Race Riots are characterized by a single, deadpan reproduction of a single image on each canvas. This is consistent with Warhol's attempt to remove as many compositional elements as possible from his work during this period.

24 This device originated in the Death and Disaster series, of which the Race Riots were a part, along with photo-based images of car crashes, suicides, tuna fish poisonings, and an electric chair, usually also printed in black on backgrounds painted in nonprimary,

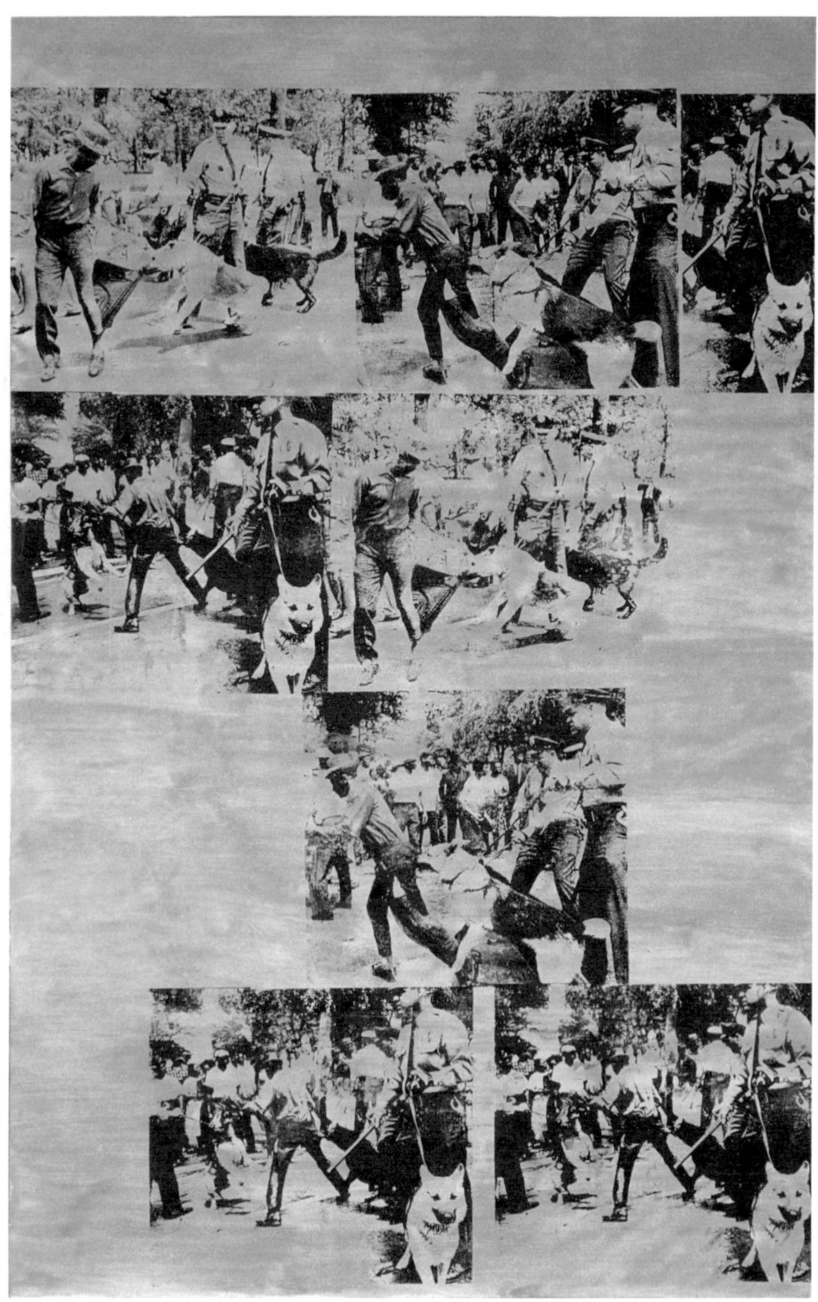

4.2 Andy Warhol, *Pink Race Riot (Red Race Riot)*, 1963. Silkscreen ink and acrylic on linen, 128¼ × 83 inches. © 2016 Andy Warhol Foundation for the Visual Arts/Artists Rights Society (ARS), New York.

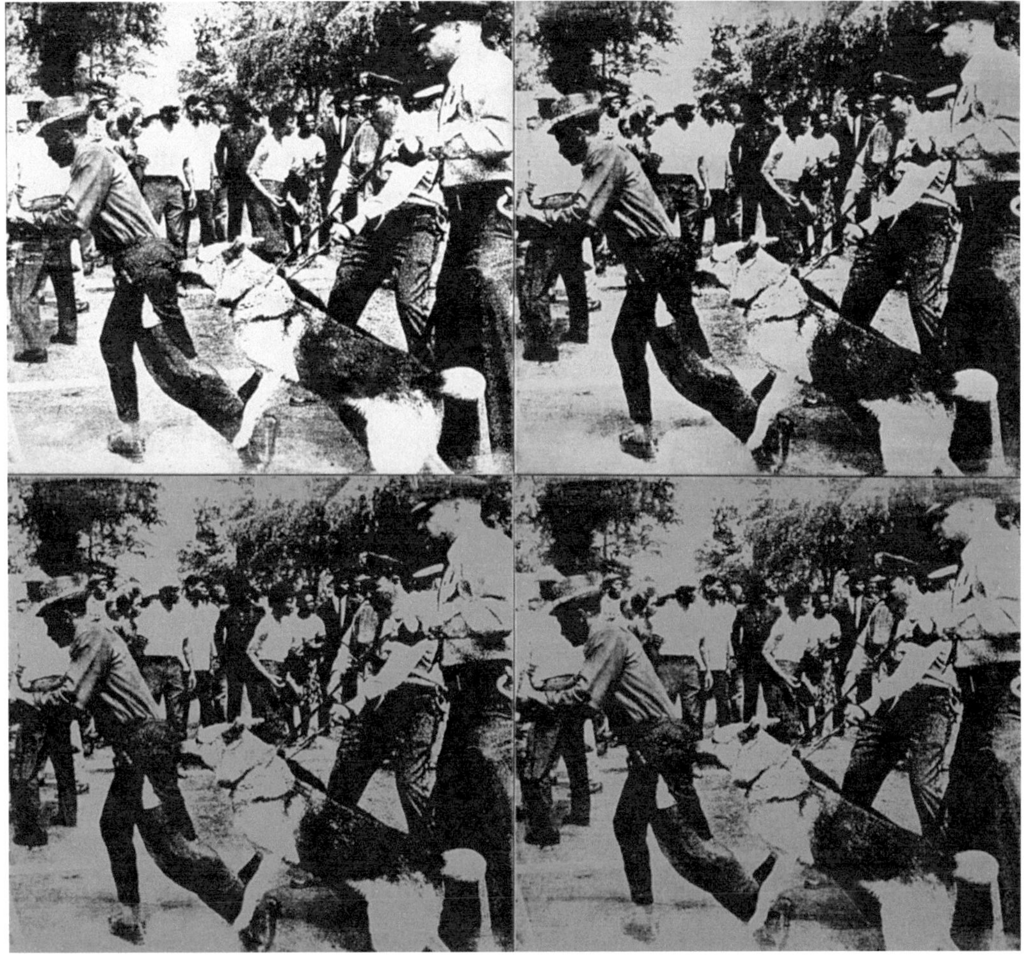

4.3 Andy Warhol, *Little Race Riot*, 1964. Silkscreen ink on linen; each canvas 30 × 33 inches. © 2016 Andy Warhol Foundation for the Visual Arts/Artists Rights Society (ARS), New York

Riots feature a thematic emphasis on a specific, violent event or occurrence (an element distinguishing them from most of his paintings of celebrities and commodities).[25]

Many of the works in the Death and Disaster series, including *Pink Race Riot* (also known as *Red Race Riot*) (figure 4.2, plate 1), received their first

---

decorative colors. The first such painting documented with a monochrome panel is *Blue Electric Chair*, included in the January 1964 Sonnabend Gallery exhibition (*CR1*, cat. no. 358, p. 331). The device has been read in various ways; see initial review by Alain Jouffray, cited in *CR1*, 331. Some paintings that feature this device had the monochrome canvas added later, at the time of purchase, as with *Red Disaster* (*CR1*, cat. no. 359).

25 On the Disaster paintings, especially their formal characteristics, see Printz, "Painting Death in America."

public exhibition in a show at the Sonnabend Gallery in Paris, which Warhol said he intended to call "Death in America."[26] His work had been engaged specifically with the theme of death and its mass publicity at least since his *129 Die*, which he had painted roughly a year earlier, not long before he began the Marilyn portraits, which were occasioned by her death, leading him to realize that "everything I was doing must have been death."[27] Although there is no death depicted in the Race Riots, Moore's photo (and others like it) served as a kind of icon for the civil rights movement and racist responses to it, which that year, as I have noted, included multiple murders of civil rights leaders and activists.

Some critics have taken issue with Warhol's use of these images. Martin Berger, for instance, writes, "Ignoring published images that spoke unequivocally to whites of black agency, Warhol selected the photographs that most succinctly articulated a safe narrative of peaceful, victimized blacks."[28] It is certainly true that other compelling images were available, even within the same article in *Life*, as Leigh Raiford shows in her powerful readings of a number of striking photos featuring black women defiantly confronting white police.[29] Perhaps with photos such as these in mind, Anne Wagner (in one of the only scholarly treatments of the Race Riots) critiques Warhol for his choice of photographs, in part because they perpetuate the "structuring

26 "Warhol and Sonnabend discussed plans for a one-person exhibition in Paris during early 1963. Sonnabend wanted to schedule an exhibition as early as possible, showing works from several series, but Warhol was more interested in exhibiting a new body of work—the 'death' series, which he was working on during that period" (Printz, *CR1*, 473). Eight of the Death and Disaster paintings, including *Pink Race Riot* (*Red Race Riot*) were exhibited in the show. Concerning the title of this last painting, the *Catalogue Raisonné* (*CR1*, 383) informs us that the "Pink" title comes from Sonnabend (and more accurately describes the clear mix of white and red paint), the "Red" title from Rainer Crone's early, important catalogue raisonné (which was incomplete and contained several errors) in *Andy Warhol* (New York: Praeger, 1970), 285–312.

27 "I guess it was the big plane crash picture, the front page of a newspaper: 129 DIE. I was also painting the Marilyns. I realized that everything I was doing must have been death. It was Christmas or Labor Day—a holiday—and every time you turned on the radio they said something like '4 million are going to die.' That started it" (*IBYM*, 19). In 1966 he noted, "the Monroe picture was part of a death series I was doing, of people who had died by different ways" (*IBYM*, 88).

28 Berger, *Seeing through Race*, 26. Berger argues that these photos of passive black victims and white racist oppressors have in some ways come to signify black politics in general, and have thus placed real limits on present and future black politics.

29 Raiford argues that "these photographs make visible long and deeply hidden transcripts between black women and white men, in which black female vulnerability to white male sexual advances bespeaks a fraught and frightening historical intimacy" (*Imprisoned in A Luminous Glare*, 83). See also her discussion of an image "of a woman whose clothes are drenched and disheveled from the force of the hoses and whose stockings are dislocated" and a policeman who "clutches his billyclub tight in his fist as he faces this woman in a condition of state-induced undress," thereby revealing "the entanglement of political and sexual power" (85).

assumptions" of American views of race and racism, which "endlessly—repetitively, redundantly—dramatize the encounter between black and white as a conflict between black and white men," ignoring the important experience of women and children.[30]

Whether or not we think Warhol should have chosen other photos, what interests me about the images he did use is the degree to which they put on display how "commonsense narratives of blackness . . . crystallize and adhere in the photograph," as Raiford puts it.[31] Warhol is not just directing attention to the event itself but is also referencing the media coverage of the civil rights movement that summer and the degree to which the most widely circulated and publicized photographs of the civil rights movement focused on the spectacular violence of white police against black men.[32] As such, the images Warhol chose are paradigmatic instances of photographs as themselves racial technologies, ways of teaching viewers how to see and feel about blackness. Moreover, these images suggestively correspond to the terms used by the leaders of the civil rights movement to describe the photographically mediated representational work that passive resistance could accomplish.

As Raiford has demonstrated in her book charting the consequential, calculated, and ambivalent engagement with photography in African American social movements, leaders of the civil rights movement helped design and produce the scenes that would lead to the capture of photographic images such as the ones Warhol appropriated.[33] In considering the role photography

30 Wagner, "Warhol Paints History," 111. Writing in the wake of the Rodney King trial and the subsequent uprising, Wagner makes a complex argument resting on a distinction between the Race Riots and other of Warhol's paintings, which she deems more successful, such as the Marilyns. These more successful paintings, Wagner argues, work as allegories: "The meanings of these works—if they have meanings—are not the particular events and individuals they illustrate—this car crash, that movie star, this can of soup. Instead, they refer outside of themselves to a particular set of conditions, which, however real, cannot be illustrated as a totality. They refer us, that is, to the system—the image world—of commodification and desire that gives them currency, and invoke that system as a set of generalities. . . . The appropriated image must be both resonant enough—and empty enough—to allow the process of allegorizing to occur" (104). The Race Riots, by contrast, because they are essentially sequential, dramatic, and narrative, depicting a complex event with multiple protagonists, do not lend themselves to being emptied out (by way of repetition) for an iconic allegorical reading. Warhol *wanted* to produce an allegorical picture, Wagner contends, but failed not only because of the particularity of this image, but because the "drama of race" itself resists such allegorization. "The rhetoric of sameness, of rote and standard repetition, can no longer be made to apply" (112).

31 *Imprisoned in A Luminous Glare*, 8.

32 Perhaps the most famous of these images, taken the same day by Bill Hudson, *Walter Gadsden Attacked by K-9 Units, Birmingham, Alabama, May 3, 1963*, was reprinted around the world (including in the Soviet Union) and was reportedly viewed and discussed by President Kennedy and his advisers.

33 Raiford examines how the leaders of the civil rights movement both orchestrated photographable scenes and took their own photographs, documenting the movement

might play, King and other leaders were well aware that "black bodies in pain for public consumption have been an American national spectacle for centuries," as Elizabeth Alexander puts it.[34] They knew that several years earlier, in 1955, photographs of Emmett Till's brutally disfigured face had a powerful politicizing effect on black viewers (as Alexander and Raiford discuss, and as writers as varied as Muhammed Ali, Shelby Steele, and Charlayne Hunter-Gault recount).[35] Alexander examines how images of black abjection such as those of Till could function as sites for "group self-definition and self-knowledge," even as or precisely because they may also occasion collective traumatic recollection of a history of white supremacist violence.[36]

But Martin Luther King Jr. did not make the case for political mobilization by way of images of black abjection. Nor did he advocate presenting images of sympathetic, suffering black victims with whom a white audience might identify, as in the model elaborated by Saidiya Hartman.[37] Instead, King argued for the production of images that captured white supremacy and white supremacists and exposed them as problems to be critiqued, stigmatized, and opposed by antiracist audiences on both sides of the color line: "The brutality with which officials would have quelled the black individual became impotent when it could not be pursued with stealth and remain un-

---

and its participants. The Student Nonviolent Coordinating Committee (SNCC), for instance, had its own photo agency, which employed the photographer Danny Lyons, who, along with Moore, captured many of the most famous images of the movement.

34 Elizabeth Alexander, "'Can You Be BLACK and Look at This?': Reading the Rodney King Video(s)" *Public Culture* 7 (1994):77–94; reprinted in *Black Male: Representations of Masculinity in Contemporary American Art*, ed. Thelma Golden (New York: Whitney Museum of American Art, 1994).

35 See Alexander, "Can You Be BLACK?," 87–90; Raiford, *Imprisoned in A Luminous Glare*, 87–89.

36 Alexander, "Can You Be BLACK?," 78. Raiford notes that "rather than being fixed by the image of degraded blackness," many would be moved to activism by seeing the images of Till, choosing to "alter and transform the meaning of black bodies in the United States" (*Imprisoned in A Luminous Glare*, 88). The lynching of Till could itself be seen as a reaction to the successes of the civil rights movement, in particular the Supreme Court's recent *Brown v. Board of Education* decision. Thus, Till's murder did not initiate an activist movement, but the existence of that movement made an activist response more likely.

37 Writing about representations of slavery (drawing especially on the well-known representation of the beating of Aunt Hester in Douglass's *Narrative*), Saidiya Hartman writes, "What I am trying to suggest is that if the scene of beating readily lends itself to an identification with the enslaved, it does so at the risk of fixing and naturalizing this condition of pained emobodiment," in that "the spectral and spectacular character of this suffering, or, in other words, the shocking and ghostly presence of pain, effaces and restricts black sentience." Ultimately, she argues, "the desire to don, occupy or possess blackness or the black body as a sentimental resource and/or locus of excess enjoyment is both founded upon and enabled by the material relations of chattel slavery." *Scenes of Subjection: Terror, Slavery, and Self-Making in Nineteenth-Century America* (New York: Oxford University Press, 1997), 20–21.

observed. It was caught—as a fugitive from a penitentiary is often caught—in gigantic circling spotlights. It was imprisoned in a luminous glare revealing the naked truth to the whole world."[38] Photography, in King's account, would achieve its effects by imprisoning official white supremacist violence in the "luminous glare" of a spotlight. Thus illuminated, whiteness is no longer the unquestioned norm but rather a problematic, glaringly visible departure *from* the norms of human behavior, to which stigma and censure should be attached.

In other words, King's emphasis was not on "giving a face" to black suffering but instead on giving a face to racism. In representing the faces of the police conducting the attack so clearly, "luminously" even, the photos Warhol appropriated for his paintings do that well. The facial expressions of the police are visible and the details fine enough to allow viewers to see whether their mouths are closed or open, to follow the direction of their gazes, perhaps even to guess what they may be feeling. By contrast, the face of the black demonstrator at the center of the action, the man under attack, is obscure in each of the three photos. In the largest, final photo in the sequence, his face is turned away; in the smaller images on the left, it is in profile and in each case dark, almost entirely black. Of the three photographs, the one Warhol later chose as the basis of the single image in the Little Race Riots (the second in the sequence) dramatizes this darkening effect most clearly.[39] In this image, the features of the man's face are almost completely covered in a dense veil of black ink.

While subjecting white racist faces to bright light, the image dramatically defaces the black man who is the object of racist violence. In so doing, it neatly allegorizes the denial of personhood, the refusal or inability to see black persons as persons, fundamental to the white supremacy the police are here enforcing. But it does so without putting the man's feelings on display for consumption or sympathy.[40] Instead, the image produces a kind of "spectacular opacity," in Daphne Brooks's evocative phrase, but an opacity

38 Martin Luther King Jr., *Why We Can't Wait* (New York: Harper and Row, 1964), 30.

39 The particularity of Warhol's choice is further underscored when we notice that in the photo by Bill Hudson taken that same day (*Walter Gadsden Attacked by K-9 Units*), the face of the black demonstrator is clearly visible.

40 Warhol's interest in this image, and the way the face at its center resists being there for the viewer's consumption, sympathy, or knowing, recalls an aesthetic strategy pursued in several of his films. I am thinking in particular of Douglas Crimp's argument in *Our Kind of Movie* against the claim that Warhol's films are voyeuristic. Concerning *Blow Job*, Crimp writes, "We cannot make eye contact. We cannot look into this man's eyes and detect the vulnerability that his submission to being pleasured surely entails. We cannot take sexual possession of him. We can see his face, but we cannot, as it were *have* it. This face is not *for us*" (7). Crimp makes a similar argument in relation to Mario Montez in *Screen Test No. 2*: "Warhol found the means to make the people of his world visible without making them objects of our knowledge. The knowledge of a world that his films give us is not a knowledge of the other for the self" (35).

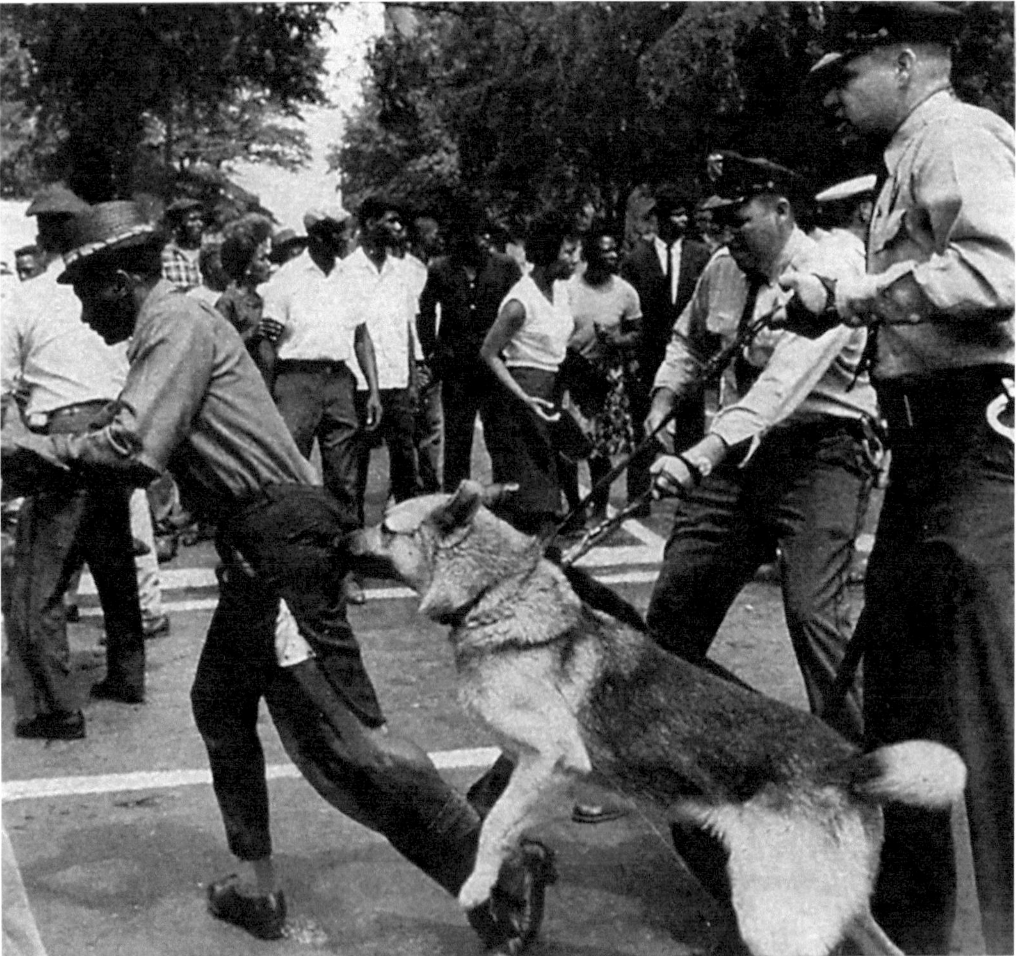

4.4 Andy Warhol, "Race Riot" source image collage (photograph by Charles Moore) (detail), 1963. The Andy Warhol Museum, Pittsburgh; Founding Collection, contribution The Andy Warhol Foundation for the Visual Arts.

that remains a site of dense figuration.[41] The image is given a further allegorical push by the fact that the police appear to be struggling to prevent the man from crossing a white line in the road. As if to emphasize that what is veiled here is precisely the face, and that the man's defacement is not incompatible with the spectacularization of his embodiment, the skin on the man's leg under the pants torn away by the dog's teeth reflects the light. Underscoring the correlation between racist violence and defacement, the faces of the members of the black crowd in the background (on which more below) are not so fully inked, as if the position of collective spectatorship

41 Daphne A. Brooks, *Bodies In Dissent: Spectacular Performances of Race and Freedom, 1850–1910* (Durham, NC: Duke University Press, 2006), 8.

may afford one a face. In multiple ways, then, in these images it is as if racist violence has a *directly* defacing effect, as if the police are themselves casting an inky shadow, bringing down the color line's "vast veil" that, as Du Bois puts it, denied black people the sun of legal protection, economic opportunity, and full personhood.[42]

Thus, to the extent that defacement is here dramatized by an inkily veiled black face, we might say, to borrow from Ralph Ellison, that the image has "illuminated the blackness of [his] invisibility."[43] Moreover, blackness has been illuminated in a way that connects the operations of key racial technologies—the police state and the photographic and print media themselves. For it is not, after all, the police who have covered the face in ink and opposed the man's defacement to the clear white-facedness of the police. Rather, these are results of a process of mediation, of light written on film and ink printed on paper.

In these photos, the white faces are not only clearly visible; they are visible inasmuch as their skin is represented by the unmarked white paper background. At the same time, the metaphor of blackness to describe persons whose skin is in fact various shades of brown is given a literal, material confirmation by the black ink. In this way, these photographic images offer a particularly dramatic illustration of the correspondence between the racial opposition between black and white and the medium-specific, aesthetic opposition between black ink and white paper.

This correspondence is embedded in print technology itself. Historical studies have shown how important the print medium has been to establishing a binary structure in which white and black are opposing colors.[44] As Richard Dyer notes, "White is virtually unthinkable except as opposition to black. This has been as true of skin as of hue white."[45] In his article on

42 Du Bois, *Souls of Black Folk*, 8.

43 Ellison, *Invisible Man* (New York: Random House/Signet, 1947), 16. See also Fred Moten: "The mark of invisibility is a visible, racial mark; invisibility has visibility at its heart" (*In the Break* [Minneapolis, University of Minnesota Press, 2003], 68).

44 On the development of black ink, and the changing significances of the color black, see Michel Pastoureau, *Black: The History of a Color* (Princeton, NJ: Princeton University Press, 2009). On the opposition between black and white, and the essentiality of blackness to understandings of whiteness, see Toni Morrison, *Playing in the Dark: Whiteness and the Literary Imagination* (New York: Vintage, 1993): "In that construction of blackness *and* enslavement could be found not only the not-free but also, with the dramatic polarity created by skin color, the projection of the not-me" (38); "Africanist character is used to limn out and enforce the invention and implications of whiteness" (52). Also see Eric Lott, who writes that white American manhood simply "could not exist without a racial other against which it defines itself and which to a very great extent it takes up into itself as one of its own constituent elements." "White Like Me: Racial Crossdressing and the Construction of American Whiteness," in *Cultures of United States Imperialism*, ed. Amy Kaplan and Don Pease (Durham, NC: Duke University Press, 1993), 476.

45 *White* (New York: Routledge, 1997), 51. See also Claudia Benthien, *Skin: On the Cultural Border between Self and the World*, trans. Thomas Dunlap (New York: Colum-

paper, ink, and print in William Wells Brown's mid-nineteenth-century novel *Clotel*, Jonathan Senchyne argues that the print medium and print culture has helped to establish a model wherein "whiteness is to be seen while unseen, providing the structural backdrop against which marks or types become legible," thereby helping shape a "sensus communis about whiteness, blackness and the structures of legibility and visibility."[46] This *sensus communis* about whiteness and blackness offers support and confirmation for the racial opposition between black and white. White is unnoticed background, an unseen given. Blackness is markedness as such. And they are opposites.

The images Warhol used in the Race Riot paintings also highlight the extent to which the blackness of black invisibility is written into the photographic medium. That is, the darkness of the demonstrator's face is not just a result of the play of light and shadows, but appears to be an effect of the biases of photography itself, one of the many effects of the fact that, as Walter Benjamin notes, the camera and the human eye see different natures.[47] As Dyer argues, in their default settings and habitual modes of use the various elements that make up the composition of a photograph—lighting, film stock, shutter speed and aperture, development and printing—"produce a look that assumes, privileges and constructs an image of white people."[48] A number of recent articles and at least one exhibition have shown how default settings and color film stock in particular have presumed a white subject as the norm, making darker-hued skins difficult to represent accurately.[49] As Kara Walker puts it, "Photographic exposure must be adjusted

bia University Press, 2002): "As in printing technology or in painting, the 'white' skin is understood as a kind of color-neutral canvas or blank sheet, a tabula rasa, and the dark skin as its colored or written-on counterpart. 'Colored' as opposed to light skin is thus interpreted as a marked epidermis; it becomes a skin that departs from the neutral norm" (148).

46 "Bodies of Ink and Reams of Paper: *Clotel*, Racialization and the Material Culture of Print," in *Early African American Print Culture*, ed. Lara Cohen and Jordan Stein (Philadelphia: University of Pennsylvania Press, 2012), 142. Senchyne discusses the efforts involved in making paper white and ink black.

47 "A Little History of Photography," *SW2*, 510.

48 *White*, 83.

49 For a summary of this research, see Syreeta McFadden, "Teaching the Camera to See My Skin: Navigating Photography's Inherent Bias against Dark Skin," *BuzzFeed*, April 2, 2014 (http://www.buzzfeed.com/syreetamcfadden/teaching-the-camera-to-see-my-skin). As McFadden and others have noted, the racial bias in photographic norms is vividly illustrated in the almost exclusive use (until quite recently) of white models in establishing the ideal settings for developing color photographs and film. In photography, these norms were established by so-called Shirley Cards (named after the first person to pose for them), reference cards "with a perfectly balanced portrait of a pale-skinned woman" (as McFadden puts it). While the problem has been most thoroughly examined (and perhaps most egregious) in relation to color film (McFadden, for instance, notes that black-and-white film seemed to be more accommodating of darker hues), it extends

to record detail and highlights without them being washed out and in the shadows, without them becoming undifferentiated black areas."[50]

These racializing aspects of photography and the print medium are highlighted by Warhol in his treatment of the images. That Warhol sought to intensify the black-white opposition here as much as possible is clear enough in his notes to the silkscreen maker, visible on the bottom of the source image: "make contrasts very black + white." The printedness of the opposition is emphasized by the way the black abstractness of the face of the demonstrator in the original photo, already intensified by the halftone printing process, is further amplified and indeed thematized by Warhol's silkscreen process, which mimics halftone printing, incorporating and magnifying the "preexisting dot pattern that appears on the source image."[51]

(and has also been noted in relation) to black-and-white film as well, although I have seen no scholarship specifically treating the differences between color and black-and-white film in this regard. But see, for instance, the black-and-photograph on page 118 of Lorna Roth's important essay on the racial bias of image technologies, "Looking at Shirley, the Ultimate Norm: Colour Balance, Image Technologies and Cognitive Equity," *Canadian Journal of Communications* 34, no. 1 (2009). Also see Roth's website: http://colourbalance.lornaroth.com/projects/shirley-card/.

Anecdotal accounts of the racial bias in photography are numerous. See McFadden's account of her mother's attempt to produce a family portrait with color film that failed to accurately capture her family's skin color, and of her own photographic practice. Or Dyer: "The problem is memorably attested in a racial context in school photos where either the black pupils's faces look like blobs or the white pupils have theirs bleached out" (*White*, 89). This problem has also been often noted by film actors and directors. Dyer cites a number of black actors, including Cicely Tyson and Joe Morton, observing how "strange," or indeed invisible, they appear when lit and filmed with the same settings used for white actors (97). Jean-Luc Godard famously refused to use Kodak film stock while making a film in Mozambique in 1977 because it was racist; his complaint was noted by London-based artists Adam Broomberg and Oliver Chanarin in the notes to their 2012 exhibit *To Photograph a Dark Horse in Low Light*, on the racism of early color photography. For coverage of their project, see *Guardian*, January 25, 2013, http://www.guardian.co.uk/artanddesign/2013/jan/25/racism-colour-photography-exhibition: "The light range was so narrow, Broomberg said, that 'if you exposed film for a white kid, the black kid sitting next to him would be rendered invisible except for the whites of his eyes and teeth'. It was only when Kodak's two biggest clients—the confectionary and furniture industries—complained that dark chocolate and dark furniture were losing out that it came up with a solution." See also Anne Hornaday, "'12 Years a Slave,' 'Mother of George,' and the Aesthetic Politics of Filming Black Skin," *Washington Post*, October 17, 2013.

50 Walker, lecture on Warhol's Shadows, Hirshhorn Museum, Janurary 11, 2012 (17:59); an mp3 of the talk was available on the Hirshhorn website for some time after the talk. For a video of a similar talk Walker gave at DIA, March 26, 2012, see https://diaart.org/media/watch-listen/video-kara-walker-on-andy-warhol/media-type/video.

51 Printz, *CR1*, 252. See also John J. Curley, "Breaking It Down: Warhol's Newspaper Allegories," in *Warhol Headlines*, on Warhol's interest in image transmission technology: "With the silkscreen Warhol could recreate the abstraction located within the reprinted press photograph—but do so through a means that artistically, even symbolically, approximated the mechanical and repetitive nature of the mass press" (34).

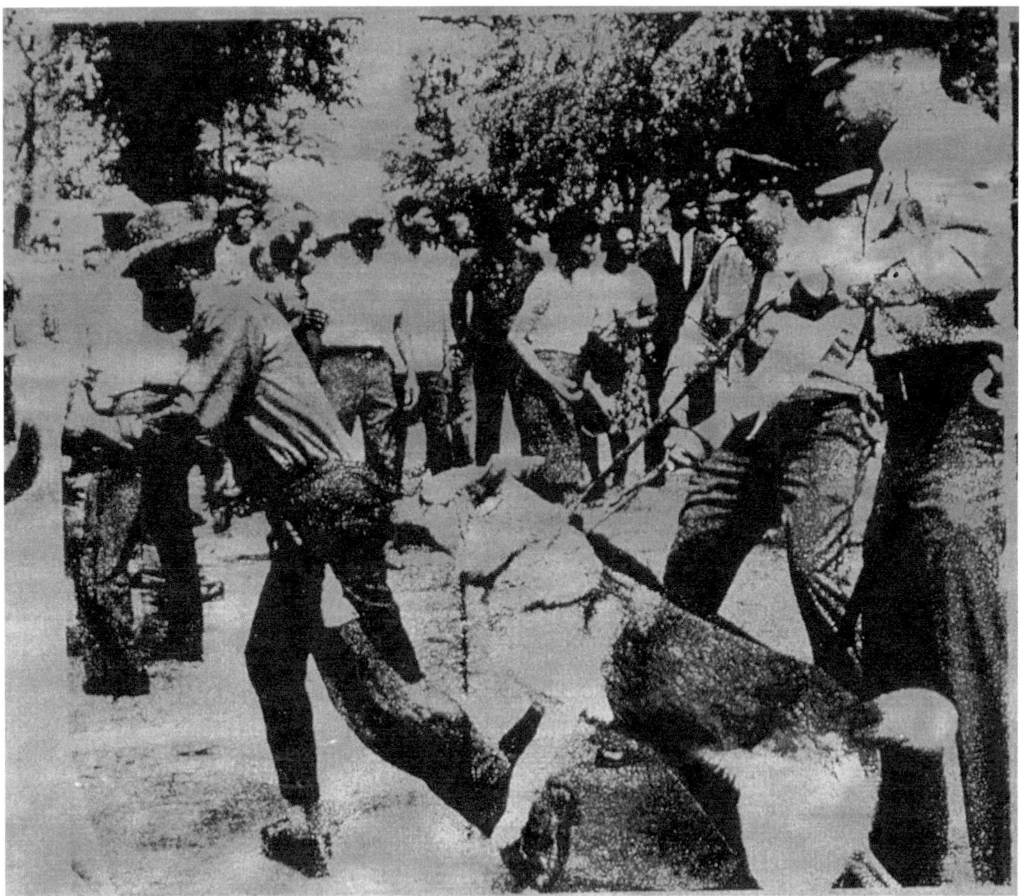

4.5 Andy Warhol, *Pink Race Riot (Red Race Riot)* (detail), 1963. © 2016 Andy Warhol Foundation for the Visual Arts/Artists Rights Society (ARS), New York.

Moreover, because varying levels of ink are pushed through the screen or rubbed on the canvas after accumulating on its underside, the image is not identical in each iteration. The minor, apparently accidental variations mean that some versions of the demonstrator's inked faced are more abstract and blocky, some less so. In the Race Riot paintings, Warhol's messy silkscreen technique calls attention to the fact that what one sees varies according to the changing mediation of the printing process and shows viewers how the inky black faces seen on the canvas do not provide an accurate picture of the demonstrator who is being attacked. In giving us a series of multiple, similar and similarly disfigured faces, Warhol's mistake-filled repetition unravels the identity of the image. Viewers might even wonder what "real" face is in fact being "represented" here.

In their own disfiguration of this face, Warhol's paintings not only represent violence but imitate and enact it on the level of the medium. Hal Foster sees an analogous effect in works such as *Ambulance Disaster*, where he notes

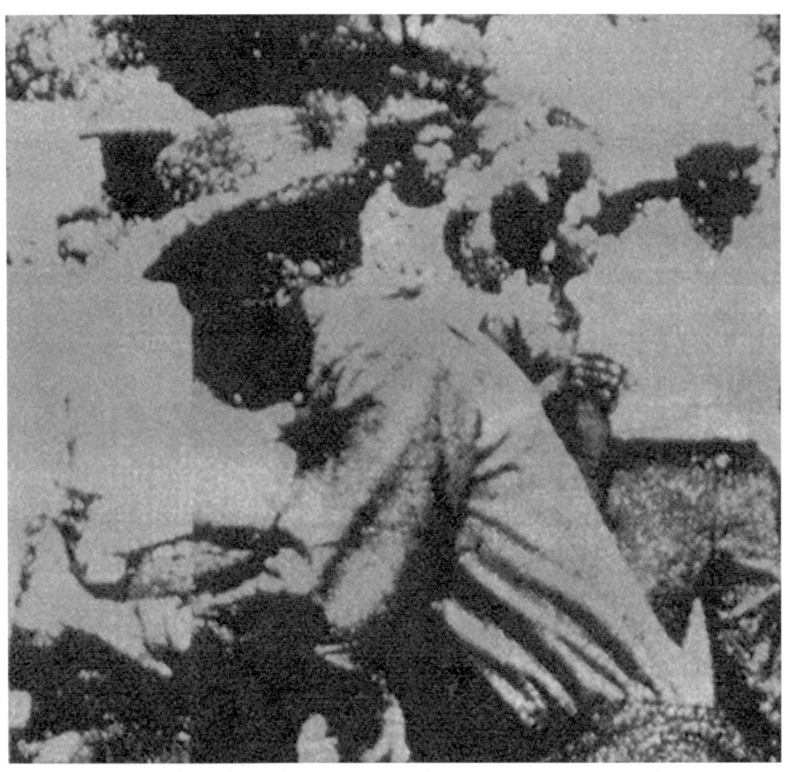

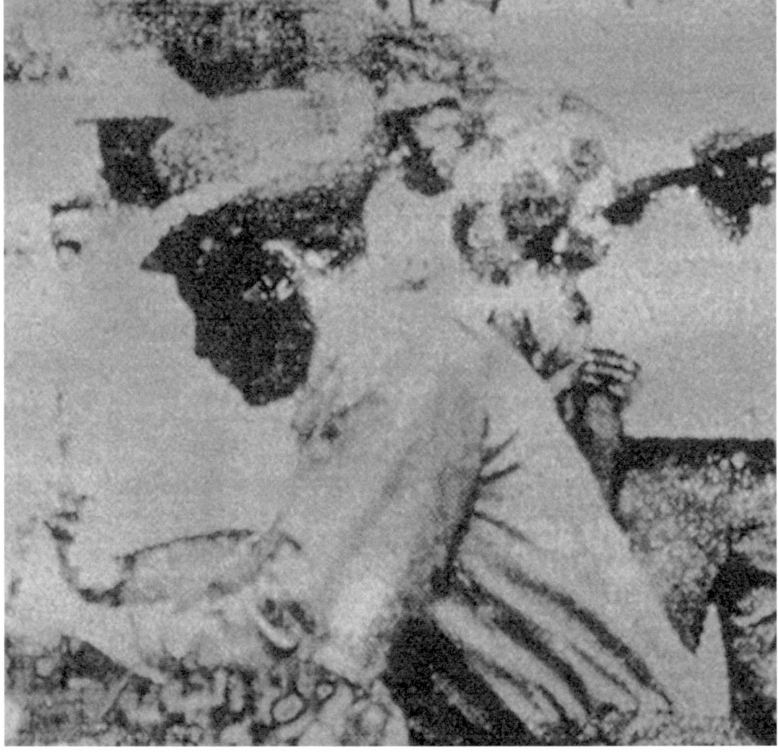

4.6 Andy Warhol, *Pink Race Riot (Red Race Riot)* (detail), 1963. © 2016 Andy Warhol Foundation for the Visual Arts/Artists Rights Society (ARS), New York.

that the silkscreen mistakes, what he calls the "pokes and pops," produce a "second order of trauma, here at the level of technique."[52] Rather than dampening or dulling the affective force of the image, the messy, mistake-prone silkscreened repetitions bring us *closer* to violence, in a material and affective sense, than the *Life* magazine images on which they are based. (Perhaps Kara Walker was partly referring to this effect when she suggested that these paintings "destroy the black viewer."[53]) In the magazine, the images pretend to represent an event objectively—look at what happened!—thereby hiding the fixing, racially reifying quality of print's own visual mediation, not to mention the strong framing effect of captions, titles, journalistic reporting, and advertisements (which I return to below).

At the same time that it highlights the racializing effects of the use of black ink, Warhol's treatment of these images disrupts the correspondence between the aesthetic black-white opposition and the racial one in several ways. To begin with, in contrast to the unmarked white paper in *Life* magazine, Warhol's backgrounds draw attention to themselves. In *Pink Race Riot*, for instance, the wash is uneven and the wide brushstrokes are quite visible, a visibility heightened by the caesuras between the printed images (a formal device uncommon in Warhol's painting during this period). The choice of colors seems pointed as well: a pale, pinkish red, a yellowy tan—these are not quite skin tones, as it were, but they are close enough to remind viewers that white skin is not white and black skin is not black (as I mentioned in an earlier note, Warhol once referred to *Mustard Race Riot* as the "tan negro painting").

In *Mustard Race Riot*, of course, it is the monochrome "blank" that most directly invites viewers to reflect on the productive presence of the background as such (figure 4.7, plate 2). On the left side, at the moment of reading the black marks as marks, the lighter background becomes the not-at-that-moment-seen surface on which the readable marks are made. On the right side, the yellowy tan announces itself as such: look at *this* yellow. The paintings thematize the non-inevitability of white background and black ink—the images are perfectly legible on this yellow—even as they foreground the function of unmarked background more generally.[54]

52 Foster, *Return of the Real*, 136. For Foster the "pops" do this work as *punctum*, by way of an interruption of the *studium*, a return of a Lacanian Real, whereas I am suggesting that Warhol's silkscreened deformations of this face imitate rather than disrupt the picture's *studium*. Foster sees mainly abjection and trauma in the "disaster" images, and expresses skepticism about their capacity to evoke compassion or mimetic correspondence.

53 Walker, Hirschorn lecture (around 14:00).

54 My thinking about Warhol's Race Riots, and the use of color and place of surface therein, has been influenced by Darby English's brilliant *How to See a Work of Art in Total Darkness* (Cambridge, MA: MIT Press, 2007), especially the chapter on Glenn Ligon and the way his text-based paintings problematize the surfaceness of the surface and the opposition between black text and white background ("Painting Problems," 201–54).

4.7 Andy Warhol, *Mustard Race Riot*, 1963. Silkscreen ink, acrylic and pencil on linen; 113⅞ × 82 (canvas with images), 113¼ × 82 (monochrome canvas). © 2016 Andy Warhol Foundation for the Visual Arts/Artists Rights Society (ARS), New York.

Reading from left to right, as if from one page to another (recalling the structure of an open magazine), viewers are not presented on the right side with language explaining the image, the next news item, another jarring image, or an advertisement seeking to engage and distract. Instead, the blank presents itself as an emotionally undemanding, adjacent space onto which one's lingering affective responses might be transferred.[55] Then, there framed, such affects may also become available for further reflection or feeling: what feeling do we have about these images, their mass publicity, and our consumption of them? One might, for instance, reflect on how often affective responses (or one's repression or disavowal of them) already do transfer in and out of experiences of mass-mediated images. How do the images of black demonstrators being attacked by police affect how readers

55 That is, the empty screen here, as in other of Warhol's work, seeks not to produce a specific affective response so much as to clear the space for *some* affective response to come into being, while also drawing attention to the need for such a space.

of *Life* feel about the images advertising floors whitened by Hoover vacuum cleaners, boots blackened by Kiwi shoe polish, or Kodak cameras, for instance?[56]

Some of the feelings that might occur and that viewers might notice in viewing these paintings are ones connected to the colors themselves. The complex paths such feelings might take are suggested by John Coplans's emotionally evocative analysis of Warhol's use of color in *Mustard Race Riot* and elsewhere:

> Warhol's instinct for color is not so much vulgar as theatrical. He often suffuses the whole surface of a canvas with a single color to gain an effect of what might be termed colored light. It is difficult to use any of the traditional categories in discussion of Warhol's usage, which bends toward "non-art" color. His color lacks any sense of pigmentation. Like the silver surfaces of the Liz Taylor or Marlon Brando paintings, it is sometimes inert, always amorphous, and pervades the surface. Though often high-keyed, his colors are at times earthy, as in one of the race riot paintings, which is covered in a flat, sickly-looking ocherish tinge reminding the viewer of a worn, stained and decaying surface. In other paintings Warhol moves into what may best be described as a range of psychedelic coloration. For the most part his color is bodiless and flat and is invariably acted on by black, which gives it a shrill tension. Further, the color is often too high-keyed to be realistic, yet it fits into a naturalistic image. This heightens the unreality of the image, though the blacks he so often uses roughen the color and denude it of sweetness.[57]

Even at first glance, the affective connotations of the adjectives Coplans uses to describe Warhol's colors—theatrical, inert, sickly-looking, high-keyed, bodiless, stained, decaying, shrill, psychedelic—suggest that if, as Benjamin puts it, color is "a winged creature that flits from one form to the next," it may

56 All of the more than fifty advertisements in the magazine (online at http://books.google.com/books?id=2kgEAAAAMBAJ) feature white models: white people smoking Salem or Marlboro cigarettes, getting loans from GMAC, talking on their Bell telephones, opening their Frigidaire refrigerators, or eating Kellogg's Corn Flakes. The color white seems unusually prominent as well: white paint, white cars and floors and refrigerators and evaporated milk. The thoroughgoing whiteness of the magazine, the public it explicitly addresses, and the segregated world in which it circulates is pointedly dramatized when, in an advertisement for Bulova watches, an ad depicts "How 65 Teens Pretty Up for the Prom," with a large photo of sixty-five young women, all white. The sole nonwhite figure appears in an advertisement for Eaton Car Air Conditioners, which depicts a drawn caricature of a "Hottentot" (with a spear in his hand and bone in his hair) to illustrate the tagline: "Big Shots / Little Tots / Huguenots and Hottentots / Lancelots and Hotsy Tots / Ocelots and Astronots / love driving *cool* when the sun burns hot."

57 John Coplans, "Andy Warhol: The Art," in *Andy Warhol*, ed. John Coplans (New York: New York Graphic Society, n.d.), 47–52, 51–52. Thanks to Darby English for his suggestions regarding the interest and importance of this passage.

carry with it not-quite-conscious affects and sensations.[58] Where do these feelings come from? What does Warhol's work do with or say about them?

Significantly, embedded in this feelingful description is the assertion that Warhol's color "lacks any sense of pigmentation." I take Coplans to be suggesting that Warhol's paint colors do not resemble skin colors in that they give no sense of there being flesh beneath them; instead, Coplans asserts, his colors are generally bodiless, flat, inert. This is a line of thought echoed by David Batchelor in *Chromophobia*, where he argues that "something important happened to color in the 1960s," when artists such as Frank Stella, Donald Judd, Dan Flavin, Yves Klein, Warhol, and others stopped using what he calls "artist" colors, which "were developed to allow the representation of various kinds of bodies in different kinds of space." As de Kooning put it: "Flesh was the reason oil painting was invented." Instead, artists turned to industrial, commercial colors, which are "made to cover large surfaces in a uniform layer of flat color. They form a skin, but they do not suggest flesh."[59] These "bodiless" colors seem to exist as pure surface, which of course is the subject of one of Warhol's most famous quips: "If you want to know all about Andy Warhol, just look at the surface: of my paintings and films and me, and there I am. There's nothing behind it" (*IBYM*, 90).[60]

Inasmuch as they appear to exist inertly on the surface in Coplans's understanding, Warhol's colors do not look like skin and do not signify like skin. That is, they do not appear to indicate the racial truth of a given body; they do not participate in the production of the racial-epidermal schema Frantz Fanon famously wrote about, which reduces a person to her or his skin and the meanings, stories, and histories such skin signals.[61] Thus, Warhol's use of color here, in Coplans's account, appears to stymie what Irene

58 Benjamin, "A Child's View of Color," in *SW1*, 50–51, 50.

59 Batchelor, *Chromophobia*, 99.

60 One might consider, too, how the emphasis on surface seems to facilitate an obfuscation or refusal of depth readings of subjectivity, especially Warhol's own, and serves as a strategy for dealing with the closet: no secrets to reveal here. For a smart reading of Warhol's interviews along these lines, see De Villiers, *Opacity and the Closet*.

61 In a well-known passage from the chapter "The Fact of Blackness," in *Black Skins, White Masks* (New York: Grove, 1967), Fanon, considering the effect of being "fixed" by the glances of the other, "in the sense in which a chemical solution is fixed by a dye" (109), writes, "Assailed at various points, the corporeal schema crumbled, its place taken by a racial epidermal schema. In the train it was no longer a question of being aware of my body in the third person but in a triple person. . . . I was responsible at the same time for my body, for my race, for my ancestors" (112). The scholarship on Fanon is impressive and extensive. On Fanon and black art, see English, *How to See a Work of Art in Total Darkness*, 31–49, and *The Fact of Blackness: Frantz Fanon and Visual Representation*, ed. Alan Read (esp. Stuart Hall, "The After-life of Frantz Fanon: Why Fanon? Why Now? Why *Black Skins, White Masks*?," 12–37). For a smart survey of the Fanon literature in relation to the way "blackness troubles vision in Western discourse," see Nicole R. Fleetwood, *Troubling Vision: Performance, Visuality and Blackness* (Chicago: University of Chicago Press, 2011), esp. 21–28.

Tucker calls racial sight, that mode of seeing in which the seeing of a skin color "renders people instantly and immediately knowable."[62]

Yet, at the same time, even as these colors do not function to produce racial knowledge, there are nonetheless affects in Coplans's description that seem to travel along paths not exactly innocent of racial meaning and feeling. Most obviously, Coplans writes of how "the blacks" "roughen" and "denude" the "sweetness" that Warhol's colors sometimes have, just after he has described *Mustard Race Riot*, an image that depicts a black man, his skin represented by black ink, being literally and roughly denuded by racially "white" (but here aesthetically "ocherish") policemen. Thus, in a striking reversal pivoting on the color black, "the blacks" have become the violent agents in Warhol's "theatrical" drama of color, as if the sense of violence is somehow indelibly attached to the color black itself. This attachment makes possible a chiasmus we are all too familiar with, when violence done *to* black bodies is justified by seeing those black bodies *as* essentially violent. Indeed, the whole history of white supremacy—right up through Rodney King and Trayvon Martin and Michael Brown and Tamir Rice and so many others—is filled with and constituted by such instances.

In the "sickly-looking ocherish tinge reminding the viewer of a worn, stained and decaying surface," we might also detect a mode of racial seeing, one traceable to the humoral origins of our modern understandings of race, where the skin's appearance is read as symptom or sign of an otherwise hidden bodily truth or history.[63] That is, the qualifiers Coplans applies to the ocherish tinge (sickly, stained, decaying) seem to be in tension with his assertion that Warhol's colors are bodiless and inert. But perhaps it is precisely this contradiction between colors that do not seem to indicate the presence of bodies and the eliciting of feelings related to skin-covered bodies that produces the painting's peculiar force—its "shrill tension." The color and the subject of the painting invites viewers to look as if they are looking at skin, even as it seems to thwart that way of looking by producing a surface without depth, skin without flesh. Thus, on the wings of this "earthy" and "sickly-looking" yellow and "the blacks" that "roughen" and "denude," racial feelings and ways of seeing have traveled to a painting that is also about "race" and "racism" even as these very colors and their use short-circuit habitual ways of reading race-as-skin. The result is an aesthetically powerful, disorienting polarity that can estrange viewers from usual modes of seeing and feeling racial difference, thereby making them newly available for contemplation, consideration, or refunctioning as the locus for a politics that makes "race" do different things.

62 Tucker, *The Moment of Racial Sight: A History* (Chicago: University of Chicago Press, 2012), 19.

63 See Sam Turner's dissertation "Red Letters, Black Ink, White Paper: Race, Writing, Colors and Characters in 1850s America" (University of Virginia, 2013), esp. 255–68, and Tucker, *Racial Sight*, 23–28.

In their focus on a surface without depth, a skin without flesh, on printing mistakes, variability, ink splotches, and bleeding across lines, Warhol's paintings may lead us to question the reliability of the correspondence between the black-white ink-paper opposition and the racial opposition. Indeed, as Warhol disorients usual modes of racial seeing, we may begin to question the capacity of *any* image technology to accurately represent skin—any skin—and in turn, to doubt skin's function as a sign of some truth or knowledge about the body it covers. As Anne Cheng puts it in her book on Josephine Baker, "The unabashed lure of the surface . . . diffuses rather than consolidates racial difference."[64] Skin, and the ontologies it appears to bring with it, begins to seem fictive, subject now to the Warholian way of seeing in which one doesn't "know where the artificial stops and the real starts," where, in fact, "everything is sort of artificial" (*IBYM*, 93). It is as if Warhol's way of seeing seeks to leave no racial ontology safe; seeing in this way, one may come to feel that "every ontology is made unattainable" (as Fanon says of the situation in a "colonized and civilized society").[65]

The possible effects of this way of seeing on differently racialized viewers may come into sharper view when we look to the context constituted by *Life*'s framing of these images. The title given to the photo spread as a whole is "The Dogs' Attack Is the Negroes' Reward." The paragraph-long caption reads as follows:

> ATTACK DOGS: With vicious guard dogs the police attacked the marchers—and then rewarded them with an outrage that would win support all over the world for Birmingham's Negroes. If the Negroes themselves had written the script they could hardly have asked for greater help for their cause than City Police Commissioner Eugene "Bull" Connor freely gave. Ordering his men to let white spectators come near, he said: "I want 'em to see the dogs work. Look at those niggers run." This extraordinary sequence—brutal as it is as a Negro gets his trousers ripped off by Connor's dogs—is the attention getting jackpot of the Negroes' provocation.

The text here makes it seem that the police actions were "scripted" by the civil rights movement itself, here described as a monolithic force called "the Negroes," and that their attack "with vicious guard dogs" was a "help" and "reward" that Connor "freely gave." "Reward" is here used half-ironically; it is true that the mass publicity generated by images such as these marked a crucial moment—"an attention getting jackpot"—in shifting the public discourse about Jim Crow racism in the United States, and that this publicity was the result of a series of calculated tactical decisions on the part of the

64 Cheng, *Second Skin: Josephine Baker and the Modern Surface* (New York: Oxford University Press, 2011), 162.
65 Fanon, *Black Skins, White Masks*, 109.

civil rights movement. What is obscured, however, or naturalized (because taken for granted), in attributing agency to "the Negroes," is white supremacy itself. Although the text puts Connor's repellent racism on display (as does the image), the caption language goes out of its way to excise white supremacy from its narrative. It is as if racism, and the violence apparent in the image, comes into existence only by way of the "Negroes' provocation." In this outrageous tautology, one fundamental to the operations of white supremacy, the "Negroes" are authors of their own assault, as if violence could only be attributed to blackness.

In this context, Connor's racist utterance does peculiar work. It communicates to *Life*'s readers not only Connor's pleasure in viewing that violence but his desire that other white spectators (including the photographer Charles Moore) witness what he understands to be an illustration and reinforcement of black abjection: "I want 'em to see the dogs work. Look at those niggers run." This desire rests upon and invokes a long tradition of spectacles of white supremacist violence against black people meant to function as a warning to black persons and their allies.[66] *Life*'s publication of the images, then, and the white viewer's seeing of them, appears to function as affirmation of Connor's white supremacist, sadistic desire. Yet, the knowledge that they are looking at a scene Connor claims to have directed for their benefit may be precisely what spurs these viewers to reject the racism that Connor presumes they share with him. That is, the mode of address may encourage disavowal, distancing, shame: "I am not racist like Bull Connor is racist. I am not the kind of white person that Bull Connor thinks I am. I *don't* want to see this spectacle." In this, the images and the story do in fact serve the purpose of focusing attention on white racism, along the lines King describes. Yet, as if anticipating this reaction on the part of its white readers, *Life* carefully avoids appearing to affirm Connor's desire by suggesting that he is not, in effect, its author ("If the Negroes themselves had *written the script* . . ."). Thus, the magazine aids white readers in disavowing their compliance with Connor's command to look at these images.

As I read it, Warhol's painting makes this disavowal more difficult, most simply by removing this linguistic framing, but also by coloring the backgrounds brightly and blowing up the images to a nearly cinematic scale. Warhol also wants us to look. But in disrupting and defamiliarizing some usual modes of apprehending images such as these by drawing attention to the violence of their mediation of blackness, while using color and repetition

66 "Countless stories of violence are made spectacular in order to let black people know who is in control, such as when Louisiana Ku Klux Klansmen in the 1940s tied bodies of lynched black men to the fronts of their cars and drove them through crowds of black children. Thus, while black men are contained when these images are made public, black viewers are taking in evidence that provides ground for collective identification with trauma. The Emmett Till narratives illustrate how, in order to survive, black people have paradoxically had to witness their own murder and defilement and then pass along the epic tale of violation" (Alexander, "Can You Be BLACK?," 90).

to facilitate the return of feelings related to the processes of racialization, as I have been suggesting, Warhol encourages a more affecting and disturbing viewing experience, one in which viewers' own sense of distance from the images may be less manageable. As Kara Walker put it, *Pink Race Riot* is "weirdly affirming, weirdly affirming the absurdity of everything—of you, of me, of violence, of art, of race, the idea of having a whole humanity, and our whole stupid history."[67] It is not that we are to "like" Bull Connor's dogs attacking demonstrators (or car crashes or executions or suicides) in the sense of "enjoying" these violent occurrences, but we are to affirm them, to be affectively open to them as events in the world.[68] This is an openness that is weird in the sense of disorienting, perhaps even deranging, because for many viewers such violence must usually be ignored in order to get through the day and be a person.[69] Warhol is inviting his viewers to like and affirm these things in the sense of having (rather than disavowing or blocking) whatever feelings one may have about them, acknowledging that they are in the world and that one is thereby already ontologically implicated in them and by them.[70]

What that more mimetically open relation might look like, and what its implications might be for viewing images such as the Race Riots, is indicated in a story Warhol tells in his interview with Swenson about witnessing violence.

> We went to see *Dr. No* at Forty-second Street. It's a fantastic movie, so cool. We walked outside and somebody threw a cherry bomb right in front of us, in this big crowd. And there was blood, I saw blood on people and all over. I felt like I was bleeding all over. I saw in the paper last week that there are more people throwing them—its just part of the scene—and hurting people. My show in Paris is going to be called "Death in America." I'll show the electric-chair pictures and the dogs in Birmingham and car wrecks and some suicide pictures. (*IBYM*, 18)

His mood set by the fantastic spectacle of *Dr. No*, Warhol sees the blood "on people and all over" and then, automatically and instantly, almost like a ma-

67 Walker, Hirshhorn lecture (16:00).

68 On affirmation in Warhol's films, see King, "Stroboscopic."

69 On this point, my reading most closely intersects and departs from Hal Foster's. Foster argues that Warhol's aesthetic procedures function as mimetic shock absorbers, "a draining of significance and a defending against affect," distancing us from the events depicted, even as his repetitions reproduce traumatic effects. "Somehow in these repetitions, then, several contradictory things occur at the same time: a warding away of traumatic significance *and* an opening out to it, a defending against traumatic affect *and* a producing of it" (132).

70 His aesthetic practice thereby recalls what Kaja Silverman calls the "ontological openness" of Gerhard Richter. Richter has compared his painting practice to the passivity of Kutuzov in *War and Peace*, whose genius, he says, lay in his ability to put his weight behind things that were already happening. Silverman, *Flesh of My Flesh*, 188.

chine, "feels *like* [he] is bleeding all over." It is as if (as Vittorio Gallese has argued in his work on mirror neurons) Warhol apprehends the feelings and actions of others *not* through an analogical thought process where he thinks, "this person is having an experience that I could be having," and then imagines what it might feel like, but through an automatic, internal, embodied simulation of them, a common experience of them. He feels *like* it is happening to him. And this is, in fact, similar to the way Jesse Jackson described the effect of images such as those in the Race Riots paintings: "When a police dog bites us in Birmingham, people of color bleed all over America."[71]

This is not empathy or sympathy as we usually use those terms; it is not about identifying with someone else's suffering, or intentionally projecting oneself into another in order to understand their emotions (the relation, Saidiya Hartman has argued, that white spectators have had to the suffering black body). Rather, here, embodied feelings are themselves essentially shared, contagious, and disruptive of the boundaries of the self. What Warhol and Jackson are describing is something like what Jean-Luc Nancy calls "compassion," which, in Nancy's sense, "is not altruism, nor is it identification; it is the disturbance of violent relatedness."[72] To feel compassion, the co-experience of a passion, is to feel a disturbance that problematizes the notion of a separate or separable self, a feeling of sharedness that might then produce a recognition that one's own being is always already tied up with the being of others. Compassion is not achieved by transcending or bridging the barriers between separate subjectivities or by creating some new way to imagine or feel the pain of others. Instead, for Nancy, following Heidegger, our being and its feelings are *already* essentially shared. The task is to avoid negating and disavowing this fundamental sharedness, the being-with that precedes and enables subjectivity. Such negations would be a key function of Jim Crow racism, but also of the numbing assault on our affective lives of the daily news.

Notably, Jackson references the collective quality of the response to these images: "When a police dog bites *us* in Birmingham, people of color bleed all over America."[73] This "us," a collective suffering body, but also a collective body engaged in active political struggle, may be metonymically represented in the Race Riot images by the crowd in the background of the image. Looking again at the image where the demonstrator's head is in profile (the second in the initial sequence), and now attuned to the significance of the

71 Quoted in Berger, *Seeing through Race*, 66.

72 Nancy, *Being Singular Plural*, xiii.

73 We know from numerous reports (some referenced by Raiford and Berger) that these images did in fact impact and politicize antiracist viewers, especially African American ones. Raiford writes, "While such images were in danger of freezing an ongoing and dynamic struggle and depicting its participants solely as victims in need of outside elite assistance, they also had the power to galvanize viewers" (*Imprisoned in A Luminous Glare*, 86).

aesthetic black-white opposition, we might also notice that his otherwise black head catches some light around the ear, eluding the veil that has otherwise blocked the light. By way of a shared illumination, this light on his ear optically links the demonstrator to the crowd we see behind him, whose full figures, as I noted earlier, are compellingly visible in their alarm and collective anger. At least one woman appears to be yelling. If the racist treatment of persons as objects is dramatically illustrated in the defacement and violence viewers see in these images, then the light cast on the demonstrator's ear reminds viewers of the sounds being made at the scene, in a striking allegory of what Fred Moten has called "the irreducible sound of necessarily visual performance at the scene of objection."[74] Perhaps the demonstrator hears the catcalls or encouragement of the people we see in the background. As Robin Kelley has noted, "When Bull Connor ordered the use of police dogs and clubs on the demonstrators, the crowd of so called onlookers taunted police, retaliated with fists, profanity, rocks and bottles, and if possible escaped into their own neighborhoods."[75]

In the images here, and in contrast, for instance, to the apparently indifferent viewer who walks by the burning car and grisly corpse in Warhol's *Burning Car* (discussed by Hal Foster in his reading of this image[76]), the members of the group in the background are clearly occupied with and compelled by the events occurring around them. But for the most part, they are not looking at what we as viewers are looking at—they gaze at something outside of the photograph's frame, perhaps another, even more urgent outrage (in other photographs of the scene one sees a melee of police violence and demonstrator resistance). Inasmuch as they look away from what we see, they do not suggest themselves as figures for us as viewers. Yet they do tell us some important things about the position of the viewer or spectator here. First, we are reminded that the viewers of this event constitute a group, a collective, and a group that is itself implicated and involved in the events unfolding before it. In this group, black being is not defaced or destroyed, but is energized and active; it is a group with which anyone angry about the white supremacist violence on view might seek to feel-with and be-with. If we take Warhol's serial repetition of these images in his paintings to reference the fact of their circulation among and reception by various audiences, then Warhol is also reproducing the fact of a multitude of spectators in the form of the painting itself, and subtly asking his viewers to connect or compare the mass viewing of the images to the multitude in the background of the image itself. Finally, the spectators and their glances indicate the par-

74 Moten, *In the Break*, 1.

75 Kelley, "Birmingham's Untouchables: The Black Poor in the Age of Civil Rights," in *Race Rebels: Culture, Politics and the Black Working Class* (New York: Free Press, 1994), 77–100, 88.

76 Hal Foster sees the apparently indifferent spectator as this painting's *punctum* (*Return of the Real*, 134).

tiality of these photographs by Moore, the sense that there is a broader field of struggle outside the frame. It is as if the image itself offers a reminder not to look for answers to the problems posed in this image *within* the image: look outside the frame, and do so together, as a group. In this, Warhol's Race Riot paintings provide a scene for viewers to look at the images there and be disturbed by them, and then, like the spectators we see in the background, to look away from the images, feeling outrage at the white supremacist state, with collective action in mind.

"The Black Marilyns"

> He first showed us the black Marilyns, and several pictures later the colored ones appeared. I said I thought they should be presented as a diptych. Andy replied gee whiz yes so he brought back the black one, stood it next to the colored one and we all saw that we had achieved a very complex, and moving statement about Marilyn so I really felt I was a collaborator! And of course we bought them both.
>
> **Emily Tremaine**, on her purchase of *Marilyn Diptych*

In the Race Riot paintings, the alignment between black ink and racial blackness is both highlighted and disturbed. The apparent blackness of black persons represented in the print medium comes to look increasingly like a printing effect, albeit a violently disfiguring one. What then, should we make of the black silkscreen ink darkening the faces of movie stars (Natalie Wood, Warren Beatty, Troy Donahue, Marilyn Monroe) we normally think of as "white" in some of Warhol's early (1962) serial portraits? Why is Marilyn's face sometimes black (figure 4.8, plate 3)?

In these paintings, among his first silkscreens, Warhol appears to be actively experimenting with the image effects that can be achieved with the technique, using variations in the buildup of ink on the screen and the density of the ink being pushed through to produce images of varying darkness, from the very dark to the barely there. In the Natalie Wood portrait, Warhol blackens Wood by overlapping multiple printings of her face, with a particularly dense cluster in the middle of the second row from the bottom.[77] In one portrait of Warren Beatty, a group of his blackened faces (*CR*, cat. no. 234) are separated, not to say segregated, off to one side. In *Troy Diptych*, darker faces of Troy Donahue (*CR*, cat. no. 239) are interspersed throughout. In *Marilyn Diptych*, the most famous of these paintings, we see an entire row of Marilyns that is rather dark in skin tone, and that in one iteration (the second from the top) her face is almost entirely black. The ink covers almost

77 This artistic darkening might remind one of Wood's then-recent star turn in *West Side Story*, where she played the Puerto Rican Maria. See Negron-Muntaner, "Feeling Pretty: West Side Story and US Puerto Rican Identity," in *Boricua Pop*, 58–84, esp. 59–66 on the casting of *West Side Story*. Negron-Muntaner notes that while Wood's costar George Chakiris, who played Bernardo, was "brownfaced," Wood was not (66).

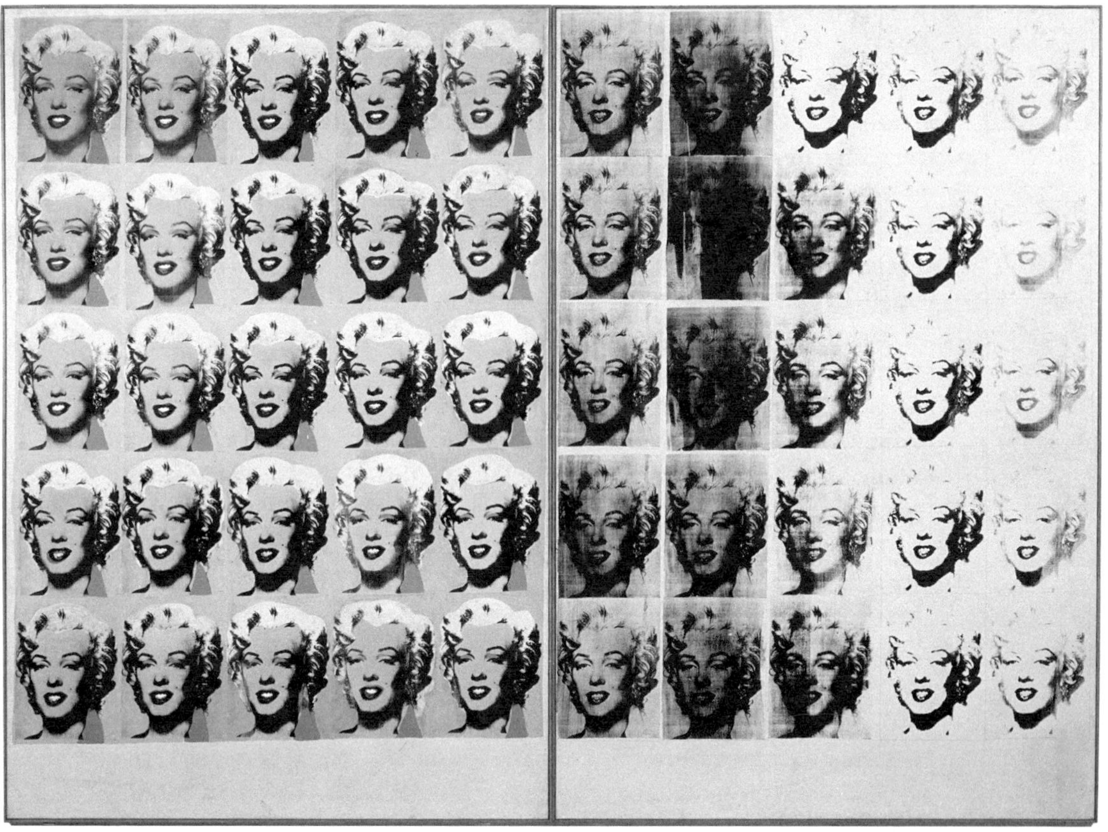

4.8 Andy Warhol, *Marilyn Diptych*, 1962. Acrylic, silkscreen ink, and pencil on linen, 81 × 57 inches. © Andy Warhol Foundation for the Visual Arts/Artists Rights Society (ARS), New York

all her features but for a gap or skip where the ink didn't come through the screen.[78] If the different arrangements seem to suggest distinct interpretative possibilities, in every instance the messy variations in the amount of ink pressed through, on different parts of the screen, make it clear that the darker, sometimes fully black faces are silkscreening "accidents."

In other paintings from this period, Warhol would use varying amounts of silkscreen ink to darken the skin of his sitters more subtly. In paintings of Liz as Cleopatra (*CR*, cat. no. 306), for instance, denser applications of ink

78 Gerard Malanga explained the effect in some detail some years later: "What happened was, the ink started tacking up on the screen. So when we put the screen back down and screened through, it would create streaks, 'cause some of the ink was drying up on the other side of the screen. And also the screen was still wet. So when we pushed the squeegee across, the paint is blocking the pores in the screen and creating what appear to be streaks. The black is where the screen is very wet. When you put the screen down it's automatically adding more paint to the image." Quoted in Scherman and Dalton, *Pop*, 127.

appear to accurately depict darker-hued skin instead of drawing attention to themselves as printing effects. A similar, subtle effect is at work in *Red Elvis* (*CR*, cat. no. 286), where Elvis gets just a bit darker as we move from the top to the bottom of the canvas. Warhol also seems to have been experimenting with different mediations of skin darkness in his films from this period, using light placement and brightness rather than silkscreen ink as the formal variable. This is especially apparent in a series such as Six Months, where changes in lighting and exposure give his boyfriend Philip Fagan a series of remarkably different looks over the series of Screen Tests.[79]

A book cover Warhol had designed in 1961 clearly indicates that he was aware of the racializing and racist meanings available in the use of black ink and that he was varying the darkness of ink to suggest a group defined by similarity. The book, *The Adventures of Maud Noakes*, is a novel by Alan Neame billed as a satirical comedy in the tradition of Evelyn Waugh and Ronald Firbank (figure 4.9, plate 4). It narrates the British heroine's "one-woman crusade to restore Africa to the Africans and win it back from the missionaries" (as the jacket copy has it). In Warhol's cover image, he uses a stamp to print a series of caricatured black faces, which together make a background for the happy white face of the novel's red-haired white heroine. The black-white opposition here is quite pointed: the white face of the heroine is drawn, not stamped; her skin is the unmarked whiteness of the background paper; meanwhile, as in the Race Riot images, black ink represents "black" skin. Where the white face is unique, the black faces are all imprints from the same stamp. Even when we consider Warhol's assertion that "everybody looks alike and acts alike and we're getting more and more that way," this image reminds us that there is nothing necessarily progressive or antiracist about the emphasis on similarity when similarity occupies the less-valued side of a binary opposition: white faces are unique, black faces all look alike.

The book cover also thereby dramatizes the particularity of Warhol's use of black ink in *Marilyn Diptych* and the other early silkscreens. In the book cover and in the Race Riots, the aesthetic black-white opposition functions as a technology to make clear distinctions between racially white and racially black faces. In *Marilyn Diptych*, however, we find a field of resemblances where the black-white aesthetic opposition no longer corresponds to a racial one. Some Marilyns are black. In this painting, black and white faces are alike, and they are alike inasmuch as they are all distinct imitations of a model Marilyn.

Because the same screen has been used to print multiple Marilyns, it is easy to look past these variations in the overall field of resemblances and miss the black faces. Anne Wagner, for example, in her essay on the Race

79 These films have not yet been restored, but see the stills and the analysis of this important work in Angell, *Catalogue Raisonné, Screen Tests*, chap. 3, "*Six Months*," 217–41.

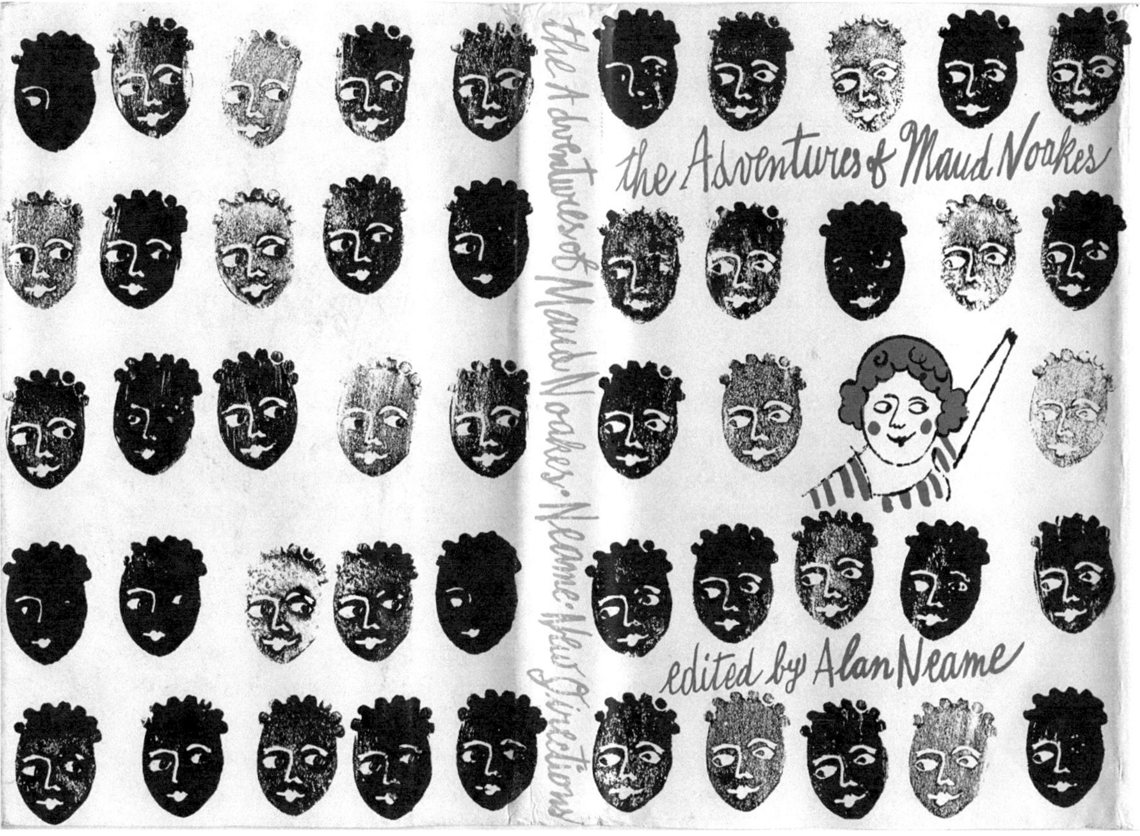

4.9 Andy Warhol, book cover (*The Adventures of Maud Noakes*), 1961. Printed ink on paper, 8¼ x 11½. Author's collection. © Andy Warhol Foundation for the Visual Arts/ Artists Rights Society (ARS), New York.

Riots, writes of the Marilyns, to which she too compares (and opposes) to the Race Riots: "One image equals the next, or at least differs from it meaninglessly."[80] Perhaps because she seems to be seeing these images within the categories of same versus different, and perhaps because she "knows" Marilyn to be "white," the color line–crossing similarities here go unnoticed. The blackness of Marilyn's black faces is seen as meaningless.

In looking past Marilyn's blackness here, I think Wagner nonetheless points to one of the ways these images achieve their aesthetic effect. Just as, in *Mustard Race Riot*, racial feelings appear to travel on the wings of color even as Warhol's surface colors do not seem to signify racially, here too, "race" may be at once simultaneously seen and not seen. In his work on blackface minstrelsy, Eric Lott has suggested that part of the force of blackface comes from the fact that the white viewer knows sameness (white like me) and sees difference (a black face), producing a kind of oscillating play

80 Wagner, "Warhol Paints History," 102.

or polarity within the aesthetic experience.[81] In a similar way, in these silkscreens, one sees an inked black face, even as one "knows" this is Marilyn Monroe. One knows that these are all images of Marilyn Monroe (or Troy Donahue or Warren Beatty or Natalie Wood) and has a set of feelings, even personal memories, about her (which might also be "about" race). But then one sees a series of faces not identical to each other, a play of imitation and iteration that crosses the line between black and white, creating images of faces that, if separated out from this field of similarities (and not of a recognizable star) might even signify as "black."[82] This polarity between what one sees and what one knows may allow a set of colliding or surprising feelings about race and the color line to appear.

The feelings evoked in a viewing of the painting might recall the experience of film spectatorship itself, of which the painting offers a provocative allegory. In painting black Marilyns, Warhol may indicate how the color line (among other boundaries) is already crossed in the space of spectatorship. As we know, in the movie theater, where viewers have become acquainted with what Parker Tyler calls "the freedom to dream and unconsciously interpret figures and events on the screen in purely subjective terms," all manner of improper, elsewhere-policed imitations and feelings may flourish.[83] The movie theater, as Jack Smith put it, "is a place where it is possible to clown, to pose, to act out fantasies, to not be seen while one gives."[84] If Warhol's serial celebrity portraits figure multiple, similar, yet particular moments of mimetic consumption (each iteration failing to "be" the celebrity model but instead "looking like" her), then *Marilyn Diptych* offers itself as an allegory for the multiraciality of mass audiences and the disidentificatory practices these audiences perform. As José Muñoz puts it, "Disidentification for the minority subject is a mode of recycling or reforming an object that has already been invested with powerful energy."[85] Disidentification, as a way of being "like" an object without trying to be "the same" as it is a

81 See Lott, *Love and Theft: Blackface Minstrelsy and the American Working Class* (New York: Oxford University Press, 1995), chap. 5, "The Seeming Counterfeit: Early Blackface Acts, the Body, and Social Contradiction," esp. 124–27.

82 In fact, because silkscreen ink had darkened the features of the (not African American) persons represented there, Rainer Crone described *Hospital* (1962), as depicting "the birth of a black baby assisted by black doctors" (Crone, *Warhol*, 29). About the series (*CR*, cat. nos. 367, 368), Printz writes that the paintings "are based on reproductions from the September 7, 1962, *Life* magazine feature in which scenes and lines from Thornton Wilder's *Our Town* were matched with photographs of 'actual events' in Oakes, North Dakota" (*CR1*, 338).

83 Tyler, *Underground Film: A Critical History* (1969; New York: Da Capo Press, 1995), 65. I was reminded of these comments by Ann Reynolds, "A History of Failure," *Criticism* 56, no. 2 (Spring 2014; Jack Smith special issue).

84 Jack Smith, "The Perfect Filmic Appositeness of Maria Montez," in *Wait for Me at the Bottom of the Pool* (New York: Serpent's Tail/High Risk Books, 1997), 30.

85 Muñoz, "Famous and Dandy," 149.

kind of "critical mimesis" that can find in spectatorship a welcome home.[86] Take, for example, the following observation by Michele Wallace, cited by Muñoz in his important essay on Jean-Michel Basquiat:

> It was always said among Black women that Joan Crawford was part Black, and as I watch these films again today, looking at Rita Hayworth in *Gilda* or Lana Turner in *The Postman Always Rings Twice*, I keep thinking, "she is so beautiful she looks black." Such a statement makes no sense in current feminist film criticism. What I am trying to suggest is there was a way in which these films were *possessed* by Black female viewers. The process may have been about problematizing and expanding one's racial identity *instead* of abandoning it. It seems important here to view spectatorship as not only potentially bisexual but also multiracial and multiethnic.[87]

Spectators, in such a model, transform and restructure the images of the stars as they possess them. Liking something, then, is not a passive act. It creates a relation that involves a transformation of the object of liking into a likeness. To borrow from Jean-Luc Nancy, the like-being that the star has now become "resembles me in that I myself 'resemble' [her]: we resemble together, if you will."[88]

This "resembling together" also constitutes the relation among spectators who enter—as spectactors—into a messy zone of mixed yet similar subjectivities. This is the zone presented in Warhol's celebrity silkscreens. Thus, because it brings into being this realm of similarities, the transformation of Joan Crawford or Lana Turner, by way of beauty, into blackness is not only a private or personal act of possession. Seeing these stars as black affects—indeed constitutes—their stardom. If, as Michael Warner notes, "we have a different relation to ourselves, a different affect" as subjects of publicity, this affect is not derived solely from the negation of one's particularity at the moment of ascension into an abstracted space of public generality, as Warner suggests.[89] Instead, the sometimes shudder-inducing charge of the experience of participation in publicity, by way of viewing or spectatorship, is generated precisely from the sense that one is mingling with all those other particularities in what may be otherwise policed or disavowed relations of resemblance.

In Warhol's paintings, the white star is presented as a site where "racial

86 The phrase appears in Butler, *Bodies That Matter*, 73; Butler borrows the term from Naomi Schor, "This Essentialism Which Is Not One: Coming to Grips with Irigaray," *Differences* 2, no. 1 (1989): 38–58, 48.

87 Wallace, "Race, Gender and Psychoanalysis in Forties Film: *Lost Boundaries*, *Home of the Brave*, and *The Quiet One*," quoted in Muñoz, "Famous and Dandy," 150.

88 Nancy, *Inoperative Community*, 33.

89 Michael Warner, "The Mass Public and the Mass Subject," in *Phantom Public Sphere*, 234. I discuss Warner's argument in "Warhol Gives Good Face," esp. 103–6.

boundaries might be both constructed and transgressed," to borrow a formulation from Lott's observations about blackface.[90] In other words, the white star's whiteness is appealing precisely to the extent to which it is not black, *even as* Marilyn's stardom means that she must also be able to allow and promote black imitations. Just as the "purest white paint"—called Optic White—that the narrator of Ralph Ellison's *Invisible Man* mixes in a paint factory, requires ten drops of a glistening "dead black" liquid, Monroe's whiteness can be achieved only by way of a supplemental blackness, which it must contain but also disavow.[91] By showing us the black paint, putting everything on the surface, as it were, Warhol's *Marilyn Diptych* invites viewers to avow the blackness that is an essential element of her celebrity.

The juxtaposition of "black" and "colored" Marilyns underscores the artificiality of Marilyn's whiteness. The propinquity not only draws attention to the blackness of the black Marilyns, and the whiteness of the background, but also thereby highlights the effect of "color" in creating racial whiteness. Where the "black Marilyns" feature great variety in the density of the ink, the irregularities in the "colored Marilyns" are less visually insistent. What keeps the inky darkenings from seeming to alter the racial significance of the images on the "colored" side of the painting are the bright pink "flesh tone" and the vivid yellow blond hair, which remain unaffected by the black shadows that dominate our apprehension of her image. Yet, even as these colors telegraph Marilyn's whiteness, they also announce themselves as artificial and mediated, "overworked Technicolor," as David Bourdon puts it (*IBYM*, 9–10). In looking at the flamboyantly artificial turquoise eye shadow and bright yellow hair, we may not only think about the Technicolor mediation of our apprehension of her figure but also remember that before she became famous, Norma Jeane Mortenson Baker had dark kinky hair, and that dying her hair blond was a crucial step in her ascension to stardom. Richard Dyer writes, "To be the ideal, Monroe had to be white, and not just white, but blond, the most unambiguously white you can get. . . . It keeps the white woman distinct from the black, brown or yellow, and at the same time it assures the viewer that the woman is the genuine article."[92] If Franz Fanon would compare the racializing effect of "the glances of the other" to the way "a chemical solution is fixed by a dye,"[93] Warhol's diptych, in presenting Marilyn's blond hair as plainly fake, indicates the mediated, fixing quality of her dye-job whiteness. Warhol thus points to the thoroughgoing mediatedness of whiteness in the world of Hollywood cinema, where it functions, as Taro Nettleton puts it, "as both a requirement for inclusion and an impossible ideal."[94]

90 Lott, *Love and Theft*, 141.

91 *Invisible Man*, 175.

92 Dyer, *Heavenly Bodies: Film Stars and Society*, 2nd ed. (1986; New York: Routledge, 2004), 40.

93 *Black Skins, White Masks*, 109.

94 "White-on-White," 18.

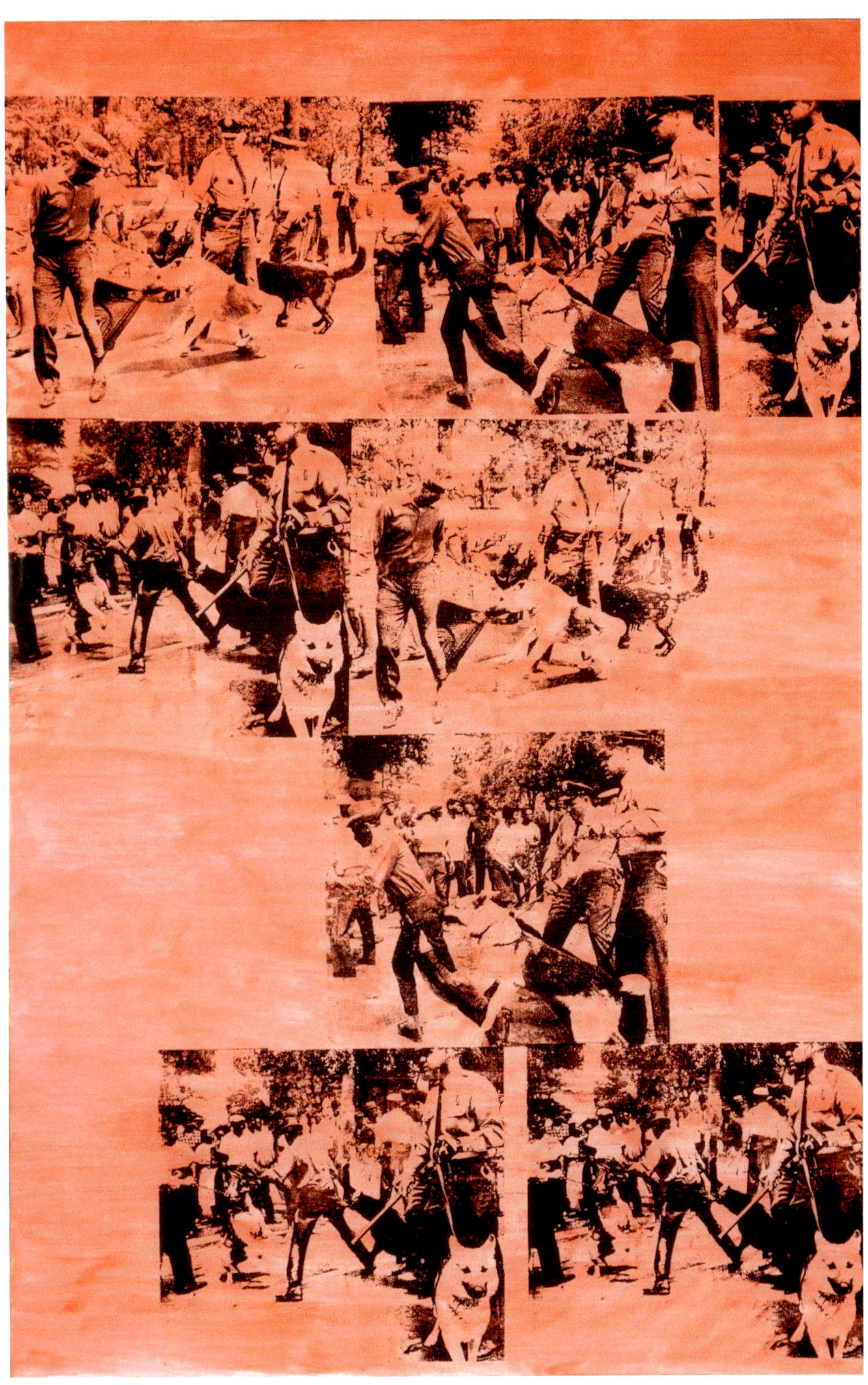

1. Andy Warhol, *Pink Race Riot (Red Race Riot)*, 1963. Silkscreen ink and acrylic on linen, 128¼ × 83 inches.

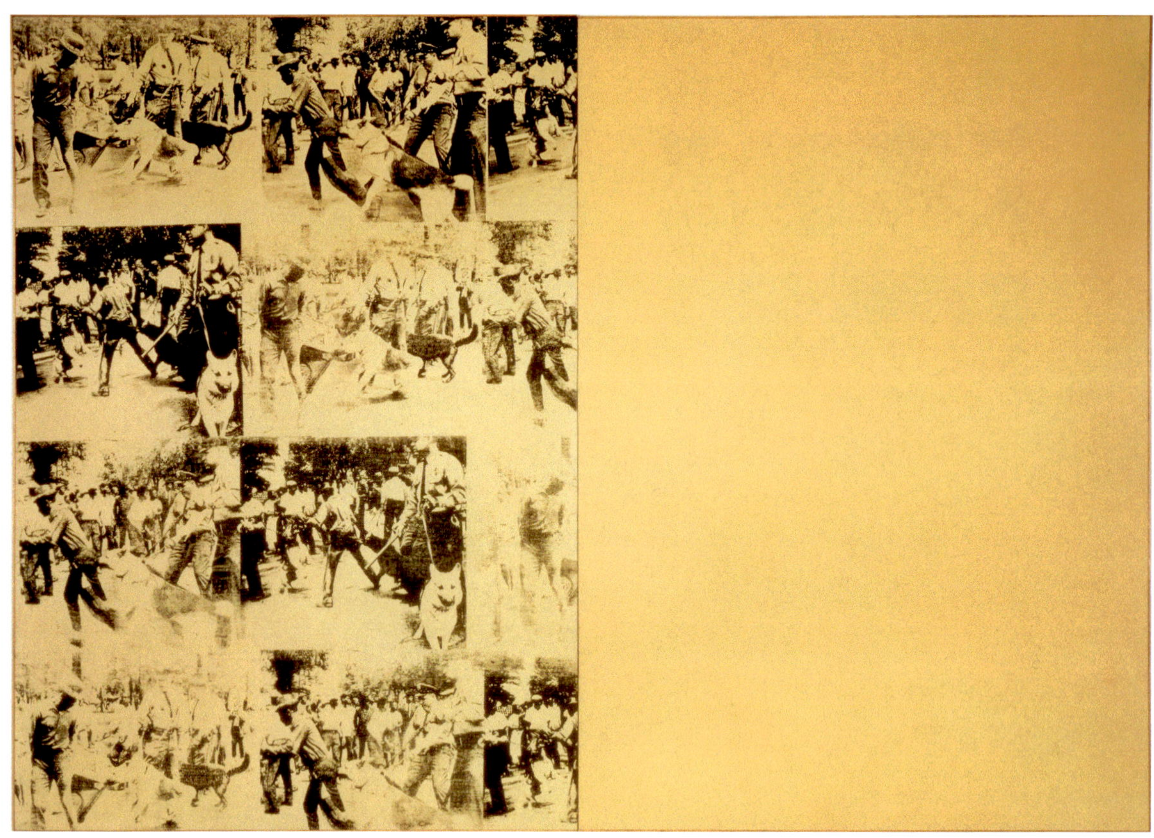

2. Andy Warhol, *Mustard Race Riot*, 1963. Silkscreen ink, acrylic and pencil on linen; 113⅞ × 82 (canvas with images), 113¼ × 82 (monochrome canvas).

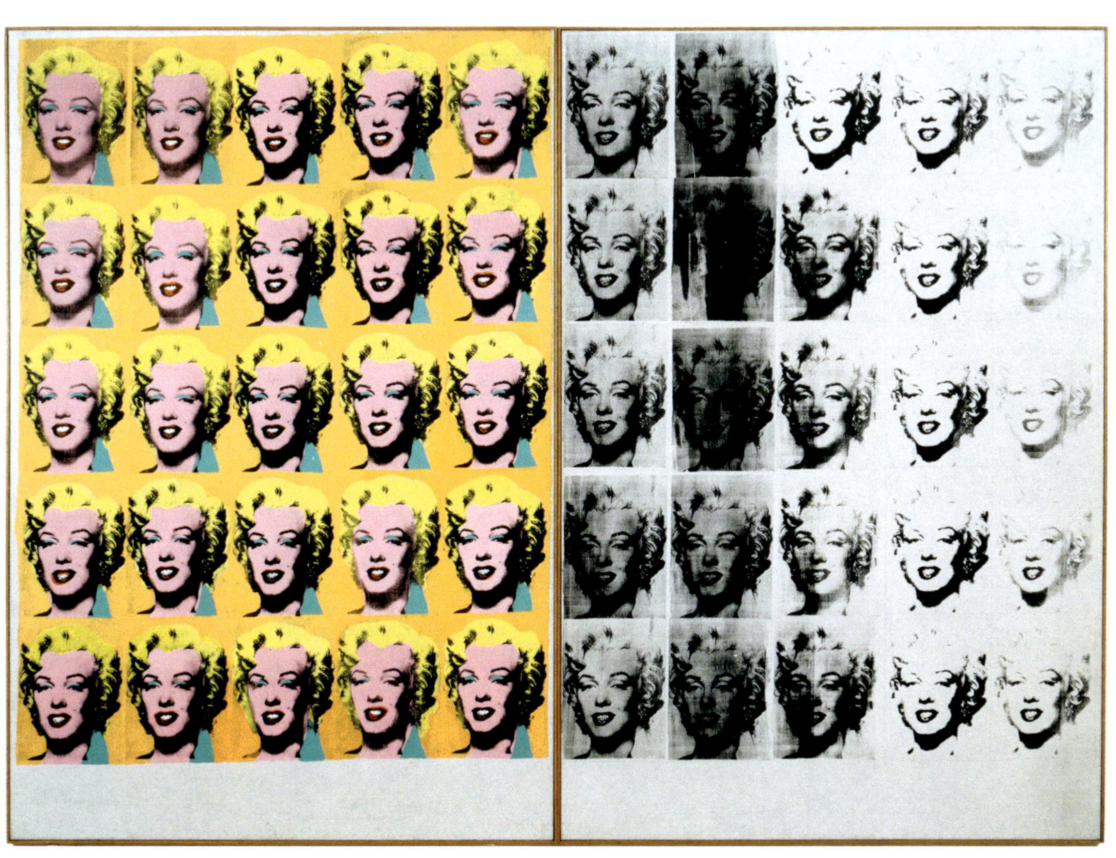

3. Andy Warhol, *Marilyn Diptych*, 1962. Acrylic, silkscreen ink, and pencil on linen, 81 × 57 inches. © Andy Warhol Foundation for the Visual Arts/Artists Rights Society (ARS), New York.

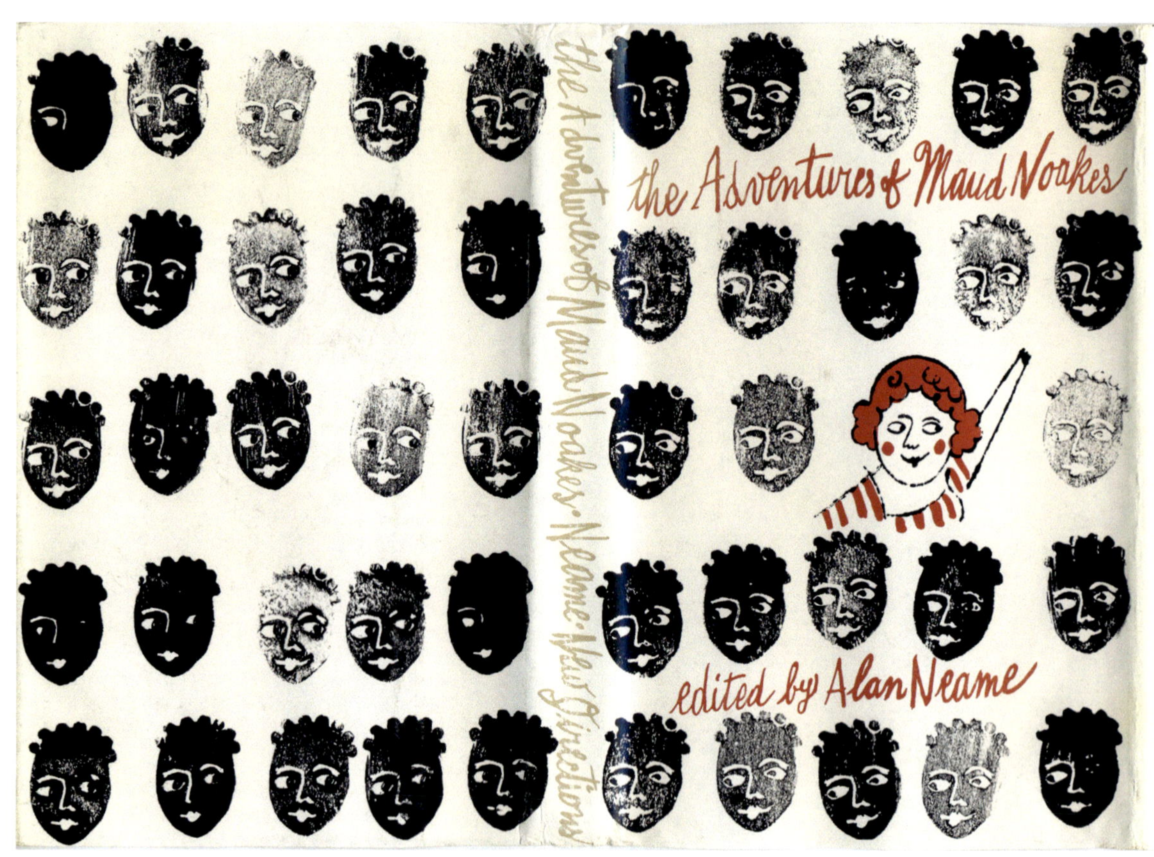

4. Andy Warhol, book cover (*The Adventures of Maud Noakes*), 1961. Printed ink on paper, 8¼ × 11½. Author's collection. © Andy Warhol Foundation for the Visual Arts/Artists Rights Society (ARS), New York.

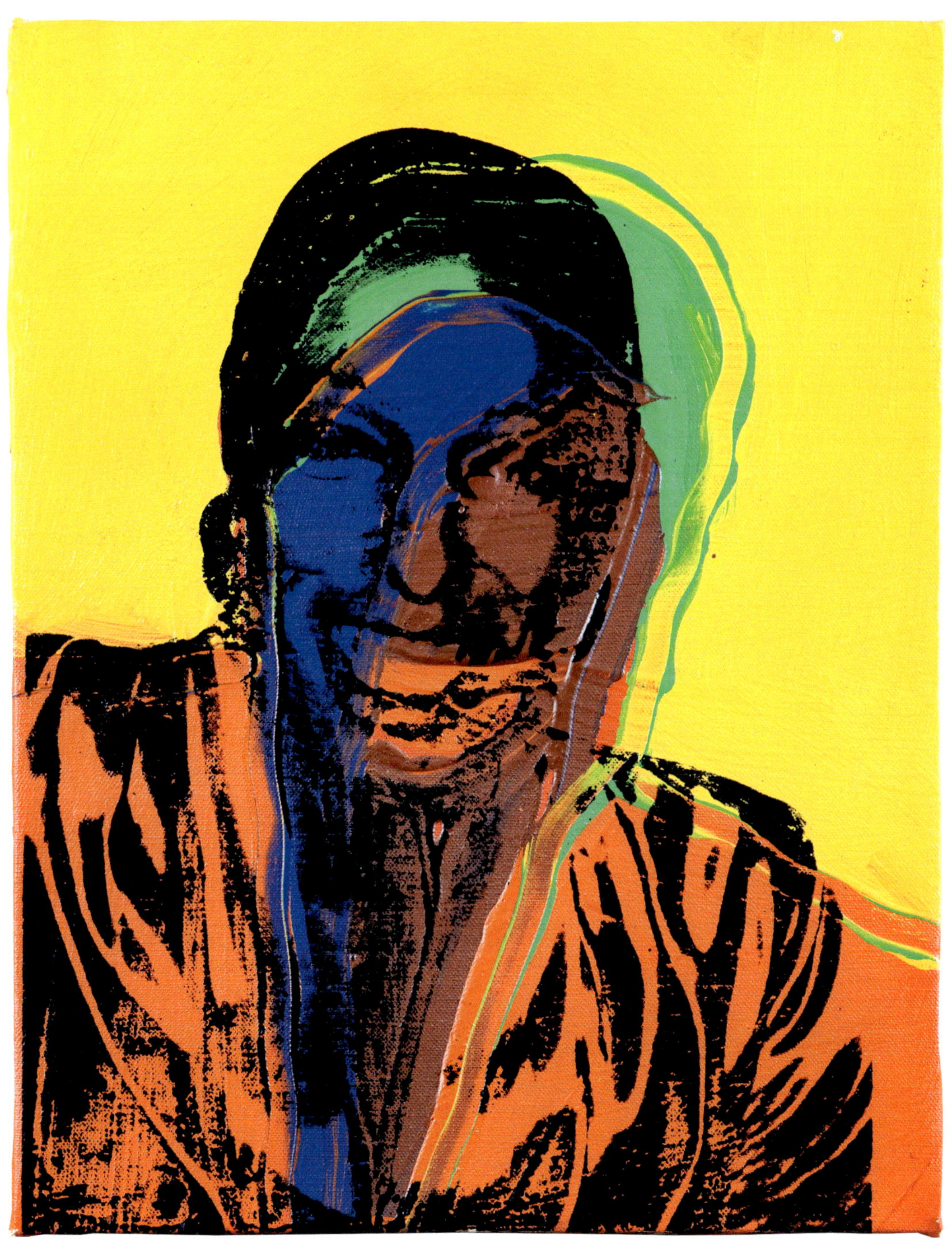

5. Andy Warhol, *Ladies and Gentlemen (Wilhelmina Ross)*, 1975. Acrylic and silkscreen ink on linen, 14 × 11 inches. © 2014 The Andy Warhol Foundation for the Visual Arts/ Artists Rights Society (ARS), New York.

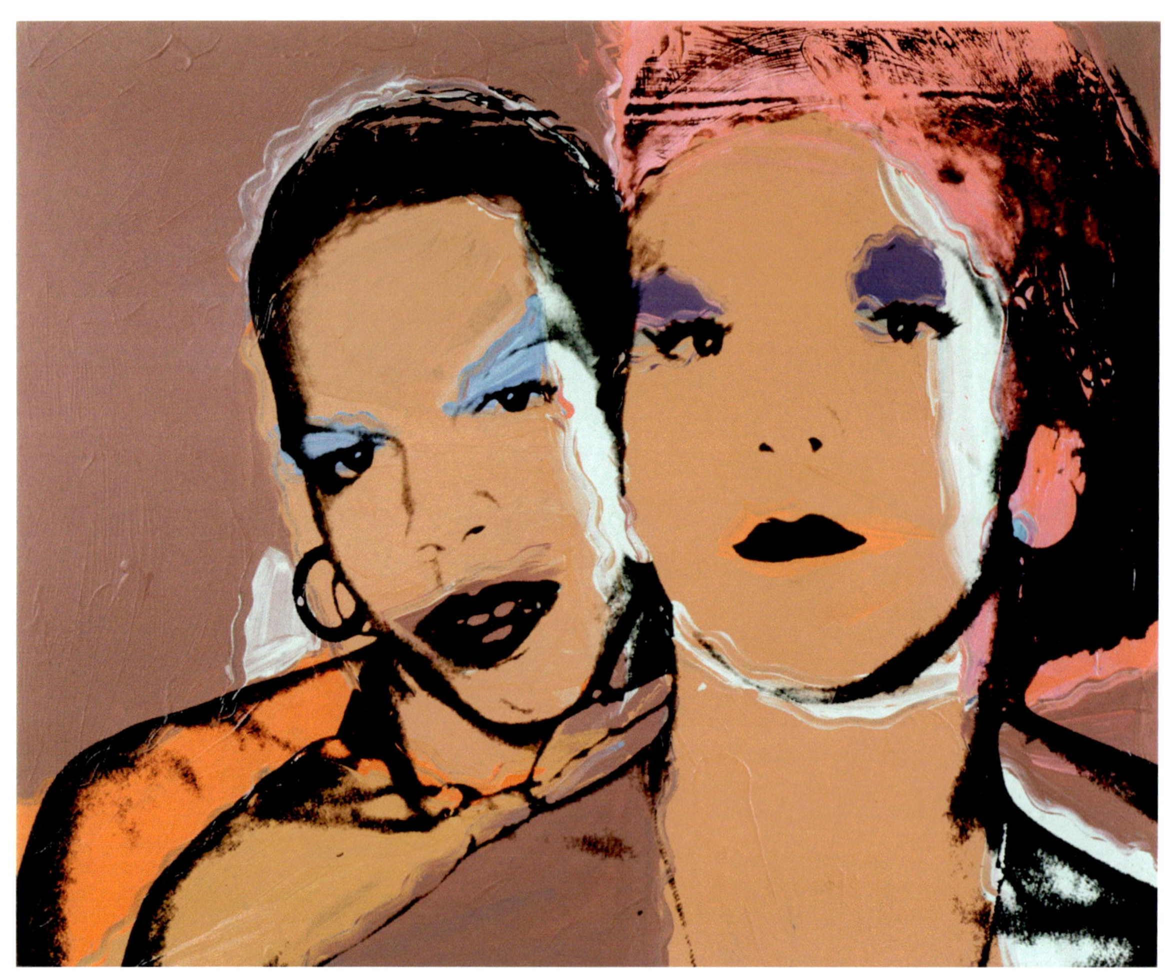

6. Andy Warhol, *Ladies and Gentlemen (Ivette and Lurdes)*, 1975. Acrylic and silk screen on canvas, 50 × 40 inches. © 2014 The Andy Warhol Foundation for the Visual Arts/ Artists Rights Society (ARS), New York.

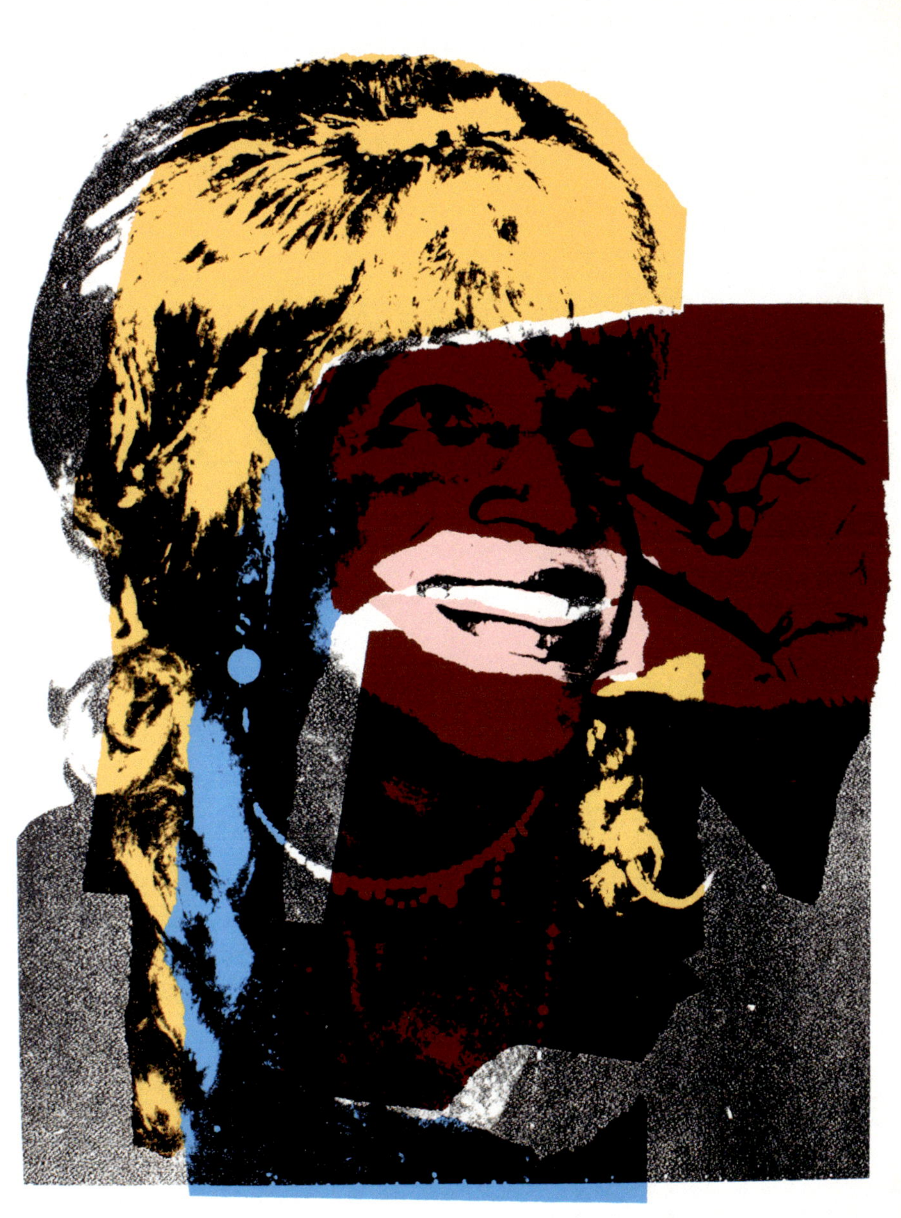

7. Andy Warhol, *Ladies and Gentlemen (Marsha P. Johnson)*, 1975. Screenprint on Arches paper, 43½ × 28½ inches. © 2014 The Andy Warhol Foundation for the Visual Arts/Artists Rights Society (ARS), New York.

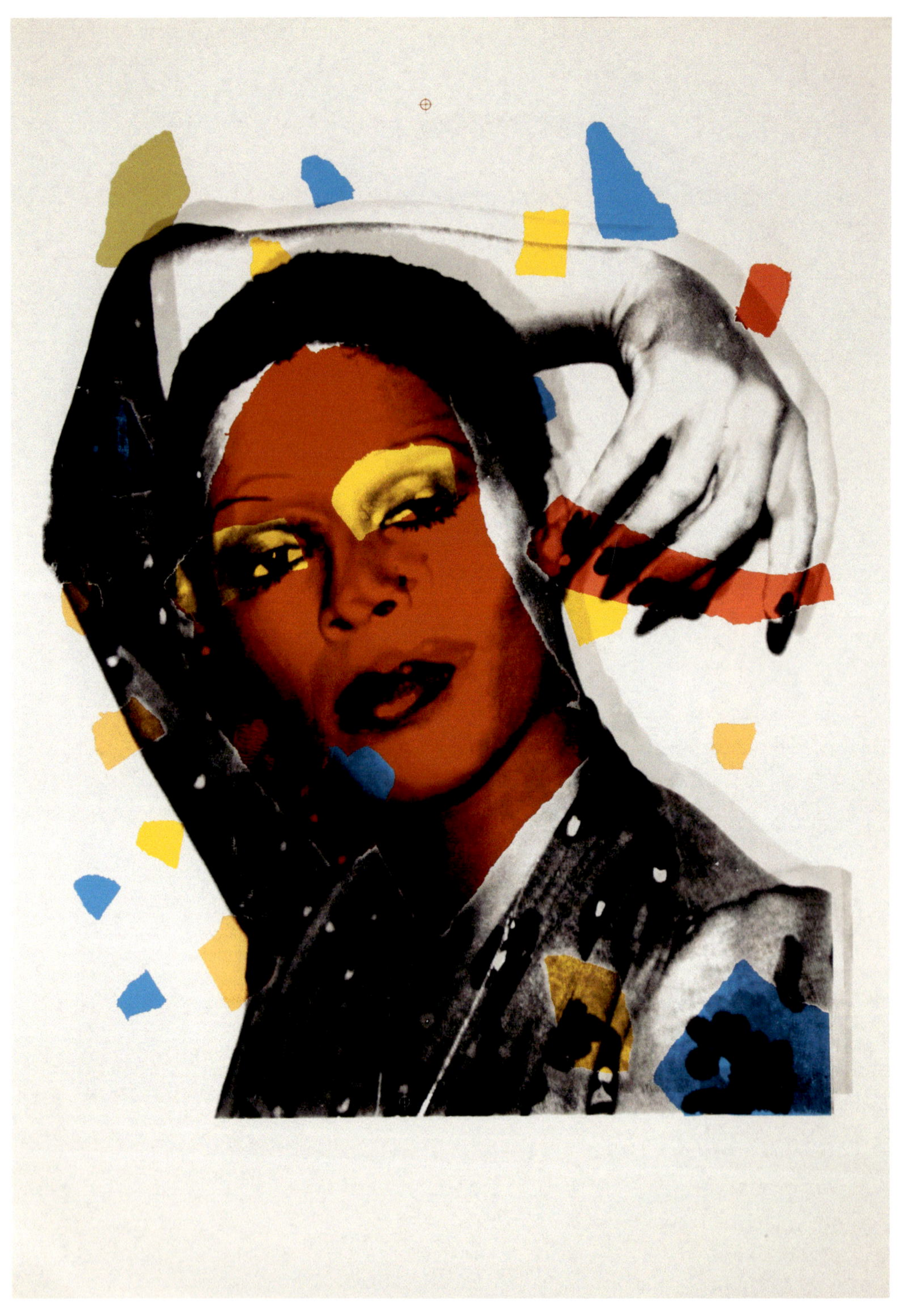

8. Andy Warhol, *Ladies and Gentlemen (Iris)*, 1975. Collage, 24 × 18 inches. © 2014 The Andy Warhol Foundation for the Visual Arts/Artists Rights Society (ARS), New York.

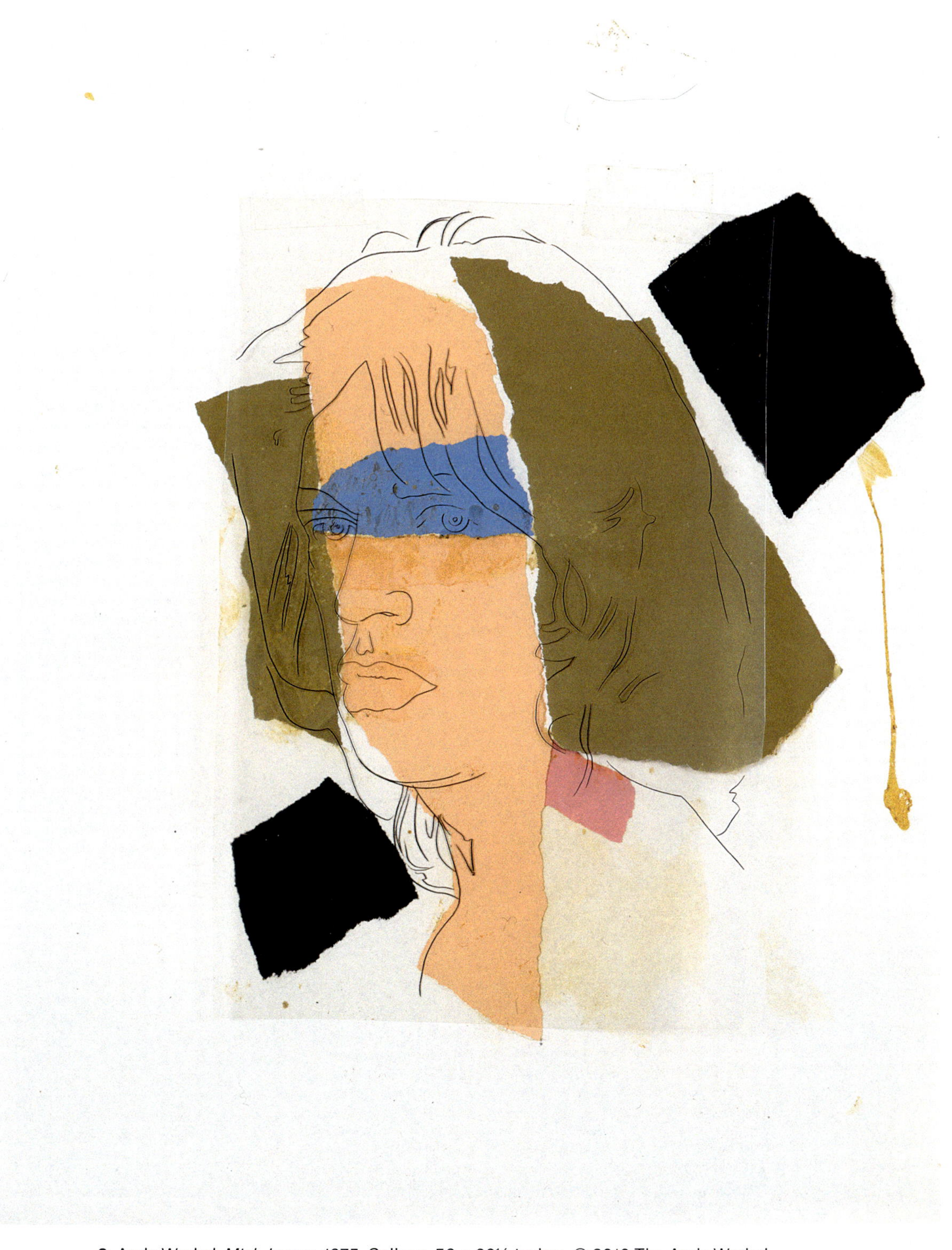

9. Andy Warhol, *Mick Jagger*, 1975. Collage, 50 × 38⅛ inches. © 2016 The Andy Warhol Foundation for the Visual Arts/Artists Rights Society (ARS), New York.

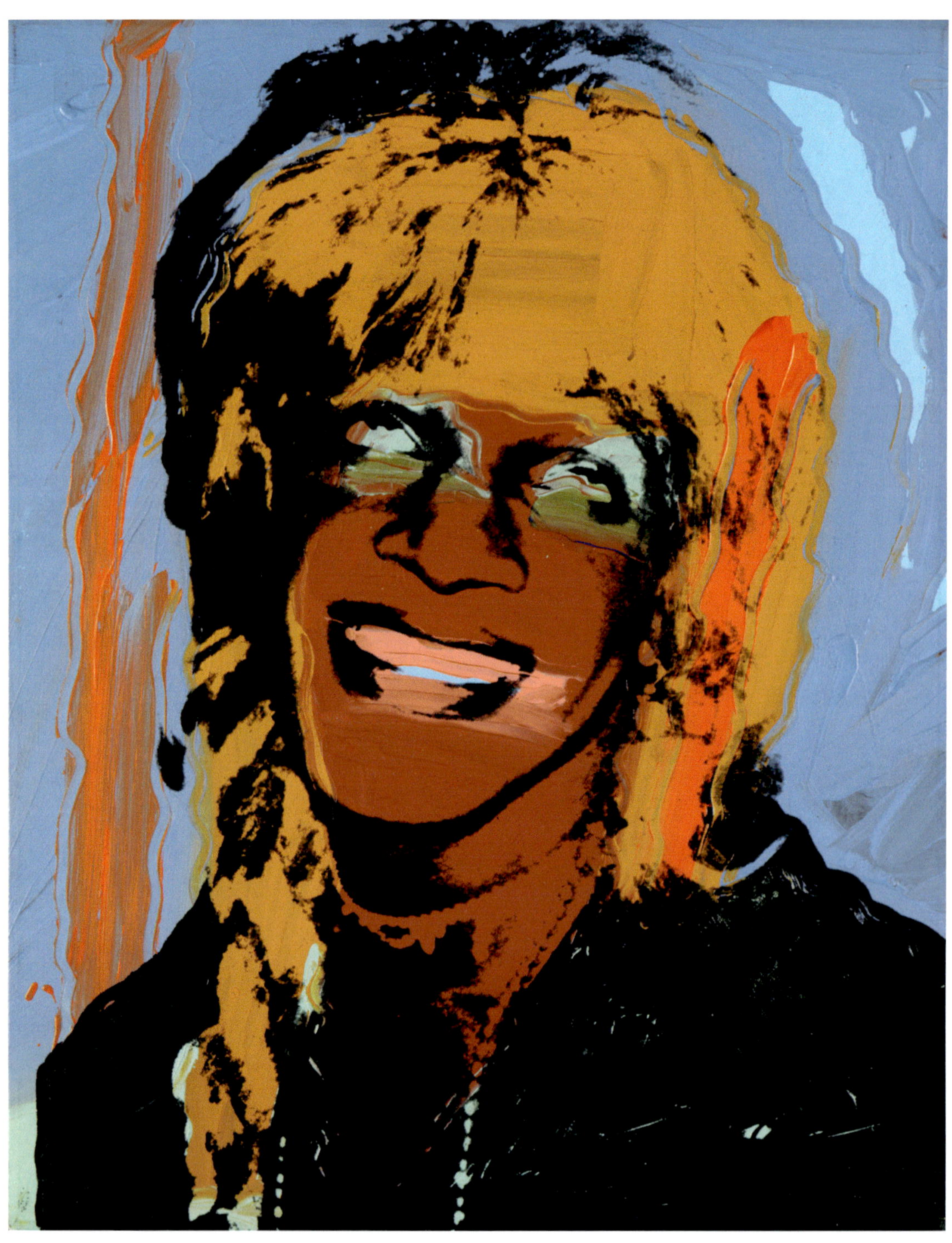

10. Andy Warhol, *Ladies and Gentlemen (Marsha P. Johnson)*, 1975. Acrylic and silkscreen ink on linen, 50 × 40 inches. Udo and Anette Brandhorst Collection. © 2016 The Andy Warhol Foundation for the Visual Arts/Artists Rights Society (ARS), New York.

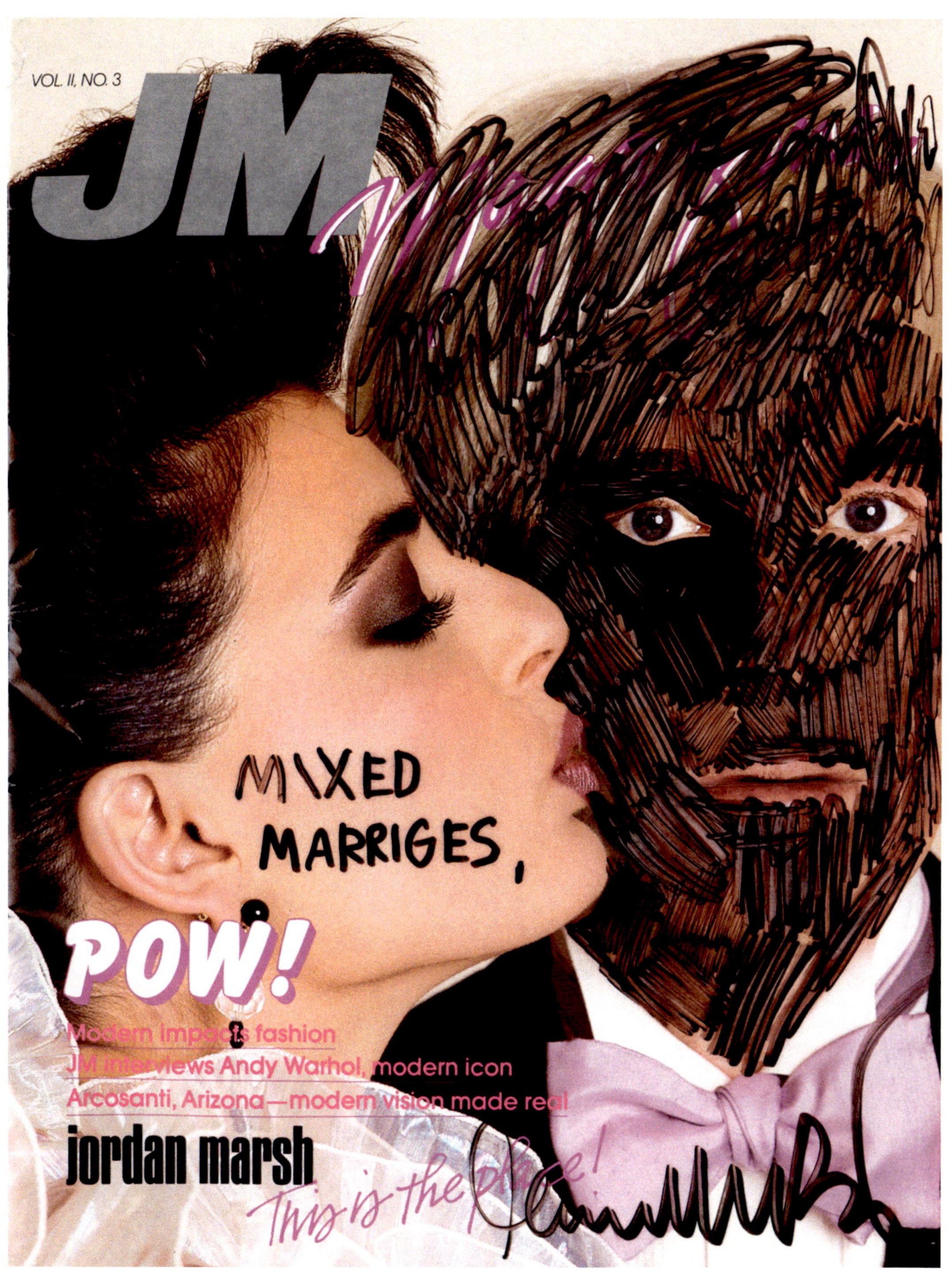

11. Jean-Michel Basquiat, *JM Magazine—Vol. 2, no. 3 (1983), featuring "Mixed Marriges" [sic] and drawing on Andy Warhol's face by Jean-Michel Basquiat*, 1983. Felt-tip marker and printed ink on coated paper, 10⅞ × 8⅜ × ¼ inches. © The Estate of Jean-Michel Basquiat/ADAGP, Paris/Artists Rights Society (ARS), New York.

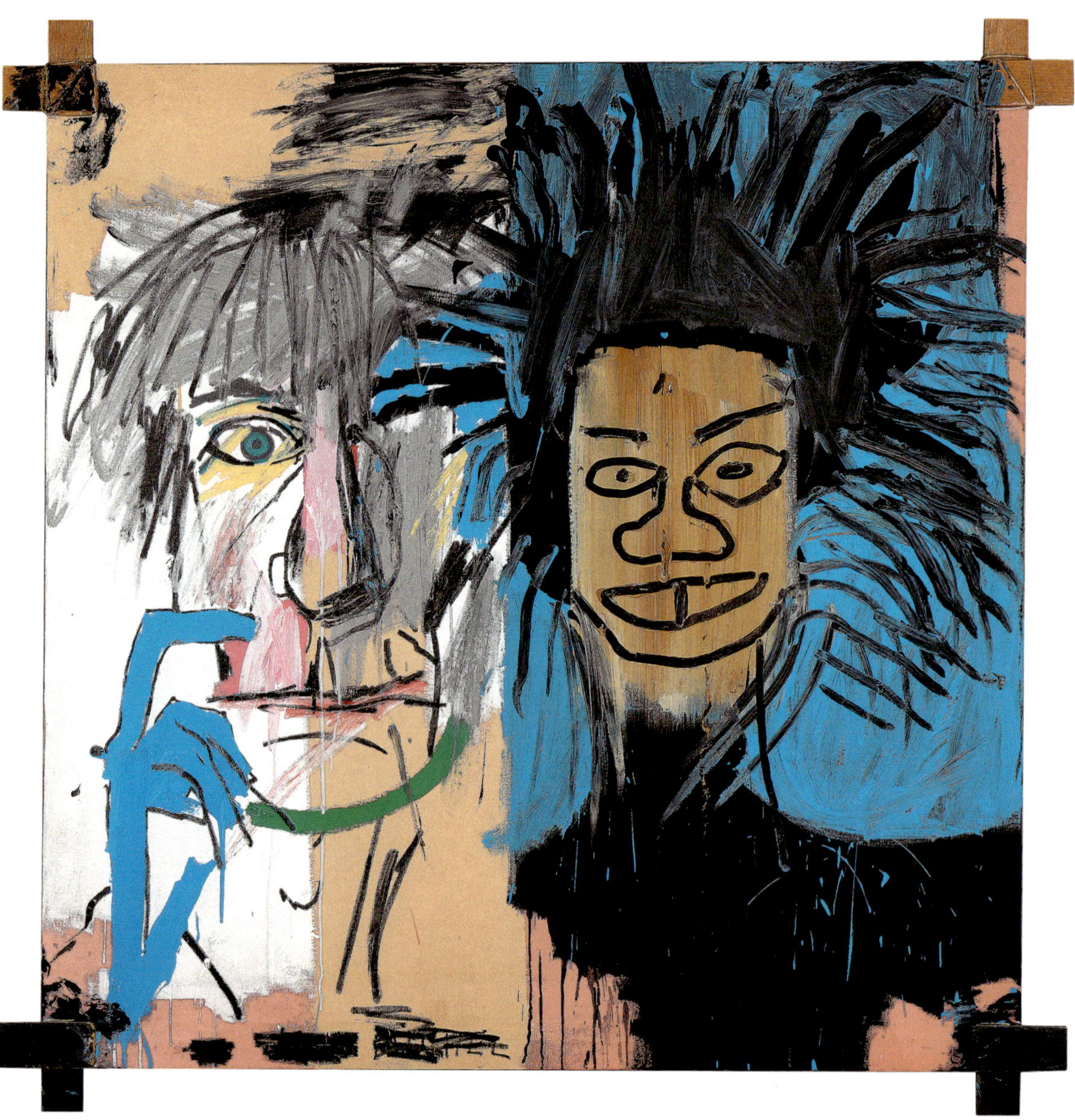

12. Jean-Michel Basquiat, *Dos Cabezas*, 1982. Acrylic and oilstick on canvas with wood supports, 59¾ × 60½ inches. Private collection. Bridgeman Images. © The Estate of Jean-Michel Basquiat/ADAGP, Paris/Artists Rights Society (ARS), New York.

If the racial significance of the color of Marilyn's skin does not seem to vary especially significantly in the colored images on the left side of the diptych, one can see that what does vary are the borders between the yellow hair and pink forehead, and the size and placement of the red lipstick, turquoise eye shadow, and matching shirt collar. If one looks closely, that is, it seems that the makeup here has been unevenly, sometimes unequally applied, that the shirt is sometimes disheveled, that the hair, mobile now like a wig, might have slipped a bit. Other facial features shift around, too. In a conversation with Warhol, David Bourdon noted, "Through misprinting . . . you somehow achieved fifty different expressions. In one portrait the green eye shadow would be printed too low, so that she looked sulky and wicked. In another, the red lips would be off-register like the rotogravure in the Sunday tabloids, where it is usual for the cover girl to have her lips printed on her cheek or chin. Sometimes the mouth was pursed, sometimes it was opened in hedonistic joy. Marilyn was given expressions that were never caught on film. (It was possible to believe that in your painting we had seen the entire spectrum of Marilyn's personality)" (*IBYM*, 9–10). These expressive, affectively charged printing accidents illustrate Marilyn's own nonidentity with herself, her multitudinous alienation from her "own" image. This nonidentity may have already been legible, in some ways, in her own public displays of "misfitting," the kinds of roles that she played (including her starring role in *The Misfits*), and her public comments on her feelings of outsiderness. According to at least one anecdotal account, this evident self-alienation may have made her unusually or especially available for disidentificatory viewing by black and queer fans, including, among others, James Baldwin.[95]

95 At least anecdotally, according to W. J. Weatherby, Marilyn's way of being a star appeared to make her available to various forms of (dis)identification. He reports that a black woman in New Orleans named Christine explained to him that "she knows what the score is, but it hasn't broken her. . . . She's someone who was abused. I could identify with her. I never could identify with any other white movie star. They were always white people doing white things." Weatherby, *Conversations with Marilyn* (New York: Paragon, 1976). Weatherby had a series of pretty intimate conversations with Monroe, in which her fellow feeling for gays and lesbians and people of color became clear. Weatherby also reports that James Baldwin identified with Monroe.

See also "A Rumbling of Things Unknown," *London Review of Books* 34, no. 8 (April 26, 2012), where Jacqueline Rose actively takes up the question of black identification with Monroe. Complicating our analysis further is the report, in a letter in response to Rose's article by Richard Gott (34, no. 9; May 10, 2012), a friend of Weatherby's, that Weatherby was "part of the gay underworld of the civil rights movement, becoming close friends with James Baldwin and Bayard Rustin (he was proud of the fact that he was the only white pall-bearer at Baldwin's funeral)," and that the "Christine" he cites was his lover, who was in fact a black man he met in New Orleans and traveled with through Georgia and Louisiana. Weatherby's fictionalized account of their remarkable journey in his book *Love in the Shadows*, published in 1966, pretends that they were a heterosexual interracial couple. This was extraordinary enough at the time; a book detailing a black and white male partnership would not have found a publisher.

Also see Dyer, *Heavenly Bodies*, on Monroe's ambivalent relation to her own celebrity,

Further emphasizing the artificial quality of Marilyn's face, in his portrait, is Warhol's mode of production itself, which played with the nature of apparently supplementary makeup and dye jobs. As we know, in these paintings, Warhol *first* paints the makeup, the skin and the hair on the canvas and then prints the halftone black screen on top, giving the image its texture and definition. As Printz notes, this "reversal of the functions and sequence between drawing and painting was noted almost immediately," by Michael Fried among others.[96] In an earlier essay, I suggested that Warhol's portraits appear at first to be instances of the hypogram, a figure that, as Paul de Man writes, "underscored a name, a word, by trying to repeat its syllables, and thus giving it another, artificial mode of being added, so to speak, to the original mode of the word." As such, Warhol's apparently decorative makeup jobs seem to denote the existence of a stable face that can be "embellished, underscored, accentuated or supplemented by the hypogram."[97] But by putting the makeup and hair color (indeed all the nonblack color) on *underneath* the lines and features of the face, Warhol's technique also seems to be an illustration of the degree to which these supplementary acts of adornment turn out *not* to be simple addition, "increase," or improvement, but are in fact foundational to the face's recognizability. These apparent enhancements or add-ons are what allow us to see and feel and know Marilyn as white, as a woman, as a star.[98] The hypogrammatic quality of Warhol's portraits quickly slides to prosopopoeia, the trope that gives or makes a face, implying that "the original face can be missing or nonexistent" (as de Man notes), thereby "inflecting all our face recognitions with an uncanny sense of the fictive."[99] In fact, we can say that in Warhol's por-

---

and Douglas Crimp, who describes seeing Mario Montez at a performance of *Turds in Hell* by Charles Ludlam and Bill Vehr, "standing on one side of the stage for what seems like hours, mute, with shimmying body and animated facial expressions, repeatedly, obsessively, miming Marilyn Monroe" (*Our Kind of Movie,* 39).

96 Printz, *CR1*, 205. See Michael Fried, New York Letter, *Art International*, December 20, 1962, 57.

97 Flatley, "Warhol Gives Good Face," in *Pop Out*. De Man, "Hypogram and Inscription," in *The Resistance to Theory* (Minneapolis: University of Minnesota Press), 44.

98 This reversal resonates with those observed by Esther Newton in *Mother Camp*, where she argues that confusions (and reversals) of surface and depth, interior and exterior, masculine and feminine, are essential to the aesthetic effects produced by the drag queen. "At its most complex, [drag] is a double inversion that says 'appearance is an illusion.' Drag says, 'my "outside" appearance is feminine, but my essence "inside" [the body] is masculine.' At the same time it symbolizes the opposite inversion: 'my appearance "outside" [my body, my gender] is masculine but my essence "inside" [myself] is feminine'" (103; brackets following quoted terms in original). What one sees and recognizes (the feminine walk, the fabulous outfit) are at once *unreal*—they do not match the masculine body underneath—and the *most real*, in the sense that they correspond to an interior essence. Appearance is an illusion, but it is a real one.

99 De Man, "Hypogram and Inscription," 44. See also Jacques Derrida, who remarks that prosopopoeia may be a fictive voice, but it is a voice "which haunts any said real or present voice" (*Memoires for Paul de Man*, 26).

traits, all facial recognitions, indeed all identities—not least racial ones—are haunted by artifice and loss.

Thus, in its suggestion that artificiality is foundation, that makeup makes the face, that racialized gender is itself a surface-oriented performance, Warhol's Marilyns (like his other portraits) present stardom as essentially imitative and imitable. In this sense, we might say that they portray Marilyn as seen from the point of view of a drag queen. Drag, it is worth emphasizing, in this understanding, is fundamentally rooted in an experience of spectatorship in which viewers can imagine being, acting, and looking like a star. In *Mother Camp* (the result of ethnographic research conducted in the late 1960s), Esther Newton observes that for drag queens, "'beauty' is the closest approximation, in form and movement, to the mass media images of glamorous women. Tastes vary, of course. Some female impersonators think that Lauren Bacall is a beautiful woman, while others prefer Elizabeth Taylor or Marilyn Monroe. The point is that the first reference of the concept of beauty is always some woman who has been publicly recognized as 'glamorous.'"[100] In order to adopt the movie star one likes as a model, repeated viewings, intense study, and multiple imitations are necessary. As a consequence, Warhol observes, "Drags are ambulatory archives of ideal moviestar womanhood. They perform a documentary service, usually consecrating their lives to keeping the glittering alternative alive and available for (not-too-close) inspection" (*Phil*, 54). In the drag queen, bodily comportment itself records an accumulation of likes—the gestures, facial expressions, styles of speech, mode of dressing, and ways of walking that have become sites of affective attachment and imitation. Drag queens thereby perform a scholarly, pedagogical function, keeping alive and making available what Warhol calls the "glittering alternative," which we might take to refer to a space of "unreal" glamour, beauty, and fame. This "alternative" space is an expansive realm of intense feeling, inviting imitation, and resemblance (as Parker Tyler and Jack Smith suggest). Drag queens, in Warhol's understanding, show others how they, too, can access this alternative, and in fact bring its glitter into the realm of everyday life. Indeed, in their commitment to being-like what they like, in the centrality of the mimetic faculty to their practice, as students of ideal movie-star womanhood, drag queens are Warholian spectators par excellence.

In its representation of a multitude of distinct yet similar Marilyns, varying in expression and hue, a series of attempts to imitate a glamorous star, and in its emphasis on a variable, non-self-identical, haunted, and artificial whiteness, *Marilyn Diptych* points not only to the multitude that Marilyn contains (as Bourdon suggests) but also to the multiracial multitude of fans and imitators she inspired. In this, *Marilyn Diptych* imagines a collectivity of drag queens. This is a collectivity that would get a more concrete and vivid representation several years later in Warhol's large series of paint-

100 Newton, *Mother Camp*, 43.

ings, prints, drawings, and collages of African American and Latina drag queens.

"Just Alike"

Usually most transvestites are friendly towards one another because they're just alike.
Marsha P. Johnson, cofounder, Street Transvestite Action Revolutionaries (STAR)

In the summer of 1974, Warhol began a large series of portraits of African American and Latino drag queens. Consisting of 268 paintings, a portfolio of ten prints, and a number of drawings and collages, the works were initiated by a large and lucrative commission from an Italian art dealer, Luciano Anselmino.[101] Works from the series were first shown in Ferrara, Italy, in October 1975, where it was enthusiastically received in the Italian art press and understood to be a forceful critique of racism and its intersection with capitalism in the United States.[102] In the United States the series has been rarely exhibited, its critical treatment scarce (something that should change with the publication of volume 4 of the *Catalogue Raisonné*, which documents and reproduces the full series).[103] Apparently, the theme of transvestites was suggested by Anselmino (who also provided the Ladies and Gentlemen

101 Anselmino was a protégé of the surrealist dealer Alexandre Iolas; the exhibition was held at the Galleria Civica d'Arte Moderna, Palazzo dei Diamanti. For a thorough account of the conception, composition, exhibition, and reception of the series, detailed descriptions of the paintings, and information about the models and the sittings, see Neil Printz's impressive entry in *CR4*, 22–203.

102 Bob Colacello: "The left-wing Italian art critics went wild, writing that Andy Warhol had exposed the cruel racism inherent in the American capitalist system, which left poor black and Hispanic boys no choice but to prostitute themselves as transvestites" (*Holy Terror*, 228). See also the remarkable book *Andy Warhol Ladies and Gentlemen*, Presentazione di Janus (Milano: Mazzotta, 1975), which opens with three photos of a melancholic Warhol, followed by an essay by an Italian critic identified as Janus, with an epigraph from Marx's *Poverty of Philosophy* on the centrality of slavery to the economy of North America and, in turn, to the worldwide development of capital. Following the essay are reproductions of paintings, prints, and drawings from Warhol's series interspersed with excerpts of texts (in Italian translation) from the black radical tradition, including Richard Wright, James Baldwin, Langston Hughes, Ma Rainey, Malcolm X, George Jackson, Angela Davis, David Walker, Martin Delany, Franz Fanon, and many others. Many thanks to Neil Printz for emphasizing the interest of the Janus catalog, and for sharing his wealth of knowledge regarding the Ladies and Gentlemen series.

103 For exceptions, see Nettleton, "White-on-White," 20–21, and Kobena Mercer's smart, brief remarks: "What makes Warhol's Ladies and Gentlemen a remarkable body of work is not the choice of African American drag queens as subject matter but the implication that 'race' and ethnicity are co-extensive with gender and sexuality as differential attributes of identity that make bodies 'readable' and culturally intelligible on the basis of their performative rather than expressive character." *Pop Art and Vernacular Cultures* (Cambridge, MA: MIT Press, 2007), 30.

title; around the Factory the pieces were referred to as the "drag queens" or "transvestites"). He would have known of Warhol's long-standing interest in drag and been familiar with the significant role played in many of Warhol's films by drag queens such as Mario Montez, Candy Darling, Jackie Curtis, and Holly Woodlawn.

Bob Colacello remembers that after initially resisting the proposal (worrying that if he painted Holly and Jackie, they would ask for money every time a painting sold), Warhol arrived at the idea of painting the mostly black and Puerto Rican drag queens from the Gilded Grape bar.[104] "Ronnie Cutrone, Vincent [Fremont] and I," Colacello writes, "would ask them to pose for 'a friend' for $50 per half hour. The next day, they'd appear at the Factory and Andy, whom we never introduced by name, would take their Polaroids. And the next time we saw them at the Gilded Grape, they invariably would say, 'Tell your friend I do a lot more for fifty bucks.'"[105] Warhol gave his own explanation of his motives in an interview published in the gay literary magazine *Christopher Street* in 1977: "I used to go to the Gilded Grape bar and the transvestites there were just so exciting looking. I decided to do some paintings of them."[106] Warhol's excitement was evident in the energy he gave to the project, the products of which more than doubled the initial terms of the commission, making it among the largest series of paintings in his career. His ambitions were not only quantitative (although Warhol certainly valued quantity as a goal in itself) but formal, which is immediately apparent in the visual exuberance of the works, which are more "painterly" than most of his commissioned portraits (although they are similar to roughly contemporaneous paintings of Man Ray and of Warhol's mother Julia). That his energy and excitement animated his bodily comportment while painting seems

104 Colacello, *Holy Terror*, 221. Colacello writes that Anselmino suggested "portraits of Candy, Jackie and Holly. Andy said Candy was dead, and Jackie and Holly would drive him crazy, asking for more money every time they heard one had sold" (221). Warhol had been very upset by Candy's death: Colacello writes that when he told Warhol that Candy was dying, "for the first and only time in the seventeen years that I know him, I saw him cry" (189). Despite his skepticism about the series at its inception, Colacello observes, "They looked so stunning in the High Renaissance Palazzo dei Diamante. It was Andy's second most beautiful exhibition, after the Maos at the Musee Galliera in Paris" (228).

105 Ibid., 228. Colacello tells a similar story in O'Connor and Liu, *Unseen Warhol*, 92. Ronnie Cutrone also remarks on his participation: "My ex, ex-wife, Gigi, and I used to hang out at the Ramrod. . . . They all loved Gigi. So I had easy access to all the transvestites. At 3 in the morning, I would chase a transvestite down the street, yelling, 'You're wonderful; we want you to pose for Warhol.' And she'd be running at me looking at me, Was I going to bash her or cast her? And I'd say, 'No, no, no, I'm serious.' So I got models for the drag queens series" (O'Connor and Liu, *Unseen Warhol*, 68). Also see Cutrone's comments on getting models in Smith, *Conversations*, 359. Neil Printz notes that Corey Tippin was also tasked by Warhol with finding models, for which he received a finder's fee of $75 (*CR4*, 26).

106 Claire Demers, "An Interview with Andy Warhol: Some Say He's the Real Mayor of New York" (Summer 1977), *Christopher Street*, September 1977; reprinted in *IBYM*.

evident in Warhol's active use of his fingers to spread, squiggle, and score the richly layered, vividly colored paints.

Part of what might have made the drag queens so "exciting looking" is the combination of impressive mimetic skill and intense affective attachment to female glamour that Warhol found compelling in drag more generally. He admired the difficult labor performed by "boys who spend their lives trying to be complete girls." These boys, he writes, "have to work so hard—double-time—getting rid of all the tell-tale male signs and drawing in all the female signs" (*Phil*, 54).[107] This particular form of artwork is doubly demanding because it involves erasure—of male signs such as stubble, Adam's apples, and genital bulges—and drawing, of female signs via makeup, clothes, and hairstyles or wigs. As boys who can look like girls, drag queens display a striking, self-conscious capacity for the creation of likenesses across the boundary of sexual difference, otherwise so rigorously policed. They are thus beacons of mimetic talent as well as exemplars of the commitment and courage required to defy social norms. Yet Warhol admired not only the drag queens who could "pass" (like Candy Darling) as beautiful women. He was just as fascinated by the moments when drag queens did *not* fully succeed in becoming the model they imitated, when "failures" in the work of erasure and redrawing instead achieved something closer to a sexual "blur" (as he put it in *POPism*, 224). In such moments of blurred disorientation, gender itself can seem both incredibly "real" in its affective force and radically artificial, contingent on the skill of a given performance.

Of course, such a male femininity would have been exciting for Warhol, in part because it echoed his own gender nonconformity, his own failures to correctly play the proper role. The imitation of female stars may have reminded Warhol of his own childhood scenes of liking and wishing to be like movie stars such as Shirley Temple ("I never wanted to be a painter; I wanted to be a tap dancer"; *IBYM*, 89) and his own ongoing, often-recounted identification with femininity, powerfully elaborated in Christopher Makos's 1981 photographs of him in drag.[108] The labor required to look like a woman that is apparent in those photographs was in some ways an intensification of the daily blemish-erasing, skin-recoloring makeup labor he describes in the opening pages of the *Philosophy*. ("Is my adam's apple that big?" Warhol wonders as he looks in the mirror while he works on his face.) Warhol

107 Also: "If you're a boy and you try to be a girl, its double work and stuff like that" (*IBYM*, 269); "They're usually such intelligent kids, they usually have more brains than other people do" (*IBYM*, 270). On drag in Warhol, see Merck, "Figuring Out Andy Warhol," 224–37.

108 On Warhol's identification with femininity, see introduction. On his collaboration with Makos, see Makos, *Andy Warhol by Christopher Makos* (Milan: Charta, 2002). Warhol used one of these photos of himself in drag for a project in *Artforum* titled "Forged Images," in which the photo appears as a kind of centerfold alongside a series of Dollar Sign paintings; see Doyle, "Tricks of the Trade," 203–6.

admired the artwork involved in drag because he was familiar with it. As a wearer of sometimes showy wigs, Warhol was also well acquainted with the importance of dazzle and distraction to drag's effects. Gerard Malanga remembers that such a distraction kept him from realizing that Warhol was wearing a wig at all. Instead of trying to fit in with something that "doesn't draw attention" like a "plain brown toupee," Malanga recalled, "Andy got outrageous silver hair." Thus, "when you looked at Andy, you didn't think, 'He's wearing a toupee,' you thought, My God, look at that guy's hair.'"[109] This seems like a paradigmatic instance of what Thomas Lanigan-Schmidt calls the "drag queen theory of art," in which, as Neil Printz writes, "multiple points of visual interest 'keep the eye moving' so that it doesn't linger on tell-tale male attributes such as large hands, an adam's apple, or stubble from the beard."[110]

At the same time, Warhol was also familiar with the sense of shame and fear of exposure that lingered around these presentational practices. Take this passage from the *Diaries*: "It was a beautiful day. Walked on the street and a little kid, she was six or seven, with another kid, yelled, 'Look at the guy with the wig,' and I was really embarrassed. I blew my cool and it ruined my afternoon. So I was depressed."[111] The mimetic talents Warhol saw on display in the drag queens he painted may have been appealing because they seemed to be a fierce and fabulous technique for the successful management of potentially embarrassing, sometimes depressing stigma (such as having one's wig called out or being "too swish" to be considered a "major painter"; *POP*, 11–12). These talents were successful in managing such stigma, inasmuch as they also created a way of being with others, one based on a shared imitation of female celebrity that radiates glamour even as it fails to achieve movie-star status.

Just as Warhol's Screen Tests provide a documentary of the persons who came through the Factory in the mid-1960s, offering us a view of the personalities who composed that counterpublic space, so his portraits of drag queens offer a remarkable picture of a specific collectivity of mostly black and Latina transvestites. That Warhol was excited about documenting the group as a group is suggested by the unprecedented scale of the sittings for this commission, which produced more than five hundred Polaroids of fourteen drag queens (all reproduced in the *Catalogue Raisonné*).[112] Where

109 Malanga, quoted in Scherman and Dalton, *Pop*, 175.

110 Lanigan-Schmidt, quoted from conversation with Printz, *CR4*, 31.

111 *Diaries*, March 15, 1983, 491.

112 Warhol collected signatures from nine of the fourteen models on at least one of their Polaroids: Broadway, Easha, Ivette, Kim, Lurdes, Monique, Vicki, Alphanso Panell, and Helen Morales (who signed another Polaroid as Harry Morales). Four of the remaining five were identified by other means: Marsha P. Johnson was a widely known activist and readily recognizable personality; Wilhelmina Ross was identified by Jimmy Camicia, who had founded a theater group in which Ross performed. Corey Tippin, who had been

the Screen Tests recorded the famous, the semifamous, and the marginal, Warhol's portraits of drag queens document a group whose lives were likely quite precarious. As poor, black or Latina, gay, and gender-nonconforming street transvestites who earned money hustling, Warhol's sitters were a multiply marginalized group.

In bringing together this group, Warhol was engaging in a representational task that finds an analogue in the work of one of his models for the series, Marsha P. Johnson. Sometimes known as "Saint Marsha," Johnson was celebrated as a key participant in the 1969 Stonewall riots (the protest against police harassment that is generally understood to have sparked the gay liberation movement) and enjoyed something of a celebrity status on the streets of the West Village.[113] In 1970, together with Sylvia Rivera (whom she had met years earlier on the streets), Johnson founded Street Transvestite Action Revolutionaries (STAR).[114] The group drew on the activist energy circulating in the wake of Stonewall and on the Gay Liberation Front's radical efforts to remake society and "build a new, liberated life-style," in which the old "gender-role system" would no longer be necessary, an openly utopian project in which "gay shows the way."[115] But STAR sought to address the particular concerns of street transvestites, who were not always represented by gay liberation groups.[116] STAR campaigned against police

---

tasked, with Colacello and Cutrone, with finding models, remembered two other models, Iris and Michele Long. Only one model remains unidentified. Information about the models and the sittings can be found in *CR4*, 26–29.

113 For accounts of Johnson's life and activism, see the biographical film *Pay It No Mind: The Life and Times of Marsha P Johnson*, directed by Michael Kasino and Richard Morrison (2012, 54 minutes; accessed at https://www.youtube.com/watch?v=rjN9W2KstqE, April 5, 2013), and David Carter, *Stonewall: The Riots That Sparked the Gay Revolution* (New York: St. Martins, 2004). The fullest history of STAR can be found in Stephan L. Cohen, *The Gay Liberation Youth Movement in New York: "An Army of Lovers Cannot Fail"* (New York: Routledge, 2008), 89–163. On STAR, also see Leslie P. Feinberg, "Street Transvestite Action Revolutionaries," *Workers World*, September 24, 2006, http://www.workers.org/2006/us/lavender-red-73/ (accessed April 5, 2013), and *Street Transvestite Action Revolutionaries: Survival Revolt and Queer Antagonist Struggle*, a zine collecting writings related to the group by Untorelli Press, http://zinelibrary.info/files/STAR.pdf.

114 Per Feinberg's account in *Workers World*: "'STAR came about after a sit-in at Weinstein Hall at New York University in 1970, Rivera explained to me, in an interview in 1998, four years before her death. The protest at NYU erupted after the administration cancelled planned dances there, reportedly because a gay organization was sponsoring the events. GLF, Radicalesbians and other activists held a sit-in at Weinstein Hall. They won the right to use the venue." See also Cohen, *Gay Liberation Youth Movement*, 111–18.

115 See, for instance, the 1971 Gay Liberation Front Manifesto (revised 1978), where the GLF argues that gay liberation requires a "revolutionary change in our whole society," including the abolition of the patriarchal family and the "gender-role system" and the creation of gay communes (https://legacy.fordham.edu/halsall/pwh/glf-london.asp).

116 See Cohen, *Gay Liberation Youth Movement*, on the place of transvestites in gay liberation (107–11). On the one hand, transvestites were "uniquely prepared to engage in the types of explosive front-line confrontation risked during the Stonewall riots,"

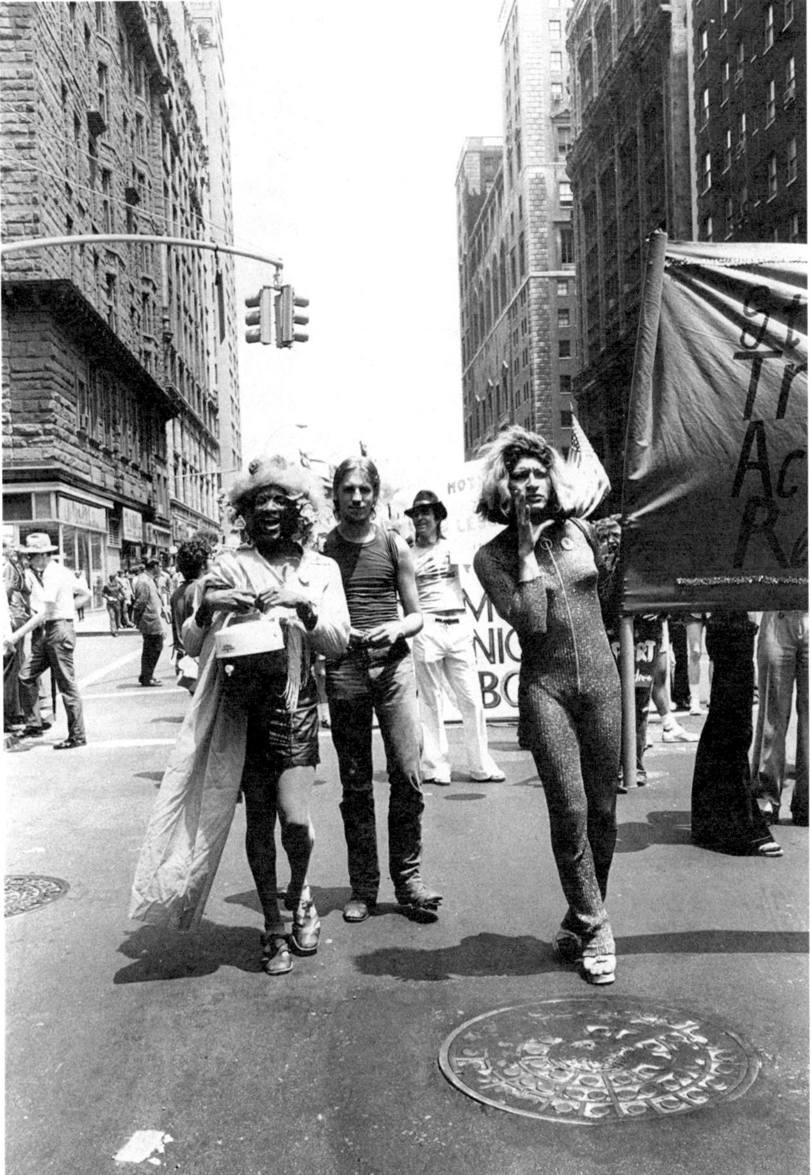

4.10 Marsha P. Johnson, Sylvia Rivera, and others, Christopher Street Liberation Day Gay Pride Parade, June 24, 1973. Photograph: Leonard Fink, courtesy LGBT Community Center National History Archive.

harassment, for the improvement of unsafe, violent prison conditions, and more generally for transvestite (which would now be called transgender)

---

and they were clearly nourished by the radical, expansive rhetoric of the gay liberation movement. On the other hand, they were sometimes seen as politically expendable, and their concerns were often not the same as those of gay men and lesbians who were less gender-nonconforming and whose lives were less precarious.

rights.[117] In 1973 Johnson spoke of STAR's objectives: "We don't want to see gay people picked up on the streets for things like loitering or having sex or anything like that. . . . Our main goal is to see gay people liberated and free and have equal rights that other people have in America. We'd like to see our gay brothers and sisters out of jail and on the streets again."[118] In addition to stressing classic civil rights such as freedom from police harassment and equal protection under the law, Johnson also asserts the right to occupy public space and engage in public sex. Moreover, she writes, " STAR is a very revolutionary group. We believe in picking up the gun, starting a revolution if necessary." Tapping into the militant rhetoric of groups like the Gay Liberation Front and Third World Gay Revolution, as well as the Black Panther Party and the Young Lords (with whom GLF and STAR marched in 1970 to protest police repression), she made it clear that nonviolent resistance was not STAR's strategy.[119]

Most urgently, STAR was oriented toward questions of daily survival, especially food and shelter. For this reason, Susan Stryker writes, Rivera and Johnson "opened STAR House, an overtly politicized version of the "house" culture that already characterized black and Latino queer kinship networks, where dozens of transgender youth could count on a free and safe place to sleep."[120] Johnson and Rivera hustled for money to pay rent and provide for food and clothing, and also hoped to use the space in the East Village (which lasted for less than a year) as a makeshift school to educate the kids, many of whom had been forced to leave home and school at young ages.[121] Thus, STAR's was a concrete group practice, oriented toward collective survival in a hostile, homophobic, transphobic, and racist environment, but also toward a radical transformation of that environment. Its praxis was queer in the utopian, anticipatory sense that Muñoz powerfully stressed; it aimed to *make* a world in which people like STAR's members would be valued. In the formal practices that characterize the Ladies and Gentlemen series, I think Warhol engaged in an analogous task: he sought to create an aesthetic world where a collectivity such as STAR's could find a home. In so doing, he would create a space in which he felt valued and welcome, too.

117 In so doing, Michael Bronski remarked, "out of almost nothing, Sylvia and Marsha essentially started, what was to become, more than 20 years later, the transgender movement that we know today." Bronski, "Sylvia Rivera: 1951–2002: No Longer on the Back of the Bumper," *Z Magazine* (2002); quoted by Cohen, *Gay Liberation Youth Movement*, 93.
118 "Rapping with a Street Transvestite Revolutionary," in *Out of the Closets: Voice of Gay Liberation*, ed. Karla Jay and Allen Young (1972; New York: Jove/HBJ, 1977), 112–20, 113.
119 On marching with the Young Lords, see Cohen, *Gay Liberation Youth Movement*, 131. See also Third World Gay Revolution (New York City), "What We Want, What We Believe," in Jay and Young, *Out of the Closets*, 363–68.
120 Susan Stryker, *Transgender History* (Berkeley, CA: Seal Press, 2008), 86–87.
121 Cohen describes STAR House as lasting from November 1970 to July 1971. It was located at 213 E. 2nd Street.

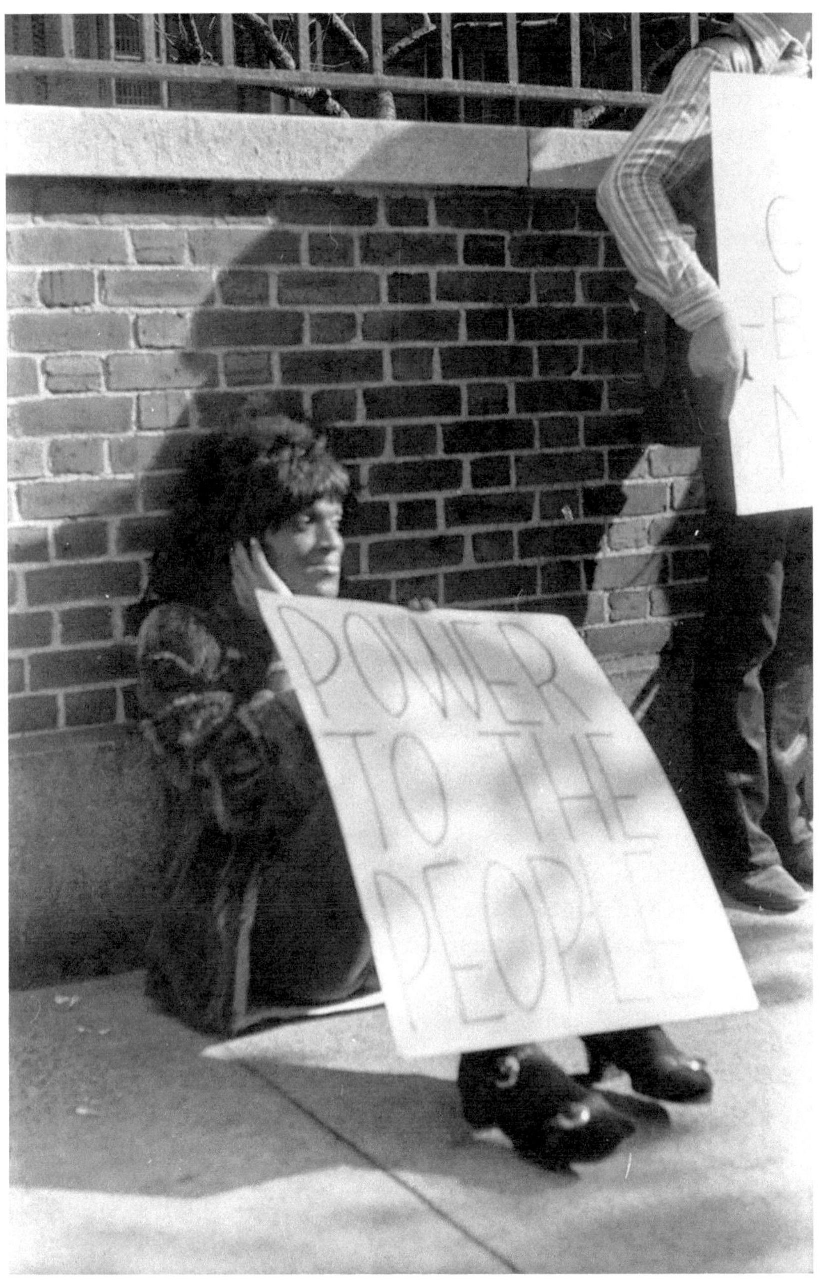

4.11 Marsha P. Johnson, Gay Liberation Front protest at Bellevue Hospital, Fall 1970. Photograph: Richard Wandel, courtesy LGBT Community Center National History Archive.

Looking through the Polaroids (and the photos that Ronnie Cutrone took documenting the sittings), one can easily imagine that, as Vincent Fremont said, Warhol made these sittings "exciting and special," so that the queens could enjoy doing "their favorite poses and act[ing] glamorous for Andy's camera."[122] The models Broadway, Easha, Ivette, Kim, Lurdes, Monique, Vicki, Alphanso Panell, Helen Morales, Marsha P. Johnson, Wilhelmina Ross, Iris, and Michele were each captured in winning star-turn poses. And when the Polaroids are transformed into paintings, drawing, and prints, we see that Warhol has assisted and amplified the drag queens' self-presentation by excising those male signs (along with other blemishes or unattractive details) that the drag queens had not themselves managed to get rid of. In the paintings, he dramatizes the female signs by drawing our attention to lips, eyes, hair, and clothes with bright hues, mimicking the eye-catching work of makeup and wigs with his paint. In his drawings, such as the depiction in figure 4.12 of Wilhelmina Ross (who emerges as something like the star of the series, the model Warhol depicted more than any of the others), Warhol repeats and appreciates the double work of drag by lavishing the attention of his pencil on such details as her eyelashes, eyes, full lips, and the design of the scarf wrapped around her head and by simply not drawing whatever male signs might have been present in the Polaroid on which the drawing is based.[123] As Wilhelmina leans on her hand, long nails dangling, framing her chin and drawing our attention again to her mouth (while partially concealing her neck), we are dazzled by her glamour. Warhol performs in these portraits a version of the work he regularly did in his commissioned portraits, where he erased wrinkles, cut off double chins, altered skin color, removed zits, and made eyes brighter and lips fuller.[124] Indeed, the labor of drag (in its doubled tasks of erasure and redrawing) could be seen as a paradigm for his portraits more generally, a connection further highlighted when we remember that his portraits, in their stylized brilliance, did not refer to a "real" face so much as to an ideal model, the "star."[125] By following their work with his, Warhol's portraiture is mimetic and methexic; he not only imitates the drag queens' practice but participates in it.[126]

Warhol's impulse toward imitation as a mode of both affirmation and participation is evident in the particular "painterliness" of the paintings

122 Press release, "Andy Warhol. Ladies and Gentlemen," Gagosian Gallery, New York, September 3–October 11, 1997; quoted in *CR4*, 27.

123 On Ross and her career as a performer, see Jimmy Camicia, *My Dear Sweet Self: A Hot Peach Life* (Silverton, OR: Fast Books, 2013), and *CR4*, 46–50.

124 See *Phil*, 51, 63, and Flatley, "Warhol Gives Good Face," for more on his portrait practice.

125 Here, I'm borrowing from my argument in "Warhol Gives Good Face."

126 See Jean-Luc Nancy on drawing, mimesis, and methexis in *The Pleasure in Drawing* (New York: Fordham University Press, 2013), 64. See also Nancy, *Listening* (New York: Fordham University Press, 2007), 10.

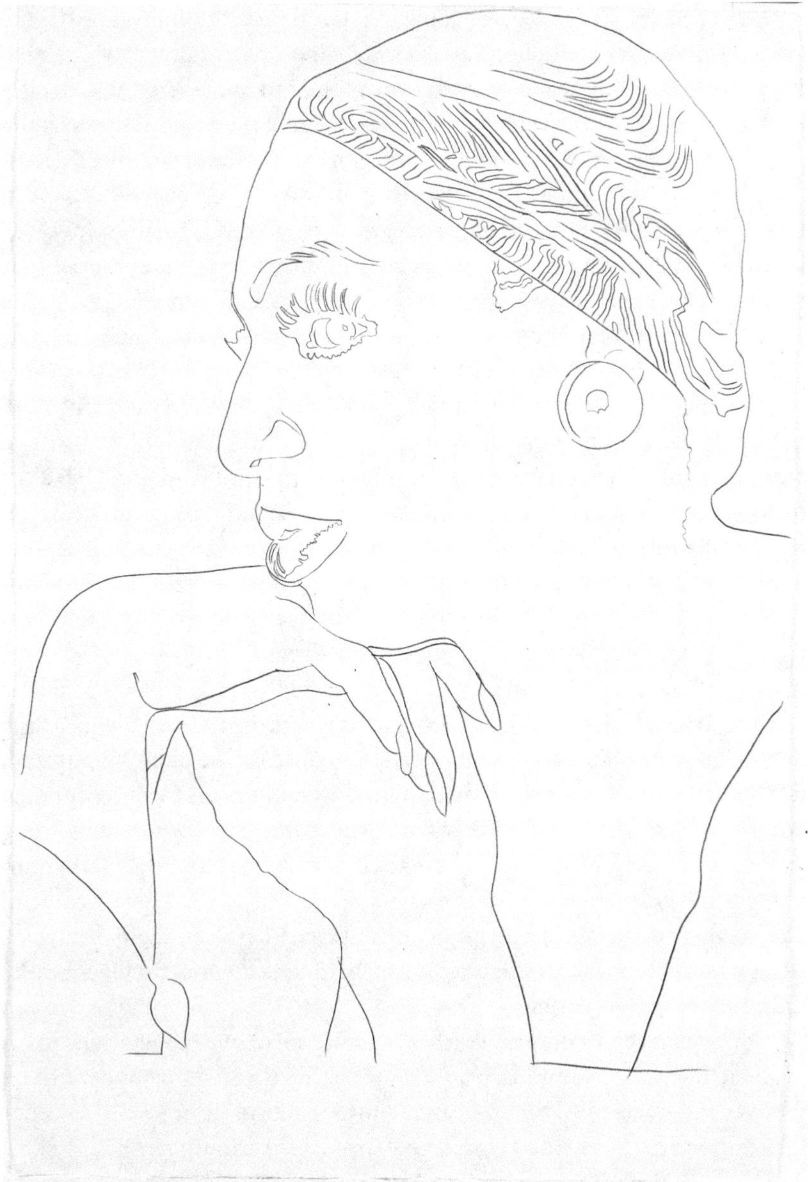

4.12 Andy Warhol, *Ladies and Gentlemen (Wilhelmina Ross)*, 1975. Pencil on paper, 40½ × 27½ inches. © 2014 The Andy Warhol Foundation for the Visual Arts/Artists Rights Society (ARS), New York.

in this series, and especially in his new approach to color. Printz notes that with this body of work, Warhol began "to superimpose local colors and the background over a base layer of color, uniformly spread over the entire surface of the canvas and directly on top of the primer" (*CR4*, 32). Warhol here abandons the aesthetic principle of white as neutral unmarked background at the level of composition; instead, like his models, he begins his artwork with a space already marked as nonwhite. It is difficult to know how the underlayers concretely affected the overall look of the paintings, what effect they exerted on the colors painted over them, but the layeredness itself *is* visible. The edges of brushstrokes and congealed lines and drops of paint are apparent, sometimes dramatically so, on most of these paintings. This is a surface that has been worked and covered, worked and covered. As an allegory of the work of drag, it suggests how the repeated imitations involved in acquiring the gestures and comportment of a given gender model may function like a lapidary re-covering that "perceptually reorganizes . . . the physical 'givens' of a body" even as it leaves visible, to the attentive eye, those "givens" that we now perceive differently.[127]

The layering effect is dramatized by the scores through the paint Warhol made with his fingers. In many paintings, these manipulations draw together paint from different layers, bringing up paint from the "base" or mixing paint from distinct areas of the canvas. Sometimes, as in the painting of Wilhelmina reproduced here (figure 4.13, plate 5; one example among many), he has scored the thick paint so sharply that the resulting ridges interrupt the subsequent silkscreening on the surface of the painting, allowing the colors on and around the ridges to show through the printed ink. Here, like a stubborn Adam's apple, bit of beard, or oddly colored patch of skin, a disruptive physicality peeks through and prevents the face from being fully defined. But in coming to the surface, it does not mar the painting. Instead, it brings surprising colors into visibility, which themselves form compelling points of visual attraction. Rather than expose the places where these drag queens may have failed to cover over their signs of masculinity, Warhol imitates and echoes them with his own painterly accidents. These beautiful and singular mistakes create points of similarity between the paintings, a reparative analogue for the way a certain "wrongness" brought together the drag queens they represent.

Underscoring this point is Warhol's disruption of our expectations in his placement of color. Sometimes, faces are painted with what appear to be more or less "accurate" references to the look of the sitter's skin. At other times, they are clearly the "wrong" colors: bright yellows, purples, greens, and blues all appear as skin surface. In many instances, across depictions of a single sitter, skin, hair, eyes, and lips change color and shift position from painting to painting, as does the silkscreen ink, which is often green or purple instead of black. Although Warhol uses bright hues like makeup, as Printz suggests, to "isolate and accentuate a selected feature of the face," such as the mouth or eyes, these eye-drawing isolations are also often significantly off register.[128] Moreover, in many of the paintings, zones of color disrupt

127 Michael Moon and Eve Kosofsky Sedgwick, "Divinity: A Dossier, A Performance Piece, A Little Understood Emotion," in Sedgwick, *Tendencies*, 215–51, 220.
128 Printz, *CR3*, 420.

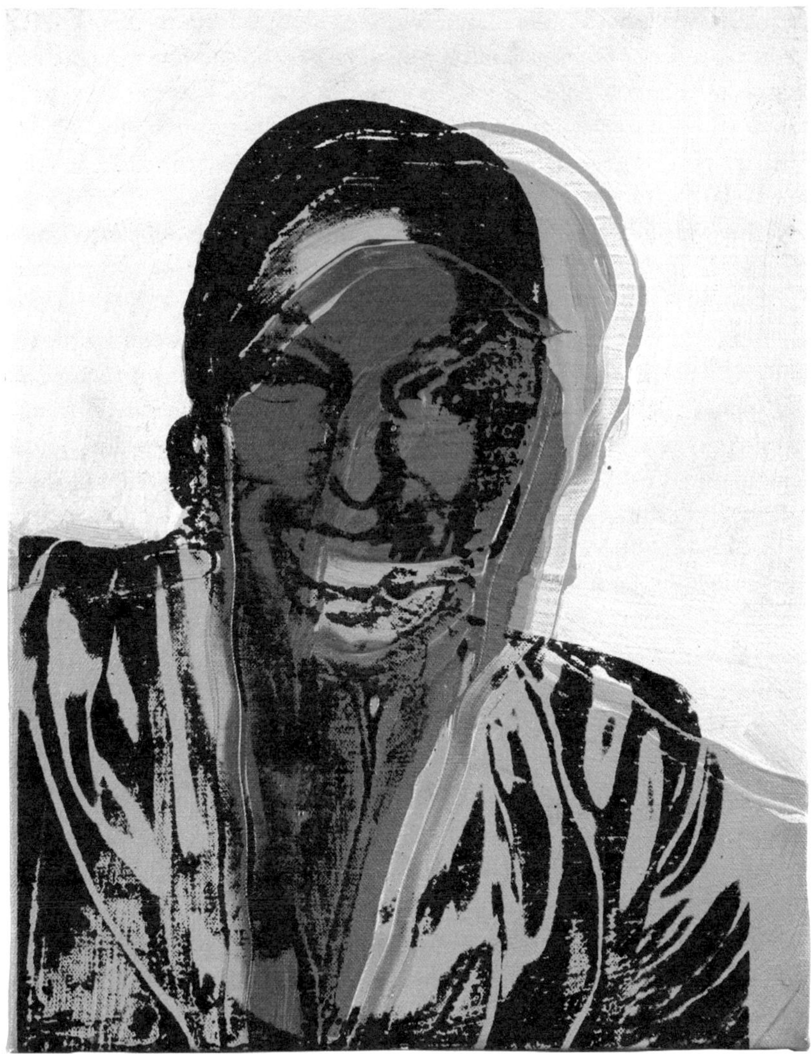

4.13 Andy Warhol, *Ladies and Gentlemen (Wilhelmina Ross)*. 1975. Acrylic and silkscreen ink on linen, 14 × 11 inches. © 2014 The Andy Warhol Foundation for the Visual Arts/ Artists Rights Society (ARS), New York.

the figure or obscure facial features entirely, giving the portraits the characteristics of a mask. Sometimes (as in many of the thirty-nine 32-by-26-inch paintings of Alphonso Panell [*CR*, cat. nos. 2870–2908], some of Wilhelmina Ross [esp. 2856–2861], and some of Lurdes [esp. 2831–2833]), the face is divided into distinct zones of color. Warhol's abstract patches seem designed for painterly pleasing and seduction, as much when they amplify our perception of lips or eyes as when they are in tension with our apprehension of the face as such. In a few instances, the screened face is barely visible because the background is so similar in color. When we put all of these uses of color together, it is difficult not to notice how important color is to our ability to discern features and recognize faces (and the role it might play in making a face female, "black," "white," or "Latina"). At the same time, however, we see that color operates on a distinct but overlapping register from the perception of facial features and the contours of the head, one that may deface as much as (or at the same time as) it makes a face. Considered together, Warhol's uses of color in these paintings seem to call into question the possibility or desirability of there being a "right" color.[129]

"Wrong" color plays an important role in Warhol's gorgeous portraits of Ivette and Lurdes. In all twenty-nine portraits of the two, based on three Polaroids, Ivette leans affectionately and intimately on Lurdes from behind. In one (figure 4.14, plate 6), Warhol's uses a vibrant, light bluish-green around the edge of their faces where we might otherwise expect to find figure-defining shadow. The effect, Printz writes, "is optical, but counter illusionistic; Warhol's finger painting signals artifice."[130] Like makeup, the bright paint here highlights certain zones of the painting's surface; however, this eye-catching color underscores the "wrong" spot, putting a pleasing artificiality on display. The painting itself imitates, without copying, the complex and showy artwork the drag queens are engaged in. Like the drag queens from the Gilded Grape ("tell your friend I do a lot more for fifty bucks"), Warhol is showing us what he will do for the money.[131]

The luminous display of painterly artificiality also visually connects the pair. As the color wiggles along the edge of Lurdes's left cheek down to her chin and then back up to Ivette's face at the point where their cheeks come together in the center of the painting, Warhol's finger has literally drawn the two together. On Ivette's cheek, at the edge of her eye, Warhol's finger seems to have dropped a tear-shaped bit of magenta (perhaps carried on the side of a finger from Lurdes's hair), which mixes into the green as it flows down the tracks laid by Warhol's finger. Fainter squiggles extend to the top of Ivette's head, where they mark the boundary between figure and ground like a soft, shimmering halo or faded crown. Moving out to the edges of the painting, Warhol has set triangles of the same light green on the two models' shoulders, framing their figures in the color that also joins them. In so doing, like Ivette leaning her hands on Lurdes, Warhol places his affectionate hands on

129 "As Warhol remarked in 1981 about the use of color in his portraits, 'I use mostly artificial colors. I'm trying to find flesh color . . . I've so many different color . . . flesh colors, but maybe one day I'll get the right flesh color'" (Lucie-Smith, "Conversations with Artists," 4).

130 Printz, *CR3*, 420. The paint may look more blue than green in some reproductions. Printz notes that in the original transparency, the paint looks to be "not as blue as phthalo green or turquoise, more like what Liquetex calls 'permanent green deep,' in a pale tint" (email correspondence with author, March 22, 2017).

131 On the connections between drag, prostitution, and Warhol's "self-production as an artist," see Doyle, "Tricks of the Trade."

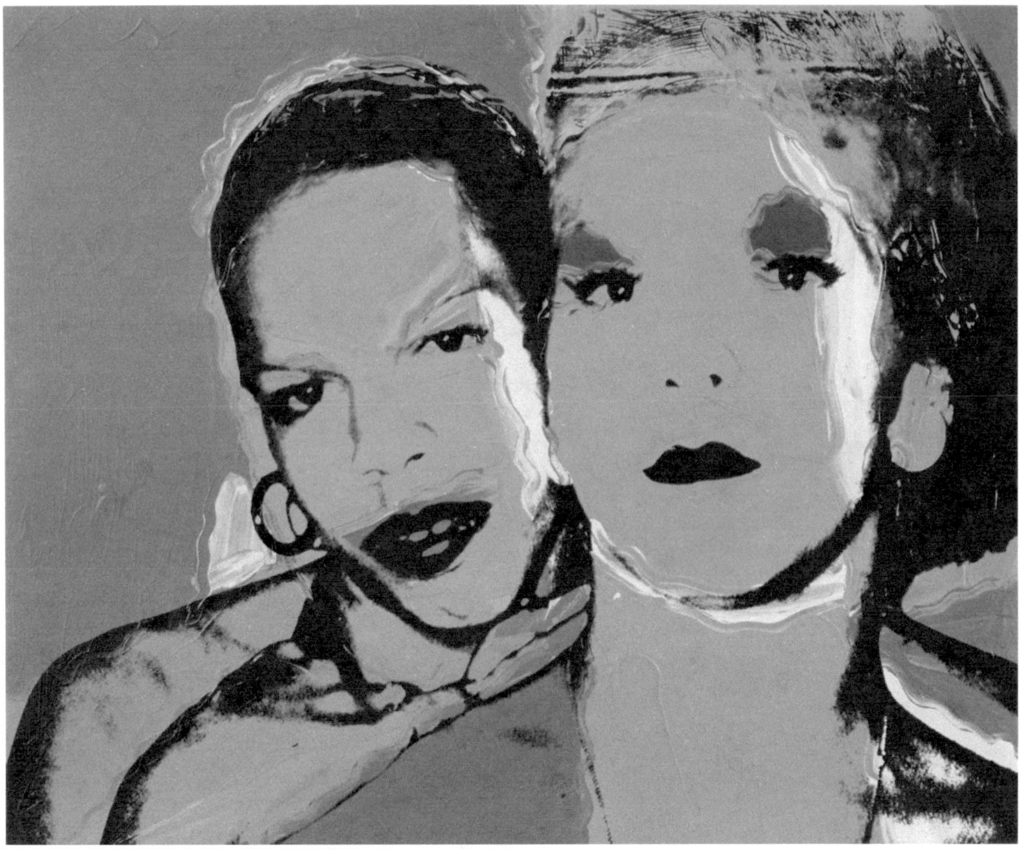

4.14 Andy Warhol, *Ladies and Gentlemen (Ivette and Lurdes)*, 1975, acrylic and silk screen on canvas, 50 × 40 inches. © 2014 The Andy Warhol Foundation for the Visual Arts/ Artists Rights Society (ARS), New York.

their collective shoulders. Here, the wrong color marks a site of connection and consolation.

In his print editions of the drag queens, Warhol uses torn paper to create patches of color under the halftone screen.[132] Each print is based on a collage in which a halftone acetate (enlarged from a Polaroid) is superimposed over the torn papers in a way that recalls the layering in the paintings. This clear layering of thin but separable, solid materials has its own way of mimicking the effects of repeated imitation, its creation of second and third skins that cumulatively create a nonhomogeneous surface. Unlike the paintings, where underlying layers of paint are mostly covered (except for places where it was mixed while wet or pokes through the screen ink), the

132 The blocks of collaged paper were first used in a print of Paloma Picasso, where they seem to reference Paloma's father—with whom Warhol was obsessed—and his famous and influential use of torn paper in the *papier colles*. Thanks to Neil Printz for pointing this out to me, and see his notation, *CR3*, 412.

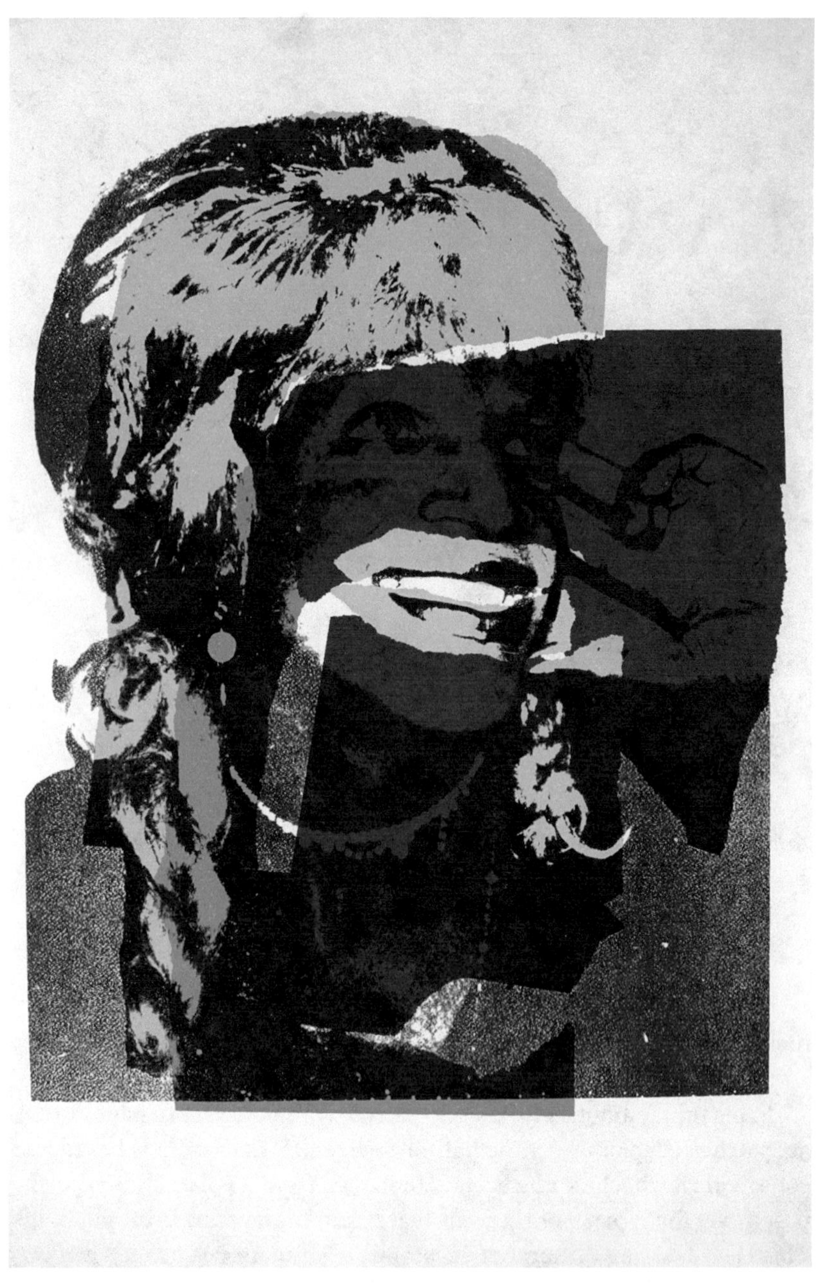

4. 15 Andy Warhol, *Ladies and Gentlemen (Marsha P. Johnson)*, 1975. Screenprint on Arches paper, 43½ × 28½ inches. © 2014 The Andy Warhol Foundation for the Visual Arts/Artists Rights Society (ARS), New York.

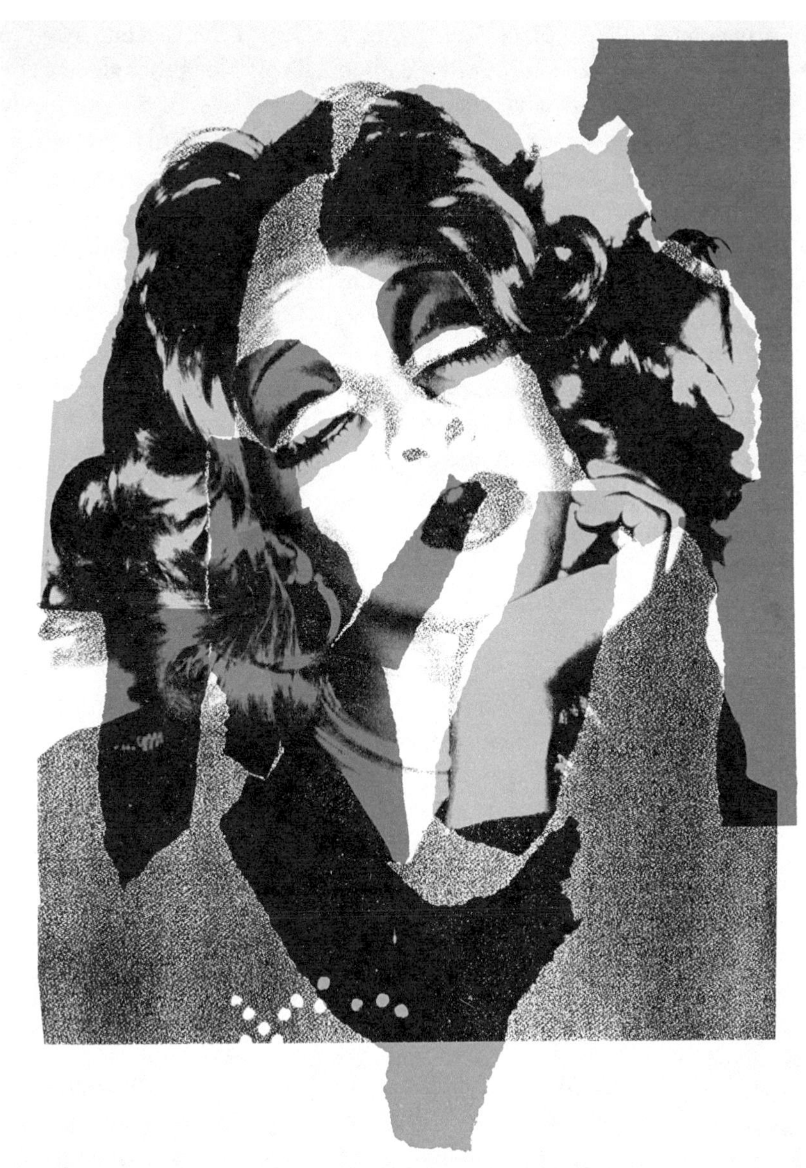

4.16 Andy Warhol, *Ladies and Gentlemen (Easha McCleary)*, 1975. Screenprint on Arches paper, 43½ × 28½ inches. © 2014 The Andy Warhol Foundation for the Visual Arts/ Artists Rights Society (ARS), New York.

layering in the collages places transparent (yet still visible) acetate over the torn paper, so that the colors underneath remain visible (although it can be hard to discern exactly what color resides on which layer of the complexly constructed collages). It is as if Warhol is showing us the shards of shimmering affective intensity lying just underneath and animating aspects of pose and expression.[133]

In one collage portrait of Iris (figure 4.17, plate 8), confetti-like patches of color surround her, as if emanating from her in a spiral originating from the bright band of red around her fingernails. Some of the torn scraps of yellow, red, blue, and a bit of gold (or parts of them) can be seen underneath the arm, as if they are supporting its provocative turn. But they also look like they are being spread around by her twirling arm, as if she had just scattered bits of glamour into the air, some of which still drips from her glowing fingertips. Around her eyes, patches of yellow draw our attention to this radiant center safely inside the arc formed by her arm, protecting and framing as it bedazzles.

Drag subjectivity in Warhol's collages and prints is composed not by the skin as cover (nor by some authentic interior waiting to be expressed), but by the patches of visibly torn, borrowed color disidentificatorily collaged together. As Printz observes, these queens are not miming individual star models but are cobbling together their own personae from different poses and female signs (*CR4*, 31–32). Drag for these black and Latina drag queens is collage work. This portrait of Iris shows how the "glittering alternative" is both appropriated and shared; it is shared by being appropriated. By sharing this fundamental shareability drag queens keep that alternative both "alive and available."

Celebrity is a powerful aesthetic and affective presence in the series; these drag queens are stars. The structure of this stardom is emphasized and complicated by the formal juxtaposition of Ladies and Gentlemen with a set of similar prints and collages of Mick Jagger, which were composed around the same time, and with which they shared at least one gallery exhibition (at the end of 1975 at Max Protetch in Washington, DC).[134] In looking at these works together, one might think, for instance, of the importance of Jagger's flamboyant sex appeal to his celebrity, and may remember that Jagger and the Rolling Stones had posed in drag before, for the cover of the single "Have you Seen Your Mother, Baby (Standing in the Shadow)," and would again a couple years later for the cover of *Some Girls*. The pairing thus seems to invoke the fan-based mimetic practices central to Jagger and the drag queens, practices that, in each case, involve a collagelike liking and imitation across the color line. Like many white music stars before and after him, Jagger's

133 There are more of these collages than were required to serve as maquettes for the prints.

134 Thanks to Eric Lott for conversation on Warhol and Jagger, and for his insightful "Andy's Mick," delivered at the Association for the Arts of the Present (ASAP) conference in Pittsburgh (ASAP/3), October 27–30, 2011.

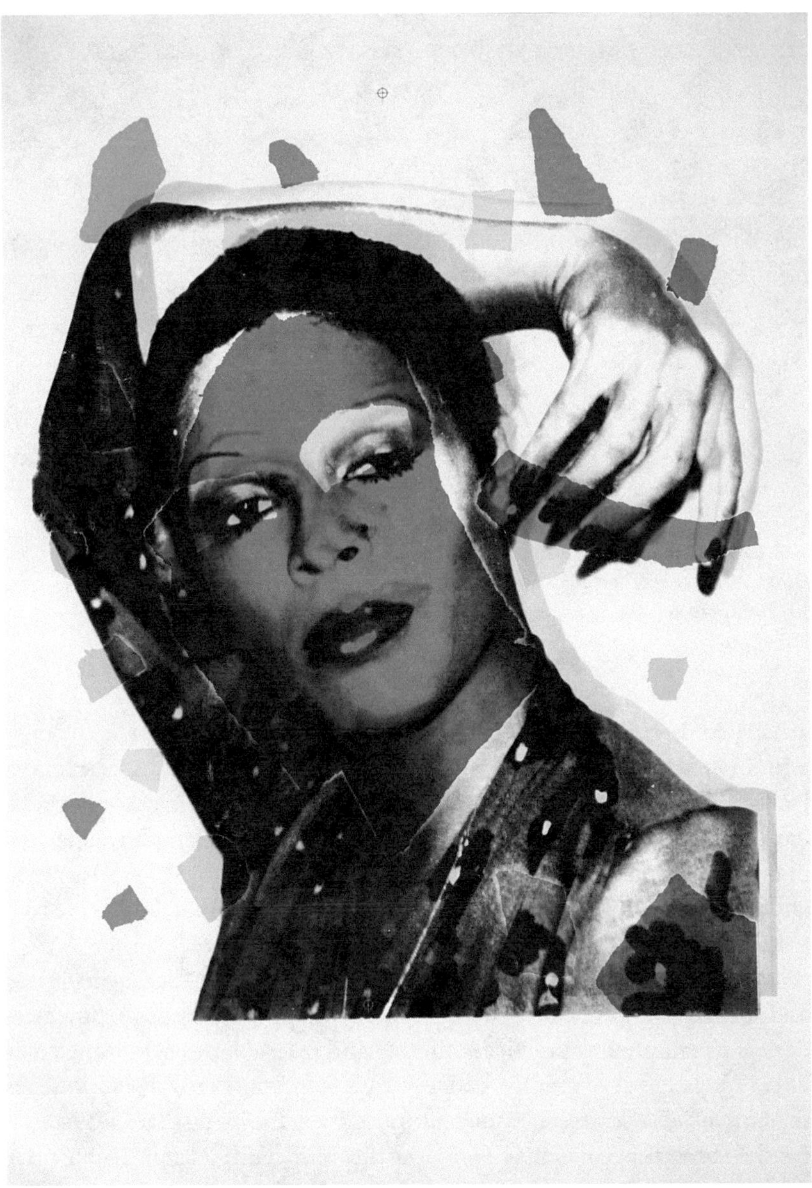

4.17 Andy Warhol, *Ladies and Gentlemen (Iris)*, 1975. Collage, 24 × 18 inches. © 2014 The Andy Warhol Foundation for the Visual Arts/Artists Rights Society (ARS), New York.

musical practices and star persona are based on an imitation of black singers and musicians. As Keith Richards recounts it in his autobiography, the Rolling Stones' musical collaboration originated in the bandmates' shared obsession with black blues musicians from Chicago and repeated listening to their records, which the Stones eagerly imitated.[135] As drag queens may

135 "As long as we were all together," Richards writes, "we could pretend to be black men." Yet, even though "we soaked up the music . . . it didn't change the color of our

max protetch 2151 p street, n.w., washington, d.c. 20037

opening dec.6, 1975

GERALD FORD POLITICAL PORTRAITS
FLOWERS
OTHER WARHOL FAVORITES

and new portfolios of:

MICK JAGGER
DRAG QUEENS

4.18 Exhibition announcement, *Andy Warhol's Gerald Ford, Political Portraits, Flowers, Other Warhol Favorites, Mick Jagger, and Drag Queens*, Max Protetch Gallery, New York, 1975. Printed ink on paper, 3¼ × 5½ inches. Collection of the Andy Warhol Museum, Pittsburgh.

archive in their bodies an ideal movie-star womanhood through layers of repetition animated by liking, so Jagger and the Stones archive an ideal of black vocality and musicianship in the performance of their music. Jagger's dancing too, owes more than a little to traditions of black performance. To many eyes, including Warhol's, Jagger's dancing resembled Tina Turner's, and while Warhol thought perhaps that she was copying him, he was pleased to hear from somebody that "*she* taught *him* how to dance."[136]

With *Marilyn Diptych*, Ladies and Gentlemen, and the Mick Jagger prints and collages, we have a set of distinct examples for thinking about how stardom is constituted by practices of liking and resemblance across the color line. I made the case that the variably dark (sometimes nearly black) faces in *Marilyn Diptych* reference the multiraciality of the liking that she inspired (at the same time that they highlight the artificiality of her Technicolor whiteness). Indeed, being available for such affective possession across the color line *and* across the gender divide was constitutive of her stardom. The Jagger portraits (especially if we pair them with the drag queens), on the other hand, seem to be less about Jagger's fans than about the black models he copied to become a star (figure 4.19, plate 9). A different paradigm is at work in the Ladies and Gentlemen representation of the expansive power of celebrity glamour. Even if one cannot identify specific white stars as models

skin." In short, "We just wanted to be black motherfuckers." Richards and James Fox, *Life* (New York: Little, Brown, and Company), 103–4.

136 *Diaries*, August 2, 1985, 666.

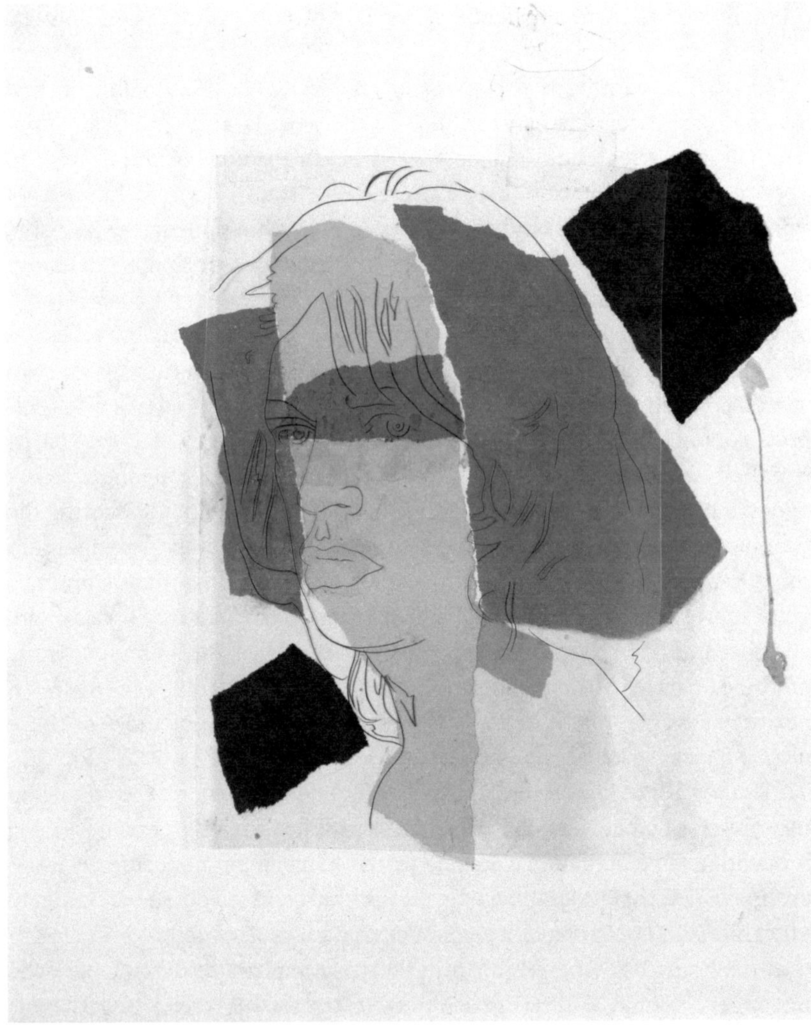

4.19 Andy Warhol, *Mick Jagger*, 1975. Screenprint on acetate and colored graphic art paper collage on board, 16⅞ × 13⅞ inches. © 2016 The Andy Warhol Foundation for the Visual Arts/Artists Rights Society (ARS), New York.

for the drag queens' self-presentations, their poses and gestures draw from a history of Hollywood movie-star glamour strongly biased toward whiteness. At the same time, one may see the looks of iconic black stars like Diana Ross and Tina Turner in the wigs and poses here. Warhol's works allow us to see these drag queens as engaged in a mimetic practice that reparatively and disidentificatorily reassembles fragmented codes of stardom, mixing and changing and recoloring them. This mimetic practice avows a black and brown stardom, one these drag queens have both referenced and created, a stardom—or perhaps STARdom—that powers the performances of femininity collected here and also provides a way for them to be-with each other, indeed to form a collectivity capable of both comfort and political action.

Indeed, in naming their organization STAR, Marsha P. Johnson and Sylvia Rivera recognized and publicized the fact that their political, oppositional, communal, and activist way of being-together rested at least in part on a shared imitation of and affection for stars. The nonwhiteness of this STARdom is interestingly underscored in Warhol's portrait of Johnson, especially in its presentation of Johnson's blond wig. Among the 268 Ladies and Gentlemen paintings, there are only two portraits of Johnson (both based on the same Polaroid), fewer than of any other model in the series. In both, Johnson smiles broadly while appearing to look skyward, perhaps even campily rolling her eyes. In one portrait, her blond pigtailed wig is a light-brown or tan just a few shades lighter than her skin (figure 4.20, plate 10). A streak of orange running through one pigtail is repeated by a longer streak over the background blue on the left side of the painting, underscoring the framing effect of the pigtails but also drawing our eyes away from them. In the other painting, Johnson's skin is a dark purplish brown and contrasts quite sharply with the blond wig, which brilliantly leaps to the foreground, an effect amplified by the bluish-green ink Warhol has used in screening the halftone. In each painting, the pigtailed wig seems to present a central compositional problem, and perhaps Warhol did not paint any more of these pictures because he was not sure how to resolve it.

The wig is not just "wrong," like any female wig on a man would be, in the sense (as Esther Newton writes) that it signifies "that the person wearing it is a homosexual, that he is a male who is behaving in a specifically inappropriate way, that he is a man who places himself as a woman in relation to other men."[137] Being blond, it is also a charged sign of whiteness on a brown-skinned body. But where Johnson otherwise appears feminine, she does not appear "white." This is not an effort at "successful" racial drag; there is nothing like an attempt to "pass." Instead, we see a paradigmatic instance of what Muñoz called disidentification, in which a potentially toxic, "dominant structure is coopted, worked on and against."[138] The wig publicly performs a disidentification with whiteness, at once representing the desire to be white, and showily announcing its failure, suggesting the degree to which that desire is not equally available to a person with brown skin, who cannot approximate a fantasy ideal of white womanhood by dying her hair blond, as Norma Jeane Mortenson Baker did in becoming Marilyn Monroe. The significance of the appeal of white femininity, and the privileges and pleasures that appear go along with it, may here be avowed and recognized. But at the same time, that whiteness is presented as itself pointedly fake, and not even glamorous. The "wrongness" of Johnson's possession of whiteness

137 Newton, *Mother Camp*, 103.

138 See Muñoz *Disidentifications*, 108, and more generally chaps. 4 ("'The White to Be Angry': Vaginal Creme Davis's Terrorist Drag") and 5 ("Sister Acts: Ela Troyano and Carmelita Tropicana"), on drag and disidentification.

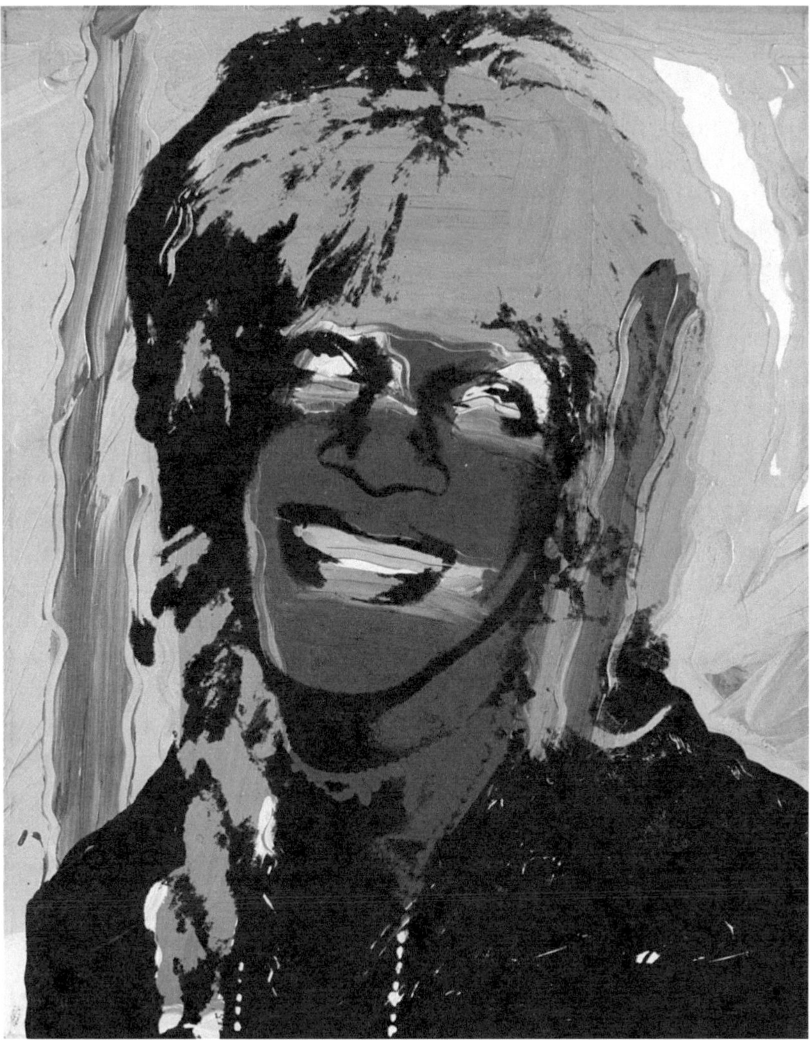

4.20 Andy Warhol, *Ladies and Gentlemen (Marsha P. Johnson)*, 1975. Acrylic and silkscreen ink on linen, 50 × 40 inches. Udo and Anette Brandhorst Collection. © 2016 The Andy Warhol Foundation for the Visual Arts/Artists Rights Society (ARS), New York. Photograph: bpk Bildagentur/Museum Brandhorst/Art Resource, NY.

here may be amplified by her wig's pigtails, which properly "belong" to a younger person, like Dorothy in *The Wizard of Oz*. It is as if Johnson wants precisely to communicate that she may not succeed in looking like a white star, but that this failure is itself the point since it succeeds in signifying and enacting her participation in a collectivity of spectators disidentificatorily attached to the glittering alternative promised by ideal movie-star femininity.[139]

139 This is analogous to the argument Muñoz makes about queer virtuosity and failure in *Cruising Utopia*, esp. 178–81.

The importance of defiance and abjection to the glamour present in such an alternative is suggested by Warhol's placement of a double-exposed Polaroid of Johnson opposite a picture of Divine (the star of many John Waters films) in one of the "red books" in which he arranged his Polaroids. Perhaps Warhol saw Johnson's "saintliness" as an analogue to Divine's "divinity," which Michael Moon and Eve Sedgwick understood to be "a feeling or attitude" that arose from a "certain interface of abjection and defiance." The product of this feeling, they argue, is the "subjectivity of glamour itself."[140] By connecting her to Divine (and to Lance Loud, who is also present in this red book), Warhol offers a small, compelling pantheon of queer heroes at this historical moment. In so doing, he also points to the nature of Saint Marsha's political work, her genial, persistent, and energetic public defiance of gender norms, her opposition to homophobia, and her support of other transvestites. In encouraging us to think about how Marsha P. Johnson may be like Divine, Warhol extends the project that I have been arguing characterizes Ladies and Gentlemen as a whole, one that mimics, complements, and seeks to participate in the project of STAR. That is, Warhol here represents a group of marginalized black and Latina drag queens in a way that shows us what brings them together: a defiant, reparative attachment to and imitation of the glittering alternative presented by movie-star femininity. This practice of becoming-like makes each drag queen like a star but also makes them like each other. These shared mimetic efforts move along "slantwise lines" to create "affective and relational virtualities," modes of conviviality and friendship, apparent and celebrated in Warhol's paintings, that were themselves the conditions of possibility for STAR to come into existence. As Johnson put it, "Usually most transvestites are friendly towards one another because they're just alike."[141]

"Like Jean-Michel"

Warhol's friendship and collaboration with Jean-Michel Basquiat marked a turning point in the career of each artist. The work they produced together developed each artist's preoccupation with the color line as an institution and technology that enables some actions while barring others. Basquiat had admired Warhol for several years before becoming his regular companion, work-out partner, and collaborator from sometime in 1983 until September 1985, when negative reviews of their joint show at Tony Shafrazi prompted Basquiat to stop seeing Warhol so frequently.[142]

140 Moon and Sedgwick, "Divinity," 218.

141 "Rapping with a Street Transvestite Revolutionary," 117.

142 One can trace Warhol's relationship to Basquiat in his *Diaries*. He mentions having lunch with Basquiat and Bruno Bischofberger on October 4, 1984. On September 19, 1985, Warhol sees the reviews of the show: "When we were at Odeon I asked for the paper, and there in Friday's Times I saw a big headline 'Basquiat and Warhol in Pas de

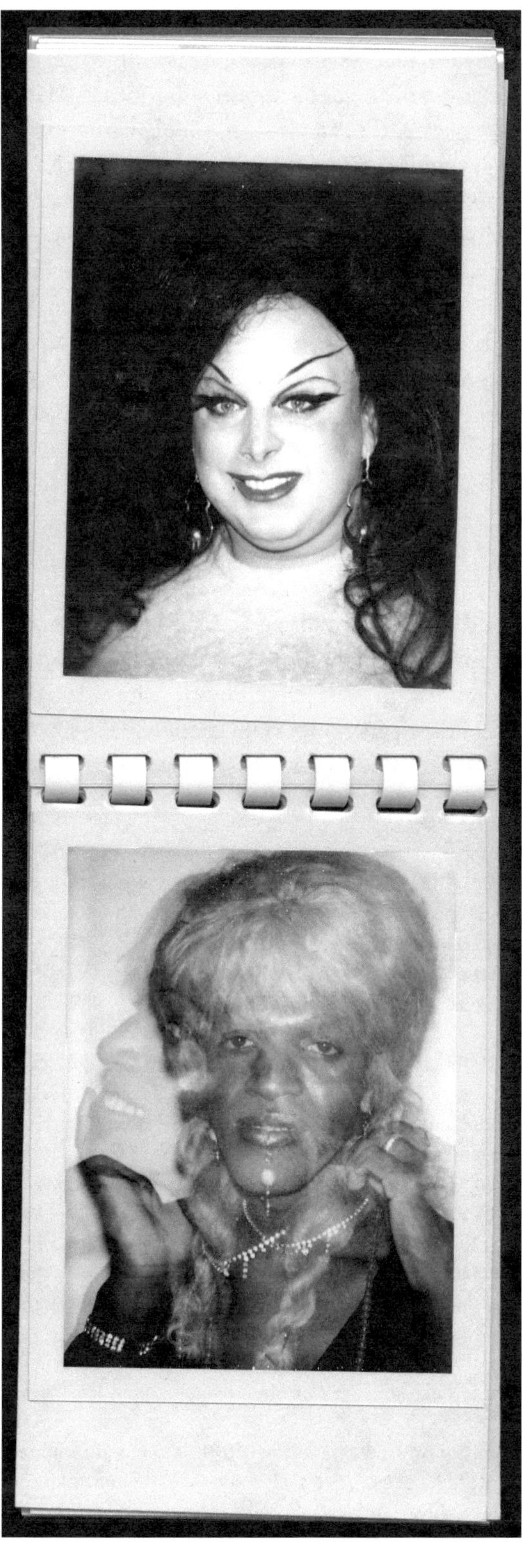

4.21 Andy Warhol, little red book with Polaroids of Divine and Marsha P. Johnson, 1974. © 2016 The Andy Warhol Foundation for the Visual Arts/Artists Rights Society (ARS), New York.

Basquiat made several portraits of Warhol, including a little-known drawing composed by using black marker to color Warhol's face on the cover of *JM Magazine*, a publication of the department store Jordan Marsh (figure 4.22, plate 11).[143] The cover features a photograph of Warhol being kissed on the cheek by a younger, white woman and promises readers an interview with "Andy Warhol, modern icon." Over Warhol's hair, Basquiat has drawn curved, Twomblyian circular lines, with what might be handwriting not quite legible underneath, while the rest of Warhol's face is covered in a series of carefully drawn straight lines, which become denser and darker around his right eye. The words "mixed marriges" [*sic*] have been written on the cheek of the model kissing Warhol, with an apparent comma dangling afterward, suggesting that the words may be supplement to the existing title, making it "Mixed Marriges, POW!" This may be read as a jokey makeshift title for an imaginary article that the cover image now illustrates, but also for the drawing itself.

In coloring in Warhol's face, Basquiat has made Warhol "black like him" in several suggestive regards.[144] For one, he has placed Warhol in an apparent cross-racial couple, a "mixed marriage," a situation Basquiat himself was frequently in. For much of the time he was Warhol's friend and collaborator, Basquiat was in a romantic relationship with Paige Powell, who worked at *Interview* and was part of Warhol's social circle. (The triangle between the three of them is a story of its own). The drawing also appears to comment

---

Deux.' And I just read one line—that Jean Michel was my mascot. Oh God" (*Diaries*, 679–80). I could not find the "mascot" reference in the review Warhol mentions, by Vivian Raynor (http://www.nytimes.com/1985/09/20/arts/art-basquiat-warhol.html). She does, however, remark that "the collaboration looks like one of Warhol's manipulations." For accounts of their friendship and collaboration, see Bockris, *Life and Death*, esp. "Andy Warhol's Last Loves," 460–70; Phoebe Hoban, *Basquiat: A Quick Killing in Art* (New York: Penguin, 1998); Jennifer Clement's account of Basquiat's relationship with Suzanne Mallouk, *Widow Basquiat* (Exeter: Shearman Books, 2001); interviews with Paige Powell (165–73) and Kenny Scharf (182–89) in O'Connor and Liu, *Unseen Warhol*; and Bischofberger's account of the collaboration on his website (http://www.brunobischofberger.com/salewarhol/swarhol.htm#wcollabtext). On Basquiat, in addition to Muñoz, "Famous and Dandy," see the essays in Richard Marshall, ed., *Jean Michel Basquiat* (New York: Whitney Museum of American Art, 1992), esp. Robert Farris Thompson, "Royalty, Heroism and the Streets: The Art of Jean Michel Basquiat," and Greg Tate, "Black Like B."; Kellie Jones, "Lost in Translation: Jean-Michel in the (Re)Mix," in *Basquiat*, ed. Marc Mayer (Brooklyn: Brooklyn Museum of Art; London: Merrell Publishers, 2005); and Laurie A. Rodrigues, "'SAMOc as an Escape Clause': Jean Michel Basquiat's Engagement with a Commodified American Africanism," *Journal of American Studies* 45 (2011): 227–43.

143 The drawing was among Warhol's possessions when he died and resides now in the Warhol Museum. Warhol makes reference to a Jordan Marsh *catalogue* in his *Diaries*, August 31, 1983.

144 I am referencing John Howard Griffin's *Black Like Me* (1961), a text with multiple resonances with Warhol's representations of skin, skin color, and crossing the color line. See Lott, "White Like Me," and Kate Baldwin, "Black Like Who? Cross-Testing the 'Real' Lines of John Howard Griffin's *Black Like Me*," *Cultural Critique*, no. 40 (1998).

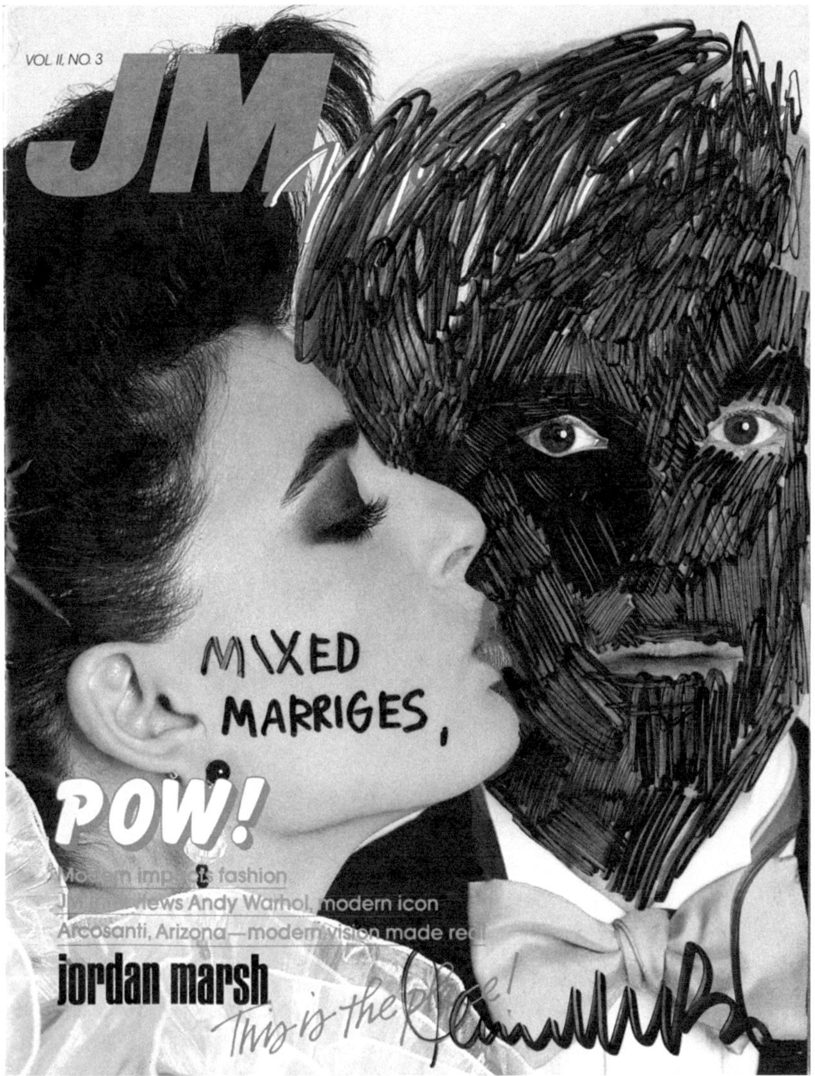

4.22 Jean-Michel Basquiat, *JM Magazine—Vol. 2, no. 3 (1983), featuring "Mixed Marriges" [sic] and drawing on Andy Warhol's face by Jean-Michel Basquiat*, 1983. Felt-tip marker and printed ink on coated paper, 10⅞ × 8⅜ × ¼ inches. © The Estate of Jean-Michel Basquiat/ADAGP, Paris/Artists Rights Society (ARS), New York.

on the cover's depiction of Warhol as part of a heterosexual couple. Basquiat marks Warhol as "queering" this heterosexual scene, suggesting that the only heterosexual couple Warhol could be a part of would be a "mixed marriage" of a gay man and a lesbian.[145] In pointing out how he and Warhol

145 Colacello reports that Warhol used the term "mixed marriage" in this sense. At one "smart Park Avenue cocktail party given by a smart couple," he reports, Warhol insisted that that host was "really after you, Bob." Warhol said "it was a mixed marriage—you

are each capable of making a couple "mixed," Basquiat makes an implicit comparison between Warhol's queer coupling with a woman and his own "mixed-race" couplings (including his coupling with Warhol). Basquiat is thus at once *making* Warhol like him by coloring him black and marking Warhol as *already* like him inasmuch as he queers the white heterosexual couple.

Warhol's markedness seems to be a primary feature of Basquiat's way of seeing him and an important element of Basquiat's affection for him, as both José Muñoz and Eve Sedgwick have suggested.[146] Warhol's unusual, whiter-than-white pastiness is subtly registered in Basquiat's first portrait of Warhol, *Dos Cabezas*, where Basquiat's skin is mainly the color of the unmarked beige background, whereas Warhol's skin stands out as uneven and splotchy, marked by pink blemishes and large white and gray patches (figure 4.23, plate 12). His later (1984) portrait of "Warhol as a banana," a complex appropriation of Warhol's use of the banana on the *Velvet Underground & Nico* cover, but also as a cock substitute in films such as *Mario Banana* (see Crimp on this[147]), is titled *Brown Spots*, a literal reference to being marked, indeed "spoiled."

In marking Warhol by coloring him—in pasty white, spotty brown, and marker black—Basquiat suggests that his liking of and likeness to Warhol involved a powerful and productive "queering of the color line."[148] The portraits function as a comment on their own "mixed marriage," in several ways. Basquiat made Warhol black by lending him some of his aura as a young, hip black artist. Through their collaboration, Warhol's celebrity and his authorship became identified with Basquiat, a development both seemed to seek. For Warhol, at least, their collaborations were most interesting when the authorship of the paintings was intentionally confused. In his *Diaries* Warhol describes their process: "I had a picture and I used the tracing machine that projects the image onto the wall and I put the paper where the image is and I trace. I drew it first, and then I painted it like Jean Michel. I think those paintings we're doing together are better when you can't tell who did which parts."[149] Basquiat not only got Warhol painting again but got him painting "like Jean Michel" ("Jean Michel got me into painting differently, and that's a good thing"; *Diaries*, April 17, 1984). Basquiat, in turn, started to

know, fags with dykes" (*Holy Terror*, 143). Warhol uses the term "intermarriage" for such arrangements in *Phil*, 191.

146 Sedgwick writes, "What Warhol allows to be called his 'faggy air' is also the air of his literalizing shame of whiteness. Yet it is not an air available for identification only to white people" ("Warhol's Shyness, Warhol's Whiteness," 139).

147 In *Our Kind of Movie* (9–11), Crimp reads *Mario Banana* as a comic version of *Blow Job*.

148 I am borrowing this phrase from Siobhan Somerville's important *Queering the Color Line* (Durham, NC: Duke University Press, 2000).

149 *Diaries*, April 16, 1984, 566.

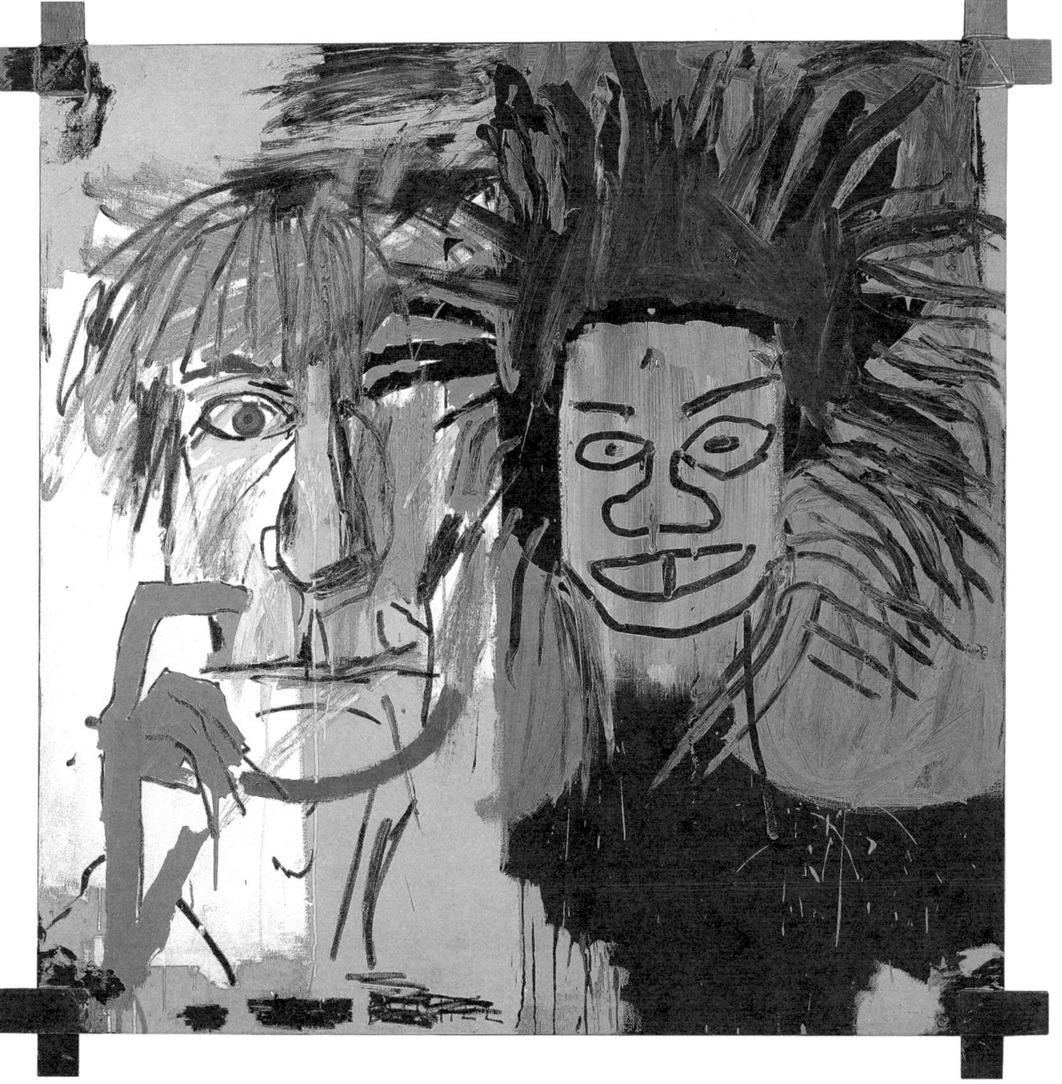

4.23 Jean-Michel Basquiat, *Dos Cabezas*, 1982. Acrylic and oilstick on canvas with wood supports, 59¾ × 60½ inches. Private collection. Bridgeman Images. © The Estate of Jean-Michel Basquiat/ADAGP, Paris/Artists Rights Society (ARS), New York.

silkscreen. In their painting practice, they were engaged in a mutual process of becoming-alike.

Their pursuit of mutual relations of resemblance was not an attempt to do away with the color line or to ignore it, but instead to show how likeness could be created and imagined across a line that had very real implications and consequences, which were experienced quite differently by the two of them. Of a party for Jermaine Jackson, Warhol remarks in his *Diaries* (August 5, 1984) that "it was one of those parties where the bouncers were all

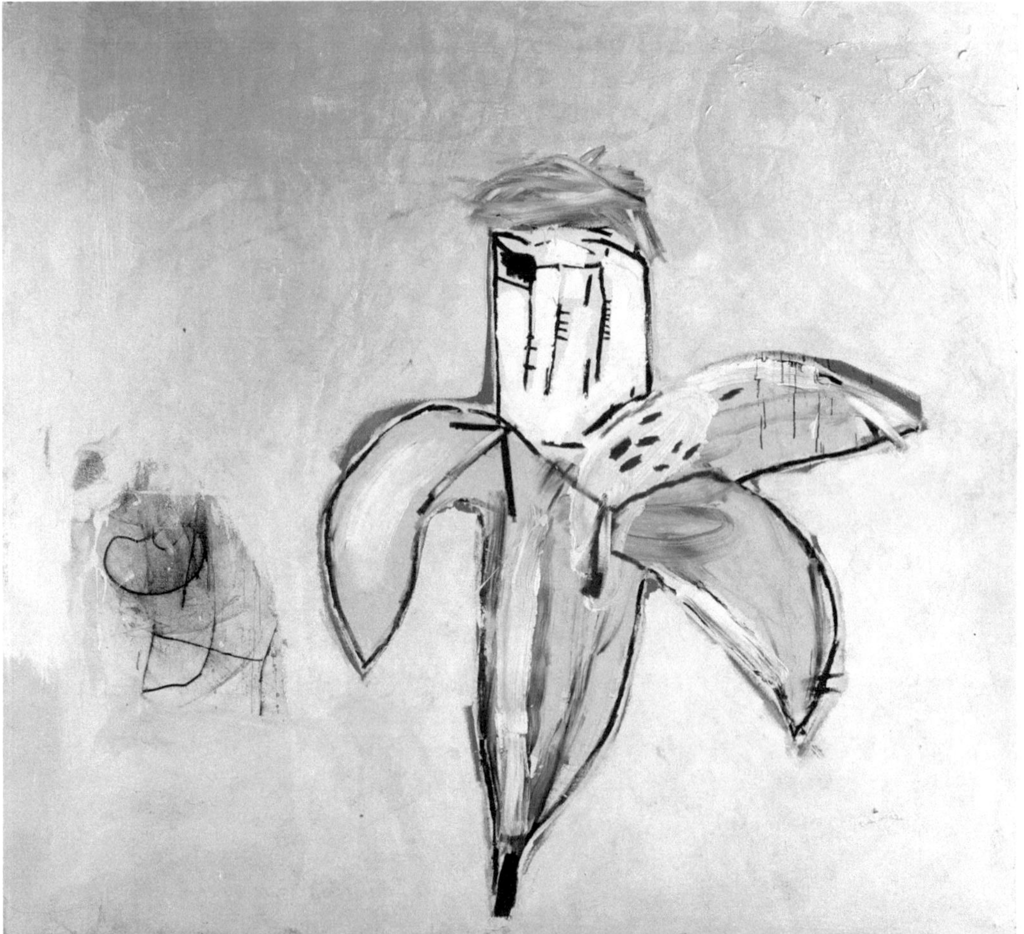

4.24 Jean-Michel Basquiat, *Brown Spots (Portrait of Andy Warhol as a Banana)*, 1984. Acrylic and oilstick on canvas, 76 × 84 inches. Private collection; courtesy Galerie Bruno Bischofberger, Switzerland. © The Estate of Jean-Michel Basquiat/ADAGP, Paris/Artists Rights Society (ARS), New York.

dumb mafia type guys who didn't know anybody. Jean Michel took us to the wrong section and they told us to beat it, and he said 'Now you see how it is to be black.'" As an artist, "seeing how it is to be black" would involve seeing the overwhelming absence of black artists from the walls of the Museum of Modern Art.[150] In making Warhol black in this drawing, Basquiat may be expressing his desire for there to be a famous black artist in the art historical canon for him to identify with, a wish that Warhol already *was* black, so that Basquiat would not have to explain to him "how it is" or color him to make

150 In *Widow Basquiat*, Jennifer Clement tells the story of Basquiat visiting MOMA with his girlfriend Suzanne Mallouk. He asks her to try counting the black men in the museum. She cannot "find even one" (34).

him so. As it was, because he was unable to find black artists in MOMA, as Muñoz notes, Basquiat found black athletes, musicians, comic books superheroes, and the "pastiest of art world megastars" to admire and imitate.[151]

In covering Warhol's face with black marker, Basquiat echoes his regular defacing of Warhol's white images with black ones in their collaborations, an operation Warhol himself invited and avowedly enjoyed (his praise for Basquiat's talent and his admiration of the work Basquiat was doing on his own and in their collaborations runs throughout his *Diaries*).[152] Typically, Warhol would silkscreen or trace an image onto the canvas, and then Basquiat would paint over or around Warhol's painting. In one of their best-known collaborations, for instance, Basquiat paints a black man playing a saxophone over the white Arm and Hammer logo, transforming the circular logo into a coin with gray bubbles floating up and away from its edges. This reimagined form of currency, with the words "commemeritive" [*sic*] and "one cent" crossed out, and the black letters of "liberty" partially outlined in red, gives the lie to the erasure of black labor by Arm and Hammer's white (supremacist) hammer-holding arm. Next to each other, the black saxophone player and white arm themselves make a kind of mixed marriage. The deadpan reproduction of the logo, now sitting alongside Basquiat's defaced logo on the canvas, looks embarrassingly, vulgarly white. It seems to ostentatiously declare its naturalization of white labor as labor as such, and to fully admit to the violence implicit in this white supremacist operation.[153] Basquiat has taken the image of whiteness that Warhol presented to him and put it under a luminous glare, making it into a very noticeable background. In this way, Basquiat amplifies the disidentificatory impulse within Warhol's appropriations, even as he points out Warhol's whiteness. But Basquiat has not covered this pretending-to-be-neutral metonym of labor with a sign of black labor (nor of black suffering); instead, we see an embodiment of improvisation and black freedom. This practice of liberty (though by no means unambiguously so, as it has been copyrighted), bears the traces of bloody struggle. Indeed, this painting is a veritable allegory of the history of the color line in the United States, figuring a white supremacist capitalism that at once excluded and exploited black people—indeed turned black persons into commodities, even as black expressive culture remained a locus of white fascination, a practice of freedom that racial capitalism could commodify but not contain. As Muñoz brilliantly writes, "Basquiat's figure, a shirtless, crudely sketched black male who plays a saxophone," produces "a melancholic reverberation"

151 Muñoz, "Famous and Dandy," 146.

152 Basquiat described the process to Tamra Davis in her film *The Radiant Child*: "He'd start one, you know, put . . . something very concrete or recognizable like a newspaper headline or a product logo and I would sort of deface it and then when I would try to get him to work some more on it, you know. . . . We used to paint over each other's stuff all the time."

153 Thanks to Benjy Kahan for sharing his insights about this painting.

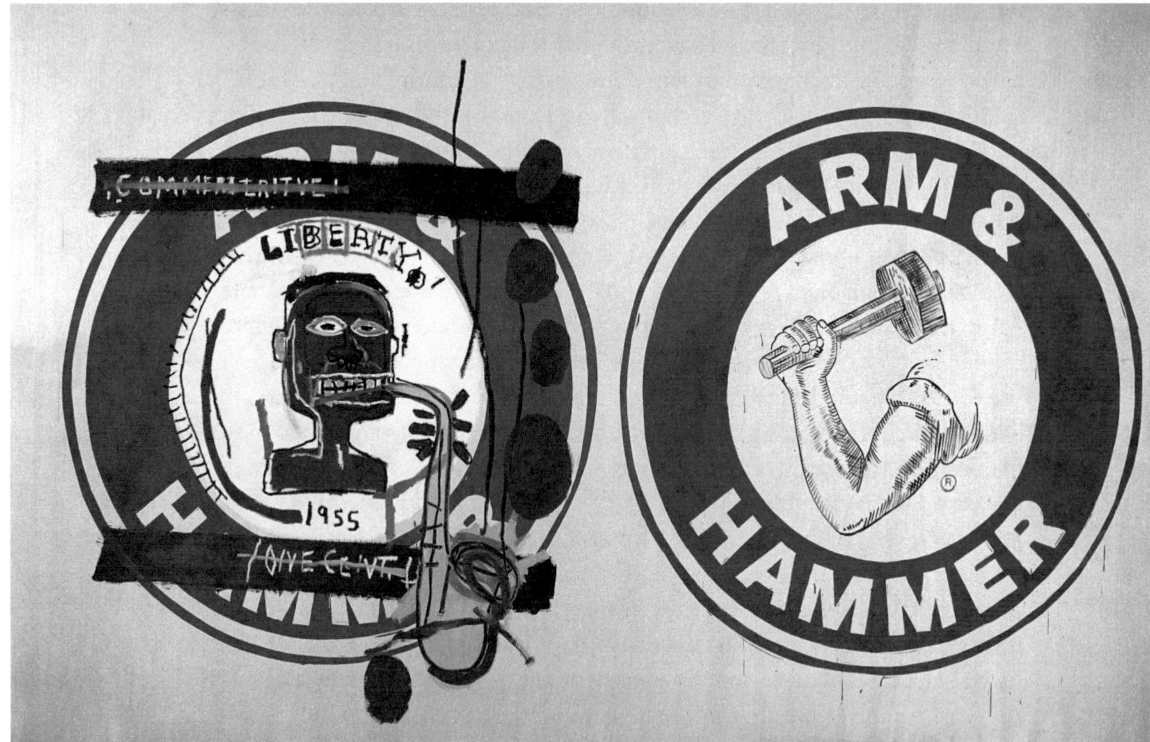

4.25 Jean-Michel Basquiat and Andy Warhol, *Arm and Hammer II*, 1985. Acrylic on canvas, 65¾ × 112¼ inches. Private collection; courtesy Galerie Bruno Bischofberger, Switzerland. © The Estate of Jean-Michel Basquiat/ADAGP, Paris/Artists Rights Society (ARS), New York. © 2016 The Andy Warhol Foundation for the Visual Arts/Artists Rights Society (ARS), New York.

that "evokes and eulogizes a lost past, a childhood, and a memory of racial exploitation and terror."[154] In the spirit of Muñoz's reading, I would add that Basquiat's figure also exuberantly exceeds the limiting confines of a commodified and exploited blackness. The sounds that this saxophone produces float away like gray bubbles (or silver pillows), ungoverned by the limits created by the boundaries of the coin.

If Basquiat's coloring over Warhol's face on the *JM* cover recalls the exuberantly melancholic face-giving defacements he practiced in collaborations such as *Arm and Hammer II*, it also references Basquiat's disidentificatory imitation of Warhol, which depended on seeing Warhol as marked, and in seeing him as such also making him so. In this, it also imitates the way Warhol's silkscreens inked over the faces of stars like Marilyn Monroe, Troy Donahue, and Natalie Wood. Like Warhol, Basquiat covers the face of a star that he likes in black ink. As it had been for Warhol, this "magic"

154 Muñoz, *Cruising Utopia*, 159.

marking was a way to feel like somebody else who similarly misfit. In marking Warhol as black and as queer, he has not only imitated Warhol's own long history of disidentificatory, marked imitations. As an act of liking, making Warhol "like Jean Michel" also publicizes the affectionate relations of resemblance he has entered into with Warhol. In putting his liking on display in this Warhol-like manner, Basquiat is showing his viewers—including Andy himself—a way to like Andy Warhol, too.

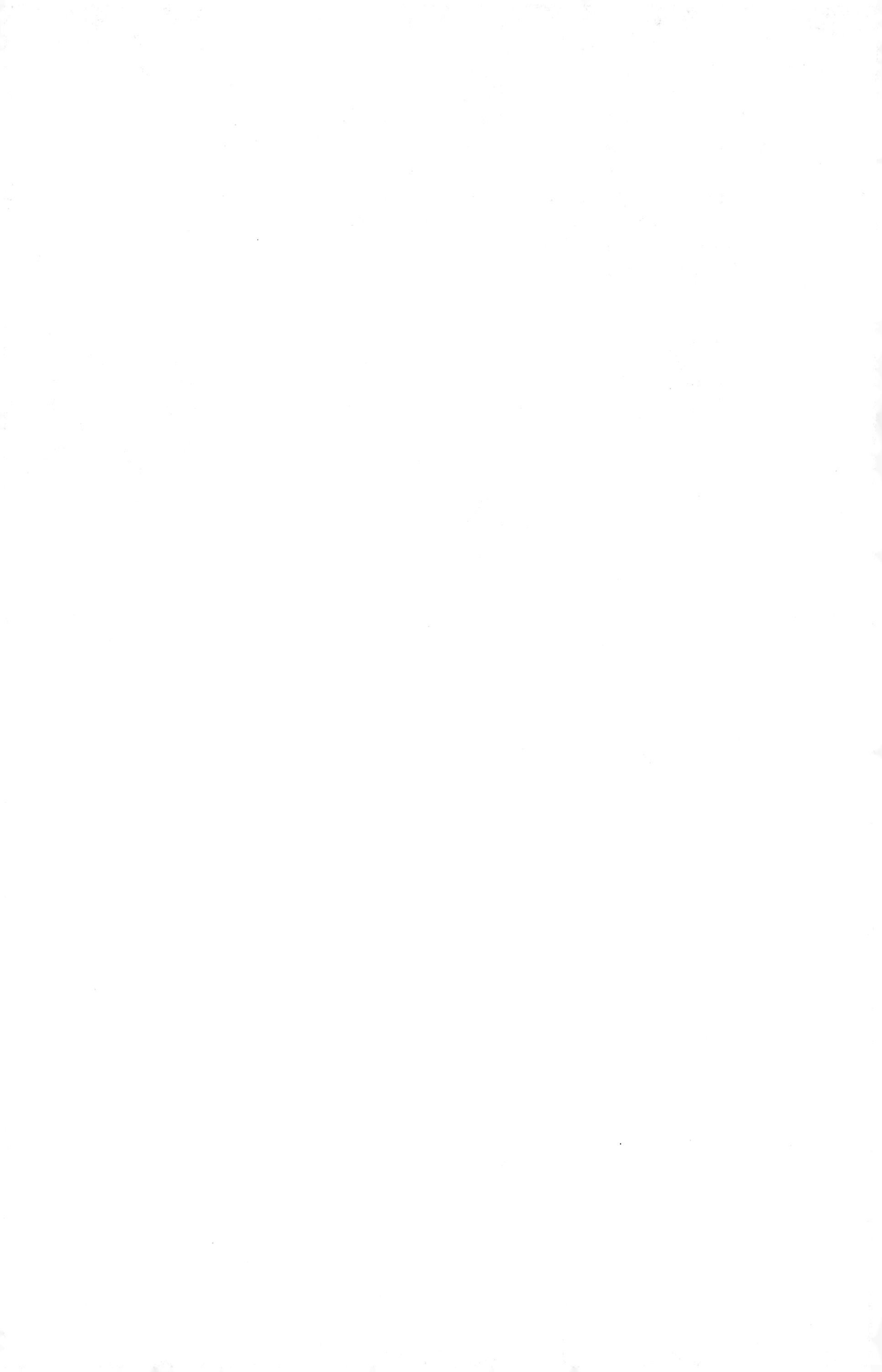

Acknowledgments

I first got interested in Andy Warhol in a seminar taught by Michael Moon and Eve Kosofsky Sedgwick during my first year of graduate school at Duke University. Under the intensely generative queer marquee they made, Jennifer Doyle, José Esteban Muñoz, and I organized a conference and then edited *Pop Out: Queer Warhol.* We were all transformed by the sequins scattered on us by Eve and Michael. Eve, who made herself abundantly and enthusiastically available for various practices of resemblance, identification, and imitation, shaped me indelibly. Michael's work on Warhol served as my initial model and inspiration. I am grateful to Jennifer for the many rich conversations and for her contagious, fierce intellectual-political commitment. I have learned so much from Mandy Berry, whose life-affirming fellowship has been a great gift. I'm also thankful for the big love made by Katie Kent's laughter, insight, and emotional constancy. Gustavus Stadler's wit, taste, and intelligence has often made a key difference. Eleanor Kaufman, Hank Okazaki, Johannes Von Moltke, Ken Wissoker, and Brian Selsky all stimulated, consoled, regaled, and challenged at important moments. I also learned from conversations with Mandy Merck, Simon Watney, Carol Mavor, David James, and Jane Gaines. I'm deeply grateful for the pleasures afforded by Jan Radway's attention, conversation, and friendship, and for the many ways she has made me smarter about everything. Among the many things I learned from Fredric Jameson's mentorship and example is that one should do one's best to be interested in everything.

The friendships formed during graduate school have had a lasting effect on how I think and feel about everything, and none more than my friendship with José. His companionship, intellectual and otherwise, was a boon to me not just because he was so smart and so gifted at idea-generating discussion, but also because he opened up a space where intellectual work was grounded in a space and a scene of friendship. Plus, he taught me to like so many things I would have missed without his brilliant, capacious, perverse, hilarious tutelage.

The idea for a book about liking and likeness in Warhol originated in a talk I wrote at the invitation of Nicholas Baume, whose counsel and encouragement on aesthetic matters of all sorts has come to be indispensable. Nicholas is one of a number of Warhol enthusiasts whose work has shaped mine. I deeply feel the loss of Callie Angell, who was so generous with her encyclopedic mind and vast knowledge of Warhol's career and circle; her remarkably careful, attentive, and intelligent work on Warhol's films is a model for us all. I am a huge fan of Neil Printz's brilliant and essential work on the *Catalogue Raisonné* of the paintings. There is no one better to talk to about Warhol, and I am thankful for his liberal assistance, advice, and insight. John Smith and Matt Wrbican, archivists at the Warhol Museum, enthusiastically shared their knowledge, and Matt's hospitality and expertise helped me to see and find any number of things I otherwise wouldn't have. I also learned a lot from hanging out with the brilliant and hilarious Ronald Tavel in Moscow for a few days.

Over the very many years I have been working on this book, giving drafts of these chapters as talks provided the occasion for constructive feedback from audiences at the Wadsworth Atheneum, Dartmouth College, the Museum of Contemporary Art in Barcelona, Harvard University, Yale University, UCLA's Center for the Study of the Contemporary, McMaster University, University of Rochester, Futures of American Studies Institute, Australian Modernist Studies Network Symposium, National Gallery of Art, Williams College, Indiana University's Americanist Research Colloquium, Performance Studies at NYU, Film Theory and Visual Culture Seminar at Vanderbilt University, Burlington Art Museum, Bryn Mawr College, Moscow Institute of Philosophy, Pennsylvania State University, African American Studies and Art and Archaeology at Princeton University, Goethe Universitat, University of Florida, Northwestern University's Summer Institute in Rhetoric and Public Culture, and UC Berkeley's English Department. At these places and others, I received helpful encouragement, challenges, and feedback from Imre Szeman, Nina Sosna, Donald Pease, Tim Dean, Scott Herring, Shane Vogel, John MacKay, Justin Neuman, John Vincent, Devin Fore, Hal Foster, Benjamin Buchloh, Michael North, Mark McGurl, Vinzenz Hediger, Homay King, Jen Fay, Lucy Mulroney, Keith Vincent, Christopher Reed, Dilip Gaonkar, Kate Baldwin, John Brenkman, Bryan Wagner, Stephen Best, Dora Zhang, Steven Lee, Rachel Haidu, Darby English, Ann Vickery, Gayl Jones, Henry Sussman, Rosalyn Deutsche, Cindi Katz, Vaginal Davis, and many others.

Wayne State University's English Department, where I have worked for the last several years, has offered a wealth of intellectual and personal support, including summer research support from the Wayne State Humanities Center and a Career Development Chair. Financial assistance from the office of the Vice President for Research, the College of Liberal Arts and Sciences, the Humanities Center and the English Department at Wayne State helped to pay for image rights and color reproductions. Many thanks to them, and to my current department chair, Ken Jackson, for his assistance and support.

I came to Wayne State because of Richard Grusin, whose convivial counsel, support, and company has regularly lifted my mood and sharpened my thought. He was one of two people who recommended the title *Like Andy Warhol* (Roger Conover was the other), and he remains a regular sounding board for much of my thinking. I have been grateful while at Wayne for the intellectual comradeship of Prita Meier, Dana Seitler, Cannon Schmitt, Sarika Chandra, Lisa Ze Winters, Donna Landry, Gerald Maclean, Barrett Watten, Les Brill, Carol Vernallis, John Pat Leary, renee hoogland, Steven Shaviro, and Scott Richmond. I was lucky to regularly enjoy the taste and wit and archival mind of Charles Kronengold for a couple years here. Lara Cohen is a champion of many things, including collegiality and friendship. For sharing their intelligence and good humor, thanks also to present and former graduate students Marie Buck, Michael Schmidt, Ryan Dillaha, Kristine Danielson, Ted Prassinos, Tara Forbes, Chinmayi Kattemalavadi, and Jon Plumb. I miss the friendship of Kathryne Lindberg, whose political commitments were felt and expressed so vitally, whose erudition and intelligence were so formidable and abundant, whose occasional anger was so piercing, whose pointed, excessive generosity was so frequent, whose profane wit so sharp and hilarious, that it just seemed impossible for her to disappear.

I feel lucky to have been buoyed many times over by conversations with Marc Siegel about Warhol and many other matters; he regularly dazzles me with his keenly queer intelligence, taste, and ethical sense. I always leave conversations with Juan Suárez smarter and more enthusiastic, too. Howard Singerman got me interested in minimalism, and his intellectual engagement remains the very paradigm of collegiality. In Moscow, Lena Petrovskaya, Oleg Aronson, Sasha Ivanov, and Valery Podoroga all offered various, crucial forms of feedback and encouragement and advice. Benjy Kahan gave a generous and careful read to a draft of the introduction. Brian Glavey's liking of the idea of liking and his own work on queer aesthetics have been a sustaining influence. Ben Lee's enthusiasm has a remarkably transformative effect on his surroundings, and I'm lucky to be lifted by it from time to time. Anthony Grudin's shared fascination with Warhol and consistent, razor-sharp feedback has been incredibly helpful. For conversations, hospitality, and encouragement, I am also grateful to Susanne Sachse, Carrie Noland, Kristin Romberg, Zahid Chaudhury, Melissa Ragona, and Henry Abelove. During a year in Princeton, I was fortunate to become acquainted with the brilliant minds of Daphne Brooks and Rod Ferguson; conversations with each of them have been transformingly sustaining. Patti Hart has done wonders for my mood. Thanks to Julia Jarcho, Wendy Lee, Crystal Parikh, and Patrick Deer for their friendship and for letting me bend their ears about affect theories and aesthetics during my time as a visitor in the English Department at NYU. Many thanks too to the students in the Queer Affect Theory Seminar there for their engagement and inspiration. In addition to their many intellectual and other assistances, Lauren Berlant and Tavia Nyong'o (with the help of Alan Klima) were my writing buddies as I finished this book, and I can honestly say that I couldn't have done it without them.

I could not imagine a better editor than Douglas Mitchell. His combination of understanding, patience, and enthusiasm is positively worldmaking. He has my deep thanks for his smart, welcoming, careful, attentive shepherding of this book into existence. Kyle Wagner's stunningly efficient, generous assistance is also very much appreciated. Many thanks, too, to Joel Score, who improved my prose with remarkable skill and intelligence.

Many of the ideas in this book came into being through conversations with Tan Lin, whose intelligence concerning matters of aesthetic experience is unmatched. I am grateful to have been able to bask in the light of Sianne Ngai's brilliance from time to time, and this book has richly benefited from the attention she gave to it and from her amazingly effective encouragement. Heather Love has been a reliable lifeline of happy conversations, support, and advice. Phil Harper's friendship has been a great source of joy over the years and I am thankful for his support of various kinds at so many different, key moments. Honestly, I don't know where I would be without the love and laughter of Eric Lott; his example, his ear, his conversation offer regular, essential sustenance. Douglas Crimp has been a steadfast supporter of me and of this book, professionally, practically, emotionally, and intellectually. I am grateful to him for that, for the example of his queer scholarship and activism, for sharing his enthusiasm for Warhol with me, and for his friendship, which has enriched and improved my life in too many ways to list here. It is one of life's great pleasures to share aesthetic experiences with Douglas, a mode of companionship that is one of Douglas's many great talents, matched perhaps only by his talent for friendship itself.

My parents, Marcia Dean and Joseph Flatley support, assist, console, and entertain in every way I could hope. It has been inspiring to see my sisters Alex Flatley and Michaela Flatley enter and transform the world. My admiration and love for my brother Jason Flatley remains a bedrock for everything I do. In the concrete, intimate daily project of making time and finding energy to write, the help and encouragement of Danielle Aubert has been most essential and most appreciated. I am thankful for her companionship, which provides a vital and regular source of pleasure, interest, comfort, and happiness. Agnes Dean Aubert Flatley has radiantly expanded my ability to be affected, and she continues to increase my dose of daily joy. With her, I have found a whole new world to like.

* * *

Portions of chapter 2 first appeared in the essay "Art Machine," in Nicholas Baume, ed., *Sol LeWitt: Incomplete Open Cubes*, exhibition catalog, Wadsworth Atheneum (Cambridge, MA: MIT Press, 2001).

Portions of chapter 3 first appeared in the essay "Allegories of Boredom," in Ann Goldstein, ed., *A Minimal Future: Art as Object 1958–1968*, exhibition catalog, Los Angeles Museum of Contemporary Art (Cambridge, MA: MIT Press, 2004).

Portions of chapter 1 first appeared in the essay "Like: Collecting and Collectivity," *October*, no. 132 (Spring 2010).

Portions of chapter 4 first appeared in the essay "Just Alike," *Social Text*, no. 121 (Fall 2014), a special issue for José Esteban Muñoz.

Abbreviations

CR1 *The Andy Warhol Catalogue Raisonné*, vol. 1, *Paintings and Sculpture 1961–1963*, ed. Georg Frei and Neil Printz (New York: Phaidon, 2002)

CR2A *The Andy Warhol Catalogue Raisonné*, book A of vol. 2, *Paintings and Sculpture 1964-1969*, ed. George Frei and Neil Printz (New York: Phaidon, 2004)

CR3 *The Andy Warhol Catalogue Raisonné*, vol. 3, *Paintings and Sculpture, 1970–1974*, ed. Neil Printz and Sally King-Nero (New York: Phaidon, 2010)

CR4 *The Andy Warhol Catalogue Raisonné*, vol. 4, *Paintings and Sculpture* [1976–1987], ed. Neil Printz and Sally King-Nero (New York: Phaidon, 2014)

Diaries *The Andy Warhol Diaries*, ed. Pat Hackett (New York: Time Warner, 1989)

IBYM *I'll Be Your Mirror: The Selected Andy Warhol Interviews*, ed. Kenneth Goldsmith (New York: Carrol and Graf, 2004)

POP Andy Warhol and Pat Hackett, *POPism: The Warhol Sixties* (New York: Harcourt, Brace Jovanovich, 1980)

Phil *The Philosophy of Andy Warhol: From A to B and Back Again* (New York: Harcourt Brace Jovanovich, 1975)

SW2 *Walter Benjamin: Selected Writings*, vol. 2, ed. Michael W. Jennings, Howard Eiland, and Gary Smith, trans. Rodney Livingstone et al. (Cambridge, MA: Harvard University Press, 1999)

SW4 *Walter Benjamin: Selected Writings*, vol. 4, ed. Howard Eiland and Michael W. Jennings, trans. Edmund Jephcott et al. (Cambridge, MA: Harvard University Press, 2003)

Index